DePaul University
*Centennial Essays
and Images*

EDITED BY

John L. Rury and Charles S. Suchar

Front Cover: Original pen and ink line drawing of the Uptown Campus taken from the Golden Anniversary Opening Day Ceremonies Program p. 15. Saturday, September 25, 1948. Artist unknown. Cover design by DePaul University Publication Services.

Back Cover: left: the John T. Richardson Library (dedicated 1992), photo by Les Boschke, Boschke photography; right: DePaul Center (dedicated 1993), photo by James Steinkamp, Steinkamp/Ballogg Photography, Chicago.

TABLE OF CONTENTS

INTRODUCTION

John L. Rury

DePaul University is presently one of the largest Catholic institutions of higher learning in the world. With nearly 18,000 students enrolled in eight colleges and schools, it is a modern comprehensive American urban university. This was not always so. One hundred years ago DePaul began as the tiny, parish-based St. Vincent's College on the north side of Chicago. It grew the way similar institutions did—by fits and starts. Its fate was tied to the city early on, and as Chicago grew and prospered, so did DePaul. But there were hard moments as well as good ones, and part of the university's identity was forged in adversity. Out of this process developed the large, complex institution that is DePaul University today.

The story of DePaul's growth and development is the subject of this volume. A tale of uncertainty and struggle, of success despite great challenges, it is also the chronicle of a particular vision of higher education, and of a set of values that has sustained this institution through bad times and good. DePaul has been led by the Vincentian fathers of the Congregation of the Mission (C.M.) throughout its existence. It has accumulated a rich tradition, and this also is reflected in the essays collected here. The publication of this book marks the university's centennial. It also affirms the lessons and the values that will carry DePaul into the next century.

DePaul is closely associated with the history of the city of Chicago and its surrounding area, and this association is an inescapable part of the story recounted here. The university has served hundreds of thousands of local men and women seeking personal and professional advancement, whether through individual courses of study or through one of its many varied degree programs. Its graduates have made major contributions to Chicago's legal, accountancy and education professions and its alumni play vital roles in communities throughout the greater Chicago region and the nation. This is an important aspect of DePaul's legacy.

Students came to DePaul from the entire greater Chicago metropolitan area, though for the first half of its existence the university primarily served residents of the city. Following the Second World War ever greater numbers came from the suburbs; and more recently DePaul has attracted a significant portion of its student body from outside the Chicago region altogether. While enrolled at DePaul, these students created a vital culture, one that in many respects represented the larger youth culture of the city and the country. And like their counter-parts at other universities nationwide, DePaul's students cultivated interests and values that changed with time. The story of the changes wrought by students constitutes another aspect of the university's history, and it too is represented in the pages that follow.

The DePaul experience has also been shaped by the overall history of higher education in this country. Like other Catholic universities, DePaul changed in response to innovations at leading national institutions and to the requirements of various accrediting organizations. In time, therefore, the university grew to resemble most other large institutions of higher educa-tion. As the university's faculty grew, it became more professionalized and began to participate in national academic organizations and networks. As a result, DePaul evolved into a more cosmopolitan institution with an increasingly accomplished faculty. This brought new recog-nition to the university, permitting it to add new programs, such as doctoral courses of study, and to attract new resources to support faculty research and scholarship.

DePaul's growth made it essential to expand the university's campuses. Starting with just one building adjacent to St. Vincent's parish church, DePaul eventually occupied more than forty structures concentrated on two Chicago campuses and several suburban satellite loca-tions. This development of the university's facilities required resources, and for much of its history DePaul's quest for new buildings was associated with a burdensome accumulation of institutional debt. But as the university expanded, particularly in the years following World War Two, its financial burden became more manageable. Today DePaul continues to add to its facilities, and it still has to rely on borrowed money to some extent. But past experience has demonstrated that this is a viable strategy for expansion and for fulfilling DePaul's urban, Vincentian mission. This is yet another lesson and legacy implicit in the university's history.

In the popular mind, of course, DePaul is associated with basketball and the many win-ning teams of Coach Ray Meyer. As most people know, Coach Meyer came to DePaul on the eve of the Second World War and stayed for more than fifty years (including an interval as special assistant to the university president). The success of DePaul's basketball teams under his guidance, first in the forties but also in the later 1970s and eighties, helped to raise the national profile of the institution. In the years prior to Meyer's arrival, however, DePaul also had winning basketball teams, and during the first four decades of the university's existence it fielded a football team. Although DePaul's gridiron Demons had limited success, they did occasionally play before large crowds at Soldier Field and Wrigley Field. Despite the fact that intercollegiate sports receive only limited mention in this book, they are important compo-nents of the DePaul story.

Throughout its history DePaul has been a Catholic institution. The meaning of the university's religious identity has changed significantly from one decade to the next, both because of changes in the institution's leadership and because of the evolution of the Church itself. Like other Catholic universities, DePaul underwent a religious revival in the 1930s. But the outward manifestation of its Catholicism moderated in the decades following the Second World War, due in part to the growing ecumenism in American life and the eagerness of American Catholics to join mainstream American culture. This trend was abetted by Vatican II, and the growing professionalization of the faculty and the university's movement toward research militated against explicit affirmation of its Catholic identity. Like most other Catholic universities, DePaul reconstituted its board of trustees in the late 1960s to place lay members in the majority, a change made to foreclose the possible withdrawal of federal and state aid because of its religious character. In technical terms, this change transformed DePaul into a private institution whose Catholic identity was less obvious. But, as several of the following chapters indicate, DePaul has discovered new ways to sustain and acknowledge its Catholic heritage. Its religious identity has continued to be a vital element of the institution's daily life.

Altogether, the past one hundred years have been a time of momentous change at DePaul. The university has grown in ways its founders could never have imagined. and in a character- istically entrepreneurial fashion it has embraced the values and often contradictory purposes of modern American higher education. Each of the chapters in this volume deals with a differ- ent aspect of the DePaul experience over the past century. Because they are organized themati- cally, the stories they tell often overlap to some extent, and the same events sometimes appear in various guises or different contexts. Still, each chapter focuses on one aspect of the university's development. Taken together, they tell its story and identify those features of DePaul's experi- ence that will carry it into its second century.

Plan of the Book

As suggested above, the book is organized thematically. Each chapter looks at the university's history from a different angle. Several of them deal with the entire sweep of the institution's existence; others are concerned with a particular period. Since the chapters are free-standing, they can be read either at random or in order, from beginning to end. One way or the other, these pages tell much of the story of DePaul over the past one hundred years.

The first three chapters, comprising the book's opening section, provide the reader with a picture of the factors that have influenced DePaul as it has grown into a major institution of higher education. The opening chapter by Richard Meister, the university's vice president for academic affairs, provides an overview of the institution's history and describes just how its Catholic, Vincentian and urban identities have changed with time. It is followed by Dennis McCann's discussion of the university's founding, and the circumstances of its early develop- ment. McCann suggests that DePaul's tradition of adaptation to its urban environment was shaped from the very beginning by its struggle for survival. Anna Waring's chapter describes the organizational development of the university and changes in its governance structure. Dr. Waring notes that a combination of internal imperatives and external forces have collaborated to shape DePaul's internal organization throughout its history. A central event in both Meister's and Waring's chapters is the crisis of 1950, when the North Central Association of Schools and Colleges nearly revoked the university's accreditation. It was after this traumatic event that today's DePaul first began to emerge. Together, the first three chapters provide the broad outline of the university's growth and development.

The book's second section, the fourth and fifth chapters, deal with campus culture and student life, aspects of the institution's experience which are only touched on in the opening section. In chapter 5, Dr. Charles Suchar uses extensive interviews with former students to document the myriad ways in which they experienced DePaul. They describe a broad range of impressions, from the loop and uptown campuses in the thirties, forties and fifties to the modern residential campus that emerged in Lincoln Park, beginning in the sixties and seventies. In chapter 4, John Rury chronicles the evolution of student life and the many activities students have engaged in over the course of the university's history. This story moves from the early days of coeducation to the dance and date era, through the political and cultural revolutions of the sixties and seventies. Though the university's experience in this regard mirrored society at large, DePaul's students also gave shape to a campus culture that was unique to their urban, Vincentian institution.

The final section of the book, organized in three chapters, deals with the evolution of DePaul from a somewhat parochial commuter institution to the large and innovative university it has become today. In the first of these chapters, Dr. Albert Erlebacher traces the development of the university during the period from 1920 to 1945. This was a time of struggle for DePaul, as enrollments fluctuated and the university was unable to reduce its persistent debt. Erlebacher discusses the difficulty DePaul's leaders experienced in obtaining and maintaining accreditation, and the successes they enjoyed in enhancing the university's religious identity. He also notes the conflicts this may have engendered. The next chapter, by Father Thomas Croak, examines the period that followed, beginning with the accreditation crisis of 1950. Father Croak examines the university's growing commitment to faculty research, a concomitant of professionalization. He also describes the physical expansion of the Lincoln Park campus, essential to the growth of programs in the arts and sciences, education, music and theater. Finally, in chapter 8, Charles Strain describes the development of teaching and learning at DePaul since the crisis of 1950—the evolution of curricular reform across the university. As Dr. Strain notes, DePaul was a pioneer in certain respects, making innovations in the teaching of religion and philosophy that gained national attention. DePaul reorganized its undergraduate curriculum several times in the postwar period and launched a number of novel curricular changes in its adult education and professional schools. In documenting these developments, Dr. Strain describes DePaul's emergence as a comprehensive institution that adapted skillfully to the changing educational and professional scene of the late twentieth century.

In the book's epilogue, Richard Meister returns to the question of the university's identity and its distinctive values. He describes the debate that has rattled Catholic higher education in the past several decades over whether modern institutions of higher education can sustain a religious heritage. DePaul, he argues, has developed its own approach to nurturing a distinctive religious identity. He suggests that the key is the Vincentian commitment to service and the idea that higher education demands public responsibility rather than private benefit. Paraphrasing the late Ernest Boyer, he describes DePaul as the "New American Catholic University," an institution dedicated to public service and the promotion of civic values. This is the vision he proposes as DePaul's contribution to American civilization in the years ahead.

DePaul has grown significantly, seemingly exponentially, from its modest beginnings. As it looks ahead to its second century, it has a rich heritage to draw from, and—if the past is any guide—a future full of changes difficult to anticipate. The university faces this, however, with a clear comprehension of its past, and a firm commitment to the values that will help it maintain a special role in American higher education.

PART I

DePaul's

Mission

and

Governance

CHAPTER ONE

DePaul University
Catholic, Vincentian and Urban

Richard Meister

Saint Vincent's College was founded in 1898 to serve young Catholic men. These students were taught primarily by Vincentians, and they commuted to their classrooms and labs from the urban neighborhoods of north side Chicago. In the years that followed, being Catholic, Vincentian, and urban revealed itself in ever-changing ways at DePaul University, the institution that succeeded Saint Vincent's. But the words "Catholic, Vincentian and urban" were not used to describe the distinctive character or mission of DePaul until the late 1970s. Even so, the values these words represent have deep roots in the institution's experience. In the chapters that follow my colleagues present their conceptions of DePaul's development during the 20th century, a period of rapid change in American higher education, in the Catholic Church, and in urban America. This essay summarizes the university's history, assessing what it has meant for DePaul to be Catholic, Vincentian and urban.

Founding DePaul: The Early Years, 1898 to 1930

Saint Vincent parish was established by the Vincentian Congregation of the Mission, on the north side of Chicago in 1875. Eight years later the Sisters of Charity of the Blessed Virgin Mary opened a parish grade school, and the Sisters inaugurated a girls' high school in 1891. Then in 1897, at the request of Archbishop Patrick A. Feehan, the Vincentians, who were known in both France and the United States for operating seminaries, agreed to establish a college and a boys' academy. The following June the charter for Saint Vincent's College was approved by the Illinois Secretary of State, for the purpose of providing a collegiate education for the sons of Catholic families on the city's north side and offering a preparatory seminary education for young men who wished to enter the priesthood. (1) This was a modest beginning for the institution that became a comprehensive university in the following century.

Enrollments grew slowly in the early years, from 70 in 1898 to 200 in 1903–1904. As other historians have noted, Saint Vincent's featured an academy and a commercial course in addition to its collegiate branch. Indeed, the commercial course enrolled the greatest number of students, a premonition of the institution's future commitment to professional education. But in 1903 Saint Vincent's faced a crisis that threatened its very survival. The new archbishop, James A. Quigley, announced plans to establish Cathedral College as the preparatory seminary for the archdiocese and to allow Jesuit Saint Ignatius College to move its secondary and collegiate program to the north side. In response to this, Peter Vincent Byrne, C.M., Saint Vincent's first president, took the institution in a totally new direction, thereby laying the foundation for a modern Catholic university. (2)

First, the Vincentians drafted a new charter, modeling it after the document that had won the Secretary of State's approval for the newly established University of Chicago, and in 1907 Saint Vincent's College became DePaul University. The new charter which called for the university to be operated by a board of trustees consisting of ten Vincentians and five laymen, did not identify DePaul as Catholic. At the same time, Fr. Byrne mounted a building campaign and sought outside funds to pay for the new facilities he envisioned: a lyceum, a theater and a classroom/lab building to serve both the college and the high school. The fund-raising campaign failed, leaving the university burdened with a debt of about half a million dollars for forty years. Nevertheless, plans went ahead to add a law school, even a medical school, as well

Earliest view of St. Vincent's church—later to become St. Vincent's College. Fr. Smith's "Farm" with the original fencing is seen in the foreground, circa 1875.

*St. Vincent DePaul Church, 1875. The building would
be converted to a classroom building to house the new
St. Vincent's College in 1898.*

as schools of oratory, music, pharmacy and dentistry. Patterning itself after Harvard and other elite institutions, DePaul adopted a curriculum based on a model that featured electives. And unlike most other Catholic colleges, only Catholic students were required to attend the one-hour-a-week lecture on Catholic doctrine. With the establishment of the university and new programs in engineering, enrollments increased from 138 in 1906 to 243 in 1907. (3)

Father Byrne and his successors in the university presidency were pragmatic and entrepreneurial; their primary goal was to keep the institution open. Catholic and Vincentian values were givens for them, and the school's urban identity meant fulfilling the need to educate students from Chicago. In doing this the university's early leaders created an institution that was responsive to its environment, and open to change. This early hallmark of DePaul is one that has endured.

During Father Francis X. McCabe's presidency, from 1910 to 1920, the university expanded its professional programs and opened a downtown campus. In 1911 DePaul affiliated with the Illinois College of Law, a proprietary college founded by Howard N. Ogden, a Baptist. When he died in 1915, control of the College of Law passed to DePaul. Undergraduate programs in commerce and music were added in 1913, and by 1917 a student could take classes in most fields of professional education at the downtown campus. The College of Law enrolled 235 students; commerce 160, and the evening and extension programs over 500. The uptown campus remained small in 1917–1918, serving only 115 students in the College of Liberal Arts and Sciences, 55 students in an engineering program, but over 200 in the DePaul Academy, a boys' high school. As John Rury has noted, many of the students downtown were non-Catholics. (4)

Subsequent chapters in this volume describe in greater detail DePaul's turbulent yet exciting developmental years. There was conflict with Cardinal George Mundelein over coeducation as the university responded to the educational needs of its diverse Catholic constituency and worked to extend the same opportunities to non-Catholics. DePaul's transformation into a university in 1907 and the expansion of its professional programs in the decade that followed were similar to strategies adopted by many Catholic universities. But DePaul was a special type of Catholic institution; its disagreements with Cardinal Mundelein and its receptiveness to non-Catholics influenced the university's later development and gave rise to what historian Lester Goodchild has called the ecumenical university. (5)

During the 1920s the Extension Division, which was on the downtown campus, expanded its offering of courses and degree programs in education and the arts and sciences, serving primarily to religious and lay women who were teachers. The downtown campus was also the site of the Commercial Division (including a secretarial school) and the Preparatory Division that offered evening students the opportunity to complete high school. Almost from its beginning, a substantial majority of the university's students was enrolled in programs offered on the downtown campus. (6)

As Anna Waring describes in chapter three, the university struggled to gain accreditation and visibility as an institution of higher education during the 1920s. To become an accredited institution, DePaul had to address a number of concerns raised by the North Central Association of Schools and Colleges (or NCA) and other certifying bodies. Thomas F. Levan, C.M., who succeeded the popular though controversial Father McCabe in 1920, was successful in securing North Central accreditation for the university and professional accreditation for the College of Commerce and the College of Law. But questions about DePaul's academic standing continued to linger in various accrediting bodies. (7)

As they were at many other universities, the 1920s were years of growth at DePaul. When Father Levan assumed the presidency, DePaul had just 130 students in the College of Liberal Arts and Sciences on the uptown campus. There were 440 high school pupils in the boys' academy and 120 in the girls' academy, and about a thousand students at the downtown campus. By the end of his presidency in 1930 the enrollments on the downtown campus had tripled; enrollment had peaked at nearly 600 on the uptown campus earlier in the decade. An increasing number of floors had to be rented at 84 E. Randolph to accommodate the growing student body. Father Levan also convinced the board of trustees to borrow additional funds for an arts and science classroom and office building on the uptown campus, which opened in 1923, providing relief for the overcrowded facilities. Two other projects on the uptown campus did not materialize: a science laboratory building and a gym which was to have been built on Sheffield Avenue, on land the university had hoped to buy from the McCormick Presbyterian Seminary. Failure to expand the uptown campus limited the development of the College of Liberal Arts and Sciences in the years that followed. (8)

The need for additional space in the Loop in the late twenties coincided with the peak of the real estate boom that was sweeping American cities. Five prominent Catholic laymen, including Frank J. Lewis, organized the DePaul Educational Aid Society in 1927 to raise funds for a seventeen story building at 64 E. Lake Street, on land that was to be leased for 99 years. Bonds in large and small denominations were issued, backed by the projected rental income from tenants who would occupy more than half of the building. Ordinary individuals were encouraged to buy bonds at the rectory of Saint Vincent parish. The society would own the building and turn it over to the university in 1947, after the bonds were paid off. Construction began in 1927 and in the summer of 1928 DePaul moved the first programs into its impressive new facilities. (9)

In 1928, thirty years after its founding, DePaul—like many other Catholic universities—seemed to be in control of its own destiny. Nearly 5,000 students were in attendance; new facilities had been added on both campuses; the debt was sizable but appeared manageable at $700,000, and the university and its professional programs were accredited. DePaul was meeting its goal of providing a wide range of educational opportunities for Catholic men and women, as well as the teaching religious. At the same time, the university welcomed into its programs non-Catholic students and sought support from the larger urban community. There was little question about DePaul's Catholic identity, and in serving first generation college students at affordable tuition rates it fulfilled the Vincentian mission. Its location and the variety of its professional programs were incontrovertible evidence of its urban character. Even if the university made little mention of them at the time, Catholic, Vincentian and urban were tangible qualities at DePaul in this period.

Manifesting the Catholic Mission in Uncertain Times, 1930 to 1944

DePaul's second period of struggle for survival occurred during depression and war. The national economic crisis that began in late 1929 hit Chicago particularly hard, and eventually had a significant impact on DePaul. In 1932 the university's faculty and staff agreed to a 10 percent cut in pay to save the institution from bankruptcy, according to treasurer Albert F. Dundas, C.M. At the same time, the university made a decision to continue supporting intercollegiate football as a part of its athletic program, despite its cost. The demand for new office space in the Loop evaporated during the Depression, leaving much of the DePaul Building vacant for years. In 1934 bondholders filed suit, charging fraud and misrepresentation, and the building was placed in receivership. Although the debt was refinanced, DePaul's downtown property remained a financial burden for years. (10)

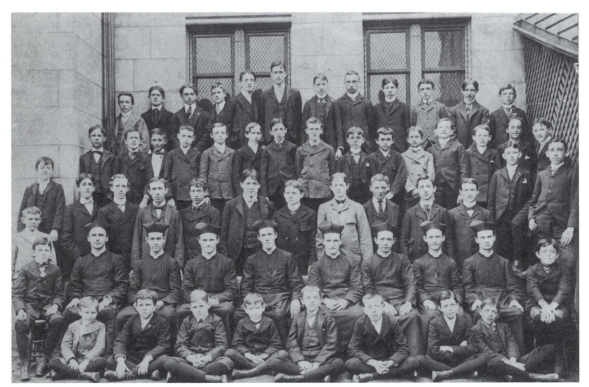

St. Vincent's first student body, 1899.

Enrollments and tuition revenue fluctuated through the 1930s, forcing a series of cutbacks, including the elimination of football in 1939. The indebtedness of 1907 that was increased with the building of the classroom building in 1923 became an annual problem, as did the financial crisis caused by the downtown building. The Great Depression put the university and its mission in jeopardy. (11)

Albert Erlebacher notes in his chapter that despite the hard times, DePaul, like many Catholic institutions, became more active in manifesting its Catholic mission. Initiated by Francis V. Corcoran, C.M., who served as president from 1930 to 1935, this renewed dedication was continued by his two successors. Father Corcoran was the first Chicagoan to head the university and the first of four successive presidents who grew up in the shadows of Saint Vincent de Paul Church. He was active in the National Catholic Educational Association and a founding member of the American Catholic Philosophical Association. (12)

In his address to the faculty in 1933, Father Corcoran placed renewed emphasis on Catholicism and on theology, philosophy and the classics.

DePaul University has been established under Catholic auspices, and its educational program and policy are determined by the general spirit of a positive and inclusive Catholic education. . . . This does not mean that the character of the school is negative and restrictive, but rather positive and inclusive. Its appeal is primarily to Catholic students and to others who are admitted without prejudice to their religious beliefs and opinions, just as the instructional staff includes many non-Catholics. . . . To accomplish the end of college instruction in harmony with this religious tradition, it is our purpose to develop courses of philosophy and religion to the utmost and to preserve for the classics, ancient and modern, the prominent place they have by rights occupied. (13)

It was also during the thirties that DePaul became a national leader in the field of religious education, founding *The Journal of Religious Instruction* in 1931. For its own students the university raised B.A. requirements from 120 to 128 credit hours, including 8 hours of religion, in 1932. Nearly half the students enrolled in evening or extension programs and one-third of those in the graduate school were members of religious orders, eliminating any doubt about DePaul's Catholic heritage among students in these programs. (14)

In 1935, Michael J. O'Connell, C.M., became DePaul's sixth president, serving until September 1944. As president, Fr. O'Connell faced the challenges of both depression and war. He convinced the board of trustees that DePaul had to respond to the criticism of the North Central Association that the university relied too heavily on the academy's (or high school) physical plant, especially its science facilities. On October 17, 1937 the cornerstone was laid for DePaul University's Hall of Science. Built at a cost of $250,000, it opened in September 1938. As a consequence, the university increased its debt from $620,000 to $830,000. (15)

World War Two posed new challenges. Keeping the university open required retrenchments. Father O'Connell moved most of the uptown campus's academic programs, except the sciences, to 64 E. Lake and leased the vacant uptown facilities to the U.S. Army for training purposes. Enrollments were reduced in any event, and the government programs housed on the uptown campus supplied a much-needed stream of income for the university.

In his last year as president, Fr. O'Connell and the board of trustees hired Stanley P. Farwell, president of Business Research Corporation as a consultant to develop a plan for DePaul in the post-war period. Farwell's 1944 report focused on how the university could take advantage of its upcoming 50th anniversary to generate civic support and develop external resources for the university. It recommended that the board of trustees be increased to 25 members, 11 of whom would be Vincentians, eight leading Catholic lay men, and six Protestant lay men. In addition the university was urged to establish University Associates, leaders in commerce, finance, industry, and the professions, to *"foster a friendly spirit of cooperation between the community and the university."* The report commented on the sad state of the uptown campus.

Outside of the Liberal Arts [today's Levan] and the Science [today's O'Connell] buildings, which are commendable structures, your Uptown campus is most unimpressive and is not such as to attract students. (16)

As Lester Goodchild's comparative study has documented, the physical facilities which supported DePaul's programs in the arts and sciences were markedly inferior to those of Notre Dame and Loyola, its two principal regional competitors. Years of financial crises had taken their toll, and the university had not been successful in raising funds. Its low tuition prevented DePaul from making significant capital improvements. And like many other Catholic universities at the time, it had virtually no endowment. (17) Father O'Connell had managed to keep the institution afloat in difficult times, as had his immediate predecessors, but much work remained to be done.

The Challenges of Growth: The O'Malley Years

As the war was drawing to a close, Comerford O'Malley, C.M., became DePaul's seventh president in October 1944. Father O'Malley had served in a variety of university administrative positions, including a term as dean of the College of Commerce. An outgoing, affable priest, he recognized the challenges, as well as the opportunities, facing the university. Post-war America was a boon for American higher education, especially for a tuition dependent institution such as DePaul—which responded quickly to meet the educational needs of returning servicemen and women. The federal government provided the resources for this boom in education under the terms of the G.I. Bill, which paid the tuition of veterans enrolled in college. DePaul had for nearly forty years offered accessible professional education for part-time students on its downtown campus and it had the space at 64 E. Lake. Enrollments skyrocketed. When the 1945 academic year opened, enrollments had nearly doubled with 8,857 students registering, including 2,384 freshmen. Over 90 percent of these students were enrolled at the downtown campus, many of them full-time, to take advantage of the G.I. Bill. The university offered morning, afternoon and evening courses. By its 50th anniversary year, 1948, DePaul was the largest Catholic university in the United States, with enrollments over 11,000, including 4,368 full-time undergraduate students. (18)

Although rapid enrollment growth strained the ability of DePaul to provide qualified instructors, and adequate academic space, it gave the university much-needed financial relief. The lingering 1907 debt was paid off, and by 1950 the university had $2.4 million in reserves. More importantly, the enrollment increases gave DePaul confidence to pursue the recommendations of the 1944 Farwell report. In 1946, on the basis of another Farwell report on the reorganization of the university, Fr. O'Malley reorganized the institution into four colleges, Liberal Arts and Sciences (LA&S) uptown and downtown, the College of Law, and the College of Commerce; two schools, the Graduate School and the School of Music; and the departments of drama, secretarial studies, home study, and nursing education, along with DePaul Academy. He also established the University Council to ensure greater administrative coordination and required job descriptions for each administrative and staff position. And he created the Office of Public Relations, partly to prepare for a capital campaign. (19) This was a heady time in DePaul's history; it seemed that the institution was finally ready to move forward.

Among the most important developments in 1946 was the creation of a board of lay trustees, which included both Catholic and Protestant lay leaders. In order to honor the 1907 charter and avoid controversy, the board of lay trustees was made adjunct to the board of trustees. The long standing board included 12 individuals: 7 Vincentians who held positions within the university and 5 laymen, one of whom was vice president and comptroller. The lay board included the 5 lay members of the board, plus 11 others. Ten of the lay members were presidents of Chicago corporations, including Stanley P. Farwell, Arthur J. Schmitt and Conrad N. Hilton; two were judges; and one was a prominent attorney. (20)

One of the first actions of the new board was to hire the architectural firm of Skidmore, Owings & Merrill (SOM) to recommend a facilities plan for the university. In December 1947, SOM proposed "A Plan for the Development of DePaul University" with a number of recommendations. Drastic alterations in the physical organization of the university were called for. The firm advised big changes:

> *[T]hat DePaul University physically integrate the Uptown and Downtown divisions in a new building to be situated in or adjacent to the Loop. . . . It is the Downtown division which is bringing recognition to the university in the educational world. . . . The consolidation of these two divisions and the College of Physical Education in a new downtown building would benefit the greatest number of students and would result in increased administrative and teaching efficiency, as well as in greater prestige for the university.* (21)

The report further stated that *"Since the area surrounding the uptown campus is deteriorating and is in urgent need of redevelopment, no further expansion of the university plant should be undertaken without a definite program to prevent the spread of this impending neighborhood blight."* A combined campus would take advantage of the Loop location and would provide facilities for the university's full-time undergraduate students, especially those in the liberal arts and sciences. SOM continued to work on the proposal and in February 1949 completed a Preliminary Design Program for the single building. After much deliberation, the university decided that this plan was not feasible given the institution's financial status; it could not afford a new building and the conversion of an existing Loop building would preclude facilities for physical education. Furthermore, abandoning its uptown campus would sever the university's long term association with the community that surrounded Saint Vincent parish and the uptown campus. (22)

DePaul University celebrated fifty years in Chicago on Saturday, September 25, 1948. This was a milestone for the university and for Father Comerford O'Malley. The archbishop of Chicago and the chancellor of the university, His Eminence Samuel Cardinal Stritch praised DePaul as *"the largest Catholic university in the world . . . [that] has sought to save society from the blight of corrupting secularism."* Mayor Martin Kennelly emphasized the role DePaul "has always played in the cultural, academic and spiritual life of Chicago," as well as its service to students and alumni throughout the city. (23)

An anniversary booklet published for the occasion noted that *"DePaul's special contribution to the Chicago community has been to provide a university education, based on Catholic principles and available at minimum cost to whoever wished it. Most . . . students come from homes with modest incomes. The majority must earn as they learn."* The booklet also listed ninety priests, one-third of whom were Vincentians, who had attended DePaul. These included Fathers William and John Robert Cortelyou, both Vincentians, and Father John J. Egan, a young diocesan priest who had graduated from the academy and spent his freshman year at the university. (24) Father Bill, a 1929 graduate of DePaul, served as dean of the graduate school in the 1960s. His brother, Father John Robert, who graduated from the university in 1943 and received his Ph.D. in biology from Northwestern University, served as professor and chair of the department of biological sciences and then as president from 1964 to 1981. Monsignor John Egan, a leading Catholic reformer, who had a long and distinguished career as an activist pastor in Chicago, joined the University of Notre Dame in 1970 as a senior fellow in theology. Later, he was appointed director of the Institute for Pastoral and Social Concerns. At the request of Cardinal Joseph Bernardin, he returned to Chicago to head the Office of Human Relations and Ecumenism. In 1987, at the age of seventy, Msgr. Egan accepted Father John Richardson's invitation to return to DePaul as special assistant to the president for community affairs. (25)

No one at the time of the university's anniversary celebration could foresee the challenges which lay immediately ahead. Within two years, DePaul faced its gravest crisis since early in the century when Archbishop Quigley had announced that he was establishing his own preparatory seminary and was allowing St. Ignatius College to move to the city's north side. The North Central Association's study of DePaul's finances in 1947–48 revealed the university's shaky financial and academic condition compared to other universities that granted graduate degrees. In its accreditation visit in 1949–1950, the visiting team recommended that DePaul lose its accreditation because of its financial instability, its small number of faculty with doctoral degrees, its low per-student expenditures, and its inadequate library. The NCA Board of Review, which included a former Loyola president, Samuel Knox Wilson, S.J., approved the recommendation, as did the annual conference of the NCA on March 21, 1950. (26)

The university community was shocked by these developments. Father O'Malley reacted quickly. Within weeks, he staved off immediate loss of accreditation and negotiated a one-year delay in which to respond to inaccuracies and to address legitimate criticisms. The NCA's major concern was the ratio of the number of students to the number of full-time Ph.D. faculty. In autumn 1950 the NCA team granted DePaul a two-year extension. By 1952 the university had significantly increased its library budget and had added thirty Ph.D. faculty members, increasing that number from 48 to 78 and the percentage from 25 to 43. The crisis had passed but DePaul's reputation had suffered. This contributed to an enrollment decrease from 9,700 students in 1949 to 6,300 in 1953. (27) The actions taken to save DePaul also moved the university closer to the mainstream of American higher education.

Despite the NCA crisis, DePaul's Catholic and Vincentian identity remained intact during these years. Father O'Malley, like his two immediate predecessors, had received his doctorate in theology from a Roman university. Like them, he continued to emphasize DePaul's Catholic tradition. Father O'Malley noted in the *1949 DePaulian* that students at DePaul were formed in the values that flowed from the charity of Saint Vincent de Paul and the wisdom of Saint Thomas Aquinas. In effect the intellectual underpinnings of the university were Thomistic philosophy and theology. As historian Philip Gleason observed, this was quite characteristic of Catholic universities of this period. It was also reflected in DePaul's faculty; the majority of instructors in the departments of both philosophy and theology were Dominican priests— perhaps the leading proponents of Thomistic philosophy. (28)

In his 1950 address at the Freshman Convocation, O'Malley emphasized that DePaul was a Catholic university, first according to the religious meaning of the term and second in a broader sense, developing its programs to address a universal commitment to education. For O'Malley, religion and philosophy were the two keys to all knowledge and in this respect DePaul was quite similar to other Catholic universities. The curricular commitment to religion and philosophy led to the creation of the Department of Theology in 1959 and the requirement that students take four, two-credit hour courses. In 1951 the Visitor (and provincial) of the western province, James W. Stakelum, C.M., recommended that efforts be made to hire Catholics to the faculty. Although many Catholics were hired during O'Malley's presidency, both he and the university remained committed to the provision of the 1907 charter that a religious test would not be applied in the hiring process. It does appear that only Catholics were hired for certain programs, but this policy was not applied to the university as a whole. Furthermore, O'Malley supported the establishment of a chapter of the American Association of University Professors in 1946, resulting in a more harmonious faculty-administration relationship at DePaul than at some Catholic institutions during the fifties and sixties. (29)

DePaul manifested its Catholic identity in other ways as well. In the 1950s, Arthur Becker, dean of the School of Music since 1921, urged DePaul to request affiliation with the Pontifical Institute in Rome to certify the quality of its sacred music program. Once the School of Music was granted this affiliation, DePaul University achieved canonical status. This meant that the university was subject to the Church's magisterium and the authority of the local archbishop; and the Pope made DePaul one of four pontifical universities in the United States, joining Georgetown University, Catholic University and Niagara. In the mid-seventies the university voluntarily relinquished its canonical status as an affirmation of its independence. (30)

As president, O'Malley linked the mission of DePaul to the mission of the Vincentians. In 1948 he stated, *"DePaul has always attracted the students of modest income and presently charges the lowest rate of tuition of any university in the Chicago area. It will always do this in conformity with the spirit of Saint Vincent de Paul."* (31) Two years earlier, he wrote: *"DePaul University is not a research institution, it has sought to maintain a sound and thorough going teaching standard supported by a high philosophy of education. . . . It must be kept in mind that the university should be a vital force in Education—academic and professional—in Chicago."* (32)

Lack of adequate facilities on both the uptown and the downtown campuses continued to plague the university and remained one of the NCA concerns still to be addressed. When Stanley Farwell was again asked to review the facility needs of the university in 1950, he identified and estimated the respective costs of seven options that would meet DePaul's space needs, including downsizing the student body, expanding the current sites, or identifying a new site for a combined campus. The direction of DePaul's future in this regard was hardly clear. (33)

During the early fifties, Fr. O'Malley asked the university's lawyers whether DePaul could or should stay in the 64 E. Lake facility after its lease expired in 1960. Though the building was large enough to allow for significant expansion, the legal entanglements were many. Should the university move its day program of liberal arts and sciences from the uptown campus to the suburbs? Or should it purchase McCormick Theological Seminary, which was considering relocating? Instead, DePaul moved aggressively to improve existing facilities on both campuses, through a $5.5 million capital campaign that was inaugurated in 1953. Frank Lewis, a successful businessman and Catholic lay leader, generously underwrote the purchase of the seventeen story Kimball Building at the southwest corner of Jackson and Wabash Avenues in 1955. After investing $1.5 million in remodeling, the university renamed it the Lewis Center. (34) The university, with $650,000 raised in the first phase of its campaign, announced that an all-purpose auditorium to be known as Alumni Hall would be built, with ground breaking planned for autumn 1955. (35) It was a major effort to remedy the lack of facilities on the uptown campus; and it was the first new building in nearly twenty years and only the third added since the building boom of 1907 that gave DePaul the Lyceum, the Theatre, and the Academy Building. More important, Alumni Hall was to be the first of a number of planned facilities: a library, a science research center, and an annex to the Liberal Arts Building. All of these improvements were intended to make DePaul a university with a strong and dynamic College of Liberal Arts and Sciences. (36)

DePaul's $1.5 million fund raising campaign for Alumni Hall culminated in a building with a basketball arena seating 5,500, a swimming pool, a cafeteria, and a number of class-rooms with offices for the physical education faculty. The university's nationally prominent Blue Demons basketball team, led by Coach Ray Meyer since 1942, had previously played in "The Barn," the 1907 Theatre Building converted into an arena. The student cafeteria had been a quonset hut informally named Wangler Hall, a legacy of the WWII military presence on campus. And the physical education program, which became part of DePaul in 1947 when it took over the American College of Physical Education, had occupied the old, dilapidated Turner Hall on Diversey Avenue. (37)

The last decade of O'Malley's presidency was a time of transition. The Lewis Center and Alumni Hall marked the end of one phase of the O'Malley presidency and the beginning of the process that led to the major strategic decisions of the 1960s. The university would focus on redefining DePaul's academic mission, developing the Lincoln Park campus, and strengthening the liberal arts and sciences.

Emerging as a Distinctive Catholic University, 1955 to 1981

The effort to rebuild DePaul's reputation as a high quality institution and to develop and retain a professionally competent faculty, fell to John T. Richardson, C.M., who was appointed dean of the graduate school in 1954. Father Richardson, ordained in 1949, had a doctorate in theology and an M.A. in sociology. He had served as dean of studies at Kenrick Seminary in Saint Louis. His tenure at DePaul was characterized by his support for faculty scholarship. In 1955 the North Central Association authorized DePaul to award post-masters, specialist degrees and certificates in education and mathematics. Father Richardson became executive vice president and dean of faculties in 1960, and in 1981 he was appointed DePaul's ninth president. Altogether, his work represented more than four decades of influence that transformed DePaul into a nationally recognized university. (38)

By the 1950s national consensus on what it meant to be a Catholic university began to come apart. Although DePaul resembled other Catholic institutions in many ways, its Vincentian values, especially its openness to students and faculty of all faiths, underscored its distinctive identity as it competed with the best Catholic and non-Catholic universities and colleges in the United States. Charles Strain notes in chapter eight that curricular innovation began at DePaul with Richardson's vision of DePaul as a university not only in substance and name, but also in its Catholicism and Vincentianism. His leadership was apparent in a two-year self-study begun in 1959, which was so critical that some within the university wished to suppress it. Father Richardson, a strong advocate of improved academic quality, argued that the self-study would force the university to adopt a comprehensive development plan that would serve it for the next twenty years.

> *If we fail to act soon, I greatly fear that DePaul will be reduced to permanent second-class status or lower . . .* [we must] *weld all departments together in achieving those goals we all desire so much: a real campus on the north side, substantial faculty improvement, new and imaginative academic programs, probably including the doctorate, support for greatly expanded research, foundation and other types of assistance that will not only keep these activities going but help them to grow.* (39)

As part of the self-study, Fr. O'Malley appointed Fathers Richardson, William Cortelyou and Theodore Wangler to revise the university's statement of purpose. Richardson used this as an opportunity to propose four goals, designating them theological-philosophical, academic, student body, and public service. Constituting a revision of DePaul's mission statement, these divisions marked the beginning of DePaul's transformation. Their formulation became a source of creative tension within DePaul, between being a university in the purely academic sense of the term, and one that is also Catholic, Vincentian and urban. One of the major innovations in the statement of purpose was its emphasis on public service, which eventually became an integral part of DePaul's mission. Richardson suggested to his fellow committee members that under this goal *"we should consider . . . the service that a University like DePaul must contribute to the community it is serving."* (40)

The final self-study document, released in 1961, stated, *"DePaul, then, is and has been a Catholic, urban University* [with 71% of its total student body being Catholic]. *Hence, its purposes and task must be understood in the light of these facts."* And it concluded with a clear vision of the university's future. *"This* [study] *represents a vigorous restlessness—even impatience—for DePaul's attainment to the circle of universities of first rank. With the continuation of this spirit, the desire for greatness that has characterized the university for the past decade, DePaul will move ever closer to this goal until it has attained it—and attain this goal, it will."* (41)

A major issue raised in the 1961 self-study involved the distance between DePaul's goals and the reality of reaching them. The self-study pointed out that *"Its* [DePaul's] *stated orientation was to the sons and daughters of the 'poor to struggling families'. . . . In practice, however, DePaul appears to serve largely the middle-income group."* Ninety percent of its students live in the city of Chicago, slightly more than half attend at night. Many of the day students also work. The study also stated, *"The commuter-school image still seems to be the prevailing one in the mind of many Board members. DePaul is this, but it is much more. What is needed is a more balanced image."* (42)

Redefining DePaul's academic mission meant strengthening the liberal arts and sciences. This in turn meant that new facilities were needed on the uptown campus, a recurring theme in DePaul's history and one that touched on DePaul's relationship with the larger Chicago community. DePaul's quest for academic recognition and distinction was unquestionably frustrated by the institution's inadequate buildings and other features of its infrastructure. These three issues, the lack of facilities, the need for interaction with the larger community, and the quest for higher academic quality, have shaped DePaul's mission as a Catholic, Vincentian and urban university, especially since the 1950s. Though fund-raising was difficult in the mid-1950s, two options that the university refused to consider were increasing the tuition and undertaking significant new debt. Father O'Malley felt that raising tuition betrayed DePaul's mission of offering educational opportunities at the lowest price possible. As for borrowing funds, few wished to repeat the nightmare of the 1907 debt that had taken forty years to pay off. In October

DePaul University buildings, including a portion of St. Vincent DePaul Church as they looked in 1904.

1955, the University Council discussed the possibility of using federal grants to build housing in Lincoln Park for its 25 or 30 out-of-state music students and 70 foreign students. This housing could also be used by the religious students who came to DePaul in large numbers during the summer. It was recommended *"that the university take the necessary steps to provide housing facilities for students and faculty."* (43)

Father Theodore Wangler, who represented the university on the Lincoln Park Conservation Association, a consortium of neighborhood organizations, reported that federal urban renewal funds, available to the community, made DePaul eligible to buy improved land from the city inexpensively. As a consequence, the board of trustees authorized hiring a planner. (44) In Wangler's formal presentation to directors of the Lincoln Park Conservation Association in May 1961, he argued that DePaul should be included in the first phase of the urban renewal process. DePaul was more than a Catholic university, it was an asset for and a partner with the larger urban community. *"Private institutions are a strong anchor for the future building up of the area because of their stability and because they are willing to expend millions of dollars in improvement and expansion,"* he observed. The Housing Act of 1959 provided that special consideration be given to urban universities, and he warned that for DePaul to survive it must expand. *"If DePaul is not included in the first project, we will come up to 1963–1965 hamstrung by the lack of facilities for college students who wish to enter. . . . When we speak of DePaul's needs we are not speaking in a selfish sense, because we are a semi-public institution serving the needs of the Lincoln Park Community, Chicago, and the nation,"* he argued. DePaul's active support of the Lincoln Park urban renewal program was its demonstration of solidarity with the community and a reminder to the association that many DePaul alumni were involved in Chicago politics. (45)

Barton-Aschman Associates, who were the planners the board of trustees had selected in 1959, presented a completed DePaul plan in May 1961. It called for acquiring a major portion of the land surrounding the university to support an anticipated increase in enrollment in LA&S and Physical Education from 1,200 to 2,000 students. It also provided sufficient space to build a science building, a general classroom building, a library, a 400 seat performance hall, and two residence halls, 350 beds for men and 250 beds for women. (46)

In December 1961 DePaul began purchasing land under the urban renewal process to implement its plan, and before the end of 1962, the university announced its campaign, "The Program for Greatness". Twelve million dollars were earmarked for a science center, a library, classrooms, a student union, an auditorium and a residence hall, $11 million for faculty salaries and distinguished professorships, $2 million for student scholarships, and $250,000 for community service programs, the latter a pragmatic response to the university's partnership with the neighborhood and the city and a manifestation of its Vincentian mission. A press release emphasized the university's commitment to community service:

The $250,000 to help finance DePaul's community-service programs will strengthen an area in which the DePaul faculty has already been prominent . . . [they] have embraced areas from psychological testing to legal symposia, from free recitals and concerts to seminars on electronic data processing, from water pollution in the Great Lakes to doing business in Japan and Hong Kong, from youth welfare workshops for neighborhood leaders to institutes on scriptural theology. (47)

In the latter years of O'Malley's presidency, Fathers Richardson and John R. Cortelyou, chairman of the department of biological sciences, were the voices of the future. Their informal leadership became official in 1964 when Cortelyou was appointed president and Richardson was reappointed executive vice president, continuing a unique partnership that guided the university for nearly thirty more years.

Cortelyou's presidency transformed DePaul. Within the first three years of his tenure, the university approved a new curricular design, established DePaul College (a general education program for all undergraduates), gained approval to offer doctoral programs, and opened the Schmitt Academic Center. In chapters 7 and 8 Thomas Croak and Charles Strain discuss the implications of these developments. A series of articles in *The Chicago Tribune* in 1965 described the excitement in the air at DePaul. The *Tribune* gave admiring coverage to DePaul's building plans in Lincoln Park and its academic programs, describing the College of Law as "the mother of the city's top lawyers." The articles also mentioned that over half of DePaul's graduates in the sciences went on for Ph.D.s and noted further changes at DePaul, such as the new curriculum and the quarter system. Selected faculty members singled out for special coverage included philosopher Gerald Kreyche, psychologists Glen Jensen and John McCauley, chemist Robert Miller and physicist Edwin Schillinger. (48)

Father Richardson, first as dean of the Graduate School and then as executive vice president, was committed to encouraging faculty to be practicing scholars and researchers as well as effective teachers. All academic programs had to be of high quality, and supported by key faculty and administrators. He worked particularly to strengthen the College of Liberal Arts and Sciences. Father Cortelyou, trained as a research scientist at Northwestern, also pointed out the importance of scholar-teachers to DePaul's survival as a university.

Both Richardson and Cortelyou acknowledged the importance of funding if DePaul's academic mission and the strengthening of its arts and sciences programs were to be successfully undertaken. An increasing number of federal programs offered a ready source of support for DePaul's quest for improved academic quality. The decision to actively pursue federal funding

Interior view of the DePaul University College Theater, erected in 1907.

gave rise to considerable dialogue over the purpose and mission of DePaul. The emphasis on research, the establishment of doctoral programs, and the acquisition of land in Lincoln Park on which to build new facilities, all challenged and shaped what came to be called DePaul's Catholic, Vincentian and urban character.

Despite the commitment of Richardson and Cortelyou to research and the sciences, some in the university and the Vincentian community expressed concerns about this emphasis. James A. Fischer, C.M., provincial of the Western Province of the Congregation of the Mission (1962–1971) and chairman of DePaul's board of trustees (1962–1967), argued that disproportionate attention to the sciences meant that the already weak departments of philosophy and theology were being unduly neglected, thus endangering DePaul's Catholic and Vincentian values and identity. Later, when funding problems required ranking the proposed facilities, the science research building program was assigned a lower priority. In an effort to salvage some of its projects, the university combined the library and liberal arts classroom/office, and designated the student center and a dormitory as the next two projects, postponing indefinitely the construction of a science research center. (49)

Raising building funds during the capital campaign went slowly, and the university relied increasingly on federal funds to fulfill its academic plans. Between 1965 and 1967 Fathers Wangler and Cortelyou lobbied the Lincoln Park Conservation Association (LPCA) and Chicago's mayor to include DePaul in the second phase of the neighborhood urban renewal plan so that the university could proceed with its planned growth by buying additional land. Father Wangler referred to DePaul's decision in 1952 to stay in Lincoln Park and a promise by then Mayor Kennelly that the city would do everything possible to keep DePaul in the city. In January 1967 Cortelyou wrote Mayor Richard J. Daley expressing concern and disappointment over the city's delay in implementing Phase II of the Lincoln Park area plan. He emphasized DePaul's commitment to remain in the community was based on the assumption that it could expand. It had already spent $1 million on property and $4.5 million on a new facility. (50)

The 1967 North Central accreditation report provides insight into the importance of federal funds and the role of borrowing in reshaping the university. It reported that the construction of the Schmitt Academic Center was the first of more than $11 million in facilities that would be completed by 1973. The Schmitt Center was made possible through a $1.4 million Title I grant and a $2 million Title III loan. Federal grants and loans would also be necessary to complete the other planned facilities. By 1966 DePaul had again turned to borrowing, as well as to federal grants, to support its academic goals. In that year, the debt had increased to $2.6 million. This was equal to approximately half of the tuition revenue generated that year. (51)

The LPCA's urban renewal plan included DePaul's expansion plans and generated considerable criticism from groups within the Lincoln Park community, as well as from some faculty and students. The poor, many of whom were African American and Puerto Rican, mobilized in opposition, as urban renewal threatened their homes and businesses. To address some of these concerns, Father Cortelyou, in a memorandum to Father Richardson and the six deans

An event at DePaul University's College Theater, circa 1920.

in October 1967, called on the university to open its doors to the community as it was open-ing the doors of the new Schmitt Academic Center,

> *N ow that the Arthur J. Schmitt Center is no longer a dream but a reality, I believe it is time to give some serious consideration to the fact that it is not an entity unto itself, . . . [I]t is an entity in the Lincoln Park Commu-nity of new dimensions and enhanced stature. It is the university in an iden-tifiable community in contrast to the university Lewis Center, which can be identified in one sense as being located in a faceless community. . . . It is a function and a commitment of the university to make its contribution to the community. Particularly true is this for an urban community. . . . You may be concerned that what I am requesting is going to make the university a social agency. In its broadest interpretation, this may be so. But the heart of what I am requesting is the bringing of people into the university to acquire learning experiences which they may carry back into the community, and translate them into social action.* (52)

Father Cortelyou also established an Ad Hoc Committee on Community Interaction. DePaul's deans were asked to contribute to the inventory of university services to the commu-nity, to encourage faculty to move into the neighborhood and to develop activities that fo-cused on the Lincoln Park area. At the same time, the university created the office and posi-tion of Community Coordinator. This office served as an information nerve center, promoting interaction between the university's programs and the community, organizing, for example, recreation activities in Alumni Hall for the children of the community. (53)

The 1960s are covered in later chapters in this volume. In chapter eight, Charles Strain discusses the importance of the Curricular Design that was adopted in 1964. It became the foundation for the new university which was destined to transform DePaul into an institution that would draw national attention. In the words of a university report, the new curriculum was designed to *"utilize the resources of the metropolitan area, which, in effect, constitute the total university campus. It is in this environment that the person will discharge his personal and social responsibility."* The report also argued that an expected consequence *"of being enrolled in a university founded by the Vincentian Fathers is evidence of the acceptance of selflessness as a present and future way of life, in the family, in vocation and in society. The notion of service within and without the university shall be considered to be a productive end of curricular offerings."* (54)

The plan redefined the roles of the philosophy and theology, calling on these disciplines to be the integrating force within this Catholic university. The plan provided the academic link to the newly emphasized public service responsibilities of the university; it supported an intellectual environment that gave rise to the doctoral programs in philosophy, psychology and the biological sciences. Philosophy was expected to impact the entire curriculum because of its importance in general education; psychology linked research/learning and public service, and the biological sciences represented the importance given to the sciences and to pure research.

The mid-sixties were an exciting time for the university and for American society at large. Revolutionary changes in the Catholic Church and in the nation mirrored internal changes at DePaul. Vatican II supported the vision of Richardson, Gerald Kreyche, the chairman who transformed the department of philosophy, William Cortelyou, who set the stage for the transition from theology to religious studies, and a group of young economists who enthusiastically endorsed and supported the Church's social teachings. Many of the new faculty saw themselves as activist-scholars championing the cause of peace, justice and civil rights. In doing so they believed they were living the values of Saint Vincent de Paul.

The campus plan for Lincoln Park had to be completed if the vision of Richardson and energetic faculty members was to become a reality. These faculty members established the university's academic reputation. DePaul University would no longer be seen simply as a commuter institution with 90 percent of its students being taught on the Loop campus. The new Lincoln Park campus, formerly known as the uptown campus, with the Schmitt Academic Center, the Stuart Student Center, and DePaul's first residence hall, made it possible to expand enrollments in the College of Arts and Sciences and the School of Education. Enrollment growth provided the resources to increase significantly the number of doctorally trained faculty. The innovative general education program, the three doctoral programs with the possibility of more to come, and the increased support for research made DePaul attractive to many prospective faculty members.

As DePaul prepared for its 1967 accreditation visit, the sense of anticipation contrasted sharply with the air of fear and trepidation that had engulfed the campus during the visits of the 1950s. By 1966 the administration and the faculty, proud of their accomplishments, eagerly awaited the expected affirmative response. The "new" DePaul was also reflected in its revised statement of purpose. *"DePaul University is founded on Judaic-Christian principles and continues to assert the contemporaneous relevance of these principles to higher education. The university expresses these principles especially by passing on the heritage of Saint Vincent de Paul which inspires perfection of the individual person through purposeful involvement with other persons and social institutions."* One of DePaul's goals in its 1967 self-study was *"To pursue learning that provides a direction for a moral and aesthetic life, for a dedication to the service of other persons, and for responsible involvement in various communities and institutions."* The report also explained the new role of faculty within the university: *"In a sense here has been change in purpose; namely, to consider the faculty and students as learners together, rather than the teacher and those who are taught."* (55) DePaul's mission statement, emphasizing Judaic-Christian principles, instead of those of Saint Thomas Aquinas, and the heritage of Saint Vincent, was clearly separating DePaul from many of its Catholic peer institutions.

The four NCA visitors, all from state universities, were impressed with DePaul during their May 15–18, 1967 visit. Their positive report endorsed moving ahead on doctoral education, as long as DePaul addressed the concerns listed in the final report. There were no surprises. The university would have to increase the budgets for those departments involved in doctoral education, to establish a graduate council, to create a university-wide research fund, and to build an endowment. The report noted a number of weaknesses, including the lack of internal collaboration and too much departmental and program autonomy, resulting in the failure to innovate in many areas of the university. Concern for students was expressed. Dormitories were needed; students should be allowed to participate in university governance. The report also commented on the high rate of attrition among students, *"DePaul is essentially a metropolitan Chicago university. . . . The combined work and course load of some students is too heavy. This may be a factor that contributes to the heavy drop-out and alarming course change record."* (56)

As with the larger society, the rosy enthusiasm and self-confidence of the mid-sixties began to turn into pessimism, disenchantment and conflict within five years. As the tensions mounted in the larger society, and especially in the Lincoln Park community, Father Cortelyou reminded the university community that DePaul's mission was public service and not community action and that it served all of Chicagoland. Because DePaul was a university, it was compelled to operate from a basis of policy and its chief contribution was in the area of education. The service programs most mentioned were those of the Mental Health Center and the School of Education, especially programs with Oscar Mayer School. (57)

John Rury in his chapter recounts the events surrounding the take over of the Schmitt Academic Center (SAC) in May 1969 by the Black Student Union. Some faculty members began to voice doubts about the quest for academic quality if it seemed to conflict with Vincentian values. In response to the sit-in at SAC, fifty-three faculty members sent a memo to the board of trustees and the officers of the university that called on *"DePaul to take action to insure that the poor of the Lincoln Park area are able to remain in the area and thus enjoy the benefits of its renewal. . . . A University named 'DePaul' can do no less."* One faculty member, long active in the affairs of Lincoln Park, sent a personal letter to Father Cortelyou urging him to move beyond the LPCA, which was viewed as representative of the middle class against the poor. He suggested that the university purchase the Alexian Brothers land instead of moving south of Belden, that it support the efforts of the poor to obtain low-income housing in the community, and that it cooperate with Waller High School to establish a pipeline for minority stu-

The Lyceum building as it looked in 1937, the site of DePaul's uptown library and some administrative offices.

dents. He concluded, *"I pray that God will give you strength and wisdom in these trying times and guide you in the important decisions that you have to make. I hope that you know that I am at your service completely."* (58)

The Campaign for Greatness ultimately failed to generate enough external support to complete the campus plan. Only three buildings were built, the Schmitt Academic Center, the Stuart Student Center, and Clifton Hall, the first large residential facility on campus. The science faculty members were especially frustrated because of the failure to raise the funds for the much needed science research center, along with a significant reduction of federal support for science research and science students because of the war in Vietnam. The Ph.D. in biology became largely a program on paper, with very few students.

By the mid-seventies, many in the university asked what was happening to the institution's Catholic and Vincentian presence. Some believed that the newly created department of religious studies and the doctoral program in philosophy had failed to become the integrating disciplines necessary for a Catholic university. They lamented a decline in the number of Vincentians on the faculty because of new hiring processes and the shrinking number of available Vincentians. And symbolic of the disappearance of visible manifestations of Catholic identity was DePaul's voluntary rescission of its canonical status as a pontifical university in 1974. Fathers Cortelyou and Richardson had requested this in the mid-sixties because of the fear of losing federal funds, and out of concerns for academic freedom. (59) Still, this decision exacerbated fears about the university's changing identity.

The Vincentians of the midwest province were concerned about their larger mission, as well as their role at DePaul. Some questioned the decision to create a lay-dominated board of trustees, even if it was done to insure eligibility for federal and state funds and to increase external support for the new DePaul. The deleting of the word "Catholic" in DePaul's statement of purpose and the replacing of theology courses by classes that studied religion as a cultural phenomenon increased the concerns. It was also difficult for Vincentians outside of the university to understand the argument of Fathers Cortelyou, Richardson, and Bruce Vawter, the newly named chairperson of the Department of Religious Studies, that Vincentian candidates could only be appointed to the full-time faculty following a national search and with the approval of the faculty. (60) In the move to improve academic quality and to emphasize the university's ecumenism, fears about the institution's changing identity persisted.

During the summer of 1975, a team of five representatives from DePaul attended a two-week seminar in Colorado, sponsored by the Danforth Foundation, titled "Values in Higher Education." The five included two Vincentians, Edward Riley and John C. Overcamp, and three lay faculty, Patricia Ewers, chairperson of English, Gerald Kreyche, chairman of philosophy, and Andrew Kopan, professor of education. This led to the naming of Father Riley to head a committee to look at DePaul as a Catholic university. The committee recommended increasing the number of Catholics on the faculty, hiring of individuals whose values were similar and supportive of the values of the university, reestablishment of a department of theology, creating an active Catholic ministry program, and offering more courses that focused on Catholicism. (61)

These discussions coincided with the collection of data to support a larger self-study being undertaken in preparation for the North Central Accreditation visit in 1976–1977. These data indicated that in 1976 only about half of the full-time faculty were Catholic with 20 percent identifying themselves as Protestant and 10 percent as Jewish. This was in contrast to twenty years earlier when nearly 70 percent were Catholic and just 2 percent were Jewish. Fifty-six percent of the students were Catholic; 75 percent of the day students but less than half of the part-time and professional students. Clearly, DePaul was changing in subtle but significant ways. (62)

Another response to the concerns over identity was a memo which outlined a plan by which the Vincentian presence could be enhanced through carrying out service to the poor. Two propositions were discussed. The first was that *"DePaul has from its foundation continuously served the poor as one of the university's distinctive religious/social purposes."* This would be continued through extending professional services offered by the university to the poor and through the active recruitment and retention of students who could not otherwise afford a college degree, by providing increased institutional aid and work-study opportunities. The second proposition was that the service, especially professional, to the poor should be done under the aegis of the Vincentians at the university. Thus, the number of Vincentians on campus would increase as these outreach programs increased. In the end, however, greater recruitment of minority students was implemented but not the other recommendations. (63)

At the same time, yet another committee, a majority of whom were Vincentians, did a study of the Vincentian presence within the university. The study concluded that there was little awareness of the Vincentian heritage at DePaul or the manifestation of specific Vincentian values, such as service to the poor, trust in the providence of God, charity, humility and simplicity. As a result, the committee made five recommendations. The first was to make definite public statements to the entire university regarding Vincentianism and how it applied to the daily operation of the institution. The second was to make use of university publications to communicate the Vincentian story. There were recommendations to increase the number of Vincentians at the university and to strengthen University Ministry. And finally the committee suggested the university review the curriculum to determine the influence of Vincentian ideals. Clearly, the university's Catholic and Vincentian character could no longer be taken for granted. (64)

This study led one Vincentian to conclude that DePaul had *"quietly slipped from being a Catholic university to being a private-independent university with no one quite aware that it happened."* (65) Thus, it seemed to some that the mission had succumbed to the quest for greater quality and academic recognition. But not everyone agreed. On looking back at the changes of the 1960s and 1970s, Charles Strain suggests in his chapter that it is important to see the pervasive professionalization of Catholic higher education—represented at DePaul by Father Richardson's vision—not as a form of secularization, but as a manifest sign of a willed commitment to carry out the educational mission of Catholic universities from within the heart of the surrounding culture.

Yet, while the various reports documented the pessimism of many about the future of DePaul's Catholic and Vincentian character, they resulted in the inclusion of strong statements on the importance of DePaul's Catholic and Vincentian identity in the North Central accreditation report and the linking of this identity to the urban mission of the university. Such statements provided the framework for discussing these issues during the 1980s.

The North Central self-study report gave the university the opportunity to articulate the link between its religious values and its urban presence. This connection was emphasized in the opening section:

> *DePaul's most distinguishing characteristics are Vincentian, Catholic and urban. Although its mission is complex, certain dominant features stand out: religious personalism, a dedication to service in the tradition of Saint Vincent dePaul, a predilection for educating first generation college students, relating religious values and ethical principles to learning, academic programs developed for career and other expressed needs of students, emphasis on strong instructional programs, significant research limited to selected areas, and a commitment to public service and close cooperation with the Chicago metropolitan community. (66)*

Thus, the terms Catholic, Vincentian and urban were linked. DePaul's Catholicism and Vincentianism were manifested by religious personalism, dedication to service, and a community orientation reflected in a variety of services offered to the community as outcomes of instruction and research. The 1977 Report also emphasized service to the community.

> *In keeping with its special commitment to serve the people of metropolitan Chicago, the university has inaugurated a number of new services and expanded existing ones. Significant among these services are a new Loop Le-*

gal Clinic; a distinctively community-oriented and greatly expanded Mental Health Center; a new psycho-educational clinic for children with learning disabilities; a neighborhood recreation program; a specially funded program to prepare bilingual teachers for inner-city schools of Chicago; and a large number of instructional public service programs offered. (67)

Under university goals, the report implied that DePaul was struggling with what it meant to be Catholic, noting that *"The Catholic character is changing and thus the university will continue its study."* (68) Under the section focusing on religious-philosophical goals, the report described the university's commitment to support *"an environment which provides members of the university with opportunities and encouragement for rendering services to other persons, and for active participation in religious, cultural, social, and political agencies and institutions."* (69) As a part of the university's programmatic goals was the commitment to be "community oriented," offering a variety of services to the community as the outcomes of instruction and research and through joint ventures with the business, professional and cultural community of Chicago. (70)

Although the 1970s were years of tension and disappointment for DePaul, it was also a period of significant accomplishments. The School for New Learning was established in 1972; the university purchased the Finchley Building adjacent to Lewis Center in the same year and acquired land and facilities from the McCormick Theological Seminary in 1976 and 1977, adding residential facilities, performance spaces, and classrooms and offices for the School of Music and other programs; the Goodman School of Drama became part of DePaul in 1978; enrollments increased, especially among African Americans and women. In 1976–1977 14 percent of the student body was African American compared to 3 percent in 1967; the number of female students in the College of Law increased from 5 to 36 percent, in the graduate business programs from 3 to 19 percent. And women made up 23 percent of the full-time faculty. (71)

Yet, despite the many positive steps taken by the university, the visiting team, although recommending continued accreditation, was quite critical. Among the concerns identified were the absence of consistent planning for the future, the lack of affirmative action (with only three African American faculty members and two professional staff members), increasing professionalism of the curriculum (with one-fourth of the majors in arts and sciences in nursing and a doubling of enrollments in commerce in five years), the curricular problems with DePaul College, and the administrative problems with nursing, the Graduate School, and the College of Liberal Arts and Sciences. Despite the advances of the sixties, significant challenges remained. (72)

On the positive side, the NCA Self-Study made it possible for the university to turn the tension over its Catholic and Vincentian mission into a positive force. The NCA Report was the first public articulation of the terms Catholic, Vincentian and urban as unifying characteristics of the university. Within two years the mission statement was revised to strengthen the connection between the academic mission and the Vincentian/urban character. It read, *"Public service shall be another important University function. This service is both grateful reciprocity to a community that has nurtured DePaul over the years, and the channel through which specialized competencies of faculty and students are further developed and directed toward others."* (73)

To respond to the NCA concerns about planning, the university made a commitment to strategic planning with the appointment of Howard Sulkin as vice president for planning. Sulkin had been the founding dean of the School for New Learning in 1972. His first planning effort resulted in 1979 in "Landmarks for Tomorrow: a Process of Planning for Improvement at DePaul." "Landmarks" gave life to the newly approved mission statement. For example, under Public Service, it called for, *"increasing ties between our academic programs and community agencies and institutions, offering more public service activities to the larger community, and regular reviewing of public services activities to insure quality."* (74)

As the 1970s ended, DePaul stood ready to embrace the future with renewed commitment to its Catholic, Vincentian and urban values. The decades ahead would bring fresh challenges, but also unprecedented recognition for the university and growth.

DePaul Emerges as a National Institution: The Richardson Years

The early 1980s marked another period of transition for the university. In 1981 John T. Richardson, C.M., the executive vice president and dean of faculties since 1960, was inaugurated as DePaul's ninth president. Patricia Ewers, the dean of the College of Liberal Arts and Sciences became dean of faculties and vice president for academic affairs. Most of the deans were relatively new to DePaul and had brought experience from a wide range of other institutions. By 1981 many of the concerns raised in the NCA report of 1977 had been addressed. A new general education program, the Liberal Studies Program, had replaced the 1967 curriculum. Administratively, the College of Liberal Arts and Sciences was strengthened with the transfer of responsibility to the dean of the college for both general education and graduate education. DePaul College and the Graduate School disappeared as administrative entities. Minority enrollments continued to increase as did the number of minority faculty and staff. However, on the downside, after a decade of enrollment increases, enrollments began to decrease in the early eighties. This occurred at the time when the university had taken on new costs, with the decision to provide a home for the Goodman School of Drama and the acquisition in 1981 of the ten-story Lyon-Healy Building on the northeast corner of Jackson and Wabash. The decreasing enrollments were troubling developments, to say the least.

Adopting themes from Fr. Richardson's inaugural address, the university's second planning document, "Forging the Next Phase," became public in October 1982. In this plan, Richardson shared his vision for DePaul. The three elements that formed this vision were the commitments to high academic quality, to providing educational and learning opportunities for students of all ages, and to be not only in and of the city, but to serve as a model of excellence as an urban university. He wrote, "[DePaul has] *flourished precisely because we are part of the yeasty environment of Chicago, and we have grown stronger because we have sought to be involved in all facets of urban life.*" In its mission, DePaul *"is a partner with other institutions of the community—business, health, government, schools, social welfare, and the arts."* Furthermore, *"DePaul's community service leadership will be enhanced by fostering existing and new community service centers related to academic programs, increasing DePaul's performing and fine arts presence in the community, and encouraging individual and organizational involvement with agencies and institutions of the community."* (75)

That same year, Richardson's vision was reflected in a section of the College of Liberal Arts and Science interim planning report titled "The Urban Mission." *"[DePaul's] unique relationship with Chicago is determined by the Vincentian ideal of mission to people. . . . Decisions that dealt with which students DePaul would recruit, how these students would be served, and where DePaul would be located have all been part of this tradition of being an integral part in the life of the people of Chicago."* The report listed a number of urban initiatives: a B.A. in urban studies, an expanded presence on the Loop campus—with new programs in computer science and taking responsibility for the M.S. in the management of public services, involvement in a number of service programs for Hispanics through grants from the Joyce and Ford foundations, and plans to propose the establishment of an urban research institute. (76)

A year later, the university issued a third planning document, "Excellence with Diversity." This report emphasized, *"Since DePaul is Catholic, Vincentian and urban, it is essential that the university not overlook its responsibilities to serve society. During the coming years, the academic areas will explore new ways to serve."* (77) Examples included the expanded programs for the Hispanic community, the establishment of the English Language Institute and the Chicago Area Studies Center. To move the university forward the plan called for a $50 million capital campaign and the establishment of an Office of Enrollment Management as a response to the decreasing enrollments. (78)

The combined efforts of the new university leaders, supported by the deans and the faculty and staff, reversed the decline in enrollments, developed a new campus plan for Lincoln Park, and started a process of obtaining corporate and foundation support for both academic and mission-related outreach efforts. DePaul in the 1980s committed itself to enhance the quality of its academic programs and to respond to the needs of the larger urban community.

Richard Yanikoski in his 1986 article, "DePaul University: Urban by Design" in *Current Issues in Catholic Higher Education,* summarized the range of activities that DePaul had undertaken. To expand educational opportunities for talented Hispanic students, DePaul had formed in 1981 (with a Ford Foundation grant) the Hispanic Alliance with Loyola University and Mundelein College. Specific programs which DePaul developed included the Hispanic Women's Program, aimed at recruiting and supporting older Hispanic women, Project STEP, a program that provided Saturday classes to high school students on campus from Benito Juarez High School, and a peer counseling program at Kelvyn Park High School. In addition DePaul's graduate program in bilingual learning disabilities provided services for Hispanic children and the Center for Hispanic Research focused on key issues affecting the Hispanic community. Outreach efforts ranged from informal student involvement in community projects through the Office of Campus Ministry to formal, course-connected programs offered by the College of Law's Legal Clinic and the Department of Psychology's Mental Health Center.

The Theatre School put on more than ninety performances of its Children's Series, entertaining more than 35,000 children, while the School of Music scheduled more than 150 public events a year. The Institute for Business Ethics, the Small Business Institute, and the Center for Economic Education also provided services and programs that served the larger community. Yanikoski concluded with *"The mission of DePaul University today is . . . to provide moral vision and intellectual enrichment to men and women of high ability, and simultaneously to render direct service to those in society who for various reasons have not yet been able to enjoy the fruits of social progress."* (79)

Following the unexpected enrollment decreases of the early 1980s, the university initiated a series of interventions that turned enrollments around by 1984 and led to the establishment of the Office of Enrollment Management under Anne Kennedy, who was appointed associate vice president. The university's goal was to stabilize enrollments at approximately 12,500 students with 4,500 full-time undergraduate students. To accomplish this and to maintain the academic quality of its programs, the university recognized that it had to expand the residential student population. In interviewing architectural firms for designing the new residence hall, the university was impressed with the presentation of FCL Architects. The firm proposed that the university should take this opportunity to develop a campus plan to insure that this building and future buildings would link the campus together and be compatible with the surrounding neighborhood.

The hiring of FCL to design both the new residence hall and the campus plan began a new phase in the relationship between the university and the larger Lincoln Park community. In the first of what came to be hundreds of meetings in the years to follow, university representatives, James Doyle, vice president for student affairs, and Kenneth McHugh, then vice president for business and finance, met with members of the Lincoln Park Conservation Association in 1984 to lay out DePaul's plans for the Lincoln Park campus. This master plan showed the location of the proposed residence hall, as well as sites for other buildings. The plan called for turning a parking lot into the site of the residence hall and creating a quadrangle with the closing of Seminary Avenue. It also called for a recreation facility, a library, a parking garage with retail stores at street level along Sheffield and graduate student housing at Seminary and Belden. Ground breaking occurred in June 1985 for University Hall and with its opening the following September, the university increased its residential population by 50 percent to 900 students. In response to the plan one neighbor wrote recommending that the university sell its few lots along Racine and buy less developed/less expensive land further west of Racine. If DePaul waits five years, the latter noted, *"the only land available then will be out in Naperville"* (perhaps a premonition of the university's decision to open a large facility in Naperville in 1997). This experience of planning with its Lincoln Park neighbors served DePaul well. The ad hoc Lincoln Park Neighbors Advisory Committee soon became an important part of a unique town/gown relationship, a good portent for the future. (80)

The university had renewed confidence as it prepared for the decennial visit of the North Central Accreditation team in 1987. It had addressed the major concerns identified in 1977; it had institutionalized a strategic planning process; it had reversed the enrollment decreases of the early eighties; and it had developed facility plans for both campuses. In addition to responding to the requirements of the NCA, the university used the self-study process as an opportunity to incorporate the study into its on-going strategic planning effort. The focus of future planning was on balancing the competing aims that were embedded in its mission statement. The 1986 mission statement, in brief, described DePaul *"as a comprehensive, urban, Catholic University dedicated first and foremost to excellence in instruction within an environment emphasizing equal opportunity and personal attention."* (81)

The self-study identified five tensions that arose from the university's mission. These were liberal learning versus professional education, research versus teaching, student quality versus student access, academic freedom and individual conscience versus Catholic and corporate identity, creative opportunities versus limited resources. The challenge to DePaul was in balancing tensions such as these: becoming a university of distinction, yet also remaining Catholic, Vincentian and urban. (82)

Following in the spirit of the 1987 Self-Study Report, the university undertook an ambitious and aggressive plan to become one of the major, national Catholic universities and a premier urban university. This occurred despite a conservative note in the NCA self-study itself.

The greatest danger facing DePaul is that its agenda may be more ambitious than its resources will permit. A central theme which emerged from the recent planning cycle is the need to ensure that the present position of the university is properly financed. The university must ensure that its resources are commensurate with its goals and plans. (83)

As part of the self-study, the university asked its seven colleges and schools to develop positioning statements identifying institutions which they would liked to be compared to, and how they would accomplish this. For the professional programs, this process was fairly easy. Commerce, law, music and theater were increasingly competitive for both the best students and faculty. For the College of Liberal Arts and Sciences, however, this task was much more challenging. Like the university, it was not evident which institutions could be considered peers, and like the university, it faced the challenge of balancing the five tensions or competing aims identified in the self-study. The college had nearly twenty-five departments and programs offering over forty degree programs, including two Ph.D. programs (the Ph.D. in biology had been dropped in 1984). Of the 3,000 undergraduate students, however, only 1,600 were full-time day students. Half of these were majoring in computer science, communication and nursing. Most of the faculty did much of their teaching in general education. Few departments in the traditional disciplines of the arts and sciences were large enough to offer an array of advanced courses on a regular basis. Most of the graduate programs had fewer than fifty part-time students. Even with the new residence hall, the 900 students living on campus did not provide a sufficient number of residents to support a viable intellectual and social community. On top of this, the campus lacked the library, science lab, and recreation facilities necessary to support a repositioning of the college and the university.

In the spring of 1987, after discussions involving Richard Heise, the chairman of the Academic Affairs Committee of the board of trustees, Patricia Ewers, vice president for academic affairs, and Richard J. Meister, dean of the College of Liberal Arts and Sciences, the college developed a plan. This plan, in turn, influenced the university's plan that was adopted by the board of trustees in the autumn of 1988. The LA&S plan called for DePaul University to become one of the top five Catholic institutions in the United States by 1998. It also emphasized DePaul's mission, *"DePaul's mission and character are unique, reflecting its own Catholic, Vincentian, and urban traditions. Academic and outreach programs support its tradition of ecumenism, its Vincentian personalism in serving others, and its commitment to fulfilling the aspirations of men and women in Black, Hispanic and Asian communities in Chicago."* Enrollment growth was the strategy that would drive DePaul's efforts to enhance its academic quality, influence and reputation. By 1998, the year of DePaul's centennial, the university would enroll 18,000 students, of whom two to three thousand would live on campus. The College of Liberal Arts and Sciences and the School of Education would serve 3,500 to 4,000 full-time students. To achieve this growth would require new academic programs and the implementation of the campus plan, beginning with a new library, additional residential facilities, a science lab building, and a student recreation facility. In turn, growth, along with borrowing and aggressive tuition pricing, would provide the funds to support new programs, the enhancement of existing programs, and the new facilities. For the university the plan called for expanding the suburban campuses that served the part-time, professional students and for purchasing and renovating the Goldblatt Building, which was an empty shell owned by the city and located along State Street, separated from the Lewis Center by an alley. (84)

In calling for the university to expand its recruitment of out-of-state students and to become nationally recognized, the plan also challenged DePaul to reflect on, articulate and manifest its Catholic, Vincentian and urban mission. The college's plan proposed that its *"Centers and Institutes . . . implement research and outreach projects that manifest the university's mission as a Catholic, Vincentian and urban University. Such centers enable faculty and students from a variety of disciplines to participate in research projects and to contribute to outreach programs."* The plan also identified the external factors that supported its vision of the future. DePaul's location in Chicago gave it access to many cultural and economic resources that would enhance its academic programs and offer many social, intellectual, and professional opportunities for students. The Lincoln Park community, which had become one of the safest and most gentrified urban neighborhoods in the United States, offered a range of social and cultural activities. And DePaul had national name recognition because of television coverage of its highly successful basketball teams in the 1980s. (85)

During the summer of 1988, the university incorporated the LA&S plan into a larger university plan. This plan was adopted by the board of trustees that autumn. At the same time, the discussions with the Lincoln Park neighbors finalized a proposal for a Planned Unit Development (PUD) that was then approved by the city. To insure continued cooperation between the university and the community, a ten-year agreement on the future development of the campus was signed in 1989 by the university and the Lincoln Park neighborhood associations. Both the university and the Lincoln Park community had come a long way since the original interactions in the 1950s. Phase I of the PUD called for construction of a new library and the renovation of a loft building on Sheffield, and conversion of the Sanctuary condominiums into use as residence halls. These projects were to be followed by a recreation and sport center, science facilities, new dining rooms, and additional parking. Betty Fromm, president of LPCA, stated, *"DePaul is to be commended on its community policies and the openness and frankness that it displayed throughout the process."* To make this agreement a reality, more than thirty-five meetings had occurred in 1988 and 1989 between community leaders and university representatives. (86)

Events moved quickly following the approval of the university plan by the board of trustees. In addition to approving architectural drawings for the new $25 million library on the Lincoln Park campus, the purchase of the Sanctuary Condominiums (62 units in what had been Little Sisters of the Poor Home for the Elderly and 17 new townhouses) and the glove factory on the southeast corner of Sheffield and Montana for residences for students, the university also approved pursuing the purchase and renovation of the vacant Goldblatt department store, a building with over 700,000 square feet of space. To pay for this ambitious expansion program the university employed aggressive tuition pricing, and increased enrollments to 18,000 by 1998, borrowing nearly $100 million, and mounting an ambitious $100 million capital campaign. Three years of tuition increases of 9, 17, and 9 percent in the period 1988–1991 moved DePaul from the low end of the range of peer private, midwestern universities (Loyola, Marquette, Bradley, and Illinois Wesleyan) to near the top. At the same time enrollment management aggressively marketed programs in arts and sciences, computer science and education in order to meet ambitious enrollment goals for full-time students. The School for New Learning and the graduate programs in business and computer science also contributed to meeting the overall enrollment projections. Under the leadership of Helmut Epp, computer science grew from a new department in the College of Liberal Arts and Sciences in 1981 to a separate school in 1994, becoming one of the largest programs in the United States. The expansion of the O'Hare campus and the opening of the Oak Brook campus provided greater accessibility to programs that served part-time students. Additional classroom, office and student support space on the Lincoln Park campus had been acquired with the purchase of the Saint Vincent grade school and a portion of the rectory from the parish and the purchase, through a gift of the Harold Reskin family, of the Blackstone Theater as the new performance and training facility for the Theater School.

Increased tuition revenue allowed the university to invest in new academic programs, to add over one hundred full-time faculty, and to support new student-related services and activities. In the College of Arts and Sciences, the modern language full-time faculty expanded from four to sixteen, and the languages offered increased from four to eight; foreign study courses increased from two to more than a dozen; an honors program was introduced; and five undergraduate interdisciplinary majors were added. These initiatives attracted residential students not only from out-of-state but also from the city and the suburbs. Innovative programs in the School of Education, especially the adoption of a clinical model of teacher preparation, along with a growing national shortage of teachers, led to an increase of students from 558 in 1987 to 1,237 in 1993. The decision to add a full-time faculty in the School for New Learning allowed it to increase enrollments from 1,040 in 1988 to nearly 1,750 in 1993. These increases in LA&S, education, and SNL more than offset the enrollment decreases in commerce and law. Computer science also showed little increase after the mid-eighties, following significant growth earlier. (87)

As Father Richardson began his final year as president in 1992, he could take great pride in his role in turning DePaul into a first-class university over a career than spanned nearly four decades. Most visible among his contributions were the physical changes of both the Loop and the Lincoln Park campuses. The Reskin Theatre (formerly the Blackstone) had been acquired in 1987 and the DePaul Center, formerly the Goldblatt Building, would be formally dedicated in 1993. On the Lincoln Park campus, the university dedicated the John T. Richardson Library in September 1992, and had added major residential facilities and new classrooms and offices in the prior two years. At the same time, the university was well underway to complet-ing the $100 million Cornerstone Campaign. DePaul indeed had become "a cornerstone of Chicago;" the Vincentian mission was manifested not only in the university's degree programs that served greater Chicago but also in its influence and visibility. The DePaul Center, along with the opening of the Harold Washington Library, contributed to a revitalization of State Street and the South Loop. Father Richardson's dream of an urban center, which would be named for his close friend Msgr. Jack Egan and funded by major grants from the Chicago Community Trust and the MacArthur Foundation, was also becoming a reality.

DePaul in the Nineties: The Presidency of John P. Minogue

John P. Minogue, C.M., a medical ethicist who had served on the faculty of the Northwestern Medical School, became DePaul's tenth president on July 1, 1993. He took over the university at the end of a five-year period of tremendous change and a time when the national economy and American higher education were in difficulty. DePaul was not immune from the problems facing higher education. Partly by design and partly because of the recession, DePaul's enroll-ments remained around 16,400 from 1991 to 1993. Fearing enrollment decreases and con-cerned about honoring the Vincentian commitment to providing affordable education, the trustees retreated from the aggressive pricing strategy of the 1988 Plan. At the same time the board's unwillingness to consider additional borrowing to pay for the second phase of con-struction that the 1988 plan called for also contributed to the stagnation in enrollments. Al-though the Cornerstone Campaign was winding down and would achieve its goal of $100 million, it failed to raise the funds that would pay off the $55 million in bonds that had been issued to build the Richardson Library and to renovate the DePaul Center. The Trustees and the new president were increasingly concerned about DePaul's indebtedness.

The trustees had selected Fr. Minogue because of his youth and energy and his new ideas; he had a view of higher education that called into question many basic assumptions under which universities in the United States operated. He believed that the university had to be-come more efficient, had to be technologically driven, and had to respond much more quickly to the changes affecting the larger society. His experience in the Catholic Church and in health care had taught him that no institution was immune from the revolutionary forces influencing society.

The first five years of Fr. Minogue's presidency marked the completion of the 1988 Plan and the laying of the foundation for a DePaul that would not just survive but thrive in the 21st century. A strategic plan, or what might be better called a strategic direction, was ap-proved by the board of trustees in 1995. It continued the quest for academic quality and the confidence that this could be linked to the mission. The opening sentence called for DePaul, by building on its strength as a a university and its Vincentian tradition, to become "a nation-ally recognized 'urban force' through zealous and self-sacrificing service to strengthen the dignity *of each individual and to impact societal systems for the betterment of a just and humane community.*" The plan set forth three broad goals, enhancing quality, manifesting mission, and insuring financial vitality and called for the university to respond strategically to nine key opportunities that would support these goals. These nine opportunities included changing demographics, DePaul's changing competition, the cost structure of higher education, opportunities for grants, contracts, and partnerships, and DePaul's record of success in international endeavors, its multicultural commitment and its Catholic and Vincentian mission. (88)

The 1995 plan recognized that the tuition pricing and borrowing strategies of the 1988 plan were no longer viable. However, the 1988 plan's third strategy, the establishment of urban partnerships, was an option. History had shown that the only way for DePaul to develop and expand the Lincoln Park campus was through effective formal and informal relationships with the Lincoln Park community and its neighborhood organizations. One example of this was the community's approval of DePaul's Planned Unit Development and the related ten-year memorandum of understanding that guided future development. This partnership led to the renovation in 1993 of a loft building on Fullerton to provide space for the Lincoln Park branch of the Chicago Public Library on the first floor and classrooms, studios, and offices for the departments of art and philosophy on the second and third floors. The DePaul/community partnership had become a model on how town and gown can move from simply mutual toleration to creating a synergy that benefits both.

In purchasing the Goldblatt Building from the city, DePaul created another innovative urban partnership. This partnership was engineered by Father Richardson and Kenneth McHugh, the vice president for business and finance. The city sold DePaul the building for $2 million and a commitment to create a "Chicago 2000 Scholarship" program. DePaul renovated the building, leased back to the city for thirty years five floors in exchange for an up-front payment of $30 million, and developed the Music Mart, a retail center on the first floor and the concourse. The six upper university floors were linked to the Lewis Center through skywalks across the alley that separated the two buildings. Because of this partnership, DePaul opened the DePaul Center in 1993, a state-of-the-art academic and student support facility, and the City of Chicago gained an administrative center, a partner in redeveloping the South Loop, and a commitment of scholarship dollars to support outstanding young Chicagoans who had leadership qualities and a commitment to public service. (89)

By 1997 a number of strategies had been adopted that allowed the university to announce the "Centennial Phase" of the 1995 Strategic Plan. Actions taken by the university included the adoption of a five-year financial plan, the implementation of a suburban campus strategy, including the opening of a Naperville campus, the approval of a tuition pricing strategy that differentiated between types of students and types of programs, the establishment of a School of Computer Science, Telecommunication and Information Systems, and the ground breaking for the William McGowan Biological and Environmental Sciences Facility.

The report of the North Central Association visiting team in March 1997 praised the university for what it had accomplished and what it intended to do in the future. In identifying DePaul's strengths, the report singled out the university's mission:

There is broad acceptance of a commitment to DePaul's Catholic, Vincentian, and urban characteristics. . . . Very strong and mutually beneficial partnerships with the people and the City of Chicago (and its surrounding communities) have strengthened both the educational experiences of the students and of the institution. DePaul has become a 'cornerstone for Chicago.'

It concluded with *"The academic programs of the university have shown continuous, sometimes striking improvement."* By the autumn of 1997, enrollments were again on the increase, with 17,800 students. Over 1,800 students lived on the Lincoln Park campus, with more than 2,000 others who had been on campus now living in apartments in nearby neighborhoods. Enrollments in the College of Commerce had increased for the first time in nine years. Computer science experienced nearly a 50 percent increase since its establishment as a school three years earlier. The College of Liberal Arts and Sciences enrolled 3,046 day, undergraduate students with another 667 in the School of Education and 550 in computer science. Twelve years earlier the total enrollment in these three programs was slightly over 2,000. Forty-eight percent of the autumn quarter credit hours were taught on the Lincoln Park campus, compared to forty-four percent on the Loop campus and eight percent on the three suburban campuses. This represented a significant change from the 1950s and 1960s when over eighty percent of the courses offered were taught on the Loop campus. And the nearly equal distribution in credit hours taken between DePaul's two student constituencies, the traditional-age full-time student and the part-time working professional, distinguished DePaul from its peer institutions both Catholic and private. (90)

The academic quality of DePaul students also had improved since the adoption of the 1988 Plan, as did their diversity. In 1997 thirty percent of the freshmen were minority students. The full-time faculty, which numbered 380 in 1987, increased to more than 520. The number of minority faculty also increased. Fewer than ten African Americans and Latinos were on the faculty in the early eighties. In 1997 eighteen Latinos and thirty-five African Americans were faculty members. The percentage of women on the faculty had increased to 38 percent, or 199 of 520. (91) And the number of Vincentians increased from one in 1981 to seven in 1997.

In many ways the 1988 plan represented, as did the curricular design of 1964, a major departure from the past. DePaul moved from being a commuter institution to becoming a national, if not international, university with a significant residential population. The plan had reaffirmed the primacy of teaching but stressed the importance of scholarship, research and creative activities. It also addressed and sought to reconcile the tensions generated by the quest for quality and its Catholic, Vincentian and urban character. DePaul's vision was to become a nationally recognized university, among the five best Catholic universities in the United States, and to do this through becoming a premier urban university. Academic quality would not be achieved at the expense of the university's urban mission.

The size of the freshmen class had nearly doubled between the mid-1980s to the mid-1990s, with more than 30 percent coming from outside the metropolitan area. Nearly two-thirds of this class lived on campus. The majority of the College of Law students also came from outside the metropolitan area, as did an even larger percentage of the students in theater and music. DePaul's pricing strategy changed from being the low-cost provider to being a "value plus" quality institution that attracted students from throughout the world.

The 1988 plan called upon the university to reflect on, articulate and take action to manifest its Catholic, Vincentian and urban character. By 1997, the Catholic and Vincentian presence was more visible than at any time in DePaul's recent past. Programmatically, in 1996 the university approved a B.A. in Catholic studies and signed an agreement with Catholic Theological Union to allow students in this program to take as electives courses offered by CTU. The university also created ties to other religious groups through its active participation in the World's Parliament of Religions and hosting a conference on Catholic-Buddhist dialogue, attended by the Dalai Lama. Faculty from the School of Education were involved with Catholic grade and high schools. Student affairs and academic affairs supported an Amate Collegiate House, which was an offshoot of a program originally supported by the Archdiocese of Chicago to foster Catholic lay leadership through providing an opportunity for young men and women to live in a Christian community and be involved in community service. University Ministry, through its DePaul Community Service Association, provided opportunities for community service to more than two thousand students each year. In addition to the DePaul community service days, hundreds of students gave significant time each week to serving others. Religious art was located throughout the campus. Vincent's Circle, a life-sized sculpture work, was sited in the courtyard adjacent to the Richardson Library and stained glass windows were incorporated into the library itself. And the library and the walls of other DePaul buildings served as galleries for religious displays. Despite the university's rapid growth and increasing complexity, its mission was clearly manifested.

A major initiative, beginning in the mid-1980s, that reflected the enhancement of DePaul's academic quality and its commitment to its mission, focused on its international programs and partnerships. (92) Prior to that time DePaul had few international contacts, few international students and few opportunities for its students to experience learning abroad, and virtually no international courses or programs. One major step to promote the internationalization of the curriculum and of the university was the hiring of John Kordek, a career foreign service officer who came to DePaul following his ambassadorship to Botswana. Kordek, a DePaul graduate, returned to his alma mater as special assistant to the president for international and governmental relations. He became a catalyst, supporting and encouraging international activities and contacts throughout the university. He was responsible for a steady stream of foreign dignitaries who visited DePaul and, in turn, invited DePaul's president and others to return their visits. Through his efforts, a host of international figures also came to DePaul to receive honorary degrees or the university's Saint Vincent DePaul Award. These included Elie Wiesel, Alvaro Arzú Irigoyen, President of the Republic of Guatemala, Sir Ketumile Masire, President of Botswana, and Wladyslaw Bartoszewski, a highly respected political and intellectual leader in Poland.

Through the efforts of Deans Leo Ryan and Ronald Patten, the College of Commerce became the most internationalized of the colleges and schools. It signed agreements with more than a dozen international universities, offered a full-time day M.B.A. in international marketing and Finance and a part-time M.B.A. in Hong Kong in partnership with the International Bank of Asia. The international business concentration in the M.B.A. program served more than 130 students in 1997. The Richard H. Driehaus Center for International Business hosted scores of international visitors each year and offered a number of short courses for DePaul students abroad. During the 1990s the Department of Finance taught bankers in Poland and international commodity traders in a summer program in Chicago. This was a wholly new direction for DePaul.

The College of Law, through the International Human Rights Law Institute, headed by Professor M. Cherif Bassiouni and Douglass Cassel, provided training for Guatemalan justices, Salvadoran and Polish lawyers, and North African justices during the mid-nineties. Research projects and international conferences, supported by the Cudahy Foundation, Joseph and Jeanne Sullivan, the MacArthur Foundation and other sources, focused on such issues as human rights violations in the former Yugoslavia, limiting nuclear armaments, and new international codes of law. These programs involved scores of DePaul faculty members and students. Law students did pro bono work through the legal clinic, the Institute for Church/State Studies, and ad hoc efforts to assist refugees. These too were new manifestations of DePaul's Catholic and Vincentian character.

The College of Liberal Arts and Sciences offered a dozen quarter-length study abroad programs and four shorter international study tours in 1997–1998. The International Studies Program had more than 120 undergraduate majors and 30 M.A. students. The Liberal Studies Program, DePaul's general education requirement, offered a range of courses focusing on comparative cultures, languages, and the international and multicultural issues. B.A. students had a new language requirement, while students in commerce were required to fulfill an international intensive requirement. The School for New Learning offered short international courses in El Salvador, Malta, Romania, and Ethiopia and hosted or consulted with representatives from a number of international universities. And each year since 1989, first the College of Liberal Arts and Sciences and then the Office of Academic Affairs, sponsored a three-week international study tour for twenty faculty and staff. Beginning in 1993 the Office of Enrollment Management became active in recruiting international students. By 1997 more than 500 international students were seeking degrees at DePaul, and another 200 were enrolled in the university's English Language Academy.

The international dimension of DePaul has provided yet another vehicle for expressing the university's Catholic, Vincentian and urban mission. Travel courses to Central America, Africa and Asia provided faculty, staff and students with insights about social issues they encountered in the United States. Faculty members have participated in the strengthening of democratic institutions in Eastern Europe and Central America, giving them experiences which enhance their teaching and scholarship. International contacts have enabled DePaul to join with other institutions in advancing its Vincentian ideals.

DePaul in 1998

In the 1980s and early 1990s, as president of the Carnegie Foundation, Ernest L. Boyer called on universities and colleges to reform themselves, to become again institutions that serve the public good rather than providing private benefits. He encouraged the enhancement of teaching, broadening of the definition of scholarship, the creation of learning communities within the university, and the reestablishment of public service to the larger society. In a number of his later articles he called for the establishment of the "New American College," as a model for the future university. (93)

Boyer's work came to have a significant influence on DePaul University. His ideas both described DePaul's thirty-year quest for integrating quality and mission and provided a framework for strategic planning. For DePaul teaching is the primary mission, scholarship is defined broadly, and a synergy exists with the larger community. The 1997 self-study report adopted the phrase, "New American University," to describe DePaul's vision of its future.

The planning retreats of 1996 and 1997, relying partially on the writings of Boyer, focused on how to build on DePaul's strength in order to become a nationally/internationally recognized university through becoming a premier urban university. As a result of the planning process, the board of trustees in October 1997 accepted three academic goals that became integral to the university's strategic plan. The first calls for DePaul to provide for all full-time students a holistic education that will foster extraordinary learning opportunities through a highly diverse faculty, staff and student body. In the second, DePaul is to be a nationally and internationally recognized provider of the highest quality professional education for adult, part-time students, and to be a dominant provider in the greater Chicago area. And lastly, DePaul is to research, develop, deliver and transfer innovative, educationally-related programs and services that have a significant social impact and give concrete expression to the university's Vincentian mission.

During the 1997–1998 academic year, faculty, staff and students, under the leadership of Charles Strain, a professor of religious studies, began to develop and implement action plans for the ten initiatives that support these three goals. DePaul, in attempting to achieve these three goals, seeks to do what few other universities have done: achieve national/international recognition as a distinctive university through its Catholic, Vincentian and urban mission. If DePaul is able to achieve this vision, it will become a model for other Catholic institutions and a model for all universities in fulfilling their promise to the larger society, that is making education a public good, not simply a private benefit.

Chapter One Notes

1. Lester Goodchild, "The Mission of the Catholic University in the Midwest, 1842–1980: A Comparative Case Study of the Effects of Strategic Policy Decisions Upon the Mission of the University of Notre Dame, Loyola University of Chicago and DePaul University" (Ph.D. diss., The University of Chicago, 1986), 227.

2. *Ibid.*

3. *Ibid.*, 250.

4. See John L. Rury, "The Urban Catholic University in the Early Twentieth Century: A Social Profile of DePaul, 1898–1940," *History of Higher Education Annual* 17 (1997) passim; Goodchild, 271.

5. Goodchild, "The Mission of the Catholic University in the Midwest," 263–267; "Patrick Mullins, C.M., Notes, Handwritten," Box 1, Rev. Daniel J. McHugh Papers, DePaul University Archives (hereafter cited as DPUA); see also "North Central Association Correspondence, 1924–1936," Box 2, O'Malley Papers, DPUA; Sandra Averitt Cook, "The Origins and Development of Evening Undergraduate Education in Chicago: 1891–1939" (Ph.D. diss., Loyola University, 1993), 239–268.

6. "Accreditation," Box 2, O'Malley Papers, DPUA.

7. *Ibid.*

8. "Proposed Laboratory (Science) Building: Correspondence, 1912–1961,"and"Property on Southeast Corner of Sheffield and Fullerton," Box 1, Administrative Support Buildings/Planning Collection, DPUA.

9. "Law Suit Against DePaul Educational Aid Society," and"Correspondence 64 E. Lake, 1953–1954," Box 17, O'Malley Papers, DPUA; "History of DePaul Building, by Rev. Michael O'Connell, 1945" DePaul History File, DPUA.

10. *Ibid.*; Goodchild, "The Mission of the Catholic University in the Midwest," 477.

11. "Report to NCA October 1949," Box 5, North Central Association Records, DPUA.

12. "Golden Anniversary Booklet," DPUA.

13. "Mission Statement: Purpose and Objectives," President Corcoran's Address to the General Faculty, September 1933", Box 1, Catholic/Vincentian Character Collection, DPUA.

14. Goodchild, "The Mission of the Catholic University in the Midwest," 443–448, 451.

15. Golden Anniversary Booklet, 7, DPUA.

16. "Recommendations Concerning DePaul University, A Report by Stanley P. Farwell, 1944," Box 4, North Central Association Records, DPUA.

17. Goodchild, "The Mission of the Catholic University in the Midwest."

18. *Ibid.*, 472–487.

19. "Revised Plan for Organization for DePaul University, 1946," Box 17, Rev. Comerford O'Malley Papers, DPUA.

20. Golden Anniversary Booklet, 7, DPUA.

21. "DePaul University Expansion Program, SOM Report," Box 1, Administrative Support Buildings/Planning Collection, DPUA, 11.

22. *Ibid.*; "Preliminary Design, SOM," Box 1, Administrative Support Buildings/Planning Collection, DPUA; "Report on Space Requirements by Stanley Farwell, 1950," and"Committee to Study Space Requirements in Downtown Building, 1950–1952," Box 17, O'Malley Papers, DPUA.

23. Golden Anniversary Booklet, DPUA.

24. *Ibid.*

25. For a biography of Msgr. John J. Egan see Margie Frisbie, *An Alley in Chicago: The Ministry of a City Priest* (Kansas City, Mo., 1991).

26. See Box 5, Box 6, North Central Association Collection for the various reports concerning the NCA reports and visits from 1949–1952; see also Goodchild, 480–482.

27. Goodchild, "The Mission of the Catholic University in the Midwest," 480–484.

28. *DePaulian,* 1949 (Chicago, 1949), 27; See also Philip Gleason, *Contending with Modernity: Catholic Higher Education in the 20th Century* (New York, 1995), 246–260.

29. Goodchild, "The Mission of the Catholic University in the Midwest," 454–458.

30. "Canonical Erection of DePaul University, Rescission of: Correspondence, 1968–1974," Box 1, Catholic/Vincentian Character Collection, DPUA; see also Goodchild, "The Mission of the Catholic University in the Midwest," 776–791, a chapter focusing on the rescission of DePaul's canonical status

31. Goodchild, "The Mission of the Catholic University in the Midwest," 460.

32. *Ibid.,* 487; "Report on the State of the University, Minutes of the University Council, October 9, 1946," Box 19, O'Malley Papers, DPUA.

33. *Ibid.;* it is interesting to note that two-thirds of the classrooms were proposed to seat more than fifty students.

34. Goodchild, "The Mission of the Catholic University in the Midwest," 484–485.

35. "Alumni Hall Correspondence, 1955," Box 17, O'Malley Papers, DPUA.

36. *Ibid.*

37. "Alumni Hall Dedication Program, December 16, 1956," Box 17, O'Malley Papers, DPUA.

38. Goodchild, "The Mission of the Catholic University in the Midwest," 484; biographical information of Rev. John T. Richardson, C.M. from the 1997 Commencement Program on the occasion of his receiving the Via Sapientiae Award, DPUA.

39. Letter from Rev. John T. Richardson, C.M. to Rev. Comerford O'Malley, C.M., dated September 16, 1961 in File "Internal Survey," Box 1, O'Malley Papers, DPUA.

40. Letter from Rev. John T. Richardson, C.M. to Rev. William Cortelyou, C.M. and Rev. Theodore Wangler, C.M., dated October 4, 1961, in File "Internal Survey," Box 1, O'Malley Papers, DPUA.

41. "The Self-Survey Study," Box 1, O'Malley Papers, DPUA.

42. *Ibid.*

43. "DePaul's University Council regarding Lincoln Park and the university, 1955–1967," Box 5, Lincoln Park Neighborhood Collection, DPUA.

44. *Ibid.;* Minutes, November 18, 1959, December 9, 1959, "University Council," Box 5, Lincoln Park Neighborhood Collection, DPUA.

45. "DePaul and the Lincoln Park Conversation Association," Box 5, Lincoln Park Neighborhood Collection, DPUA.

46. "Uptown campus Plan, 1961," Box 5, Lincoln Park Neighborhood Collection, DPUA.

47. Minutes, Property Owners Meeting, October 5, 1962, File Procedure for Land Acquisition," Box 19, O'Malley Papers, DPUA; "Program for Greatness, Proposed Release," Box 19, O'Malley Papers, DPUA.

48. "DePaul University: Six articles by Frank Hughes, *The Chicago Tribune,* 22–27 August 1965," DePaul History File, DPUA.

49. "University Council, 1955–1967," Box 5, Lincoln Park Neighborhood Collection, DPUA. The revised plan was discussed by the Council on February 12, 1964. Despite these efforts, DePaul failed to purchase additional land. See "Urban Renewal Correspondence, 1970–1979," Box 5, Lincoln Park Neighborhood Collection, DPUA.

50. "Arguments for Including DePaul in the Second Phase of the Neighborhood Renewal Plan, 1965–1966," Box 5, Lincoln Park Neighborhood Collection, DPUA; Letters, July 10, 1967,

51. "1967 NCA Report," 77–91, Box 15, North Central Association Collection, DPUA.

52. Memorandum, Rev. John R. Cortelyou, C.M. to Rev. John T. Richardson, C.M. and deans; "Deans' Committee: Interaction with the Community, Correspondence," Box 5, Lincoln Park Neighborhood Collection, DPUA.

53. Minutes of October 19, 1969, Deans' Committee, *Ibid.*

54. "1967 NCA Report, Exhibit 17, A Curricular Design for DePaul University, April 13, 1964," Box 15, North Central Association Collection, DPUA. A committee comprised of Fathers William Cortelyou, Patrick O'Brien, and John T. Richardson, Irma Halfter, and Gerald Kreyche submitted the Curricular Design to the DePaul Faculty in April 1964.

55. "Report to the NCA, 1967," Box 15, *Ibid.*

56. "NCA Visit and NCA Report, 1967," quote from p. 29, *Ibid.*

57. "Deans' Committee: Interaction with the Community, 1967–1968," Box 5, Lincoln Park Neighborhood Collection, DPUA.

58. Letter from DePaul Faculty to Board of Trustees and Officers of DePaul University; letter of May 26, 1969 from William Waters, Professor of Economics, to Rev. John R. Cortelyou, C.M., "Dean's Committee: Interaction with the Community," *Ibid.*

59. "Report on DePaul as a Catholic University, Part I, Appendix: Is DePaul Catholic?"; and "Canonical Erection of DePaul University, Rescission of: Correspondence, 1968–1974," Box 1, Catholic/Vincentian Character, DPUA.

60. "General University Policy to Specific Types of Service to the Poor, 1975," *Ibid.*

61. "Report on DePaul as a Catholic University (Rev. Edward Riley, C.M., chairman),"*Ibid.*

62. "Self-Study Report to NCA," Box 21, North Central Association Collection, DPUA; In 1958–1959 of the 214 full-time faculty, 105 were Catholic laymen and women, 41 were from religious orders, 33 were Protestants, and 3 Jewish. Internal Survey," Box 1, O'Malley Papers, DPUA.

63. "General University Policy to Specific Types of Service to the Poor," Box 1, Catholic/Vincentian Character Collection, DPUA.

64. "Vincentian Study," *Ibid.*

65. Quote from "Appendix: Is DePaul Catholic?," "Report on DePaul as a Catholic University, 1975–1976," *Ibid.*

66. "Mission Statement: Statement of Purpose, 1977," 2, *Ibid.*

67. *Ibid.,* 12–13.

68. *Ibid.,* 14.

69. *Ibid.,* 15.

70. *Ibid.,* 16; "NCA 1976–1977 Self-Study Report," Box 21, North Central Association Collection, DPUA.

71. "Final Report, 1976–1977," 21–30, *Ibid.*

72. "NCA Report and Letter of Approval," *Ibid.*

73. "Mission Statement: Draft 1979," Box 1, Catholic/Vincentian Character Collection, DPUA.

74. "Landmarks for Tomorrow, 1979," 13, Box 1, Administration Planning Collection, DPUA.

75. "Forging the Next Phase, 1982," 3–4, 18, 23, *Ibid.*

76. "Planning for the 1980s: An Interim Report of the College of Liberal Arts and Sciences," 29–33, *Ibid.*

77. "Excellence with Diversity, 1983," 30, *Ibid.*

78. *Ibid.*, 61.

79. Richard Yanikoski, "DePaul University: Urban by Design," *Current Issues in Catholic Higher Education* 6:2 (9 January 1986), 5–8, DePaul History File, DPUA.

80. "LPCA Correspondence, 1982–1988," Box 5, Lincoln Park Neighborhood Collection, DPUA.

81. "DePaul University Mission Statement, 1986," 11, Box 2, Catholic/Vincentian Character, DPUA.

82. "Self-Study Report to the North Central Association, December 1986," I, 12–13, Box 29, North Central Association Collection, DPUA.

83. *Ibid.*, 13.

84. Memorandum of May 6, 1988 from Richard J. Meister to Patricia Ewers, A Planning Model for the College of Liberal Arts and Sciences," quote from p. 1. Later drafts of the university's Plan included the expansion of the Loop Campus through the purchase and renovation of the Goldblatt Building.

85. *Ibid.*

86. "DePaul's Ten Year Development Plan," Released by the Haymarket Group on August 10, 1989, Box 1, Lincoln Park Conservation Association Collection, DPUA.

87. DePaul University, Office of Institutional Planning and Research, "Fact File: A Profile of DePaul University, 1992–1997." Each autumn, OIPR issues a new report, covering five years, including the autumn quarter data.

88. "A Strategic Plan for DePaul University: 1995–2000."

89. "Goldblatt Building: Newspaper Articles, 1991," Box 5, Lincoln Park Neighborhood Collection, DPUA.

90. Report of a Visit to DePaul University from 27–29 January 1997 for the Commission of Institutions of Higher Education of the North Central Association of Colleges and Schools.

91. DePaul University, Fact File, 1997.

92. See "The Annual Report of the Committee on International Programs," issued each year during the 1990s.

93. Ernest L. Boyer, "Creating the New American College,"*Chronicle of Higher Education* (4 March 1994), A48; Ernest L. Boyer, *Scholarship Reconsidered* (Princeton: The Carnegie Foundation for the Advancement of Teaching, 1990); Dale Coye, "Ernest Boyer and the New American College," *Change: The Magazine for Higher Education* (May/June 1997) 21–29.

CHAPTER TWO

THE FOUNDLING UNIVERSITY

Reflections on the Early History of DePaul
"Make No Small Plans"

Dennis P. McCann

R ushing to and from classes, and all the other busyness that keeps DePaul University bustling from day to day, one still has the opportunity to stop by a courtyard just off the main corridor in Schmitt Academic Center (SAC) where a statue of Saint Vincent dePaul holding an infant invites us to prayer or, perhaps, to a recollection of the university's distinctive history and sense of mission. The statue is iconic, very traditional, and paternalistic. It was meant to memorialize the pre-Vatican II Church's official designation of Saint Vincent as preeminently "the apostle of charity," and it does so by recalling the work that he helped St. Louise deMarillac organize in protecting the orphans and other homeless children of Paris. Saint Vincent is holding the infant in a manner remindful of statues of the Blessed Virgin Mary or her chaste spouse, Saint Joseph, holding Baby Jesus who is also Christ the Light of the World.

The statue delicately suggests what liberation theology was later to make explicit, namely, that the poor are, in the eyes of faith, the very presence of Christ among us. Yet the reality of poverty and what it does to the poor remains veiled, for the infant also symbolizes an innocence that absolves us as soon as we respond—as Saint Vincent is depicted—with a simple, intensely personal gesture of protection. The cry of the poor, as symbolized by the infant, is not yet an occasion for political mobilization or Christian social action. This Saint Vincent invites us to perform a personal act of charity, directed to the foundling's immediate need for warmth, shelter and hospitality. The mood is still one of compassion and not yet reciprocity, of love, and not yet justice.

The many layered meanings conveyed in Saint Vincent's paternal embrace of the foundling can be inferred by contrasting it with the most recent Saint Vincent memorial to grace the Lincoln Park campus, a bronze arrangement of Saint Vincent with several DePaul students, in yet another courtyard, this one the sunny garden placed between SAC and the new Father John T. Richardson Library. There's nothing traditional about this Saint Vincent, except possibly his cassock. For he is seated and clearly involved in a conversation in which students speak as well as listen. The pose suggests that he is intellectually engaged by them, a veteran teacher who still can learn something new from each new group of students. The students are diverse in gender and ethnicity, just as the university hopes to be. They are casually posed, too grownup to ever again be held in Saint Vincent's arms. They don't need protection, but they do seek an education whose aims ultimately they will decide for themselves.

Both statues are idealized and romantic. They conceal DePaul's reality as much as they reveal it. Nevertheless, the contrasting aspirations they depict may offer clues to the history of DePaul University's unique claims to a Catholic identity and an authentically Vincentian sense of mission. In what follows, I focus on the founding of DePaul University, and thus will tend to emphasize the meanings conveyed in the traditional statue of Saint Vincent. But since these reflections are meant to contribute to the relevant aspects of the university's search for a usable past, they cannot help but reflect my experience in a DePaul that is closer, in fact, to the aspirations conveyed in the bronze ensemble of Saint Vincent and today's students.

The title for this chapter is meant to be a pun. Instead of "the founding of the university" I call this "the foundling university." For my research into DePaul's early history suggests that the origin and development of DePaul University is not the result of some grand design, or some allegedly Vincentian genius for, of all things, strategic planning. Rather DePaul University is, as it was from very early on, the foundling in Saint Vincent's arms, a child abandoned by its own father, the archbishop of Chicago. This foundling survived thanks largely to the somewhat unorthodox nurturing it received from surrogate fathers, the priests of the Congregation of the Mission who labored here in the first decades of the 20th century. I hope to show that the early history of DePaul was unusually traumatic, and the effects of that trauma continue to shape the university's sense of identity, or its lack of identity, in often imperceptible ways. Though this foundling university grew up a street-wise kid from Chicago, one hopes that even as she learns to accept her roots, she will never forget them.

The Founding of a University

The facts upon which I wish to build this revisionist view of the university's early history are generally familiar and largely undisputed. Let me summarize them as they are recounted in Stafford Poole's authoritative essay, "The Educational Apostolate: Colleges, Universities, and Secondary Schools." (1) Poole observes that the hope of establishing some sort of college for "daystudents," the sons of Chicago's burgeoning Catholic immigrant population, was already part of the founding mission of Saint Vincent dePaul Church in 1876. This hope was not to be realized until Patrick Feehan, archbishop of Chicago (1880–1902), authorized the Vincentian priests to establish Saint Vincent's College in 1898, an institution that would educate both laymen and candidates preparing for the Roman Catholic priesthood in the Chicago archdiocese.

The Vincentians accepted this edict with the understanding that Saint Vincent's College would be the Catholic institution of higher learning for the rapidly developing north side of Chicago, an arrangement paralleling the role that Saint Ignatius College had filled for Chicago's west side Catholics since 1870. The provincial, Thomas Smith, C.M., levied a substantial tax on the 14 existing Vincentian institutions of the Western province to pay for the college's first buildings, and on June 30, 1898, a charter to operate a college was granted by the State of Illinois. Saint Vincent's College first opened its doors on September 5, 1898, the date the university centennial celebrates. The first college staff consisted of Thomas Finney, C.M., and six scholastics, that is, six seminarians from the province's motherhouse, Saint Mary of the Barrens, Perryville, Missouri, who were in the final stages of their priestly training. Fr. Smith himself acted as supervisor until January 1899, when he appointed Peter Vincent Byrne, C.M., as the college's first president. Fr. Byrne became the central Vincentian figure in the early history of DePaul University.

The college's first years of operation were encouraging, and the new president, following Father Smith's lead, began an ambitious program of expansion. In quick succession, Father Byrne broke ground for a new administration building and expanded the curriculum by adding departments of mechanical, electrical, and civil engineering. In 1907 he authorized construction of the auditorium. The architecturally avant garde design had near-disastrous consequences. It made poor economic sense and generated intense controversy within the Vincentian community and other ecclesiastical circles. 1907 was the year when Saint Vincent's College secured a revision in its charter, reopening in September as DePaul University. Under the banner of its new identity, Byrne continued to innovate, first, by appointing five laypersons to the board of trustees, an unprecedented move at the time among American Catholic colleges and universities, and second, by introducing the elective system into the curriculum, in order to bring DePaul into what Byrne regarded as the mainstream of American higher education. Finally, the college erected four new buildings and hired additional faculty at high salaries. By 1908, the university had amassed a debt of over half a million dollars as a result of Byrne's policies. As other authors in this volume note, this extraordinary sum was not paid off until the 1940s.

To prove that he was serious about the leadership role in American higher education that he envisioned for DePaul, Byrne allowed the study of religion to be marginalized by refusing to exempt course offerings in religion from the logic of the elective system. Religion courses at DePaul became, in Poole's words, "an extracurricular affair." Furthermore, the university's new charter explicitly pledged that an applicant's religious affiliation, or lack thereof, would have no bearing on admission to DePaul. These moves made Byrne's leadership even more controversial, and when the financial panic of 1907 shrank both DePaul's enrollment and its reputation among its creditors, Byrne was criticized as a "poor administrator." He was forced to resign in May, 1909. The foundling university now found itself bankrupt.

Byrne was succeeded in the presidency by John Martin, C.M., whom the provincial—the

The Rev. Peter V. Byrne, C.M., President 1899–1909.

same Father Finney who had been part of Saint Vincent's original teaching staff—placed under tight restrictions regarding university finances. The provincial also tried to restore DePaul's credit rating by securing a short-term loan of $100,000 from a bank in Saint Louis. Father Martin may have felt that, with the university's creditors satisfied for the time being, he was free to ignore the provincial's interdiction against further borrowing. When Finney found out about a $25,000 loan arranged by Martin with a Chicago bank, the new president was removed. In September 1910, Francis X. McCabe, C.M., replaced him. Father McCabe managed to procure the resources to continue Byrne's policy of expansion and academic innovation, illustrated by the establishment of the university's schools of music, commerce, and law. He oversaw the creation of the "Loop campus" in 1913 to house the commerce and law programs, and introduced coeducation in 1911 with summer schools for Catholic women who sought accreditation as teachers. Though DePaul suffered the normal loss of students to the military as the country mobilized for World War I, by the end of McCabe's tenure in 1920, DePaul, like the rest of the country, was poised for a period of consolidation and solid growth, if not prosperity.

Peter Vincent Byrne and Vincentian Higher Education

This account so far may suggest that the foundling university is better characterized as a runaway than as a child abandoned by its father. Though the condensed chronology presented here may make Byrne seem like a visionary—albeit a remarkably willful one whose obsession with growth nearly precluded any future at all for the university—it wasn't just blind ambition that drove him to desperate measures. Saint Vincent's College was essentially doomed by the actions of Feehan's successor, the new archbishop of Chicago, James Quigley (1903–1915). Archbishop Quigley had been trained by the Vincentians and, as former bishop of Buffalo, New York, he had served ex-officio as chancellor of another Vincentian institution, Niagara University. Despite—or, perhaps, because of—his personal familiarity with the Vincentians, Quigley in effect revoked the ecclesiastical mission of Saint Vincent's College, by establishing his own archdiocesan preparatory seminary in 1905, the Cathedral College that later was to bear his name. This meant that the Archdiocese of Chicago would no longer send its seminarians to study at Saint Vincent's. The other half of the college's dual mission, its mandate to educate Catholic laymen, was also severely undermined by Quigley's decision in 1906 to permit the Jesuits to move Saint Ignatius College from Chicago's west side to the north side. Despite protests from Father Finney, the archbishop felt no obligation to honor his predecessor's promises. Unless some alternative could be found, Saint Vincent's would have to compete with Saint Ignatius for students and tuition fees, a rivalry that did not bode well for the future of either institution.

Whatever Quigley's motives may have been, Byrne was not about to let the college die. His move to recharter the institution as DePaul University salvaged from the archdiocese's apparent indifference to Saint Vincent's an unusual opportunity for educational innovation. That opportunity, I believe, can only be fully appreciated by understanding Byrne's actions in the context of an impasse that had dogged Vincentian educational institutions throughout their history in the United States.

The statue of St. Vincent DePaul & Foundling originally stood in front of the Academy building. It was erected in memory of Fr. Robert Brennan. The statue currently stands in the garden area between Levan Hall—the old Liberal Arts and Sciences building and the Schmitt Academic Center.

Before accepting the presidency of Saint Vincent's College in Chicago, Byrne had served brief terms as president of Saint Vincent's College in Cape Girardeau, Missouri (1886–1889) (2) and as rector of Kenrick Seminary in Saint Louis (1894–1897). (3) The histories of these two institutions were intimately interrelated, a fact that bears testimony to the pre-Vatican II paradox that confronted Catholicism's desire to educate its seminarians in first-rate academic institutions that excluded laymen and laywomen. This goal was virtually impossible, given the economics of privately financed higher education at the time. Consequently, a "mixed" college that educated laymen along with candidates for the priesthood often resulted when the Vincentians sought to found a seminary in the Western Province of the United States.

The history of both the Vincentian motherhouse, Saint Mary of the Barrens, and Saint Vincent's College at the Cape confirm the old saw, "He who pays the piper calls the tune." Local benefactors who controlled the resources on which Vincentian institutions depended usually were not interested in endowing a seminary. But they were very eager to secure the services of seminarians and priest-teachers in a college that would educate their sons and the other young men of the region. The Vincentian pattern, in the western province at least, seems to have been one of circumventing its benefactors' preferences where possible, and acquiescing to them when necessary. In short, they often combined institutional missions to make ends meet. Throughout the 19th century, both Saint Mary of the Barrens and Saint Vincent's at the Cape reflected the tensions and institutional instability that apparently resulted from trying to accommodate both the benefactors who wanted a secular college and the bishops—as well as the Congregation of the Mission's own superiors—who every now and then demanded that the Church's ideal of seminary education be rigorously pursued.

When Byrne was appointed president of Saint Vincent's at the Cape, he inherited an institution that for nearly 50 years had attempted, with some success, to serve both masters. Since its founding in 1843, Saint Vincent's had been mostly a "mixed" institution, with certain brief periods when it functioned exclusively as either a secular college or a seminary. (4) Examining the college's archive at Saint Mary of the Barrens, one finds no evidence that foreshadows Byrne's allegedly visionary leadership at DePaul University. Instead, what appears is a generous, open-hearted attempt to make the inherited system work and improve it incrementally. This effort was played against the background of episcopal decisions that would eventuate in the creation of Kenrick Seminary and the consequent withdrawal of the seminarians to Saint Louis. The founding of Kenrick in 1900 doomed Saint Vincent's College at the Cape, for it was unable to survive by serving only lay college students. Byrne's presidency had come and gone roughly a decade before Kenrick was opened, but the archives suggest that he could easily read the handwriting on the wall.

Byrne's own approach to the college's uncertain future seems to have been to emphasize its strengths as a mixed institution. The Saint Vincent College catalogue issued in Byrne's last year in office (1888–89) spells out an educational mission in which the curriculum is divided into three different tracks, "The Ecclesiastical, the Collegiate, and the Commercial." (5) The only change evident in the catalogues issued during Byrne's administration are the graphics. The Byrne catalogues feature impressive pictures of the college's laboratories for chemistry and physics. The mission statement, with its reassurances about the "unremitting care and vigilance" directed toward the morality of students and its outline of the three tracks, is unchanged. Byrne may have already imagined a radically different future for American higher education, but there is no hint of a visionary program at Saint Vincent's at the Cape. Particularly instructive is the absence of the elective system he was to introduce at DePaul University, with its *laissez-faire* implications for the role of religious instruction in the curriculum.

Judging from the college's daybooks (6) in which the student prefect was expected to keep a journal recording the high points of the academic year, Byrne was enormously popular among the students. He played the paternal role expected of him very well, as chief presider over the college's religious and secular rituals, and the dispenser of the chief boon—unexpected days off from classes—that were so cherished by boarding students in those days. At the same time, the daybooks reveal why the mixed system was essentially unworkable. The student prefects, all of whom were seminarians, unfailingly recorded their irritation with the boisterous and sometimes troubled behavior of the lay students. Alcoholism, then as now, was a major problem for college students. With an understandably exalted sense of their own dignity as candidates for the priesthood, the student prefects complained that the president was not rigorous enough in enforcing the rules, expelling trouble-makers, and otherwise disciplining the lay student population to the satisfaction of the seminarians. It is not surprising that such complaints occasionally found their way back to the bishops, who saw in them justification for abandoning the mixed system and establishing stand-alone seminaries. The student prefects, of course, represented only half the story.

The rest is revealed in what little correspondence survives from the Bryne administration. (7) Presidents in mixed institutions such as Saint Vincent's at the Cape had little choice other than to turn a blind eye to all but the most flagrant violations of proper decorum. Byrne's correspondence is littered with letters from all-too-busy parents, the professional elite of the Mississippi valley, who were bent on using the college as a convenient reformatory—handy precisely because it was a boarding school—for their wayward children. Byrne could hardly expect to win the hearts (or open the pocketbooks) of his lay benefactors if he expelled their sons from school! One imagines Byrne using his considerable charm to keep the tensions from spilling over into major scandal. For the mixed institution to succeed, he had to spend considerable energy from day to day searching for a *modus vivendi* for both seminarians and lay students. It must have been a thankless task, if ever there was one.

The archives provide no direct evidence that would explain why Byrne's presidency ended in the summer of 1889. The catalogue for the following year merely notes the name of his successor, Francis Nugent, C.M., and the minutes of the board of trustees make no remarks at all on the change in administration. The daybook, however, does provide a basis for fruitful speculation. In the months preceding Byrne's departure, there is no hint that his term in office is about to expire. There are no preparations for farewell receptions or other signs that would accompany an expected and orderly leave-taking. It does, however, yield indications of Byrne's heightened participation in Cape Girardeau's civic affairs, and tantalizing references to campus visitations by representatives of the "normal school" or teachers' college in the area. If Byrne were attempting to open the college still further to lay students and the educational needs of the local civic community, his actions would certainly have made it more difficult for the provincial to convince bishops to keep sending seminarians there. Perhaps Byrne already understood that the mixed system was untenable and was hoping to steer Saint Vincent's onto a more straightforwardly secular path of development.

Whatever the reasons for Byrne's departure from Saint Vincent's at the Cape, he was soon to play a crucial role in the founding of Kenrick Seminary in Saint Louis. The intricate maneuvering that led to Archbishop Kenrick's decision to entrust its founding to the Vincentians is not part of this story. Suffice it to say that once the contract was signed that formally authorized the Vincentian initiative in 1892, Byrne, along with his successor at Saint Vincent's at the Cape, Father Nugent, was appointed to raise funds for the seminary buildings. In that capacity, Byrne and Nugent goaded the Provincial, Thomas J. Smith, C.M., to take special measures to insure the educational effectiveness of Kenrick's curriculum. Byrne understood that simply protecting seminarians from the contamination of lay students was no guarantee of academic quality. Byrne's complaints, which often went over Father Smith's head to higher authorities in the Congregation of the Mission, eventually led to his appointment as seminary rector in December 1894, a post that he held until Smith replaced him with Nugent in 1897. Stafford Poole's account of Byrne's rectorship at Kenrick, from which these facts are taken, (8) does not explain the reasons for either Byrne's appointment or his later dismissal. Much as Byrne may have irritated the provincial by acting on his own at both the college and the seminary, their differences did not keep Smith from later naming Byrne president of Saint Vincent's College in Chicago.

Sister Margaret Beudette, S.C., poses with cast bronze sculptures she created of St. Vincent dePaul and two contemporary students. The sculptures are part of St. Vincent's Circle, a landscaped plaza on the university's Lincoln Park campus donated by Board of Trustees Chairman Richard A. Heise and dedicated to the students of DePaul. (1995)

What can this examination of Byrne's previous forays into academic administration tell us about his role in transforming Saint Vincent's College into DePaul University? When Byrne assumed the presidency of Saint Vincent's in Chicago in January 1899 he possessed, or at least had the opportunity to benefit from, the wisdom of hindsight. The college in Chicago was ostensibly founded with the same dual mission that Byrne had faithfully attempted to carry out at Saint Vincent's at the Cape. Byrne knew that it would be difficult, if not impossible, to execute that same mission in Chicago while striving for academic excellence above all. Therefore, when Archbishop Quigley unilaterally rescinded Saint Vincent's ecclesiastical mission, Byrne was well prepared to focus the college as an institution on its other charge: to serve the educational needs of Chicago's Catholic lay students. When Quigley later authorized Saint Ignatius' move to the north side of Chicago, Byrne knew that the only path still open to Saint Vincent's involved deliberately transforming itself into something that Saint Ignatius emphatically was not, namely, a university.

It is at this point that Byrne's distinctive educational vision and the way he tried to implement it at DePaul becomes relevant; but before examining that vision, it would be useful to recall the name that Byrne originally proposed for the new university. Saint Vincent's was to reopen as the University of North Chicago, a title that Byrne hoped would emphasize its aspiration to serve all the people of Chicago regardless of their religious affiliation, and also to strive for academic excellence to rival the achievement of a certain other university recently established on the south side of the city. Byrne's proposal was rejected by the provincial, Father Finney, who felt that something more Catholic was needed in the name. It was Justin Nuelle, C.M., the college's prefect of studies, who suggested DePaul University, and so it has been known ever since. (9)

Byrne's Vision and the Character of DePaul

Lester F. Goodchild succinctly captured the nature of Byrne's educational vision when he observed that "Byrne defined the Catholic character of the university as a university conducted under Catholic auspices." (10) Goodchild's account of Byrne's policies proves essentially accurate when it is considered in light of surviving material in the university archives, especially the eyewitness accounts of Daniel McHugh, C.M. (11) Goodchild, however, also attempts to situate Byrne's policies within the so-called Americanist heresy condemned in 1899 by Pope Leo XIII. This interpretation does not appear to be warranted by the facts. (12) Byrne was essentially a pragmatist, an educational innovator blessed with an entrepreneurial spirit. The exigencies of marketing another Catholic university on the north side of Chicago and finding it a niche different from the one Archbishop Quigley had secured for the Jesuits of Saint Ignatius College are, in my view, sufficient to account for Byrne's innovations.

Any doubts that pragmatism can lead to radical innovation are dispelled by considering carefully what Byrne had in mind when he chartered a Chicago university under Catholic auspices. The Articles of Incorporation themselves are modeled on those of the University of Chicago and set a strikingly secular tone for DePaul University. They commit the university, among other things, "to provide, impart and furnish *opportunities* for all departments of higher education *to persons of both sexes on equal terms.*" (13) There was no precedent whatsoever for coeducation in American Catholic higher education at the time, yet this promise was to become a reality at DePaul only four years later, in 1911. The composition of the board of trustees was equally innovative, consisting as it did of ten Vincentian priests and five laypersons. This arrangement tended to ensure not only the transparency of the board's deliberations, but also the university's faithfulness to DePaul's charter long after Byrne's term of office had ended. What made DePaul something truly different from other Catholic institutions that called themselves universities, however, was Byrne's commitment to curricular reform which, in turn, reflected and further intensified the decentering of religious development, particularly instruction in Catholic faith and morals, in the academic program.

The rationale for Byrne's modified elective system was laid out in fulsome detail in Father Nuelle's "Report of the Director of Studies to the President" (February 1, 1909) which Father McHugh preserved substantially verbatim. (14) Nuelle first made it clear that the changes had Byrne's "hearty sanction and cooperation." His report took the form of a reflection on educational philosophy, contrasting "the old college and its advantages" with "the new system that prevailed in the larger universities," in order finally to advocate, predictably, a policy of moderation, "In Medio Virtus Stat." Given the rather authoritarian tenor of traditional Catholic education at the time, the document as a whole is remarkably student oriented. The major advantage of the elective system was that by encouraging students to choose courses consistent with their personal interests and professional goals, student motivation for scholastic achievement would be increased. At the same time, each student would work with a faculty advisor who would help him or her make the best curricular choices. Student advising was envisioned as the most important internal accountability structure, but the electives program remained a "modified" or limited system precisely because elective studies were not available to the student until after the two-year curriculum of "prescribed studies" had been successfully completed. Philosophy, Latin, Greek, English, and mathematics made up the group of prescribed studies. Philosophy, in particular, was reaffirmed as the core of the university's commitment to providing a liberal education.

Summarizing the arguments favoring Byrne's modified elective system, Nuelle pointed out that elective courses made up only "about one-half of the time to be spent in college work," hence, the system was simply an analogous application of the educational requirements that the Church expected of candidates for the priesthood. After requiring six years (four in high school and two in college) of prescribed studies considered essential to a liberal education, the theological seminaries then offered just one specialized set of "electives." In this way, they provided required courses in ecclesiastical studies that insured the appropriate qualifications for the Catholic priesthood. A modified elective system, by implication, merely universalized this ideal by offering a range of options to prepare students for the full spectrum of modern professions. This argument—no doubt, an ingenious one to make to the provincial—was a telling indication that Byrne was thinking about the elective system in terms of the modern student's need for professional training.

Nuelle's remarks on the pivotal role of philosophy in the prescribed part of the undergraduate program further demonstrated Byrne's essentially Catholic understanding of the modified elective system. Philosophy courses, in Nuelle's calculation, constituted "about one-eighth of the DePaul student's time spent in college." (15) More important than the number of courses was their subject matter. Nuelle described what was essentially the standard curriculum in neo-Scholastic philosophy prescribed by the Church for the college education of seminarians. He observed that there were advantages in studying these subjects from Latin textbooks, for philosophizing in Latin *"results in closer scrutiny, a more just weighing of words and, therefore, a deeper comprehension."* Lest there be any doubts about DePaul's commitment to the Church's canonical view of neo-Scholastic philosophy, he added that *"the prescribed philosophy should be the philosophy of common sense, not a grindstone of abstractions, possibles, etc., well calculated to evolve a narrow psychologue, or subjectivist—but there is little danger here."* (16) The subjectivist possibility, of course, was precisely the can of worms that neo-Scholastic manuals warned was the logical outcome of modern post-Cartesian philosophy. In Nuelle's view, there was "little danger here," of rampant subjectivism, which supported the assumptions that not only would the Vincentian priests themselves continue to teach philosophy but also that the streetwise sons of Chicago's immigrant communities whom DePaul hoped to attract would be unlikely to be taken in by effete and useless speculation.

What Nuelle, and by implication, Byrne had to say about philosophy is entirely consistent with the official status given to the philosophical study of Saint Thomas Aquinas' work, mandated in Pope Leo XIII's encyclical, *Aeterni Patris* (1879). Thomism, in short, was regarded as the philosophical articulation of "common sense," as anyone could easily discover simply by studying it thoroughly with an open mind. Such a program of philosophical study formed the backbone of DePaul's undergraduate program and the core of its claim to a Catholic identity. Thomism's intellectual strength—as perceived by the Vincentians and all other American Catholic educators at the time—accounts for Byrne's self-confident embrace of academic excellence and his relative indifference to the academic study of religion. Religious instruction was necessary for the proper practice of the faith; it was meant to provide neither a world view nor the intellectual weaponry for defending one's faith with compelling arguments. Since only philosophy—namely the true *philosophia perennis* codified in Thomistic Scholasticism—provided that defense, only philosophy was to be part of the prescribed curriculum. Catholic religious instruction, like opportunities for Catholic devotions, mass and the sacraments, could safely be regarded as extracurricular. It was required of all students who elected to identify

The Rev. John J. Martin, C.M.,
President 1909–1910

themselves as Catholics, but such religious instruction was simply not central to the Catholic identity of DePaul University, at least as Byrne and Nuelle conceived it.

Byrne's Gamble for Greatness

The most definitive statement of Byrne's educational vision is contained in his "First Annual Report to the Trustees of DePaul University, 1908–1909," (17) which was issued just three months before he resigned from the presidency. This document confirmed Byrne's ambitions for DePaul, which he hoped would achieve a prominence equal to Northwestern University and the University of Chicago; it suggests further that the motive for the university's rapid expansion was market driven. He portrayed rapid enrollment growth as the key to institutional development. The report also made the case that DePaul University was primarily an urban institution serving the needs of all of Chicago's citizens. The trustees were reminded of the university's charter and its promise that "no religious test is applied to either students or teachers." But DePaul's openness to religious and cultural diversity did not stem from any philosophical considerations about the nature of human liberty, any more than did Byrne's decision to implement a modified elective system. The report suggested that both were a result of a pragmatic calculation that, without such policies, enrollments simply would not grow as fast as they must if DePaul were to become a university in fact as well as in aspiration.

Byrne's pragmatism was particularly evident in his strategy for tapping the financial power of Chicago's civic elite. He believed it was in their collective self-interest to support DePaul precisely because the university was poised to play a unique role in main streaming or pacifying Chicago's immigrant communities. Byrne, like many other American Catholic leaders at the time, touted "the conservatism of Catholic teaching, especially in matters of political, moral and social import," implying that the university might be Chicago's most effective weapon against social anarchy. This was designed to reassure the civic elite that though DePaul intended to be a genuinely open university, its Catholic students—who would no doubt continue to remain in the majority for some time to come—would receive wholesome instruction in a form of social Christianity that was officially anti-Marxist, anti-socialist, and keenly sensitive to the potential excesses of popular democracy.

Byrne's "First Report" was also significant for what it did not say about the problems that were, it seems, about to end his presidency. The half million dollar debt was acknowledged in the course of an exhortation to the trustees to find new ways to discharge it. But there was no hint of the extent to which the university's debt was a direct result of Byrne's ill-fated decision to build the College Theater (or auditorium, as it was also called). The largest single document in McHugh's "Notes" was an eighteen page narrative outlining the story of the auditorium and its near disastrous effect on the university's finances. (18) McHugh, who as university treasurer had immediate access to the accounts, estimated the cost of building the theater at over $100,000. He also emphasized the need for such a building and its central position in Byrne's vision of DePaul as a university that integrated the best of both liberal and professional education.

The theater was intended to symbolize the university's commitment to excellence in music and drama, "part of the cultural heritage of man," as well as debating and oratory, "powerful tools in law, politics and other fields of human endeavor." An architecturally significant building with a seating capacity of 1,500, the auditorium was regarded as one of the largest and most beautiful theaters in Chicago. It also proved to be Byrne's undoing. What went wrong?

According to McHugh's recollections, Byrne felt that he could easily pay off the debt on the building from the revenues that a full schedule of events at the theater would bring in. He knew that the Bush Temple Theater, where Saint Vincent's College had held its commencements, cleared over $30,000 a year. But the Bush Temple stood at the corner of Chicago Avenue and Clark Street; the auditorium, by contrast, was somewhat out of place in a quiet residential neighborhood still considered off the beaten path, at least for theater goers. As McHugh ruefully observed

St. Vincent's football squad. The new Lyceum and College Theater are visible in the background.

in hindsight, "Over at Lincoln Avenue and Fullerton, there might have been a chance, at least for a while." The revenues generated fell ludicrously short of Byrne's expectations, and the university's inability to service the debt on the new building was further exacerbated by the economic downturn of 1907 which, predictably, caused DePaul's credit to evaporate.

The auditorium also compounded Byrne's difficulties with the Vincentians. He and the university were already called to answer for the absence of religious instruction in the new curriculum. When Finney, the provincial, made his canonical visitation in 1908, he characterized the situation as "rather deplorable," citing the lack of a "system of discipline" and the neglect of "religious training of the boys," which he considered "no slight deficiency in a Catholic college." (19) Interestingly enough, Finney apparently attributed these failings to Byrne's preoccupation with finances and institutional development and did not view them as the predictable consequence of Byrne's innovative academic policies. Indeed, Finney did not seem to appreciate the significance of rechartering the college as DePaul University, even though—or possibly because—he had served as the first Vincentian priest on the faculty of Saint Vincent's College. His report to the Vincentian Superior General, Antoine Fiat, C.M., minimized the significance of the name change, as if it were merely an accommodation to local custom. (20) Obviously, the change was intended to be far-reaching and the new institution's program would, in fact, constitute a ground breaking innovation in Catholic higher education. Either Finney wasn't paying attention, or at the time of the rechartering he still trusted Byrne and was willing to cover for him in Rome.

Byrne, however, was no longer given the benefit of the doubt after Finney's canonical visit a year later. The rumors getting back to him about Byrne's plans for the auditorium must have been particularly irritating in light of what he had already seen for himself. The controversy over the theater became particularly heated among the confreres, once they got wind of Bryne's plan to cover its costs by renting it out to commercial theatrical groups whose performances were not directly under the control of the university. Working with theater people and other such low-lifes was pushing openness to the point of recklessness.

As the provincial's faith in him was disintegrating, so, according to McHugh, was Byrne's health. He discreetly noted that Byrne had become ill in the autumn and winter of 1908, spent several months convalescing in Saint Joseph's Hospital, and was succeeded in office by Martin, in May 1909. He also recorded a comment, made years later by Nuelle, that best explains Byrne's removal from the presidency: *"I have some vague notions that the failure of the College Theater had much to do with stalling the really grand dreams which a really saintly—if unlucky— priest had entertained for the glory of God and the salvation of college students."* (21)

Ironically enough, the auditorium was the place where DePaul's commitment to equality of educational opportunity for both men and women, as set forth in its charter, was eventually fulfilled. McHugh recounts that in 1911 DePaul hosted the annual meeting of the National Catholic Educational Association, a large gathering that included some 1,100 Catholic nuns, many of whom were so impressed with the new facilities in the Lyceum and auditorium buildings that they enrolled in DePaul's first summer school, given for "sisters, lay teachers, and advanced students." Of course, the summer school, which paved the way for DePaul to become coeducational in 1917, didn't just materialize from thin air. On December 28, 1910, Archbishop Quigley expressed a desire to see DePaul provide degree-related extension programs that would allow Catholic women to meet the educational requirements for hiring and promotion in the Chicago public school system. The board of trustees, Goodchild reports, met that very day and approved plans for the summer school. It enrolled 125 religious and lay women in July 1911, was accredited by the superintendent of the Chicago public schools in fall 1911, and conferred the first DePaul collegiate degrees on women in spring 1912. (22) McHugh nicely captures the spirit of the event, which finally vindicated Byrne's visionary but risky building program: "[The] *History of DePaul was in the making. [The] Theater or Auditorium building and Lyceum had been quite a care for nearly five years, but now they began to pay dividends in a manner hardly visualized by their founders and promoters.*" (23) Continuing innovation, often born of necessity, was Byrne's vision and legacy for DePaul.

A Foundling's Legacy

Does this account of Saint Vincent DePaul's foundling university make its past useful to DePaul in the next century? I think so. Facing the uncertainties of DePaul's infancy may be painful, but helps to account for many of the tensions that affect the university's present and future. Then as now the university's ambitions far outstrip its resources. Although DePaul may no longer aspire to compete on an equal footing with either Northwestern or the University of Chicago, it anticipates taking a unique leadership role in American higher education well beyond the constraints imposed by the university's relatively modest endowment and operating budgets. Then as now, all of us who care about DePaul worry about its Catholic identity: in what sense, if any, can DePaul, the diverse urban university, meaningfully claim to be Catholic? Retrieving DePaul's institutional memory of its perilous birth may afford us a degree of comfort by affirming that there have been few points in the university's history when its Catholic identity has not been analyzed and disputed.

Our aspirations relating to public service in Chicago today, described in Richard Meister's opening chapter, may require just as much flexibility on the question of Catholic identity as the exigencies of yesterday's crisis over institutional survival. Byrne could risk being flexible because he was confident of the superiority of the inherited Catholic intellectual tradition that was reflected, primarily, in the philosophy curriculum. A strong program in Scholastic philosophy, he reckoned, could be relied upon to give direction to the university's innovative elective system. Today the university may be less able to live with ambiguity, precisely because confidence in the Catholic intellectual tradition has apparently been seriously eroded, and not just at DePaul. The days are long gone when philosophy programs at Catholic colleges and universities reflected a distinctively Catholic approach to intellectual life. Nothing, alas, has emerged to take their place.

So Saint Vincent's foundling, now all grown up and on her own, must face her second century with certain unresolved questions about her ancestry and who or what she may yet turn out to be. The university's Vincentian heritage does not provide easy answers to such questions, but now as then it will continue to beckon with a love for DePaul that is sometimes more, and sometimes less, than justice.

University Seal, 1920.

Chapter Two Notes

1. Stafford Poole, C.M., "The Educational Apostolate: Colleges, Universities, and Secondary Schools," in, John E. Rybolt, C.M. (ed.). *The American Vincentians: A Popular History of the Congregation of the Mission in the United States, 1815–1987* (Brooklyn, New York, 1988): 291–346.

2. Francis V. Nugent, C.M., "History of Saint Vincent's College, Cape Girardeau, Mo.," in Marshall Solomon Snow, *Higher Education in Missouri: United States Bureau of Education: Contributions to American Educational History: No. 21* (Washington, D.C., 1901): 173–191, in the DeAndreis-Rosati Memorial Archives, Perryville, Missouri (DRMA, II C (MO) 3, Box 54).

3. Stafford Poole, C.M., "Ad Cleri Disciplinam: The Vincentian Seminary Apostolate in the United States," in, John E. Rybolt, C.M. (ed.), *The American Vincentians*: 97–162.

4. John E. Rybolt, C.M., "Saint Vincent's College and Theological Education," n.d. 33 page mss. in the DeAndreis-Rosati Memorial Archives, Perryville, Missouri (DRMA, II C (MO) 3, Box 55).

5. "46th Annual Catalogue of the Officers and Students of Saint Vincent's College, Cape Girardeau, Missouri. 1888–1889," 15 page document, in the DeAndreis-Rosati Memorial Archives, Perryville, Missouri, (DRMA, II C (MO) 3, Box 24), p. 6.

6. "Archives 6/5/78–5/20/89, CAPE.04," and "Archives 5/21/89–8/22/05, CAPE.05," in the DeAndreis-Rosati Memorial Archives, Perryville, Missouri, (DRMA, II C (MO) 3, Box 32).

7. "P.V. Byrne, C.M.: Correspondence," a folder containing various handwritten letters, in the DeAndreis-Rosati Memorial Archives, Perryville, Missouri, (DRMA, II C (MO) 3, Box 32).

8. Stafford Poole, C.M., "Ad Cleri Disciplinam:" 137–143.

9. Stafford Poole, C.M., "The Educational Apostolate:" 322.

10. Lester Francis Goodchild," The Mission of the Catholic University in the Midwest, 1842–1980: A Comparative Case Study of the Effects of Strategic Policy Decisions upon the Mission of the University of Notre Dame, Loyola University of Chicago, and DePaul University," (unpublished dissertation, University of Chicago, 1986) 252.

11. Daniel McHugh, C.M., "DePaul University, 1898–1920: Some Historical Items," an unpublished collection of notes and personal narratives, n.d., in the DePaul University Archives (DPUA).

12. A clarification is called for here, because this thesis mars Lester F. Goodchild's otherwise reliable and insightful analysis of DePaul's early history. Here is the gist of Goodchild's view:

"Byrne was a man enamored with the intellectual life and the liberal Catholic spirit. Byrne's sentiment reflected the "Americanist" ideas which swept through a signficant segment of the American Catholic chuch during this period. . . . They [the Americanists] called for a rapprochement between American Catholicism and the American way of life. The "Americanists" emphasized the glory of the intellectual life and the pursuit of higher education which other American bishops, especially those of German decent (sic), opposed. . . . The Americanists possessed a quasi-ecumenical spirit, a concern for the material prosperity and development of American Catholics, and a vision of the American Catholic responsibility to lead world-wide Catholicism into a rapprochement with the modern world, a world which was most clearly evident in the American experience. These ideas ignited Byrne as president of Kenrick Theological Seminary." Goodchild, "Mission of the Catholic University in the Midwest," 238–9.

My own view is that these "Americanist" ideas are either so vague as to be the common property of virtually all Church leaders at the time, or, when specified in identifiably Americanist ways, insufficiently warranted as Byrne's own. In the former category of vagueness, I place a passion for the intellectual life and a concern for the material prosperity of American Catholics, which, no doubt, even bishops of German descent were committed to. In the latter category of distinctively Americanist ideas, I place the vision of an American Catholicism assuming a global leadership role in modernizing the Roman church worldwide. This was, in fact, an idea derived from the thoughts of Father Isaac Hecker, and overzealously championed by certain French liberals who provoked the Papal condemnation of "Americanism." What Pope Leo XIII in 1899 condemned as "Americanism" is quite specific, even if—as prominent American Catholic leaders, like James Cardinal Gibbons, at the time insisted—no one here holds such an extreme view. Leo condemned the idea "that a certain liberty ought to be introduced into the Church, so that, limiting the exercise and vigilance of its powers, each one of the faithful may act more freely in pursuance of his own natural bent and capacity." See Pope Leo XIII, "Testem benevolentiae," January 22, 1899, in *Documents of American Catholic History*, John Tracy Ellis, ed., Milwaukee, 1956, 556.

In other words, the Pope felt that "Americanists" were advocating the wholesale democratization of the Church, by introducing a certain liberty" into it that Americans take for granted in the ordering of their civic institutions. Such a proposal on its own merits may hold some attraction to American Catholics, both then and now. See for instance, Dennis P. McCann, *New Experiment in Democracy: The Challenge for American Catholicism* (Kansas City, Missouri, 1987), but I see no evidence either that Byrne wasted much time on it or that his vision of DePaul, and its inspiration, is unintelligible apart from it.

What prompted Goodchild to link Byrne, prior to his Presidency at DePaul University, with others accused of Americanism is first, Byrne's Irish ethnicity which he holds in common with many other Catholic leaders so accused, like Cardinal Gibbons and Archbishop John Ireland, second Byrne's impatience with the low estate of academic preparation on the part of Catholic seminary professors, and third, Byrne's consequent support for requiring faculty assigned to teach at Kenrick to attend courses at the Catholic University of America, allegedly a hotbed of Americanist thinking. The only concrete evidence that Goodchild can muster is Byrne's meeting with Ireland in September, 1895, in Saint Paul, Minnesota, on the topic of clergy education. Well, as the rector of Kenrick Seminary, what else would he be conferring with the archbishop about? Certainly not the overthrow of the Catholic hierarchy! Goodchild could also have appealed to Byrne's civic mindedness, as demonstrated by his extracurricular activities in Cape Girardeau. But openness alone, I would hope, does not warrant condemning—or glorifying, for that matter—Byrne as an Americanist heretic.

This disagreement over Byrne's alleged Americanism is not trivial. For it does make a difference in Goodchild's interpretation of Byrne's policies, especially his depiction of Byrne's actions during the transition from Saint Vincent's College to DePaul University. Goodchild correctly notes that Byrne's administration of Saint Vincent's College faithfully followed the mandate for a mixed institution given by the provincial, Father Smith, until Smith's death in 1905. But then Goodchild speculates, "Part of the reason for this involved Leo XIII's (1901–1903) condemnation of Americanism. . . ." Goodchild, A Mission of the Catholic University in the Midewest," 241. The insinuation is that Byrne did not act upon his "Americanist" vision of DePaul University any earlier because of cowardice, as if Byrne were afraid to reveal his own attachment to the ideas that Leo had just condemned. There is no basis whatsoever for this assumption. Byrne's actions admit of a simpler explanation, and a simpler explanation may be preferred because Byrne, it seems to me, may be a simpler character than Goodchild imagines. Byrne, in short, was a faithful Vincentian who carried out the assignment that he had been given. He began to act on his own, only when his original mission had been rendered moot by Archbishop Quigley's reckless actions. When he did begin to innovate, his policies conform to no distinctively Americanist agenda in Catholic higher education, for there never was such a thing. His innovations were a desperate gamble, now that the Archbishop had acted, attempting to define a market niche in Chicago for a small Catholic college that could only survive if it risked becoming a university administered under Catholic auspices.

13. Goodchild, "Mission of the Catholic University in the Midwest," 248; italics mine.

14. McHugh, "DePaul University, 1898–1920," "Transitional Period" (A), pp 1–11, and "Transitional Period" (B), pp. 1–9, in DPUA.

15. McHugh, "DePaul University, 1898–1920," "Transitional Period (B)," p. 2, in DPUA.

16. *Ibid.*

17. McHugh, "DePaul University, 1898–1920," "Transitional Period (B)," pp. 10–16, in DPUA. I am including the full text of the "First Annual Report" as an appendix to this paper, because of its historic significance.

18. McHugh, "Lyceum and Theater," pp. 1–18, in DPUA.

19. Goodchild, "Mission of the Catholic University in the Midwest," 250.

20. This seems to be the clear implication of Finney's report to Fiat, as quoted in Goodchild, "Mission of the Catholic University in the Midwest," 249: "Cum hujusmodi instituta apud nos nomine "Universitatis" solent designari confratres nostri precibus quorumdam presbyterorum dioceseos et secularum et religiosorum, morem gerentes, nomen Collegii mutandi consilium inierunt. Posthac ergo titulo "DePaul University" fruetur; minime dubium quin exitus hujus instituti futurus sit felix et faustus.˙

21. McHugh, "DePaul University, 1898–1920," "Lyceum and Theater," p. 11, in DPUA.

22. Goodchild, "Mission of the Catholic University in the Midwest," 268.

23. McHugh, "DePaul University, 1898–1920," "Lyceum and Theater," p. 18, in DPUA.

First Annual Report to the Trustees of DePaul University, 1908–1909 (Dated: February 1909)

To the Trustees of DePaul University, Gentlemen:
In this my first official communication, transmitting to you the reports of the heads of the several departments of the University for the year just closed, you will find details entered into, explanations given, and plans discussed which ordinarily might be considered uncalled for, but which I deem highly important as conveying to you a fuller understanding of the character, status and workings of the University than some of you may have already possessed.

AIM OF The University: NUMBERS.
A large number of students have a pecuniary advantage, and if all other conditions obtained, would be a decided advantage indeed.

To conduct a University requires the expenditure of a large amount of money. If making money beyond the requisite for maintenance were the prime object, large numbers would assuredly be the great desideratum. Numbers, sufficient to create interest, excite emulation and stimulate ambition in the various departments and courses of study, are a practical necessity. But numbers principally, or indeed to any appreciable extent for the sake of revenue, would be a genuine hindrance to the realization of the real object of a University—which is *to make scholars*. To become a scholar a man must be a student.

When the administration is not overanxious for the revenue derived from large numbers, it will not hesitate to dismiss from the halls of the University the indolent and the indifferent. And this process of weeding out the slothful and the incapable cannot fail to produce a wholesome influence on the entire student body. Besides, such a procedure has the additional advantage of giving an enviable reputation to the institution and of, in consequence, attracting earnest students to its various departments. My purpose, however, in making these statements is not to deprecate numbers. Would we had large numbers, but of the sterling kind. Efforts are now about to be made to secure such from the city of Chicago and from the small towns and country districts of Illinois and the bordering States. Indeed, it is from the outlying places principally that we expect to fill our technical and professional schools with students who know the value of time and appreciate the advantages which the University offers, and who therefore will [be] men of definite purpose—studious, earnest, bent on the acquisition of the one thing they seek—a good liberal or professional education.

AIM OF The University: LIBERAL EDUCATION.
I have said liberal or professional education, which I believe I should not have expressed the thought in this form. In strict truth, liberal and professional education should not be dissociated. A liberal education may be had, indeed, without knowledge of the technicalities of the individual professions, but a knowledge of the underlying and governing principles of all professional studies is indispensable for a liberal education; whereas a professional education that is limited to the requisites of the profession is not education in the proper sense of the word and its possessor is not, strictly speaking, an educated gentleman. No one recognizes this truth more clearly than the professional man himself. Not long since, a gentleman who occupies a prominent and lucrative position in his profession volunteered to me the information that he considers himself, and is regarded by others as an excellent engineer; but he is often made to blush for his deficiencies in other branches of knowledge.

Truth is one and homogeneous, and the liberal scholar is he who loves truth and seeks truth wherever it is to be found; and who seeks it for its own sake, not, as too often is the case with the specialist, for the sake of mere lucre. Time however is a factor which enters largely into the question of education, and the professional student necessarily finds it difficult to devote himself to liberal studies, except at the expense of and to the sacrifice of his professional duties. At all events, the aim of DePaul is to lift higher the standard of higher education; to make the entrance requirements to its colleges as high as the exigencies of time may permit; and of the elective courses to encourage the choice of those that tell most for a liberal education: philosophy, English literature, history, political economy, sociology, besides the ancient classics.

NEEDS OF The University.

For future development, and even for the satisfaction of present conditions, the institution is in sore need of additional facilities. Prime among these, and of urgent and imperative necessity, is an *academic building*. This necessity you will find plainly set forth in the report of the dean of the medical faculty (Dr. Hugh McKenna) and in that of the general director of studies of the University (Rev. Justin A. Nuelle, C.M.).

The cost of such a building and necessary ground need not exceed $50,000. As a preliminary condition however, for the erection of the academy, our Visitor (Very Rev. Thomas Finney, C.M.) insists on the obliteration, or a very substantial reduction of our indebtedness. Our debt at present amounts, in round numbers, to $500,000. Of this sum, about $175,000 must be paid forthwith. Some of our creditors are waxing impatient, and peremptorily demand a settlement of their accounts

Gentlemen, the task is before you of devising, and putting into immediate operation, ways and means for establishing the University on a solid financial basis. The amount of money needed is small in comparison with the magnitude of the work. This institution can do more with thousands than other institutions, of like character, can do with tens of thousands. In explanation of this statement, take the item of salaries alone. DePaul today has thirteen officers and professors, including the president, who receive no salary whatever. Were these to receive an average salary of $2,000—and the figure is conservative—to pay the thirteen salaries would require an investment at four per cent of $650,000. To the judicious and reflecting mind, therefore, our financial condition, though seriously embarrassing, should not be alarming

MEANS.

A permanent endowment of the University, or any of its colleges, is not to be hoped for at this time But something may be done even now, and more later on, toward establishing Chairs in the several departments by direct donations, or by bequests, and devises of real estate.

CHAIRS WHICH MIGHT BE ENDOWED: Chair of Anatomy, Astronomy, Biology, Chemistry, Christian Doctrine, Economics, Engineering Departments,

English, French, German, Geology, Greek, History, Latin, Philosophy, Physics, Pure Mathematics.

ENDOWMENT FUND required for each of the above:

Each Chair endowed shall bear the name of the person who endows it or of the one in whose memory it is endowed; as, e.g., The Abraham Smith Chair of Political Economy.

The expenses of the Schools of Oratory, Music, Pharmacy and Dentistry, when established, and the salaries of instructors in all departments, may well be provided for by tuition fees.

The present necessities of the University, however, to which I have already invited your attention, call for immediate action, and can brook no delay.

RELIGION. This institution is Catholic and must ever remain Catholic. Regular instructions in Catholic doctrine are given to the Catholic students. They have also Chapel exercises, Mass and a sermon, once a week. But, true to the letter and spirit of the charter of the University, no religious test is applied to either students or teachers. No provision is made in the record forms for noting the religion of the students or professors. In fact, there are a number of non-Catholic students in the University, and the President and Faculty do not know what religion these profess; while two of the reports, herewith submitted, are signed by two non-Catholic gentlemen, as heads of departments.

In this great city of Chicago there are hundreds of wealthy, liberal-minded and thoughtful men, Catholic and non-Catholic, who are not influenced by the specious objection that the University of Chicago and Northwestern University are ample to satisfy all the demands of higher education, because they know that these excellent institutions do not cover the entire field; that a large class of our citizens, for conscientious or financial reasons, cannot patronize them; men, too, who recognize the consistency, the stability and the conservatism of Catholic teaching, especially in matters of political, moral and social import.

These men can readily understand the immense good DePaul University can do for the entire community, when fully organized and operating in all fields of knowledge, free from the trammels of debt. They would, therefore, contribute cheerfully and generously to the funds necessary to this end.

But how are these men to be reached and made cognizant of the facts? This is the question which you, gentlemen, are to consider and determine. If I might venture a suggestion, would it not be well to organize, if possible, a Finance Committee, composed of a number of gentlemen, representing some at least of the great interests of the city—merchants, manufacturers, bankers, etc., etc.—the personnel of the committee to be made known to the general public through the press, and all donations received to be acknowledged also through the press.

I would likewise propose for your consideration the advisability of associating with the University, in some official capacity, say, as an Advisory Board, a number of gentlemen of prominence, wealth and education, not for the direct purpose of the material benefit they might bestow upon the institution, but rather for the moral influence their names would have in giving tone and prestige to the institution in the estimation of the public.

ADMINISTRATION.

It is of supreme importance that the affairs of the University be conducted on strictly business principles. Accordingly, the requisite set of account books has been provided and a bookkeeper engaged for the purpose of keeping an exact account of all moneys received, and to what purpose applied; of receipts from tuition and fees; donations and foundations or endowments, and of disbursements for ordinary expenses by direction of the Executive Committee, which committee shall meet monthly, or as often as necessity may demand or utility advise; the allocation, however, of considerable amounts to be always the duty of the Trustees and the Advisory Board; the books to be audited at stated intervals by the Auditing Committee; all of which is to be done in strict accordance with the provisions of the By-laws.

Respectfully submitted,
P. V. Byrne, C.M. President.

CHAPTER THREE

ADMINISTRATION AND GOVERNANCE AT DEPAUL

Building and Sustaining a University

Anna L. Waring

The transformation of DePaul from small, struggling St. Vincent's College to the second largest Catholic university in the United States is a story of the creation of a university and its search for identity. DePaul has been administered and governed by a number of persons and organizational entities, and its presidents, especially in the early days of the university, played broad and powerful roles in the development and design of the institution. Each of DePaul's first six presidents served in the dual role of president of the board of trustees and president of the institution, giving him wide authority over the development of university policies. As the university's governance structure became more complex in the years following World War Two, this arrangement changed. Today, like other large Catholic universities, DePaul has a multi-faceted system of internal and external governance.

The question of university governance is usually associated with boards of trustees. DePaul has had such a board since its incorporation as a university in 1908, and for much of its history—through a number of reorganizations—the majority of its members were Vincentians. To bring greater lay participation into the university, a board of lay trustees was formed in 1946. Though fundraising was the primary function of the lay trustees, a reorganization of that board begun in 1964 eventually gave lay trustees a more active role in the governance of the university. The two boards were eventually combined, but through most of the institution's history the board of trustees (later "Members of the Corporation") and the board of lay trustees linked DePaul to the Congregation of the Mission and to the larger world.

There is also the matter of the university's administrative structure. Since 1930, DePaul presidents have relied on advisory councils for suggestions and help with decision making. Three councils—the University Council, the Administrative Council, and the Joint Council—were established by presidents Corcoran, Cortelyou and Minogue. These councils, composed of senior academic and administrative leaders, set polices that guided and organized the university's internal administration. The University Council and the Administrative Council served slightly different functions, policy development and administrative coordination respectively. The university Senate, Faculty Council, and Staff Council were added in the 1960s to expand governance beyond the officers and administrators who served on the presidents' councils.

To focus exclusively on the mechanisms of internal governance and administration, however, would be to neglect a large part of the DePaul story. External organizations such as accrediting bodies and professional associations also played a major role in shaping the university, forcing it to transform itself to meet the standards they established. Finally, there was the influence of the Catholic Church, though it was less of a force than one might expect, given DePaul's foundation as a Catholic institution.

In short, the history of administration and governance at DePaul has been characterized by internal and external streams of influence. The internal actors and organizational bodies made the decisions that turned DePaul into a university, and the external forces were the models that shaped the early institution, challenging it to ask what it meant to be a university.

Internal Administration and Governance:
From Presidential Authority to Multiple Constituency Dialogue

Governance and administration in the broadest sense are defined as the decision-making processes and the structures for carrying them out. Many think that governance in higher education is limited to boards of trustees. In colleges and universities, however, governance is shared among a number of groups: trustees, administrators, faculty, and in some instances, students, though boards of trustees have taken to transferring some of their involvement in decision making to other groups.

There is a tendency for the literature on administration and governance in higher education to assume that these functions are mutually exclusive when in reality senior administrators and faculty, the groups who develop policy, are also most often responsible for the implementation of that policy. Especially, as front-line actors, administrators often find themselves having to create policy through their day-to-day actions. Throughout most of its history, DePaul has had a system of shared governance and administration (see list of DePaul presidents, table 1). While an arrangement that gave one individual so much control was not the usual pattern for American universities, it was rather common in Catholic institutions. The sponsoring religious orders in Catholic colleges and universities maintained control of their institutions until the 1960s when they transferred governance authority to boards composed principally of lay members. (1)

The colleges and universities that have survived over the course of the twentieth century have tended to adopt growth and diversification as strategies. While this has enabled them to endure, their continued existence has come at a cost. Burton Clark (2) has suggested that growth affected universities administratively in four central ways, with respect to size, value systems, specialization, and bureaucratization. First, as they increased in size, colleges evolved from a unitary to a federal structure. The 20th century saw the development of professional schools and the proliferation of academic disciplines, which called for a departmental type of organization. Faculty were identified primarily with their academic departments rather than with the institution as a whole, and as a reflection of this change the authority structure became correspondingly more diffuse.

Table One *Presidents of DePaul University*	
1898–1909	Peter V. Byrne, C.M.
1909–1910	John Martin, C.M.
1910–1920	Francis Xavier McCabe, C.M.
1920–1930	Thomas F. Levan, C.M.
1930–1935	Francis C. Corcoran, C.M.
1935–1944	Michael J. O'Connell, C.M.
1944–1963	Comerford J. O'Malley, C.M.
1964–1981	John R. Cortelyou, C.M.
1981–1993	John T. Richardson, C.M.
1993–present	John P. Minogue, C.M.

Second, when the central authority structure gave way, universities developed multiple cultures and value systems for faculty. In addition, other groups, especially administrators and students developed distinct cultures as well. Each of these three groups exerted its own demands on the institution. A larger faculty resulted in greater diversity of thought among its members with respect to disciplines, identification with the goals of the college or university, and compliance with the expectations of the institution. As the number of administrators grew, each having his or her own responsibilities, there was an inevitable separation into different functional areas that were often at cross purposes. Finally, students from all kinds of backgrounds started coming to colleges and universities. They often held widely different beliefs about why college was important (whether it was to secure a profession, become educated, escape the family, or a host of others). This diversity often put students at odds with faculty and administration thinking about what it meant to be college educated.

Third, the growth in the number of disciplines and different types of schools and programs made academic work increasingly specialized and the faculty more professionalized. Faculty members developed into experts who created knowledge as well as shared it in a limited area. These new faculty members, unlike their older colleagues—who had shared a less differentiated classical curriculum—had considerably less in common with others in the university community, even their faculty colleagues.

Fourth, the subcultures created by sheer physical growth, multiple value systems and specialization, required a bureaucracy to coordinate them. Since members of large universities tend to have little contact with or knowledge of others in their institution, broad-based collegial decision making was increasingly difficult. Shared decision making, even among such traditionally close-knit groups as the faculty, was increasingly replaced by rule-driven decision-making processes. Thus, as universities grew larger and more complex, they also became more bureaucratic.

As it grew larger DePaul, like most other American universities, became more differentiated. Clark's framework accurately describes the internal growth and development of the university during its first hundred years, a process that can be identified as DePaul passed through several distinct stages. These stages correspond to some extent to the periods described in chapter 1 and can be linked with particular university presidents. A general pattern in the development of governance structures emerges as each of these periods is examined individually. Consequently, the discussion that follows focuses on the evolution of the internal administrative bodies at DePaul over the past century, although certain external forces that helped to shape the university's growth and development will also be described. A more complete consideration of external influences will follow.

The Era of Centralized Leadership: Early DePaul Presidents, 1898–1930

Ten men have held the position of president of DePaul University during its first century. All have been members of the Congregation of the Mission, or Vincentians, the religious order that founded the university. With the exception of Father John Martin, C.M., who left the university after only one year, DePaul's early presidents embodied the dominant forces that built and sustained the institution. Each of these early presidents faced financial pressures and external threats, such as difficulty obtaining and keeping the accreditation that permitted DePaul to continue functioning as a university.

The Reverend Peter Byrne, C.M., became president of St. Vincent's in 1899 and remained in office until 1909. He was an especially influential figure. As Richard Meister and Dennis McCann have noted, Byrne presided over the transformation of St. Vincent's College into DePaul University and provided the initial academic vision for DePaul by attempting to model it after the leading colleges and universities of the time. The traditional liberal arts college in the late 1800s educated a small homogeneous student body, using a single common curriculum for all, and DePaul was established in this mold, even though it also featured a course in commercial studies and a boys academy. A small institution, it served primarily a local clientele. But Byrne, who had a more ambitious vision for DePaul, was hamstrung by the university's need for money. He unsuccessfully sought to establish a college of engineering and a medical school.

Byrne was the first president of both DePaul University and of its board of trustees, exemplifying the dual structure of administration and governance that characterized DePaul

The Rev. Francis Xavier McCabe, C.M., President 1910–1920.

during its early history. The board, organized to pay off the $400,000 debt that the university had incurred as a result of its startup, was also committed to expand curriculum offerings beyond the liberal arts and sciences, and engineering and to establish a department of economics to combat socialism and anarchism. While curricular issues were significant, the primary duty of this new group was fundraising. At their inaugural meeting, the trustees formed a committee consisting of President Byrne, Charles C. Mahoney, Walter J. Gibbons, William Dillion, John V. Clarke, and John McGillen. Mahoney, Gibbons, and Dillion were identified as attorneys. Clarke was president of Hibernia Bank and McGillen was a general agent for the United Surety Company of Baltimore, Maryland. They were "to solicit aid for the university from such persons as are able to contribute, without regard to their nationality or creed." (3) Though they were men of some prominence in Chicago, they were unable to generate sufficient interest, and the fundraising campaign was ultimately unsuccessful.

Father Byrne was replaced by Father John Martin who stayed only a year. The Vincentian Visitor sent Martin to DePaul in hopes that the new president would be able to reduce the institution's oppressive debt. Martin's tenure as president was cut short, as Dennis McCann has noted, and he did not remain at DePaul long enough to institute any significant curricular changes. His departure opened the way for the institution's second charismatic leader and the next phase in its early development.

DePaul's third president, Father Francis McCabe, whose tenure (from 1910–1920) was longer than the presidencies of either of his predecessors, redirected the university's efforts toward less costly professional programs such as law, education, and business at the undergraduate and graduate levels. Under its two previous presidents, DePaul had explored the possibility of establishing schools of medicine and engineering as ways to distinguish itself, but these courses of study never provided the number of students required to offset the costs associated with their development. McCabe's presidency introduced changes in faculty composition at DePaul that eventually led to the departmental form of administration, primarily through the university's acquisition of free-standing professional schools. With several semi-autonomous schools, the unitary form of administration and governance had to give way to a federated structure, one that connected faculty members and other university employees more closely to their academic departments than to the institution as a whole. McCabe and the Vincentian community that governed DePaul had little choice but to move in this direction; the institution's long-term survival depended on it.

The addition and relative independence of its new professional schools brought new challenges to the university. Though DePaul reiterated its commitment to coeducation and religious diversity in 1910, the pledge to educate both sexes on a nonsectarian basis had been written into the university's original charter. The education of women at DePaul became a palpable reality, however, when President McCabe responded to Bishop Quigley's request that DePaul provide bachelors degree programs for Catholic laywomen to improve their chances for promotion in Chicago's public schools. (4) These aspiring baccalaureates were not only accommodated in separate summer sessions at the uptown campus, they were also taught wholly apart from the male student body of the College of Liberal Arts and Sciences. As John Rury notes in this volume, when full-blown coeducation was finally put in place in 1917, despite the protests of Archbishop George Mundelein, DePaul became the first Catholic university in the United States to educate college men and women together. Here too, it was in great measure the need for additional enrollments that encouraged this departure from traditional Catholic educational policies.

When DePaul merged the Illinois College of Law and the Illinois Law School to create the new DePaul Law School, a large number of non-Catholic students were brought into the university. The addition of these students improved the institution's fiscal position, helping to reduce its debt by nearly doubling its size. In return, DePaul made Howard N. Ogden, head of the Illinois College of Law, the first non-Catholic member of the board of trustees. (5)

At DePaul these new academic programs attracted more students, including women, who in turn contributed additional revenues that helped to control the university's debt level. A larger faculty introduced diversity of thought among its members. As women, students and faculty from other religious backgrounds began to expand and diversify the

The Rev. Thomas F. Levan, C.M., President 1920–1930.

value systems of the institution, the academic culture, administrative culture, and student culture—Clark's categories—manifested themselves and placed different demands on the university. While still a Catholic institution, DePaul was now a university with a diverse faculty, an increasingly varied curriculum and a sizable number of non-Catholic students.

DePaul, like other American universities, experienced significant expansion during the 1920s. Father Thomas F. Levan, C.M., who assumed the presidency in 1920, held the office for a decade. Though its debt load continued to be quite high, Levan managed to keep the university functioning during this period of considerable growth. DePaul added a new classroom building to the uptown campus during Levan's presidency (a building now named for him), and built a new "skyscraper" campus for its downtown programs in 1928. This made it impossible to retire the university's financial obligations. Even so, Levan was able in 1926 to secure accreditation from the North Central Association of Schools and College (NCA), the regional accrediting body for most of the institution's programs. This was a critical step, even though DePaul's relationship with NCA was not a smooth one during the next several decades.

Inclusion on the list of approved colleges and universities gave DePaul increased credibility. But in 1929, three years after it had won official NCA approval, it had to submit to another review. Letters between President Levan and George F. Zook of NCA indicate that the hard fought battle for accreditation was an ongoing one, compelling the university to continue efforts to get and keep certification of its academic programs. In his December 23, 1929, letter, Mr. Zook informed President Levan that DePaul had to agree to reinspection because of the "percentage of classes not meeting North Central standards." NCA was also concerned that the College of Liberal Arts and Sciences and DePaul Academy were too closely linked, especially since the high school was one of only four in the state that was not accredited. DePaul had an unusually high number of student athletes on scholarship (18 of 56 scholarships went to athletes), and NCA inspectors believed that the university's practices with respect to granting extension credit were suspect. (6)

In letters to Zook in March (7) and April 1930 (8), President Levan argued forcefully on behalf of DePaul. He complained that the NCA reviewer was too harsh and unprofessional, and finally in November he pledged to revamp both teaching and administration. Levan assured Zook that the registrar had been warned to exercise "utmost care" in the admission of students, and he promised further that class size would henceforth be limited to no more than 35 students. (9)

Problems with the NCA were only the tip of the administrative iceberg, however. With over five thousand students on two campuses enrolled in eight different colleges and schools, the university had become too large and complex to be run by one person, no matter how authoritative or charismatic. A new administrative structure had to be developed to accommodate the institution's growth. Creating an effective, responsive and innovative organization became the task of DePaul's next generation of leaders.

The Beginnings of Shared Governance: The Middle Presidents

While it was President Levan who made the promises to Mr. Zook and the NCA, it was Father Francis C. Corcoran, DePaul's fifth president, who was responsible for keeping them. Father Corcoran was brought to DePaul to reorganize the university administration. In his November 1930 letter Levan made the following observation to NCA's George Zook:

> *The Administration of the university has changed at the beginning of the present scholastic year by the appointment of a new president. His primary task has been the reorganization of the school from within, by the appointment of Boards and Committees, a more exact division of specialized tasks, and by the active function of the enlarged University Council. It is our hope that what is being done in this respect will meet the Association's fullest approval. (10)*

The reorganization of the university under Father Corcoran was the first of many attempts to improve administration and governance throughout the institution. In the decades between the 1930s and the end of the 1960s efforts were undertaken to limit the power that the institution's first few presidents had been given. DePaul's board of trustees was reorganized on two occasions, and internal and administrative governing bodies were put in place. During the presidencies of Father Francis C. Corcoran, C.M., Father Michael J. O'Connell, C.M., and Father Comerford J. O'Malley, who served in DePaul's middle years, the university became increasingly complex as it acquired new academic and administrative departments. Burton Clark has characterized this kind of expansion and differentiation as the third developmental stage: as academic work becomes increasingly specialized, it demands a more scholarly and professionalized faculty. When scholarship and teaching preclude faculty assumption of administrative responsibilities, the university's bureaucratic structure has to expand to assume these roles.

With the appointment of Father Corcoran in 1930, DePaul began its rapid transformation into a more complex university. It adopted up-to-date methods of management and public relations, creating the first of a number of administrative councils to coordinate the institution's multiple and diverse activities. Though the names of these bodies have changed over time, their functions have not. First as the University Council and later the Administrative Council and the University Senate, each entity advised the president, developed university-wide policies, and disseminated information. Of the three councils, the University Council is the most interesting because the battle to reconcile tensions between centralization and decentralization—as well as early efforts to form a credible university—took place during its existence.

The Rev. Francis V. Corcoran, C.M., President 1930–1935.

The University Council was formed in 1930 and not dissolved until 1970, when its functions were split between the Administrative Council and the University Senate. As the only internal university-wide policy making body until 1964, it included representatives from the various colleges and schools of the university: liberal arts, commerce, law, music and the Secretarial School. The roster of council members (see table 2) offers an insight into DePaul's relatively simple administrative structure at that time. With only one vice president, a registrar, a dean of the graduate school and a dean of women, there was not sufficient personnel to manage a large and complex institution. The University Council offers the first evidence that a federal structure had developed at DePaul as a result of growth. As the number of new schools increased, improved coordination among the deans and administrators was essential. The council became the forum for discussion of university-wide concerns, including questions raised by NCA or other external bodies. Significantly, since Vincentians were a minority of the council's members, at least through most of its existence, the leadership of the university was a mixture of priests and laymen.

Father Corcoran created the University Council as a way to bring some of DePaul's administrative problems under control. In his address to its first meeting in October 1930, Corcoran emphasized that the University Council was essential to the overall administration of the university. It was to focus on DePaul's general welfare rather than on specific departmental concerns. (11) Though the council was conceived as an administrative body, its function broadened to include academic matters and governance as well. In a pre-bureaucratic era when there were few institutional rules and lines of responsibility were often unclear, there were few issues it did not consider.

The early minutes of the council depict a group formulating rules and requirements that kept DePaul functioning as an institution. It created policies and was responsible for overseeing their adoption. In this respect, the University Council was typical of many senior-level groups for which the line between administration and governance was blurred. For example, the council's agenda at its fourth meeting focused on efforts to achieve uniformity and consistency for the university at both its Loop and uptown campuses. Each campus and the schools at each location had developed different methods and procedures for handling recruitment of students, making up its calendar for classes, and setting policies governing students and faculty.

Table Two *Initial Members of the University Council 1930–1931*

Very Reverend Francis V. Corcoran, President

Rev. Thomas C. Powers, Vice President of the University

Rev. James M. Murry, Regent of the College of Commerce*

Rev. Daniel J. McHugh, Regent of the Secretarial College

Rev. Alexander P. Schorsch, Dean of the Graduation School

Rev. Martin V. Moore, Regent of the College of Law

Rev. Thomas Devine, Regent of the School of Music

Rev. Emmett L. Gaffney, Dean of the Liberal Arts

Mr. Howard E. Egan, Associate Dean of Liberal Arts

Mr. William F. Clarke, Dean of the College of Law

Mr. Harry D. Taft, Assistant Dean of the College of Law

Mr. Arthur C. Becker, Dean of the College of Music

Mr. Harvey L. Klein, Dean of the Secretarial College

Mr. William M. Murphy, Dean of the Department of Education

Miss Margaret A. Ring, Dean of Women

Mr. John C. McHugh, Registrar

Much of the council's early work, therefore, involved attempts to reconcile these differences and create standards for the entire institution. This, of course, had been one of the NCA's concerns, and professional organizations and other groups outside of the university were also interested in promoting more uniform standards of performance.

The minutes of its meetings highlight the critical and the mundane issues that often were brought before the council. Among the critical problems these administrators faced were accreditation of the law school, strategies to handle declining enrollment and the reduced revenues associated with it, development of new degree and other academic programs, coordination of a common calendar, and a set of procedures to govern the schools and colleges.

Equally compelling, however, was the frequency with which this body concerned itself with seeming minutiae: producing bulletins with consistent language among the various

---

*Regents were responsible for the religious and moral tone of students and served as advisors to students. They were not to be involved with the administration of any of the schools or colleges.

schools; developing consistent purchase order forms; establishing schedules for baccalaureate and convocation services; striving for consistency in general information and announcements, even with make-up examinations. It performed such tasks in addition to supervising the formation of boards in charge of undergraduate and graduate education. Publicity, another concern of this group, marketed the university to the public as a way to increase enrollment and supply the funds to keep the institution open. In the absence of a bureaucratic organization to perform such tasks, attention to such issues was necessary. It was in these meetings that the processes and procedures that regularized critical administrative aspects of the university began to be hammered out. All of these matters, even those that may have appeared trivial for senior decision-makers, contributed to standardizing administration and governance in the university.

Though these issues were clearly administrative, the council also concerned itself with academic topics commonly regarded as more appropriate for deliberation by the faculty. It examined the criteria for setting academic ranks and involved itself in creating new courses to enhance the university's curriculum. By 1946, in the absence of a university-wide forum in which faculty could be heard, the University Council was dealing with both academic questions and administrative issues.

The council, consisting originally of both deans and regents from the various colleges, had a membership of 11 to 18, with commerce, music, the Secretarial School and the Department of Education each having one representative. Both deans and assistant deans from the larger colleges of liberal arts and sciences and law were on the council. The dean of women (the only female on the council), the registrar, and the vice president of the university completed the group. The president, who served ex officio, usually addressed only the first meeting of each academic year and did not attend thereafter. As new administrative positions were created, such as university examiner or director of athletics, these men joined the council. The deans were the only faculty representatives on the council, and there were no student spokespersons.

Though the president rarely attended council meetings, his presence loomed large, especially during Corcoran's tenure. Father Corcoran, who assumed DePaul's presidency during the Depression, sought to lead it toward improved financial health. He saw the University Council as a unifying body that could act for the university as a whole. The minutes of the University Council during the Corcoran presidency are peppered with requests and demands from the president exhorting the members to standardize procedures and to improve the way the university operated. Throughout academic year 1933–34, Corcoran urged council members to hold regular departmental meetings, clarify the range of responsibilities for department heads, reorganize various departments to reduce financial pressures, have faculty submit articles to local newspapers as a way to promote the university, and initiate procedures and standards for governing student groups. (12) The first steps toward a federated organizational structure at DePaul were uncertain, even though the University Council was given broad powers. The members, at least at the outset, were still mindful of an authoritative president who took command, even telling them how often they should meet.

Corcoran's moves toward standardization of policies and procedures throughout the university initiated bureacratic or rule-driven control. As enrollments grew, there were more student groups and, as John Rury has noted, the university needed policies to govern their behavior. As their numbers grew, faculty members looked for more traditional departmental organization. A growing and heterogeneous institution required a coordinating focus, hence the importance of departmental meetings. Rule-driven management and multifaceted control demanded leadership control throughout, however. DePaul still had to develop leaders who could act independently.

While the University Council's purpose was to improve the overall coordination and functioning of the university, it never seemed able to find the right mix of independent action to implement the president's ideas. Corcoran always opened the first council meeting of the year with a statement of the council's aims, laying out some of the issues on which he wanted it to act. But its performance remained tentative, even as late as 1962, when Father John T. Richardson, as chairman of the University Council, planned changes to its operation and makeup to make it more effective. (13)

When Father Michael O'Connell came to DePaul early in 1932 to serve as vice president of the university and chairman of the University Council under President Corcoran, he proposed that the council create permanent committees to review topics regularly brought before it. (14) He aimed to create a common administrative foundation for the entire university by establishing committees on admissions, curriculum and degrees, convocation, downtown building and public relations. Athletics, student relations, student activities and faculty relations were added to the committee structure later. The committees were precursors to many of the administrative units that conduct today's routine operations at DePaul. In addition, O'Connell suggested creating an Internal Survey Committee (a forerunner of DePaul's current Office of Institutional Planning and Research) to review ways of improving internal procedures and to reevaluate academic requirements for the faculty at each rank, establishing guidelines for admission, matriculation and program fees on all campuses.

Feverish efforts to expand and improve committee design, function and purpose, and ongoing attempts to set a course for the faltering university could not offset the financial crisis it faced during the 1932–33 academic year. Growth during the twenties had relieved some of the financial pressure but it by no means protected DePaul from the more extreme economic swings that affected the nation and the world in the following decade. The university endured financial hardship along with many other institutions during the Great Depression. By fall

The Rev. Michael J. O'Connell, C.M., President 1935–1944.

1932, it was nearly bankrupt, the result of a sharp decline in enrollment. University Council minutes for December 15, 1932 (15) report that all departments showed a one-third drop in income below expected revenues, making further borrowing impossible until the banks saw evidence of retrenchment in the university. So DePaul set out to reduce expenses by decreasing the number of courses offered, reducing the number of assistants in deans' offices, and reducing faculty salaries. The newly formed but untested council was forced to take on a major crisis.

Reverend O'Connell assumed the presidency in 1935, after Corcoran resigned due to illness. As in previous administrations, financial distress shaped much of the O'Connell presidency. Though enrollments stabilized for a time following the crisis of 1932 and the university achieved a tenuous solvency, they dropped once again as the United States geared up for war in the late thirties and early forties. O'Connell urged the University Council to advise students that those who stayed in school also served their country. There seemed to be no end to the problems faced by the university.

It appeared at first that World War II posed a mortal threat to DePaul, yet it turned out in the end to be the university's salvation. O'Connell, and following him, President Comerford O'Malley, placed DePaul at the service of the federal government for training purposes. But after the conflict, DePaul—like many other institutions—became a site for educating returning soldiers. As noted in other chapters, these veterans doubled the student enrollment of the university and at last put DePaul in a position of financial strength. The new students required more administrators and faculty to look after them, sorely straining existing administrative structures and procedures. But with the basic bureaucratic apparatus of the university firmly in place by the end of the O'Connell presidency, subsequent presidents had only to modify, adjust and expand the existing structure, leaving them free to improve the university's overall academic quality and to maintain its financial solvency. The institution's fiscal stability was secure for the moment, but a new crisis loomed, this one having to do with its academic programs.

The struggle that had characterized the Levan presidency (1920–30)—earning and keeping North Central accreditation—resumed during O'Malley's term. The term of

Comerford O'Malley, the last president to serve during the middle period of the university's first century (1944–63), was marked by this threat, even though it was only temporary. The president and others in the university had to focus intensely on upgrading the institution's educational program. In 1949, DePaul found itself threatened with the loss of North Central Association accreditation. NCA Director Norman Burns' April 1949 letter to O'Malley indicates there were a number of serious issues:

> *A*s you will note, DePaul University stands quite low on a number of items in the area of faculty. Furthermore, the standing on the items relating to expenditures for library salaries and to educational expenditure per student is low in comparison with other institutions. (16)

Nearly a year after the Burns letter, the NCA took action against DePaul. At the March 1950 meeting of the Commission on Colleges of the North Central Association, the members voted to remove DePaul from the list of accredited institutions. (17) This plunge in DePaul's fortune was featured in the local newspapers and caused the university widespread embarrassment. President O'Malley filed an appeal the day after the NCA's decision.

Lean financial years had caused DePaul to spend little on its academic programs, resulting in standards below those for comparable institutions. DePaul was ranked in the 25th percentile with respect to stated purposes of the university and their usefulness in planning. The report's text criticized the university's statement of purpose, calling it vague and so inclusive that it would be of no help in "determining policies or activities." Other criticisms were even more telling. The North Central Association ranked DePaul's faculty at the 10th percentile or below for graduate training and educational experience of its teachers, membership and programs pursued in learned societies and the all-important faculty-student ratio. DePaul was at the lowest possible level for faculty members holding doctorates, and those with masters degrees (23rd percentile), publication of books (11th percentile) and articles (32nd percentile), and membership in professional organizations (23rd percentile) were also unsatisfactorily low. Not surprisingly, the NCA report found DePaul's general education curriculum inadequate (18th percentile) and rated no student personnel services above the 29th percentile. DePaul fared better in some administrative areas, except for educational expenditure per student (18th percentile) and stable income per student (16th percentile). (18)

Dr. George A. Works, director of study for the North Central Association (who had participated in the DePaul review process since at least 1934), regularly evaluated the university's progress toward meeting the North Central Association's demands. It was not until 1951, however, that DePaul's NCA accreditation was finally restored. In a letter dated April 18, 1951, Manning M. Pattillo of the NCA listed the terms for reinstatement:

The report of the re-survey indicates that progress has been made in strengthening the institution in the year that has elapsed. However, the Commission wishes to assure itself that the improvements initiated during the year will be carried forward and that other urgently needed changes will be made in the program of the institution. It therefore recommends that DePaul University be continued on the accreditation list for two years and that another survey be made in the Autumn of 1952. (19)

DePaul was required to make regular reports to the North Central Association throughout the early 1950s. During the 1954–55 academic year, the university received accreditation for five years, relieving some of the intense pressure to perform to external standards. Still, as other authors in this volume have noted, the threatened loss of NCA accreditation was particularly traumatic and influenced DePaul's leaders for decades to come.

In addition to external threats, O'Malley had to contend with a decline in his authority when the board of trustees was reorganized in 1946 to reduce presidential power. Briton I. Budd, one of the five lay members of the board, initiated the appointment of an outside management consultant, Stanley Farwell, president of Business Research Corporation, in 1944, to reorganize the administration and governance of the university. Farwell proposed a plan for reorganizing the institution to make it more effective, and conceded to Budd's insistence that the university should be more successful in marketing itself and raising funds to support its academic programs. The reorganization plan included restricting the president's authority to the management of internal administrative matters and placing him at the head of the university, supported by a vice president and dean of faculties who would be second in command. The proposal retained the University Council and acknowledged its role as the highest internal policy body. (20)

In a further administrative change, Farwell called for the creation of a "Board of Lay Trustees" (he later became a member of this newly formed board). It was a separate entity and exercised no authority to obligate the university financially or programmatically. That authority continued to reside in the board of trustees, henceforth called the "Board of Legal Trustees." Whereas the legal trustees were the owners of the university, the lay trustees were primarily fundraisers and public relations advocates. The following statement of purpose spells out the role of the board of lay trustees:

*T*he purpose of the Board of Lay Trustees is to promote and advance the objectives of DePaul University as an educational institution in Chicago. The immediate objective of the Board and its committees are centered upon the needs of the university for public recognition and support and for additional facilities in the way of buildings, land and equipment. (21)

The first meeting of the board of lay trustees was held on December 18, 1946. (22) Members were drawn from business, the law, and the DePaul alumni. A banker, a real estate executive, and a comptroller represented the business community. The legal profession was represented by a circuit court judge and a lawyer. Besides the president, the dean of the DePaul Law School, William F. Clarke, and a representative from the DePaul Alumni Association, Stacy Osgood, were members. Briton Budd set the work of the board of lay trustees in context, suggesting that DePaul was at a crossroads and that it needed to take aggressive action "to consolidate the university's position and to keep it moving forward." The lay trustees were particularly concerned about the deteriorating neighborhood around the uptown campus and about extricating the university from its lease on the Lake Street building. In addition, they began thinking about preparing for the institution's golden jubilee, about the need for faculty housing, the lack of an auditorium, and the need for an athletic field house.

During its nearly 20-year existence, the board of lay trustees addressed many of the important financial and physical plant issues that faced the university: whether or not to buy a building in the Loop during the 1948–49 academic year; it celebrated the university's release from debt when it paid off its last outstanding obligation, a coupon held by Northwestern Mutual Fund, in 1948; and it worried constantly about the fluctuations in enrollments that determined in large measure whether the university was in the red or in the black during any given academic year. Finances continued to be of concern to the lay trustees all through the 1950s. The $100,000 deficit the university showed in 1950 was due largely to a decline in enrollment. The 1953–54 academic year finally saw another balanced budget, although enrollment did not show a substantial upswing until 1955. Fewer college age students, the result of a decline in birth rates during the Great Depression, and military service (the Korean War) were cited as reasons for the drop in enrollment during the early fifties. (23)

DePaul could not afford to rely mostly on tuition to fund its operations, and President O'Malley and the board began exploring ways to raise money for the university. The board of lay trustees decided to launch a $5,250,000 fund drive in 1953 to focus on upgrading the university's physical plant by constructing buildings and acquiring land. The money raised by

A page from the DePaulia student newspaper announcing the expansion of the University's lay board of trustees. March 8, 1946

the campaign would be portioned out, with $4,250,000 for infrastructure improvement and the remaining $1 million for endowment. (24)

To improve its fundraising capability, the board of lay trustees increased its membership from 16 to 21 and added a committee on board organization in 1954 to coordinate the growing number of board committees. During the 1959–60 academic year, board size was finally fixed at 60, though President O'Malley had hoped for a 100-member board.

The board of lay trustees turned its attention to two pressing matters during the 1960s: raising additional money from corporations and the question of the Lincoln Park campus. In 1962, it established a Business-Industry Liaison Committee to solicit funds from corporations, motivated by a meeting between DePaul board members and Dr. Frank Sparks of the Council for Financial Aid to Education at which they discussed how to increase corporate support to higher education in Chicago. As Thomas Croak notes in chapter 7, DePaul made a commitment by 1963 to stay in the Lincoln Park area and to improve its uptown campus. The board of lay trustees reviewed proposals that called for purchasing an apart-

For decades, summer school enrollments at DePaul included many religious. Sisters teaching in Chicago's Catholic School System and

ment building for dormitories, building a library-classroom facility, a student union, and a power plant. Government funding for colleges and universities, and changes in urban renewal laws that allowed DePaul to purchase land at substantially reduced rates, facilitated the transformation of the Lincoln Park campus. By July 1963, the university had acquired all the land, except for one parcel, in the area bounded by Fullerton, Belden, Kenmore, and Seminary. (25)

The commitment to expand and refurbish the Lincoln Park campus and the arrival of a new president set the stage for changes in the administration and governance of DePaul during the middle and late 1960s. When he assumed the presidency, Father Cortelyou, President O'Malley's successor, created the Administrative Council to manage the changes taking place on the Lincoln Park campus. The need for federal dollars brought about another reorganization of the lay board in 1967 in a further effort to increase lay participation and governance in the university. The era of strong presidents was giving way to the shared governance that characterized the administrations of DePaul's next three presidents.

taking education courses accounted for a large number of students.

The Later Presidents: Creating the Modern University

The periods of continuing growth and change that marked the presidencies of John R. Cortelyou, C.M., John T. Richardson, and John P. Minogue, C.M., confirmed Burton Clark's prediction that specialization, multiple value systems, and increasing size would spawn numerous subcultures. Coordination and vigorous bureaucracies would become common in large universities as a consequence, Clark has argued. At DePaul, the University Council had been the dominant administrative group for more than thirty years, but beginning with the Cortelyou presidency in 1964 and continuing into the present, new administrative structures were added, even though they made DePaul's governance more rule-driven and fragmented.

Father John Cortelyou (president from 1964 to 1981) was the first DePaul president with an advanced degree in an academic discipline (biology) rather than in theology. As Thomas Croak notes, his commitment to the sciences served as a catalyst, inspiring a rise in the quality of all academic programs, but especially the sciences. Father Cortelyou also presided over the expansion and modification of the university's internal governance structures. The formation of the Administrative Council and the University Senate and the growing interest of the student body in the curricular and administrative issues that affected their education accelerated changes in DePaul's management structure.

A small group of administrators, concerned about the building program at the Lincoln Park campus and renovation in the Lewis Center on the downtown campus, formed the Administrative Council, a new university-wide body. The university was engaged in an aggressive building campaign on the Lincoln Park campus to build dormitories for 200 students, a new building for classrooms, faculty offices and a library, and a new central heating plant. With all of this construction activity, there was a need for close coordination of the projects and the costs associated with them.

The Administrative Council, consisting of President Cortelyou, Executive Vice President John Richardson, Vice President Theodore Wangler, Secretary-Treasurer Albert L. Dundas, and Comerford O'Malley, former president and now chancellor, held its first meeting in February 1964. (26) It undertook decisions about salary and benefit levels for faculty, administrators, and clerical staff, heard about proposed changes in the board of trustees, discussed the format for the inauguration of President Cortelyou and, of course, monitored progress on acquiring and developing property in Lincoln Park.

The structure of this body, including its limited size, was reminiscent of the old model of authoritative control in university affairs. The Administrative Council once again centralized decision making in the hands of a few individuals, almost all of whom were Vincentians. However, as the control exercised by Vincentian priests at DePaul continued to decline, Father Cortelyou recognized that the leadership of the institution was heading toward lay control. In a statement to the board on January 17, 1964 he said:

Every year more and more of the academic leadership at the university is passing from the Vincentian priests to the laymen of the faculty and in the administration. This transition is the result of a shortage of capable Vincentians at the university and the insistence of the administration that the best persons be given positions of authority regardless of their clerical or lay status. This situation has redeeming features, for it assures the laymen greater equality with the clergy and greater responsibility in determining the development of the university. (27)

As the internal organization of the university developed, the Administrative Council expanded to include additional senior administrators who filled newly created vice presidential positions. The heads of enrollment management, student affairs, institutional research and planning, and development joined the Administrative Council as these departments came into existence. The decline in Vincentian influence and participation at the university is evident in the Administrative Council membership. Mostly Vincentian in 1964, by the end of the Administrative Council's existence in 1993, the president and the "Senior Officer for Mission" were the only Vincentian priests remaining at the administration's senior level. (28)

The Administrative Council oversaw most areas of administrative function. Father Richardson, executive vice president and chief academic officer for the university at the time of its formation, reported changes in academic programs to the council. In 1964, for instance, he was instrumental in its rejecting a nursing program, and he recommended adopting a quarter system for all schools except law in 1965. The council also dealt with faculty concerns. To help faculty members raise money to support their research, the Department of Sponsored Programs and Projects was proposed in 1970. At its final meeting (June 1993), plans for expanding DePaul's international academic offerings were brought up. Even though the Administrative Council discussed and made recommendations related to academic concerns throughout its existence, it functioned more in an advisory capacity on academic matters than as a decision making body.

As regards external governance, another substantial change in the board of trustees was introduced during the Cortelyou presidency. Much of the drive to transform the board originated in DePaul's need for government funds to help support academic and administrative programs. But it also corresponded to the drift toward greater lay participation in all areas of university life. As a corollary to increased lay participation in administration of the university, more lay involvement in the governance of the university was called for.

As early as 1963, Father Cortelyou, Father Richardson and members of the board of lay trustees discussed ways to improve the operations of both the lay trustees and the board of legal trustees. The trustees were not involved enough with the university and consequently their efforts at fundraising were hampered. More outside or lay representation on the legal board of trustees was recommended in a 1963 self-study. A number of changes to both the legal board of trustees and the board of lay trustees were proposed between 1964 and 1967. Finally in 1967, the board of lay trustees was completely reorganized in accordance with a plan devised by Claire Roddewig and an ad hoc committee of the board that he chaired. The former board of legal trustees, renamed the "Members of the Corporation," retained the authority to select both of DePaul's boards. In addition, as a way to retain their influence in the university, two-thirds of the Members of the Corporation were to be Vincentians. Governance and management of the university, however, was transferred to the newly formed board of directors, which replaced the board of lay trustees. The board of directors was given a degree of authority that put it on a par with traditional boards of directors at other colleges and universities. Specifically, the board was empowered to select the president of the university, a choice no longer limited by the restriction that the president must be a Vincentian. For the first time, DePaul University was an institution primarily under lay control. (29)

Finally, Father Cortelyou's presidency saw a further set of changes related to administration and governance. The University Senate, created in 1968, expanded the number and type of people who were involved with the internal functioning of the university. This body represented an attempt to combat the fragmentation that Clark suggested is an outcome of growth, and was designed to bring faculty, staff, and students more fully within the governance of the university. Each of these three groups was represented on the senate, an entity that was emblematic of the new accessibility to governance structures that was occurring on college and university campuses in the 1960s. The University Senate eventually succumbed to its own ineffectiveness and was disbanded in 1983. Nonetheless, it consolidated the increasing desire for faculty involvement in administration and governance that had evolved over the past 20 years. In addition, the University Senate set the stage for the increased participation by faculty and staff, and to a lesser extent students, in leading and managing a new DePaul that was increasingly manifest in the closing decades of its first century.

As early as 1946, a faculty committee made recommendations to the University Council about matters affecting faculty members. This relationship was formalized in 1950 with the creation of the Administration-University Senate, made up of representatives from both the administration and the faculty. Vice President Krammer and Comptroller Sharer represented the administration, but faculty members varied from year to year (usually there were five faculty participants). During the 18-year history of this body, members addressed such matters as secretarial and other support services for faculty, salary and benefits, the role of academic freedom at DePaul, and policies related to tenure and promotion. In May 1965 (30) the faculty group reported considerable enthusiasm among its constituents about the possibility of organizing an academic senate to better serve faculty interests, a suggestion that contributed to the eventual formation of the University Senate.

Various committees and councils took up the issue of an academic senate over the next four years. In October 1965, members of the University Council learned that the faculty had requested a faculty senate but had not developed a formal proposal. At the same meeting, Father Richardson proposed that the Student Activity Council select some students to serve in "a liaison capacity with the faculty and administration, that the Faculty Advisory Council select three faculty members, and that the president of the university appoint three administrators to meet with duly appointed student representatives." (31) The idea of joint meetings between faculty, administrators, and students influenced the composition of the University Senate.

In April 1966, Father Richardson sent a memorandum to the University Council indicating the formation of a steering committee for the senate to guide the development of the University Senate, to ensure both faculty and administration involvement. (32) In addition to faculty members Father Joseph Brokers, William Hayes, Lawrence Ryan, Cornelius Sippel, and Robert Tiles, the steering committee included University Council representatives Father Richardson, Father Theodore Wangler (vice president for student personnel services), Jack Compare (budget and finances), and Martin Lowery.

In December 1967 Dr. Bunion, chair of the Faculty Advisory Council, proposed an academic faculty senate so that faculty and administrators could share authority in the operations of the university. (33) Faculty members, it was felt, should have authority over curriculum, degree requirements, and standards of student achievement. Further, control over standards for promotion, tenure, academic freedom and other areas that affect the life of the faculty were to be in faculty hands, along with the grievance process as it related to faculty members. In addition to the areas in which the faculty would have direct authority, there were other areas such as budgets, student affairs, physical plant, and public statements of the university, over which it was believed the faculty should have indirect authority.

In the end, the idea of a university governing body involving faculty, staff, and students won out over an academic senate consisting only of faculty. The University Senate Committee, which met first in February 1968, was chaired by faculty member Albert Erlebacher. (34) It spent approximately two years determining membership in and the structure of this body. On February 16, 1970, after the committee approved the final document, it voted to disband as a committee. Professor Erlebacher, who had been its chairman, assumed the presidency pro-tem of the University Senate in June of that year.

According to its by-laws, the University Senate was to consist of 26 faculty senators, 13 student senators, 12 administrators as ex officio members (vice presidents and deans) and 2 staff who were to represent all elements of the non-professional staff of the university. To make the University Senate a functioning and manageable body, a committee and subcommittee structure was put in place for faculty affairs, academic programs and regulations, student affairs, human relations, finance, physical plant and development. (35) Similar to the committees developed for the University Council in the 1930s, they dealt with aspects of administration and function that were becoming increasingly important.

The University Senate, with its combination of both advisory and legislative powers, was designed to permit individuals to contribute to the formulation of decisions, to make policy and to facilitate communication throughout the university. In its advisory capacity, it would counsel the president and through him the board of trustees. It would advise on matters both external (relationships with other institutions, finances, plans for physical expansion, and public relations) and internal (changes in curriculum and degree requirements).

The president delegated legislative powers to the University Senate and he reviewed senate decisions and retained veto power over them. Any decision not acted on by the president within 30 days became university policy. The University Senate's legislative authority covered academic faculty and student affairs. Its control in the area of academic affairs dealt with academic programs, curriculum, and standards for student admission and achievement. Its role with respect to faculty gave the University Senate the right to create policies related to academic freedom, tenure, morale, and the welfare of the faculty. In the area of student affairs, it focused on counseling, paracurricular activities, discipline, and the general welfare of the students.

The University Senate attempted to develop collegial decision-making at DePaul by placing representatives of the various constituencies squarely within the decision-making process. As the language of senate by-laws demonstrated, however, the only way to activate collegial decision making given the growth in the university was through a rule-driven bureaucracy. Burton Clark has designated this use of bureaucracy the fourth stage of growth in a university, in which rules are promulgated to bind together different subcultures of the institution and dictate how they will interact with each other. At DePaul, there were very specific guidelines for faculty and students having to do with election to the senate and extent of authority as a member of this body. On the other hand, the by-laws were rather vague with respect to lower-level staff whose representatives were allotted only two of the 65 positions. The by-laws did not specify any area of legislative power specifically reserved for staff, nor were the provisions for electing staff as clearly laid out as they were for faculty and students. The University Senate was disbanded in 1983 during the Richardson presidency because it did not address the issues and concerns of each group of participants satisfactorily, and because its large membership and consequent unwieldiness interfered with its ability to function.

Father John Richardson, who was named president in 1981, was the first president to be chosen by the board of trustees under its new authority rather than appointed by the Vincentian provincial. Richardson had come to DePaul in 1954 and played a critical role in the university for many years before assuming the presidency. Father Richardson, like Father O'Connell, one of his predecessors as executive vice president, had been an influential academic administrator. As Charles Strain notes in this volume, Richardson oversaw a number of the curricular reforms initiated during Father Cortelyou's presidency. In addition, during his term as executive vice president, he headed the University Council and was an active member of the Administrative Council.

Father Richardson had been an activist as second in command and he was an activist as president. Under Cortelyou and Richardson, DePaul put into effect doctoral level programs in philosophy, psychology, and computer science and brought to fruition the plan Richardson had developed during Cortelyou's presidency. During Richardson's tenure the university officially adopted the concept of growth as a means of upgrading DePaul's academic offerings. Growth meant more students, which meant more income for DePaul; this money was to finance improvements in physical plant and permit an increase in the size and quality of the DePaul faculty. Growth in the university also called for more administrators. By naming three women, including an African American and an Asian American, to vice presidential posts, Richardson pioneered racial and gender diversity at DePaul's senior administrative levels.

Early in his presidency, Father Richardson took the first steps toward elimination of the University Senate. (36) He appointed a committee consisting of Carol Abbinanti, Virgil Johnson, Barbara Lewis, James McGing, John Markese, Federick Miller, David Sonenshein, and Simone Zurawski and charged it with making specific recommendations for replacing or restructuring the senate. In February 1983, the committee released its "Report of the Committee on Replacing or Restructuring the University Senate." (37) Opening with a discussion of academic governance, the members stated some of the basic assumptions that guided their recommendations: the University Senate can be effective only within the larger context of governance at DePaul; faculty, students, staff, and administrators should share in governance; and the board of trustees is the university's ultimate authority. While the committee acknowledged the influence of such external agencies and forces as legislative bodies, regulatory agencies, courts, accrediting bodies, and other social forces, it chose not to deal with them. The report also noted that faculty members had become less involved in the University Senate and more involved in their departments and schools. In the section on governance at DePaul, the committee wrote:

Among virtually all of the individuals consulted by the committee, and in every group interviewed, representing all constituencies on the campus, there is a clear consensus that the University Senate, as presently constituted, is ineffective as the principal mechanism for faculty, staff, and student participation in governance at DePaul. Inadequacies most frequently cited are that it is too large and unwieldy; the diversity of representation is a problem, particularly in view of the fact that there are not other structure (sic) for faculty participation in governance; it does not effectively represent staff. (38)

In light of the disenchantment with the University Senate, the committee recommended that it be disbanded.

> *T*he Committee is satisfied that the present circumstance is not the fault of any person or group of persons. Rather it recognizes that the University Senate is no longer adequate as a governance structure to deal with issues of the time. It is the recommendation of the Committee that the University Senate be discontinued, and replaced with separate, discrete organizations to serve the four constituency groups that make up the campus community: faculty, staff, students, and administrators. (39)

In place of the University Senate, the committee recommended that separate governance structures be created for faculty, staff, and students. The report described each of these structures. The suggestions made for faculty and staff became the blueprints for the Faculty Council and Staff Council, the bodies that replaced the University Senate.

The committee report recommended that Faculty Council members be elected by the faculty and advise the administration on those aspects that affected faculty, in which faculty might have expertise, or those with implication for the educational mission of the institution. Curriculum, instruction, academic programs, degree requirements, educational policies, faculty status (including appointment, reappointment, promotion and tenure), and admission standards were to be the primary responsibilities of the Faculty Council. According to the report, faculty would routinely deliberate with the administration on such matters as the development of the budget, institutional priorities and planning, and selection and retention of administrators. The administration could request advice from the Faculty Council or the council could offer such advice independent of the wishes of the administration. Finally, the report suggested that participation on the Faculty Council be recognized in the reward systems of the university.

In the section on participation of students in governance, the report recommended that a "Student Association" be created, an instrument to communicate students' point of view rather than a "governing body." The Student Association would have primary responsibility for formulating the regulations that affect student life, student-sponsored activities and programs and student publications. The Student Association and the administration would work together to establish standards and procedures governing student discipline, student disciplinary procedures and appointments to key positions in student affairs. Like the Faculty Council, the Student Association could advise the administration in such matters as curriculum, establishment and development of programs, procedures for evaluation of courses, procedures for evaluation of students, the appointment and retention of faculty and administration, and quality of academic life as it affected students.

The "Report on Replacing or Restructuring the University Senate" attempted to address a major senate shortcoming: lack of involvement of staff in the governance of the university. As it had for faculty and students, the report recommended that staff have its own governance structure, with the establishment of a "Staff Council" to be elected by staff members. The staff would work with the administration to make decisions that affected staff, particularly with respect to working conditions. In addition, the Staff Council would advise the administration and faculty regarding the effect new programs would have on academic support resources such as library, computer services, and the like. By recommending the creation of the Staff Council, the committee members acknowledged that the staff had concerns that had not been addressed satisfactorily by previous administrations (deans and those who served on the Administrative Council) and, therefore, needed its own body to advance the interests of its constituents.

In light of the committee's recommendations to form separate councils, a faculty committee was convened at President Richardson's request. Its members, Joan Lakebrink (education, and chair of the Faculty Steering Committee to Establish a Faculty Council), Jurgis Anysas (chemistry), James Belohlav (management), Patrick Callahan (political science), Edwin Cohen (accounting), Jeanne LaDuke (math), Raymond Grzebielski (law), John O'Malley (Goodman), and Stephen J. Leacock (law) who resigned and was replaced by Ray J. Grzebielski, set the structure and objectives of the Faculty Council. (40)

During January and February of 1984, this steering committee revised suggestions that had appeared in the 1983 report and offered more specific commentary on the rights and responsibilities of faculty. The document they produced divided faculty responses into three types: primary, participatory, and advisory. Primary responsibilities covered all governance in the area of academic and scholarly activities and faculty personnel matters within the university. Participatory responsibilities allowed the faculty to "participate regularly with the administration and other appropriate bodies in the University" to establish priorities and to formulate policies related to allocation and use of human, physical, and fiscal resources, selection and retention of administrators, creation of offices and other major changes in the university structure. Any matter of interest to the faculty or pertaining to the university and its purpose such as policies related to intercollegiate athletics would be within faculty purview. In an advisory capacity, the Faculty Council could counsel the administration whenever asked or when the faculty felt it was appropriate. (41)

Though the Faculty Council was designed and set up by a faculty committee, President Richardson was actively involved in its development. In his May 5, 1983 memo to Patricia Ewers (dean of faculties) and Howard Sulkin, another academic administrator, Richardson wrote:

> *A*s you can see from the attached, I have written both of you into my
> Guidelines for the Faculty and Staff Council. My experience with faculty
> and staff groups leads me to the absolute conviction that unless key adminis-
> trators provide leadership and actively participate in these organizations, they
> will not be effective. (42)

Later that month (May 17) Richardson asked Deans Griffith, Meister, Miller, Ryan, Sarubbi, and Watts to distribute a final draft of the recommendations to each of their faculty members. Though Dean Justice at the School for New Learning received a copy of the memorandum, this school did not yet have full time faculty members, so the draft was not circulated in the School for New Learning. Richardson observed in a memo that accompanied the draft, "We are somewhat pressed for time because my calendar calls for getting the reactions of the faculty to the proposal before the faculty disperse for the summer. Hence the June 1 deadline. We have been at this too long already." (43)

The Faculty Council held its first meeting on October 26, 1984. (44) Some members of this first council—for example, Professors Lakebrink and Sippel—had been involved in earlier attempts at faculty governance as members of either the University Senate or the committee to develop the Faculty Council. Junior faculty who were newer to the governance process at DePaul but who were part of the larger national movement to open governance structures in higher education also served on the Faculty Council. (See table 3, list of members of first Faculty Council.)

The Faculty Council addressed issues of its internal governance as well as issues affecting the larger university during its first year. At its first meeting, the council elected William Hayes (by a narrow 9–7 margin over Joan Lakebrink) chair and appointed members of the Committee on Committees (Sullivan, Lakebrink, Messmer, Vitullo, Bennett, and Flynn) to begin recruiting faculty to serve on its various and still-to-be-formed committees. Finally, the council assumed the responsibility (previously held by the Faculty Affairs Committee of the University Senate) to participate in the nomination of the president of the university and appoint faculty candidates to university-wide committees and boards. Hayes appointed Erlebacher to be temporary secretary at the following meeting. (45) Father Richardson, who attended the meeting, agreed to a course reduction for the president of the council to accommodate his additional administrative obligations and suggested that the Faculty Council consider making the secretary's position a nonfaculty one. Richardson said that he was willing to explore a system of early consultation with the faculty to expedite decision making. Throughout the rest of that academic year, the Faculty Council continued to organize itself and became increasingly involved in academic governance issues.

It created the Committee on Status of Faculty, organized a process for consultation on the reappointment of David Justice as dean of the School for New Learning, and approved a Masters of Science in Management Systems, revision of the faculty handbook, the appointment of a faculty representative from the School for New Learning and the appointment of a student as a non-voting member of the Committee on the Status of Faculty. Over the next decade, the Faculty Council supplemented programs and policies with the aim of improving the university's academic quality and its treatment of faculty. (46)

During this period, university staff members were organizing the Staff Council through their Staff Steering Committee which consisted of William Duffy (payroll), Portia Fuzell (admissions), Judith Rycombel (libraries), Georgette Rohde, (School of Music), and Brenda Sanders (Rehabilitation Services Program).

Founded in 1983, Staff Council was created to represent the staff and promote its concerns, to facilitate staff participation in governance, planning and decision making, to serve as a liaison between staff and faculty, students, and administration, and to preserve an atmosphere of personalism in the university community. Any staff member below the level of vice president was eligible for election to the Staff Council, which was made up of 12 exempt mem-

---

Table Three *Initial Members of Faculty Council*

Commerce:	*Education:*
William Hayes	Joan Lakebrink
Thomas Kewley	Jack Lane
Robert O'Keefe	(alternate: Kopan)
Mark Sullivan	
Gemma Welsch	*Law:*
(alternates: Luft, Markese, Waters)	Vincent Vitullo
	David Coar
Liberal Arts & Science:	(alternate Ginsberg)
Larry Bennett	
Albert Erlebacher	*Music:*
Elaine Fila	Donald DeRoache,
John (Jack) Leahy,	George Flynn
Cornelius Sipple,	(alternate: Lyne)
Rose Spalding	
(alternates: Anderson, Bille, and Crossan)	*Goodman:*
	Janet Messmer
	James T. Ostholthoff
	(alternate: Fielding)

---

bers and 12 non-exempt members. Although the Staff Council was created to increase staff participation in the administration and governance of DePaul, it did not inspire the same interest among staff as the Faculty Council did among the faculty. Only one group of staff, the librarians, responded to the proposed establishment of a Staff Council. They wrote a memorandum responding to the "Report of the Committee on Replacing or Restructuring the University Senate," voicing their opinions about the role proposed for the librarians on the Staff Council. (47) They argued for exempt and nonexempt staff representation on the Staff Council, adding that librarians, as the largest single group of academic professionals, should have permanent voting representation. But, they asserted, limiting participation of librarians to Staff Council excluded them from active participation in planning and developing academic programs. Finally, they pointed out that the library is the only large unit in the university whose chief administrative officer is not represented on any policy-making body.

In recent years the Staff Council has become more active, recommending staff representatives for most major university-wide committees and creating for itself a more active role in university governance. Since 1994, staff members have participated on the Joint Council, the Benefits Committee, the Sexual Harassment Advisory Board, and the Information Technology Academic Advisory Group. Current Staff Council president Kelly Moore has commented that the council is still working to fashion its appropriate role. (48)

Father John Minogue became president of DePaul in 1993. He was the second president elected by the board of trustees rather than appointed by the Vincentian provincial. The board chose the president, but the presidential selection committee first presented the three finalists to the university community for its comments. In contrast to Father Richardson, his predecessor, whose transition to the presidency was eased by his long tenure at DePaul, Father Minogue was new to the university and to administration in higher education. His professional training was in the area of theology and he had been a clinical professor of ethics at Northwestern University, where he had worked on a day-to-day basis with parents of unborn babies afflicted with severe medical illnesses. It was work that demanded quick decision making as lives often were at stake. Minogue's propensity for action early in his tenure sometimes found him at odds with a university culture that was slow and collegial in its decision making processes.

Father Minogue made a number of administrative changes early in his tenure. He reorganized the senior administration into administrative and academic lines with an executive vice president heading each of these areas. This restructuring of the senior administrative leadership resulted in a number of long-term members of the senior leadership leaving the university or assuming new positions. He dedicated his efforts to expanding the number of suburban campuses and computerizing the university, increasing the staffing in these areas as a way to implement these plans.

Also, Minogue replaced the Academic Council with the Joint Council. The Joint Council, a larger group than the Administrative Council, had a membership that was closer in its makeup to the old University Council. The two executive vice presidents (operations and academics), five vice presidents (planning, student affairs, enrollment management, development and university relations, and human resources), the deans of all the schools and colleges, the president of faculty council and the senior executive for university mission comprised the membership of the first Joint Council, though it expanded later to include the controller, the associate vice presidents for enrollment management and organizational development, and the special assistant to the president for diversity. For the first time since the demise of the University Senate, DePaul students were represented in a senior decision making body when the president of the Student Government Association became a member of the Joint Council. The Joint Council, with both policy endorsement and operational functions, touched all important facets of the institution. The early agendas of the meetings had sections for policy and procedure, academics and operations areas, strategic planning, deans and administrative councils, and ongoing effectiveness. (49) Each academic and administrative area was to present to the Joint Council its short- and long-term plans for operation. The council commented and made recommendations, though each of the deans and managers of the functional areas set individual agendas. Each unit made reports designed to increase understanding among the senior administrators of the university and to anticipate the strategic planning process that would occur over the next few years.

In some ways, the start of the Minogue presidency crystallized the transition that was taking place at the university. DePaul had been growing steadily for the previous 10 years, and there was a sentiment on the part of many long-term faculty and staff that the university was changing from "the little school under the El" to an organization different from what they were familiar with. There was concern as well that expansion to the suburbs was in conflict with the institution's mission of serving Chicago students. Faculty were concerned that teaching on multiple campuses would weaken their connection to their home departments. Some wondered whether a commitment to multiculturalism would mean a commitment to quotas. Finally, many members of the DePaul community felt that focusing on computers, improving administrative procedures, and reducing the university's operating costs would lead to a university climate in which the importance of the individual would be diminished. (50)

During the first years of the Minogue presidency, discussions about what DePaul had been and was to become took place in a number of university forums. Each of the councils—faculty, staff, and joint—allocated time to react to proposed changes and make recommendations of its own. Open sessions on the strategic plan and town hall meetings on diversity provided opportunities for a wide variety of faculty and staff to engage senior administrators about the future of the university. By the 1990s DePaul was no longer an institution built on and dominated by the larger-than-life presidents of its early years. Governance was now in the hands of the administration, the faculty, the non-teaching staff and, to a more limited extent, the students. In this respect, DePaul, like most other American higher education institutions of its size, conformed closely to Burton Clark's general model of institutional behavior. DePaul had moved from an institution where administration and governance was embodied in the president and a small number of priests, through stages that brought increasing differentiation in the faculty and administration. This process, while allowing more voice to people who were excluded from decision making in the earlier days at DePaul, resulted in clearly identified groups—faculty, staff, students—representing the interests of their constituencies. On the threshold of its second century, DePaul had become a fully modern university with all the benefits and challenges attendant to such a transformation.

External Factors Affecting the Life of the University

DePaul, like other universities, has grown substantially since its founding. Burton Clark's model of the organizational dynamics of growth provided a framework for interpreting DePaul's evolution. But this framework has two drawbacks. First, it fails to acknowledge the role of external forces in higher education in general (and DePaul in particular) with respect to administration and governance. Second, it fails to take note of the religious identification that plays such a significant role in an institution such as DePaul. DiMaggio and Powell (51) argue that organizations in a given field tend increasingly to resemble one another. They call this trend toward uniformity "isomorphism" and explain that there are three types: coercive, normative, and mimetic. Coercive isomorphism occurs when external agents with power over a given domain make the organizations in that domain comply with external standards. Accrediting bodies, local, state, and federal governments are primary sources of coercive isomorphism for colleges and universities. Normative isomorphism is most closely associated with professionalization. When a profession adopts standards of behavior for its members, these standards tend to become codified, limiting members' freedom to explore alternative ways to deliver services. Finally, mimetic isomorphism addresses the tendency for new or less successful organizations to emulate their more successful counterparts as a way to increase their legitimacy. Mimetic isomorphism can save time for organizations that need to develop standard operating procedures quickly.

DePaul has been profoundly influenced throughout its existence by external forces. The direction the university took in its early days was determined by the expectations and requirements of external groups: the Catholic Church, the local Catholic bishop and regional accrediting bodies. DePaul's resemblance to other colleges and universities is in part the product of coercive, professional, and mimetic isomorphism. The Catholic Church and the North Central Association were the most influential sources of coercive isomorphism in DePaul's formative years.

When Chicago Archbishop Feehan asked the Vincentian Visitor, Thomas J. Smith, to open the day college in Chicago that became St. Vincent's, it was because the archbishop wanted another institution to help educate the growing number of Catholic immigrants in Chicago.

(52) The church hierarchy frustrated DePaul's efforts to model itself after lay universities, and between 1903 and 1905 Bishop Quigley, who succeeded Feehan, influenced the educational philosophy of the college by pointing it back toward a more religious orientation for the training of priests. (53) When Quigley permitted a Jesuit institution (which later became Loyola University) to be established north of DePaul, President Byrne of DePaul recognized the arrival of a threat to his university's survival but was unable to alter Bishop Quigley's decision. Quigley then suggested that DePaul become more effective in its ability to compete with Loyola by creating extension courses for Catholic laywomen to prepare them for principalships in Chicago's public schools. (54) Clearly, the decisions and recommendations of local Catholic leaders were extremely influential in DePaul's early history.

The Vincentian Visitor had the authority within the Vincentian community to assign priests to leadership positions at the university. These appointments ensured that Vincentian and Catholic principles would pervade the university. When Rev. James W. Stakelum made himself chair of the board of trustees in 1954 in an attempt to exert greater Catholic control over the university, his tenure was cut short as the movement to bring more lay involvement to the governance of the university prevailed. (55) But his efforts point out the strength of the relationship between DePaul and its Vincentian sponsors, who exercised direct control over DePaul for more than half of its existence. This measure of control by the Vincentians and the Church has diminished in the last half of the century for a number of reasons. First, reorganizing the board of trustees has transferred governance of the university to lay people. Though the board has chosen a Vincentian president of DePaul on both of the occasions it has had to exercise its new prerogative, it has been under no formal obligation to do so. (56) Second, the trend toward religious diversity among students, which goes as far back as 1910 when non-Catholics entered the university with the law school, has continued. Current figures indicate that only 43 percent of DePaul's student body identifies itself as Catholic. (57) Third, the university faculty has become increasingly diverse with respect to religion and ethnicity. Finally, as Richard Meister has noted, the number of Vincentian priests has declined precipitously since the early days of the university. During DePaul's 1997–98 academic year, there were only thirteen Vincentians out of a faculty and staff numbering more than two thousand.

The entity most responsible for pushing DePaul into a degree of conformity with other colleges and universities, however, has been the North Central Association of Schools and Colleges, the major accrediting body for high schools, colleges and universities in the midwest. Though approval by regional accrediting bodies is not mandatory, virtually all eligible educational institutions seek accreditation as a reliable and objective measure of the quality of their programs. Approval by accrediting bodies confers legitimacy on educational organizations.

The discussions between DePaul's presidents and the accrediting bodies during the 1950s demonstrate that they significantly influenced DePaul's academic program and administration. Philip Gleason (58) makes the case that Catholic colleges and universities struggled throughout the first half of the 20th century to adopt standards that accrediting bodies would approve.

DePaul's professional programs had been accepted by the NCA in 1932 and the entire university was granted unconditional NCA accreditation in 1933. On the occasion of this accomplishment, President Corcoran stressed the need for the university to work out " . . . its own destiny by doing everything possible to further its standing and its usefulness to the community." (59) The university's continuing problems with NCA were testimony to the challenge it faced in keeping accreditation while fulfilling its mission.

The North Central Association was a looming threat to the university that affected its internal functioning from almost the beginning. A year after official acceptance into NCA, for example, President Corcoran was regularly requesting the University Council to enact changes in general academic and administrative standards and to limit the award of what the accrediting team had criticized as an excessive number of honorary degrees (DePaul tended to give honorary degrees at each of its three graduation exercises). DePaul began creating its administrative positions with an eye to thwarting criticism from the accrediting bodies, and it created the position of "Inspector of Scholastic Records" in 1934 to assess courses from junior colleges " . . . to forestall unfavorable criticism by accrediting officers." Despite such efforts, the university almost lost its accreditation in the 1950–51 review period. DePaul responded to NCA reactions to its poor library facilities, inadequate space, and insufficient resources by increasing fundraising to direct greater resources into these areas. The 1952 campaign launched by the board of lay trustees specifically addressed these matters.

The second issue raised by the NCA team struck at the heart of DePaul's problems, attacking the quality and integrity of the university's academic program as delivered by its faculty. As noted earlier, the team expressed concern about the small number of faculty with advanced degrees. Since many of DePaul's faculty were part-timers or were teaching at the instructor level, the president pressured the deans of each of DePaul's schools and colleges to hire individuals who had degrees in hand and to encourage already employed faculty to complete their degrees, as Thomas Croak notes in chapter 7.

DePaul also made administrative changes internally and at the board level to eliminate practices that the report had labeled unsound when it questioned the propriety of having the president serve as chair of the board and the vice president and comptroller sit on the board of trustees and at the same time report to the president. (60)

The regional accrediting body and the Catholic Church, both powerful influences on DePaul's administration and curricular offerings, were not the only organizations that forced compliance to external criteria. In order to make itself attractive to students, faculty, and larger professional bodies, various colleges and departments actively sought membership in professional associations. These associations made conforming to their professional standards a condition of membership. These newly emerging professional association standards affected both DePaul's academic and administrative programs and typify the isomorphism that is a result of normative pressures.

University Council minutes in 1930, for instance, (61) stated that the law school had been placed on probation because it did not meet the standards of the Association of American Law Schools. Among other questionable activities, DePaul was allowing examination credits in lieu of classes and was accepting nonacademic credit toward degrees. After a year's worth of hard work, the law school's membership was unconditionally reinstated. The School of Music became a member of the National Association of Schools of Music in 1933, (62) and in 1934 DePaul agreed to follow the rules set forth by the Western Conference with respect to athletic competition.

The university leadership sought membership in the growing number of groups and associations that, as corollaries to the professional academic organizations, were advocates for colleges and universities. DePaul was a member of the Association of Catholic Colleges and Universities, the American Association of Colleges, and a variety of Illinois based consortia. Each of them had standards for admission and membership, and the university worked hard to transform itself to meet these requirements. For a number of years DePaul was denied membership in the American Association of University Women because it had too few women in leadership positions, prompting President O'Malley to express his dissatisfaction to the University Council at the university's inability to meet this organization's standards. (63)

The mimetic form of isomorphism has institutions looking to other organizations to see how they should appear and function. DePaul created its programs, set its tuition, and altered its curriculum most often with an eye toward what other colleges and universities were doing. For example, in 1933 DePaul adopted the process the University of Illinois had established for selecting honors graduates in the College of Liberal Arts and Science. (64) In 1934, the law school considered creating a law review publication in hopes of garnering the kind of prestige such publications gave to the University of Chicago, the University of Illinois, Northwestern, Harvard and other leading institutions. (65) In 1934, President O'Connell suggested that DePaul create a pool of faculty to comment on current social and political issues, and shortly thereafter DePaul faculty members joined colleagues from Northwestern and the University of Chicago on a local radio talk show to discuss social and religious issues of the day. (66)

The tradition of taking other universities as models dated back to the founding of the university. DePaul made adaptations to the university of Chicago's charter, using its terminology in the sections on incorporation and curricular direction. President Byrne turned to Harvard and its elective system as DePaul's guide into the world of universities. Local universities such as the University of Illinois directly influenced programs and academic policy at DePaul when their registrars occasionally refused to certify DePaul students' transfer credits. DePaul exercised a corresponding influence on other institutions. Newly formed junior colleges and schools that trained women religious designed their courses to ensure that DePaul would accept their students' course credits.

DePaul seldom looked to other Catholic colleges and universities for models, however. Though on occasion Loyola was mentioned as a resource, it was usually in the field of tuition pricing and never with respect to administration or curriculum. Instead, the young university sought private non-Catholic institutions and local public universities as role models, since these institutions were also DePaul's direct competitors for students. On a number of occasions, DePaul looked to elite eastern universities such as Harvard and Yale, especially when the university sought models for its academic programs. When plans emerged to create an honor society, for instance, it was pointed out that Northwestern had such a society, and then DePaul proceeded to adopt much of Northwestern's honor society protocol.

While not the dominant forces in shaping DePaul's administrative and governance structures, external forces helped the institution conform to the design and structures of other colleges and universities in the area, a requirement for attaining legitimacy and success. (67) DePaul's reputation improved after it successfully met the challenges of accrediting bodies and professional associations. In this respect external factors exerted a very significant influence on the development of the university.

Conclusion

Administration and governance at DePaul University has developed thanks to internal actors and external agents that combined over time to compel the university to adopt conventional administrative and governance procedures. The power of the presidency diminished in proportion as others—faculty, staff, and lay people—became involved in the internal management of the university.

The unitary structure that, according to Burton Clark, characterized colleges and universities in the 19th century was evident at DePaul well into the 1930s. But at about that time a trend materialized that encouraged shared decision making and implementation among a growing constituency in the university community. Though at first only senior administrators and deans participated, by the 1970s governance was being distributed over a wider range of groups in the institution. Participation by these discrete groups brought previously excluded actors into university life. The University Senate's aim of reintroducing a more unitary approach to decision making had, by the 1980s, installed an entrenched federated structure at all levels of the institution. Growth, which had been a survival strategy, further fragmented the members of the university into distinct subcultures.

Accreditation pressures from the North Central Association in the 1950s and the need for federal money to support the development of the physical plant in the 1960s brought more board-level lay control to the university. External groups and associations, which had developed their own standards for admission to their ranks, required DePaul to make further changes to obtain certification from such organizations. The pressures of isomorphism made DePaul look administratively and academically like most of the other mid-sized American universities that had triumphed in their own struggle for survival.

Chapter Three Notes

1. Clarence J. Fioke and Richard A. King, "Shifting Governance and Control in Church-Related Institutions of Higher Education," Annual Meeting, American Educational Research Association, 1982.

2. Burton Clark, "Faculty Organization and Authority" in *The Study of Academic Administration*, The Fifth Annual Institute on College Self Study, Western Interstate Comission for Higher Education, Colorado, 1963.

3. "First Meeting of Board of Trustees, February 25, 1908," Board of Trustees, Box 2, DePaul University Archives (DPUA).

4. Lester Goodchild, "The Mission of the Catholic University in the Midwest, 1842–1980: A Comparative Case Study of the Effects of Strategic Policy Decisions Upon the Mission of Notre Dame, Loyola University of Chicago, and DePaul University." (Ph.D. Diss. The University of Chicago, 1986.) 264.

5. Lester Goodchild, "The Mission of the Catholic University in the Midwest," 268.

6. George F. Zook letter to Levan, December 23, 1929. O'Malley, North Central Correspondence 1921–1936. O'Malley Accreditation files, Box 2. DPUA.

7. President Levan letter to George F. Zook, Office of the Secretary, North Central Association of Colleges and Secondary Schools, March 17, 1930 North Central Accreditation files Box 1, DPUA.

8. Levan letter to Zook, April 16, 1930, North Central Accreditation files Box 1, DPUA.

9. Levan letter to Zook, November 26, 1930, North Central Accreditation files Box 1, DPUA.

10. Levan letter to Zook, November 26, 1930, North Central Accreditation files Box 1, DPUA.

11. "Minutes of the First Meeting of the University Council of DePaul University, October 16, 1930," Minutes of University Council, DPUA.

12. "Minutes of the First Meeting of the School Year 1933–34, October 19, 1933," Minutes of the University Council, DPUA.

13. "Minutes of the Seventh Meeting of the University Council, April 11, 1962," Minutes of the University Council, DPUA.

14. "Minutes of the University Council, April 14, 1932," Minutes of the University Council, DPUA. Also see "Minutes of the University Council, October 1, 1940," Minutes of the University Council, DPUA.

15. "Minutes of the University Council, December 15, 1932," Minutes of the University Council, DPUA.

16. Norman Burns April 14, 1949 letter to O'Malley "Report by NCA 1948–49," NCA files, Box 7, DPUA.

17. "NCA Vote to Repeal Accreditation—March 1950. Part 1 of 2," NCA files, Box 7 DPUA.

18. "Report by NCA 1948–49," NCA Report on DePaul University by George A. Works, NCA files, Box 7.

19. Manning M Pattillo, Jr. Assistant Secretaty NCA letter to President O'Malley, April 18, 1951. "NCA Board of Review Ruling, March 1951," NCA files, Box 9, DPUA.

20. Farwell Proposal for New Board Structure 1944–47. Board of Trustees, 1908–1968, Box 2, DPUA.

21. "By-Laws Board of Lay Trustees 1946–1949," Board of Trustees, 1908–1968, Box 2, DPUA.

22. "Minutes of Board of Lay Trustees, December 18, 1946," Board of Trustees, 1908–1968, Box 2, DPUA.

23. "Minutes of Board of Lay Trustees 1946–1966," Board of Trustees, Box 2, DPUA.

24. "Minutes of the Board of Lay Trustees, May 15, 1953," Board of Trustees, Box 3, DPUA.

25. "Minutes of the Board of Lay Trustees, May 23, 1961," Board of Trustees, 1908–1968, Box 2, DPUA. Also see "Minutes of the Board of Lay Trustees, July 1963," Board of Trustees, 1908–1968, Box 2, DPUA.

26. "Minutes of the Administrative Council, February 18, 1964," Administrative Council files, DPUA.

27. "Minutes of the Board of Trustees, January 17, 1964," Board of Trustee Files, DPUA.

28. "Minutes of the Administrative Council, July 31, 1964," Administrative Council files, DPUA.

29. "Minutes of Administrative Council, December 22, 1965," Administrative Council files, DPUA. Also see "Minutes of the Administrative Council, May 28, 1964," Administrative Council Files, DPUA; and "Report of Committee Appointed by Legal Board of Trustee to Study and Recommend Change in the Corporate Charter and By-Laws of the University," Board of Trustees files, DPUA; and "Report and Recommendations of DePaul University Legal Committee Considering Charter Revisions," February 20, 1967, Board of Trustees files, DPUA.

30. "Minutes of the Administrative University Senate, May 27, 1965," University Senate files, DPUA.

31. "Minutes of the University Council, October 13, 1965," Minutes of the University Council, DPUA.

32. Father John T. Richardson memorandum to the University Council, "Commission to Committee for Developing a University Senate," April 19, 1966, University Senate files, Box 1, DPUA.

33. Dr. A. Bucinno memorandum to University Council, December 6, 1967, Faculty Advisory Council Correspondence & Memos, University Senate files, Box 1, DPUA.

34. "Minutes of the Committee on a University Senate," February 23, 1968, University Senate files, Box 2, DPUA.

35. "By-Laws of the University Senate," University Senate file Box 7, DPUA.

36. "Minutes of the University Senate, November 10, 1982," Univeristy Senate files, DPUA.

37. "Report of the Committee on Replacing or Restructuring the Univesity Senate," February, 1983, Faculty Council files, DPUA.

38. *Ibid.*, 16.

39. *Ibid.*, 17.

40. Father John T. Richardson memorandum to prospective faculty members, July 14, 1983, Faculty Council files, DPUA.

41. "A Governance Structure for Faculty, DePaul University," February 28, 1984 draft, Faculty Council files, DPUA.

42. Father John T. Richardson memorandum to Patricia Ewers and Howard Sulkin, May 5, 1983, Faculty Council files, DPUA.

43. Richardson memo to DePaul University Deans, May 17, 1984, Faculty Council files, DPUA.

44. "Minutes of the First Meeting of the Faculty Council, October 26, 1984," Faculty Council files, DPUA.

45. "Minutes of the Faculty Council, November 7, 1984," DPUA.

46. "Minutes of the Faculty Council, 1984–85 academic year," Faculty Council files, DPUA.

47. "Staff Council By-Laws," Staff Council Web Site, http://condor.depaul.edu/~stafcncl/scc.html.

48. Kelly Moore, President, Staff Council, personal communication, October 1997; also see "Memorandum from University Librarians to Committee on Replacing or Restructing the University Senate," May 17, 1983, Faculty Council files, DPUA.

49. "Minutes of Joint Council Meeting, August 18, 1993," Personal papers, Anna L. Waring, Public Services Graduate Program, DePaul University.

50. Memorandum for Professor Susan F. Bennett to J. Patrick Murphy and Anna L. Waring, February 24, 1994, Personal papers, Anna L. Waring, Public Services Graduate Program, DePaul University.

51. Paul DiMaggio and Walter W. Powell, "The Iron Cage Revisted: Institutional Isomorphism and Collective Rationality in Organizational Fields," *American Sociological Review* 82: 147–60.

52. Goodchild, "The Mission of the Catholic University in the Midwest," 208.

53. *Ibid.*, 210.

54. *Ibid.,* 245.

55. Father John R. Cortelyou, "Why a University Needs Trustees," Minutes of the Lay Board of Trustees, October 20, 1965, Board of Trustees files, DPUA.

56. "Minutes of the Board of Trustees, April 19, 1967," Board of Trustees files, DPUA.

57. "A Snapshot of DePaul University 1997–1998," University Relations Brochure, DePaul University.

58. Philip Gleason, *Contending with Modernity: Catholic Higher Education in the Twentieth Century.* (New York, 1995).

59. "Minutes of the University Council, May 4, 1933," Minutes of the University Council, DPUA.

60. "Minutes of the University Council, May 3, 1934," Minutes of the University Council, DPUA.

61. "Minutes of the University Council, October 6, 1930," Minutes of the University Council, DPUA.

62. "Minutes of the University Council, Janaury 12, 1933," Minutes of the University Council, DPUA.

63. "Minutes of the University Council, May 3, 1934," Minutes of the University Council, DPUA.

64. *Ibid.*

65. "Special Meeting of the University Council," December 4, 1934, Minutes of the University Council, DPUA.

66. Minutes of the Second Meeting of the School Year 1933–34," Minutes of the University Council, DPUA.

67. DiMaggio and Powell, "The Iron Cage Revisted," *passim.*

DeP

PART II

CAMPUS

CULTURE

AND

STUDENT

LIFE

CHAPTER FOUR

"The Little University Under the El"

The Physical Institution of Memory

Charles S. Suchar

Over thirty-four years ago (in 1964), as an eighteen year old youth from Chicago's East Rogers Park community, I got off the "El" at Fullerton Avenue, walked down the steps, through an alley, and headed for my very first experience as a student of DePaul University. Having come an hour before my first counseling appointment and in nervous anticipation of the beginning of a new life experience, I had the time to walk around and explore the area.

My first reaction to DePaul was one of disappointment. This was it? Only two buildings were actively being used for classes, plus Alumni Hall, the gymnasium. It was pretty small, quaint, not much of a place. I knew that there was also a downtown office building. I only learned later that the Lincoln Park campus, or "uptown" campus as we called it, also included two buildings on Sheffield Avenue, the Lyceum (library, administrative offices, art dept. at the time, razed in 1987) and the "barn," the College Theater (razed in 1979). That was everything. I remember asking about the cafeteria, to grab a drink before my appointment, and was directed to the basement of Alumni Hall. I discovered that this was the social hub of the campus (the largest gathering place for students anywhere). My high school cafeteria had been three times the size of DePaul's.

The College of Liberal Arts and Sciences had all of its administrative offices on the first floor of the four-story Liberal Arts Building (Levan Center, today); two very tightly packed sets of offices on either side of a small corridor. I later discovered that the faculty and department offices were to be found in several two- and three-story brick houses (taken over by DePaul) located on the west side of Kenmore Avenue, stretching north toward Fullerton Avenue from the Liberal Arts Building (with two departments per apartment/floor in some cases). I was rather shy and didn't visit these buildings and offices very often. All my classes were located in two buildings, no more than twenty yards apart, and I ate my lunches (brought from home) in the basement cafeteria of Alumni Hall. I spent about 85 percent of my time at DePaul in these three buildings, and the remainder at one of some half dozen tables that comprised the entire reading area in the aging Lyceum, the uptown campus library.

The early disappointment in the size and quality of the physical campus soon changed to an appreciation of how easy it was to know where people and things were and when to find or encounter them. The limited space of the campus helped establish, for me at least, a routine that reflected a very predictable sense of where fellow students could be found in between classes, who would be found at which tables in the cafeteria at lunch (both students and faculty) and who would be sitting at a particular library study/reading table. I came to know when the "barn" would be open for recreational basketball pick-up games and who would more than likely be found hanging out there. Since we were on the semester system, the regularity of these predictions was further enhanced.

The effect of the "feel and look of the place" on me, the sensed environmental atmosphere, was significant. I had come from a religiously conservative Jewish family and from what even my friends referred to as Chicago's Jewish ghetto at the time—Rogers Park. The decision to come to DePaul was not without some element of adolescent rebelliousness and yearning for independence. My parents, quite frankly, would have preferred to have me enroll at the University of Illinois at Navy Pier downtown. The thought of attending a private, Catholic university held an element of the "foreign" for them, as well as for myself—but for me, especially, that was its particular charm and exoticism. Going away to school was financially out of the question. Attending DePaul was, in that case, a way of being "away" but staying very much at home.

Initially, the everyday atmosphere of DePaul, as I experienced it, made me feel as though I had, indeed, entered another world. This was, in part, abetted by the look and atmosphere of the classrooms and hallways. The presence of religious icons and crucifixes, in almost every classroom and nearly every hallway, was, of course, a taken-for-granted reality for my Catholic classmates. The images of St. Vincent dePaul and the Virgin Mary in the Liberal Arts Building and in the Hall of Science (O'Connell Building) lecture hall, were an everyday reminder of DePaul's Catholic identity, but a somewhat exotic one for me. I came to cherish this place very much, with its deliciously strange atmosphere, the warmth of its people, its coziness and quaintness, its distinct character. The environment has had a lasting effect and influence on me. I, like tens of thousands of others, became and remain attached to this place.

DePaul: A Sense of Place

This essay will explore the "sense of place" of a group of DePaul Alumni whose collective memory spans approximately 50 years of the school's 100-year-old history. It is based on oral history interviews with these individuals and is supplemented with archival documentary information. (1) The interviews focused on the alumni's recollections of their experiences in the classrooms, lunchrooms, laboratories, common areas and other facilities of the university, but more uniquely, the spaces, and multipurpose places, that, together, went into making their physical and sociocultural and psychological environment: the physical institution of memory and identification. (2) But what is a "sense of place" and why should we examine it as a piece of DePaul University's history?

One of the most significant characteristics of DePaul in its one hundred year history, is the fact of its physical growth, particularly over the last thirty years. It has become a cliché to contrast the "little university under the El," a commonplace characterization of DePaul for its first 70 years, with the expanded, contemporary campuses at Lincoln Park, downtown Chicago, and in the suburbs. But to a student, being at DePaul—regardless of when it was, or the particular campus she or he attended—had a particular significance, we might assume. Their "sense of place" is the relevance of the physical space to the activities and relationships that they remember being situated and experienced there. That sense is, of course, retrospective; it has been filtered through years of additional experience. It may have been influenced by recollections of very particular architectural features, physical limitations, environmental conditions as they are perceived to have influenced one's everyday engagement in activities, special events, or institutional rituals. It includes social relations that a place signifies, but emphasizes the impact that space and place have on these social relations and on the lived experience of institutional membership, passage, socialization, and self-transformation.

Various social scientists refer to this impact of place and "sense of place" as "place attachment." (3) This term refers to people's affective bonding and identification with environmen-

Students in front of the Liberal Arts & Sciences building in the 1940s, from Lorraine Bond, private collection.

tal settings. In this essay, it will refer to the attachment and meaning DePaul University's physical environment has inspired in its alumni. This sense of place and place attachment has a dual nature, in the words of one scholar, *"involving both an interpretive perspective on the environment and an emotional reaction to the environment."* (4) This essay will draw specifically on such perspectives, and on emotional reactions to the physical and social environment of DePaul. It will explore DePaul's built environment as alumni, through a span of fifty years, recollect it. It is the story of student memory of the place and experience that to them was the DePaul they knew. It is, in particular, the story of that period in DePaul's history when it was known as "the little university under the El." The essay will attempt to characterize the "sense of place" engendered by this DePaul of limited size and means, a DePaul now thirty years older, significantly grown in stature, and still cherished in the memories of students who directly experienced it.

The essay is organized by my partition of the physical history of DePaul into three periods. The first, 1898–1928, extends from DePaul's founding to the time when it moved into the first permanent structure in downtown Chicago that it did not lease but owned, the 64 E. Lake Street building. The second period, 1929 to roughly 1955–1958, was a period of slow-paced physical change that culminated in the building of Alumni Hall and a move from 64 E. Lake Street to the Kimball Building (Lewis Center) at 25 E. Jackson Boulevard. Finally, the third period, 1958–1967, marked both the interval immediately preceding DePaul's greatest physical expansion and transformation (the building of a residential campus, Schmitt Academic Center, Stuart Center, the purchase of McCormick Theological Seminary property and related developments) and the end of the era when DePaul was still considered "the little university under the El."

These periods in the history of DePaul's physical growth also reflect corresponding changes in the makeup of its student population, in academic and curricular programs—both at DePaul and in higher education nationally—and in its changing faculty, to say nothing of a changing city, nation, and world. More specifically, however, the physical environment of Chicago, the transformations in its neighborhoods, population, industry and economy, all have a bearing on the physical environment of DePaul's campuses and landscape. The very fact that DePaul was located in Lincoln Park, a changing Chicago neighborhood, in one of the most important commercial, financial, and cultural centers in the country, whose downtown "Loop" was also re-creating itself, makes its history of physical change a part of changing urban America. In fact, this essay will demonstrate the exceedingly close affinity that DePaul has always had with Chicago, and its immediate physical, social, cultural, and economic environment.

The interviews with alumni, whatever the historical period they were students, revealed an unequivocal and explicit functional co-dependency between the university, the city and its people. They also demonstrated the ties between the university and the lives and actions of those who were associated with it as faculty, staff, or students. One of the most significant outcomes or conclusions I reached in analyzing the oral history transcripts is that DePaul's history is irrevocably and inseparably tied to its location within an urban setting. It has had an ecological and functionally interdependent relationship to the social, cultural, economic, political, and religious institutional infrastructure of Chicago. DePaul's students, as well as the university itself, adapted to their respective environments in mutually need-fulfilling ways. Limitations imposed upon students and the university due to a lack of monetary resources, were responded to with solutions that were possible only because of the opportunities available in a large, complex, and vital urban environment, and the resourcefulness of students and the university alike. The city of Chicago became for DePaul students and faculty an "extended campus," rich with possibilities, that probably would not have been available elsewhere. The children of working-class and middle-class immigrant Chicago, usually the first generation to have had the opportunity for a college education, found the urban setting of DePaul, its proximity to neighborhood, work, and home, an enormous resource, indeed, an outright advantage. It became an environment used by many as a social psychological source of support throughout the new experience of higher education, through hard times and good times, through the making of short-term and lifelong friendships, and the making of oneself. It was an entry point to learning and a career.

Where I rely heavily on alumni interviews for information, I have organized material by campus, discussing uptown and downtown campuses individually; the sections on each campus include descriptions of the specific buildings and places. Finally, I have allowed the alumni themselves to describe how the extended campus marked their experiences as students.

1898–1928: *Making the Most with Limited Means*

The original St. Vincent's College Hall was located at the corner of Webster and Osgood Street (the present Kenmore Avenue). The address of the building was 244 E. Webster Avenue. (5) The structure, originally built as the church, was dedicated on April 30, 1876. Prior to 1885 it had housed the first parochial school for the parish, and in the 1880s its basement served as a multi-purpose hall. The building was designed originally as a multi service building with classrooms on the first floor and the church proper on the second floor. (6) The back of the structure had a chapel and living rooms for priests. The Vincentian fathers had, from the beginning, an eye toward getting the most out of their modest structures. They made changes to the building when it became Saint Vincent's College Hall in 1898: they remodeled it and added a story.

With the dedication of the new St. Vincent's Church on May 19, 1895, the original building was made available for the new Catholic college. The remodeled building had a third floor that served largely as an auditorium, having a small stage and about five hundred seats. McHugh (1935) indicated that the classrooms were on the floor below, which had served as the church for twenty years. The first floor was partly offices and classrooms.

The institution opened with an enrollment of 72 students (the first graduating class in 1899 included two degree recipients). McHugh described the early campus's prime attraction as the athletic field:

> *During the noon recreation and after classes, it was customary for the young professors to mingle with the students. Baseball was a favorite sport. Mr. Murray, C.M., and Mr. LeSage, C.M. especially excelled [LeSage would later be named to one of the first two major appointed positions in the university, the manager of the Athletic Association]. There was a fence in the early days directly behind the college building. The corner of the lot toward Belden and Sheffield Avenues was rented out to a gardener. In fact, it seemed that we could not go very far without running into rows of garden truck and flowers. (7)*

It should be pointed out that the location of a truck farm on campus fit in well with the tradition of Vincentian presence in the area. The five-acre plot that formed the original campus of DePaul had been known in the 1870s as "Father Smith's Farm," named after the Vincentian priest who founded the parish. The entire five-acre plot had been purchased for $38,000. Again, the practical needs of an institution with limited resources are apparent in McHugh's illustration. Minutes of early faculty meetings reveal an all too frequently mentioned concern with "The low state of revenue." This was a phrase used to explain the reason why many things could not be accomplished in the first few years of the institution's history and why adaptations, new solutions, and make-do's were needed.

Nevertheless, the original college building was torn down in 1906 and was replaced by what was described by the Very Rev. Peter V. Byrne, C.M., the first president, as a "bigger and better" one, still used and known today as Byrne Hall. One institutional historian mentions that the new imposing structure, then called the College Building, was "built of Bedford stone and quarter-sawed oak" and added "elegance and durability" to the campus (the one building, as it was). (8) In fact, the oak beams delayed construction for a period (city permits denied), since these were in violation of city ordinances after the Chicago fire. Steel beams replaced the wooden beams at an additional cost of $20,000, not an inconsiderable sum at the time. (9)

In the following year, 1907, the Lyceum (library/administrative offices) and the College Theater (referred to by generations of later students as the "barn") were completed. In that same year, in a move that reflected, at least in part, the school's positive frenzy of construction (three brand new buildings in a period of two years), its name was changed from Saint Vincent's

College to DePaul University. The ambition and vision of the Vincentian community leaders, most notably Father Byrne himself, was apparent in both stone and symbol. This was an expansive and expensive vision; as other authors in this volume have noted, the university struggled with the debt incurred by this development and growth for many years to come.

The College Theater (2219 N. Sheffield Avenue) was a major addition to the university and to the immediate north side neighborhood in which it was located. Designed as the auditorium by the architect J.E.O. Pridmore, the building was appointed originally as a theater with "924 fancy opera chairs" (and eventually, a capacity for 1,500), "first quality silk velour draperies and silk plush curtains," and chandeliers (ordered from Mandel Bros. Home Furnishings). (10) The dome and proscenium arch of the auditorium contained murals that the Chicago *Inter Ocean* is said to have described as "the largest canvases ever attempted in Chicago."

DePaul students at play on Kenmore Avenue in the late 1940s. Lorraine Bond, private collection.

At the opening of the theatre, Chicago composer Frederic Grant Gleason's opera "Otho Visconti," was performed; the *Chicago Tribune* critic, Forrest Dabney Carr, was much more impressed with the theater than the performance. The headline of his story read "Priests' Theater a Beauty." The newspaper accounts of the theater praised its aesthetics and safety: There were said to be 24 exits and the aisles widened toward the rear of the structure to permit " . . . easy egress for large crowds." (10)

As Dennis McCann notes, the College Theater's life as cultural center for performances was plagued by difficulties, but it too was designed for multi-functional use. In the opulent setting of artistic murals, silk, glass, and bronze, soon there were to be basketball games, boxing matches, military drill formations, religious retreats, commencement exercises, oratorical contests, dances, and a host of other activities. Getting the most from the structure was to become a DePaul tradition.

The Lyceum, built in the same year, was adjacent to the College Theater, and was originally intended to be a social center as well as a library. A *Chicago Daily Journal* story for June 6, 1907, titled "A Common Sense Church," by Finn Egan, described the Lyceum as equipped "for all the social pleasures residents of the neighborhood may indulge." (11) As a description for the building, along with similar descriptions for the College Theater, the phrase itself gives the distinct impression that the community, not just the young university, saw these structures as "neighborhood institutions." A description of the Lyceum in 1907 inventories its multiple uses: the basement had "baths" and a locker room, the first floor had a parlor, lounging room and assembly room (soon to become the expanded library), the upper floor had rooms for meetings and "dancing parties." (12) It is said that the building had space for serving meals. A document written by Rev. D. McHugh indicates that "The College Grill," located within the structure, did not last:

[It] was given up before long, as a losing proposition. The large room was used for various parish and school purposes, for instance, an afternoon luncheon for the girls of St. Vincent's High School before it became known as DePaul High School for Girls.

McHugh's papers indicate that the original purpose of the "College Grill" was intended to be more than a cafeteria for students:

The idea was to take care of the patrons of the Theater and others who might come here instead of going to a hotel or restaurant. Linens, table silver, and glassware were the best, furnished by the same Mandel Brothers. The Chef served an excellent dinner to the first Board of Trustees of DePaul University in [this] northwest room on the second floor in 1908. President John V. Clarke of the Hibernian Bank was there, with other lay trustees. (13)

Finn Egan's story included the line *"the men can smoke upstairs and the women can sew on the first floor."* It was, after all, 1907, and since women would not be admitted to the university until 1911, it suggests that the facility was used by community residents, men and women alike, as a social center in the first years of its existence.

Documents indicate that the Lyceum was used, variably, as space for classes for the high school in 1910, for the parochial school around that time, by the Music School from 1912 till September 1930, and by the students in Army Training Corps (later called the ROTC) in 1918. (14) In summer 1930, plans were made to locate the library on the second floor. This took place during the presidency of Father Corcoran, who also converted a room in the building into his executive office. The treasurer's office was located nearby. The building thus served as both library and administrative offices until just after the Second World War.

In 1923–24, the university erected the Liberal Arts Building. This was to be the primary home of the liberal arts college for some forty-three years. It contained five floors of usable space (four floors plus basement), with the first or main floor used as administrative offices for the college. This left room for approximately twelve to sixteen classrooms. Some rooms in the basement and on the top floors served miscellaneous functions during this period and on into the 1950s and 60s (such as meeting rooms for student organizations and for certain social events).

Until the Hall of Science building was erected in 1938, all of the humanities and social science courses were taught in the Liberal Arts Building. Science students, until 1938, used the science facilities of the high school in Academy Hall, now called Byrne Hall. The high school and college, in fact, shared several facilities, including the athletic field behind the academy, the College Theater, and some rooms in the Lyceum. The close relationship between the high school and university is evident in the early DePaul yearbooks, which featured both institutions. They also shared faculty, many of whom were Vincentians, who moved between the secondary and higher educational missions of the community.

A Presence in Downtown Chicago

DePaul became a presence in the heart of downtown Chicago, the "Loop," when the Illinois College of Law, a private proprietary school, became affiliated with the university. Within a year, in 1912, DePaul also established a College of Commerce downtown. The schools were originally located in a series of rented buildings in the heart of the Loop: first, in the Power Building at 37 S. Wabash, and then, under terms of a five-year lease (1915–1920), space was rented in the Tower Building at 6 N. Michigan Avenue.

In the meantime, DePaul had inaugurated a new late afternoon program for teachers on the north side campus (bringing a number of women into the institution, beginning in 1911). But with a physical presence downtown, it was decided to move that program to the Tower Building, as well. The university quickly found, however, that it needed additional room downtown to accommodate its growing programs. Space was leased at 84 E. Randolph Street in the Taylor Building (1920–1928) which also housed part of the John Crerar Library. Proximity to library facilities was a significant benefit to law and commerce students and scholars alike. The building also housed the British Consulate and a medical supply company.

Under its new president, The Very Rev. Thomas F. Levan, DePaul added several new programs at 84 E. Randolph: a downtown liberal arts program which served teachers primarily, a Secretarial School, and a Loop High School. These additions provided significant resources to the university, while responding to important societal and community needs for education and training.

The downtown programs enrolled a variety of students, with varied backgrounds. But the vast majority of these students—in law, education, commerce, and the Secretarial School—had a common focus on professional/career education and training, and a great many of them worked part or full time in the central business district. For most of these students, the everyday routine of school, work, and the commute back and forth to their neighborhoods, usually by public transportation, were the mainstay of their DePaul years.

The commute home highlighted one highly significant feature of DePaul's early campuses: they were eminently accessible by streetcar, bus or train. In fact, the university's location next to the major elevated train line connecting north and south Chicago (and running through the heart of its central business district), and its proximity to the terminus of major streetcar lines, helped to account for its early success in attracting students. The uptown campus was within blocks of at least three major streetcar terminals, as well as other surface lines, that brought students from the south, north and west sides of the city. The earliest advertisements for DePaul in local papers always mentioned that its "location [was] unsurpassed [with] central and easy access." The Bulletin of Saint Vincent's College of 1906–1907 included the following:

> ### ACCESS
> *The College may be reached by the Northwestern Elevated railroad, the Webster Station [before Fullerton was the stop] of which is but one-half block from the college grounds; by the Larrabee Street, Sedgwick Street, Lincoln Avenue, Clark Street, North Avenue, and Fullerton Avenue surface lines; and, through means of transfer, by all the surface lines of the Union Traction Company. (15)*

The advantage of a central location, at the junction of north to south and west to east public transportation, also served to integrate the everyday needs for access to school, work, and social activities for students and faculty alike. This made it possible for an "extended campus" to exist, one that will be discussed later.

According to Father Michael O'Connell, an early Vincentian chronicler of DePaul, the real estate market in downtown Chicago was booming in the period between 1924–1929, just before the Depression, resulting in inflated building values and spiraling rents. (16) Advisors to the Vincentian community urged a long-range investment plan in which available parcels of land at 64, 66, and 68 East Lake Street might be built on to satisfy the university's growing need for downtown space. The Vincentians organized the DePaul Educational Society, with a prominent group of Chicago financial/real estate advisors, and this nonprofit society purchased the land. The seventeen-story building erected at 64 E. Lake Street would eventually cost over a million and a half dollars to construct, and since it was financed through bonds, the university incurred additional debt.

The plan was to have DePaul use a portion of the seventeen floors (the second through seventh floors as a theater hall, administrative offices, space for music, drama, the Secretarial School, and liberal arts; and on the 13th, 14th, 15th, and 16th floors for commerce and law, with a social activity space/lounge on the 17th floor), leasing out the rest of the space as offices to businesses to help defray the initial investment and future maintenance of the building. The first floor was leased to Pixley and Ehlers restaurant, and floors eight through eleven were held for leasing.

By 1928 DePaul was thus firmly established as a two-campus institution. In fact, counting the numbers of students served at each of these two sites, the recently acquired downtown location had the largest student population. The uptown campus served only about 600 university students, along with the academy, while the new 64 E. Lake Street building counted several thousand.

The 64 E. Lake Building, due both to its location and the workaday schedules of its students, was in use for significant portions of each day during the work week. Morning and early afternoon hours were used for commerce and law classes, typically for full time students. Late afternoon and evening division courses were scheduled for part time students in a variety of programs, including teachers interested in liberal arts and education classes. This was not the case at the uptown campus, where generations of DePaul students—with the possible exception of science majors taking laboratory courses—rarely had classes beyond the early afternoon hours. This, too, changed when facilities expanded, beginning in the late 1960s.

In the first quarter century of DePaul's history, the pattern of growth and program expansion shifted from the uptown campus at the beginning of the period to the downtown campus at the time of DePaul's Silver Jubilee. The downtown building had more than three times the usable classroom and office space than uptown facilities in 1928. The meaning of physical space in DePaul's early years grew from a very basic organizational or institutional trait: new organizations often have to be resourcefully multi-functional in the way they form and situate themselves, particularly those with limited resources. The physical structures of "the little university under the El" demonstrated complex patterns of multiple use. Out of necessity— due to limitations of size and other resources, but also to the educational and community

*The 64 E. Lake Building opened in
1928 in the north Loop. Chicago's
central business district.*

missions, values and commitments of the Vincentian fathers—decisions were made to do as much as possible within the physical space that comprised DePaul in its first quarter century.

1928–1955: DePaul of Memory—Streetcars, Sidewalks, and Stairwells

When DePaul alumni were asked to remember their everyday experiences and daily routines as students, they commonly began with a description of traveling to campus. For students in the 1920s through the 1950s, commuting from home typically meant travel from urban neighborhoods and parishes on public transportation. (17)

Nick Deleonardis (COM 1951) described DePaul, in fact, as the "streetcar university," recalling fondly the everyday routine of taking the "Chicago Surface Line" or trolley to school. (18) For many, such recollections were filled with memories of friends with whom they made such trips to school. Carole Nolan (LAS 1954) remembered taking the "Old Red Rocket" streetcar in her St. Basil's Parish neighborhood on the south side of Chicago to 63rd and Ashland, transferring to 63rd and Loomis where she would take the "El" train to school. (19) At the "El" she would often meet her DePaul classmates Mary Belose and Bob (Robert) Klonowski (who later married) both of whom took science classes with her. For many alumni, the urban identity of DePaul was epitomized in part, by this travel between home and campus neighborhood, whether uptown or the Loop. This shared commuter routine served a

Entrance to the 64 E. Lake building. DePaul occupied the north Loop site for over a quarter century.

social bonding and equalizing function. They saw each other as generally from similar circumstances and backgrounds, although they were obviously from an array of specific ethnic, religious, and social class enclaves in the city and surrounding communities. It was because of such experiences that many, like Bud Kevin (LAS 1938/LAW 1941), would characterize DePaul as a "city school for city people." (20) Nick Deleonardis called DePaul a "working class, middle-class sort of place, not uppity." This is echoed in Bernard Carney's (COM 1942) comments that *"I've always regarded it [DePaul] as a working person's university. That's probably one reason for my affection [for] the school, is that it has never tended to be elitist."* (21) This "urban," "working class/middle class" and "non-elitist" characterization of DePaul was part of a larger, common framework that formed the basis of alumni memories of DePaul's physical quality and character.

The most common attitude expressed by the alumni I interviewed was that they had no illusions about the physical limitations of DePaul: for most, just being in college was considered a privilege. They were quite accepting of what many, like Carole Nolan (LAS 1954), called a "no frills" kind of institution. The most typical comments are reflected in Ed Schillinger's (LAS 1944) statements:

We were not critical. It was fine. There was a room with windows and heat in the building, nice chairs. We had no complaints . . . by today's standards it was probably kind of seedy . . . [but] nobody complained, now, mind you. . . . And I think a number of us used reverse snobbery. We'd turn up our nose at all the riches down in Champaign [state university], for example . . . This was, and still is, a fine institution. The fact that it was . . . first generation to go to college, for the most part, [to] this Spartan, little university under the EL. All those are true, but that kind of obscures the fact that we had a good faculty here dedicated to the students. And they didn't mess around. (22)

When alumni were asked to characterize in a general way the campus on which they attended classes, they used many interesting terms. Several described the "campus" as consisting of the sidewalk and walkways and thus spoke of a "sidewalk" or "concrete" campus. This was especially true in warmer weather when the non air-conditioned buildings on both campuses made the sidewalks a welcome escape from the heat. In reference to the uptown campus, the walk in front of the Liberal Arts Building and the one paralleling the wall of the athletic field on Kenmore Avenue were described as the only "campus" outside of the buildings.

Rita Barr (COM 1939), referring to the 64 E. Lake Street building, described it as a "columnar campus," a downtown office building seen as a vertical campus. (23) In such a structure, the campus was confined to the hallways and passageways inside the building. Gerry Radice (COM 1949), a student at the Lake Street building ten years later, described the campus in the following manner:

> *Our campus was the stairwells . . . the building was rectangular. It was harsh. It was very basic . . . I mean basic [chuckles]. It wasn't much else, except chairs and rows . . . walls, too little space for too many people . . . very crowded.* (24)

Radice and others described corners in the hallways and particular landings on certain stairwells as places where students would congregate on a regular basis (the elevators were notoriously slow at 64 E., and the stairs were frequent substitutes).

These general characterizations of DePaul's campuses set the stage for the particular places and spaces that alumni remembered most vividly. To capture these more specific recollections, we examine each campus's structures as remembered by a cross-section of alumni.

The Uptown Campus

In the early part of the period between 1928 and the mid-1950s, the uptown alums remembered a campus largely consisting of the Liberal Arts building, the College Auditorium, Lyceum, and the athletic field behind St. Vincent's Church. For students taking science classes before 1938, the academy's science facilities were recalled fondly, as was the Hall of Science after that year. One additional structure stood out significantly in alumni memories toward the end of the 1928–55 period: Wangler Hall, a temporary, multipurpose structure erected towards the end of the second World War and located just behind the Liberal Arts building. This building served as a combination cafeteria and social/recreation center until the period just after the building of Alumni Hall, when it was demolished.

It is not surprising that in the earliest part of this 1928–1955 period, a good many memories of DePaul's uptown campus focused on the Liberal Arts Building. Most of a typical student's time was spent in its classrooms, hallways and stairwells. This was especially true before Wangler Hall appeared.

In a telling commentary, alumni stated that the Liberal Arts Building and its classrooms reminded them of their high schools; when asked to characterize the classrooms, they made comparisons to their secondary school experiences. This meant that the rooms were standard

View of 64 E. Lake building.

classrooms with chairs, a blackboard, lectern and a table/desk at the front. In other words, rather quite ordinary. More specifically, however, they compared these rooms and the furniture to their Catholic high schools. Tom Joyce recalled his first year on campus in 1928 (the building was four years old at the time), describing the Liberal Arts Building in these terms:

> *It might not be huge as far as [the] standards of today, but I thought it was an excellent building, good rooms and well kept, and well built. I was in the construction business later in life, and I would consider it sturdy built . . . The classrooms were not large . . . I would say there were thirty or forty students per class. (25)*

After a few more decades of student use, Carole Nolan (LAS 1954) described the same building this way:

> *W*ell, I'll tell you, DePaul looked really, if you'll excuse the expression, seedy to me after Longwood [the Catholic high school she attended]. Because, you know, when you go to a high school with nuns, everything is completely [neat] and the floors were so waxed. And nobody ever walked on those floors with their boots or their dirty shoes or anything. And when I got to DePaul, everything was kind of old and, you know, the desks were carved up. I remember this one priest. He used to be smoking during class and he'd put his cigarette out in the top drawer. [Chuckles] And coming from an all girls school where everything was perfect and you had to wear your white gloves, it was different. So it was a little culture shock . . . I was kind of appalled coming from my high school at the way that it looked. (26)

Tony Behof, who attended the DePaul Academy high school and then began his DePaul studies in 1955, remembers the Liberal Arts Building thus:

> *A*ll the classrooms, of course, had a crucifix in them and . . . it was common for all Vincentians to start the class with prayer. Some of the lay teachers did, but not many. [In referring to the rest of the building:] Well, I think it was not terribly comfortable. It was, well, . . . not air-conditioned. There were some times when it was just uncomfortable in the middle of the day . . . The classes were a little crowded . . . they were filled . . . [and] many of the classes were [not] seminar classes; back then they were all conventional talking heads. There were risers [elevated platform from which faculty would teach or write on the blackboard], of course, in the classrooms and the instructors would come in and, of course, trip over the first step. It never failed . . . [There were] no elevators. And so there was always the problem of being on the fourth floor . . . In some ways, I think the classrooms were very much like the ones I had in high school. [Suchar: Were there places in the building that people congregated or hung out?] I can only think of hallways. (27)

Other alumni, when asked to remember salient features of the Liberal Arts building, recalled the stained glass window with religious motif on the first floor, the narrow lockers that were shared with other students, the meetings in the hallways and on the stairway landings in between floors, and the difficult climb to the top of the building. In other respects, however, the building elicited relatively few comments. It is perhaps not unfair to say that it was, in comparison to other structures, a notable "unnotable;" a more or less taken-for-granted feature of the campus. The same could not be said for some of the other buildings on the uptown campus between the 1920s and the 1950s.

The nostalgic sentiment expressed for the College Theater, or "barn," as it was known to many generations of DePaul students, and Wangler Hall, stand out in the recollections of alumni. The memories were not always pleasant ones, but they have stayed with former students for many decades. As noted earlier, the barn was a multipurpose, multifunctional structure, that served the Vincentian community in various ways, as well as the local neighborhood and community at large. It was also, next to St. Vincent's Church, perhaps the most significant architectural site and aesthetically striking structure on campus. Tom Joyce recalled that in 1928 he enjoyed going there.

[T]here were some very nice dances, and very beautiful girls . . . I was surprised they took the building down . . . I thought it . . . could very well be a historical building. The building . . . kept the values of the neighborhood high, and I thought it was very helpful for students. But I suppose the cost of keeping it up may have cost [too much] . . . just like they gave up the football team.

Tom Joyce further remembered the barn as the site for his beloved boxing matches. Born in County Mayo, Ireland, he had come to Chicago and the DePaul neighborhood as a young lad and soon became interested in boxing. After a serious amateur career that had him traveling around the country and in Europe, he came back to the DePaul neighborhood and caught the attention of the president, Father Michael J. O'Connell. O'Connell gave Tom a scholarship to the university in exchange for helping out with the boxing team and assisting football coach Jim Kelly, another Irishman. While he was with the team, the barn became the site of many boxing matches, and drew huge crowds when the likes of Harvard and Northwestern were the opponents. Tom recalled that the boxing team practiced behind the stage in the barn and that the structure was used by a wide variety of students for many purposes, but especially basketball games, drama presentations, as well as the ubiquitous student dances. (28)

Fran (Armsrong) Kevin (LAS) declared that in 1936 the barn was, effectively, the social center of the uptown campus. She vividly remembered the Friday afternoon and evening dances that were held there:

> *Campus dances, . . . we used to have them at the gym [another term used for the barn]. We had a Spanish club, and I was a freshman then. And we just all of a sudden decided to hold a dance, and the gym was never booked that far in advance, and we didn't spend a lot of money decorating it . . . And we, I think it was a week or two later, we had a dance . . . Usually the dances were on Friday evening, for . . . informal dances . . . we had a lot of them.*

Fran also recalled the student-produced dramas and musicals that were performed in the barn. These were among the more popular student events on campus. She described, with considerable enthusiasm, the way in which she and fellow students put together an original play/musical/comedy "All At Sea" in 1937. In Fran's words, *"It was interesting, it was fun, and they made money for the school."* (29)

Bernard Carney (COM 1942) also recalled that in 1938 the "auditorium" (another name for the barn or College Theater) was used for dances by both the high school academy students and the university, but had greater significance for him, as it had been for Tom Joyce, as the site for basketball games and other athletic activities. Carney's memories of the structure in the 1930s are not, however, all that positive. As the manager of the football team (DePaul's last one in 1938), he reported that the athletes did not appreciate the terrible locker room facilities in the building next to the barn (basement of Lyceum) and the fact that they had to walk outside to gain access to the building. Also, the main auditorium was evidently not always very well heated and this caused the athletes additional consternation. (30)

Edwin Schillinger's memories of the barn went back to 1937, when he began his DePaul Academy career, and extended to 1944 and his graduation from liberal arts and sciences.

> *It was . . . a nice old building. The barn . . . was used for basketball games. The University played small colleges there. The big ones they played down at the Stadium. It was used by the Academy for the First Communion, for their Friday Communion breakfast. And it was used for all intramurals. I won a number of trophies there, I might add [laughs].*

Ed further recalled that during the Second World War the building was used by the ASTP (the Army Specialized Training Program) and the Signal Corp civilians that had largely taken over the uptown campus. Much of the liberal arts college had been moved to the downtown campus during the war to make room for the large number of military personnel. (31)

Many generations of DePaul students remember the barn as the site of ROTC drills. Tony Behof and Jack Dickman both recalled that participation in ROTC was a major part of their DePaul experience in the first two years of college (1955–56—both were 1959 LAS graduates). Tony also remembered that the special drills for the rifle team were held in the barn and that the rifle target practices were held in the basement of Saint Vincent's Church, the site of the target range. Behof reminisced,

I was on the rifle team. I joined everything just to get out of the normal drill, which I couldn't stand. I enjoyed the military science classes. I thought they were taught at a very high level. If you wanted to learn something, you certainly could. But we frequently would drill in the Barn. (32)

Jack Dickman (LAS, 1959) also remembered the ROTC Pershing Rifles, a drill team, and the Scabbard and Blade organizations that he associates with the barn, along with the more routine ROTC drills that were conducted there. (33)

The DePaul structure that received the most detailed and enthusiastic commentary and is recalled with great nostalgia by alumni from this era, however, was Wangler Hall. This temporary structure was not even listed on several "official" documents indicating the chronology of DePaul University buildings; nor was it on other published listings of campus buildings. It is remembered, however, as a hub of student activity and as the site where students ate meals, even though there wasn't an "official" cafeteria on the uptown campus prior to the opening of Alumni Hall in 1956.

Uptown DePaul students in the late 1940s and early to mid-1950s, when asked to describe a typical day on campus, would invariably mention Wangler Hall as the center of their campus social activities. Tony Behof described this structure circa 1955:

Well, my recollection is it was one large room. People, I think, called it a Quonset Hut and it may have had steel sides or steel roofing, but it wasn't what I think of a Quonset Hut. I think of a half cylinder-type building. And I never thought it was like that at all. Now I don't know exactly why it was built. I was told it was built shortly after the war. It seemed to me like there were too many tables for the size of it . . . it was very crowded. (34)

Many students remembered the unique way in which Wangler Hall functioned as a cafeteria. Evidently, before the noon hour, food service trucks would drive around to the back of Wangler and dispense sandwiches, hotdogs, donuts, and drinks through windows in the rear of the structure. Others remember most students bringing their lunches from home and eating in Wangler Hall. Carole Nolan, describing the building from her experiences in the early 1950s, said that Wangler was not particularly attractive:

It was the "rec hall" and it was a wreck! And that's basically where we all would congregate. We'd play cards and talk. . . . That was where we spent lots of time. We spent a lot of time playing cards. Pinochle we were playing in those days. So Wangler Hall was just a place that we would go to. And even though it was noisy and kind of steamy at times, you know, you'd find people studying there too. The library just didn't lend itself to study. (35)

In the period between 1928 and 1955, three additional uptown structures and several "areas" or places inspired "campus" reminiscences by alumni. Chief among these were the Lyceum or library building adjacent to the barn; the Hall of Science; Saint Vincent's Church; and the athletic field (future site of Alumni Hall).

Alumni commentary on the Lyceum suggested that the DePaul student body during this period did not spend extensive amounts of time in what was then the official DePaul library. The space devoted to student use for reading and studying was very limited. The few available tables, and the combination of severe restrictions on conversations, an overly warm and stuffy area, and the noise and vibration caused by the frequent elevated trains passing by the building did not make for a particularly inviting environment.

Fran (Armstrong) Kevin, remembering the Lyceum and the strictly enforced silence in 1936 (in the presence of her husband Bud, also a student in that period) noted these problems.

Remember Miss Schnur [librarian]? She wouldn't let you open your mouth. . . . If you did she sent you out. She did; she was really strict. . . . It [the library] was a one-floor, you know . . . when you climbed up these stairs and it was all on this one floor. (36)

Carole Nolan remembered the Lyceum circa 1950–54 especially well, not only because she worked there part-time, but also because of the controversy surrounding it with regard to re-accreditation by The North Central Association: it was judged to be particularly inadequate during the 1949 accreditation review. Carol described it in bleak terms:

[It was a] Spartan place. . . . The Library just didn't lend itself to study. . . . It was out of the given path. . . . It just didn't have the atmosphere for studying like the new one. . . . I spent lots of time downtown in the public library. (37)

Other alumni also remembered very few students actually using the facility. It appears not to have been a very popular venue for them.

The Hall of Science Building was built in 1938. Students prior to that date had their science and lab courses in the Academy Building. Fran (Armstrong) Kevin recalled the science facilities circa 1936:

I don't know when it was built [Hall of Science], but, it wasn't there when we were there. And we . . . were in that old . . . it was the top floor of the part of the Rectory in the Priest's house in the Academy . . . And it was really wood floors and . . . ugh, the equipment was pretty bad. The Chemistry was on the first floor. And we . . . used to laugh, because we swore that the priest who was in charge, his name was Father Ardones, he was from Puerto Rico. He . . . swore he trapped these cats that he gave us to dissect, because they really weren't in good shape. . . . I can remember going there and taking a class in Anatomy one night and bringing my dress and changing clothes to go to a formal with Bud. (38)

Carole Nolan, a chemistry major, had similar recollections.

I don't think they were, you know, so up to date in the kind of equipment that they had . . . they were adequate . . . I mean it wasn't a beautiful lab. You wouldn't walk in and say "Oh!" But it had everything . . . we needed. (39)

But not everyone thought the university's science facilities were deplorable. Tony Behof, a physics major, has fond memories of the Hall of Science or "Science Hall" as it was more commonly called:

> We spent a lot of time on the first floor, or basement if you want to call it that, primarily because of the science library. But we would generally congregate in the science library . . . So I have fond memories of the first floor, the second floor, and the fourth floor, which is where the chemistry, general chemistry class was. What I would call now the second floor, up that flight of stairs when you come in, had a large lecture room. It sat [about] 100. (40)

If the science labs received mixed reviews, there was one DePaul structure that drew much positive commentary from former students, particularly the older alumni: Saint Vincent's Church. Not surprisingly, the church was particularly important to Catholic students. Of course, the changing policy of the Vincentians with respect to religious practice for Catholic students affected their experience with the church as well. (Catholic religion courses were mandatory for Catholic students until the late 1960s). The changing significance of such practices as religious retreats, formal university ceremonies that were held in the church, or, of such religious student organizations as the Legion of Mary, also affected the role of Saint Vincent's for students. But one thing is quite clear from student comments about the church: it was seen as one of the most aesthetically pleasing DePaul structures. On a campus most often described as "Spartan," "basic," "barebones," "functional," "simple," and "pragmatic and practical," Saint Vincent's Church was seen by many students, Catholic and non-Catholic alike, as a structure of some artistic and spiritual significance.

Carole Nolan, for instance, ranked the structure high on her list of important DePaul places and spaces:

> It was just a beautiful building . . . it was just, you know, kind of warm as opposed to the rest of DePaul . . . it gave you a place to go and to contemplate and to have more peace and meditation . . . to get yourself ready for the next part of life there. (41)

Other students also remember the building as a place of quiet and solitude, a pleasing refuge from the everyday bustle of class, work, and studying. The beauty of its stained glass windows, the grace of its altar, and the open space of its sanctuary were a distinct contrast to the utilitarian character and limited quarters of the remainder of the uptown campus structures.

Downtown: The 64 E. Lake Street Building

In the period 1928–1955, the downtown Chicago campus of DePaul at 64 E. Lake Street housed the greatest number of academic programs and, by a substantial amount, the largest number of students. (42) Commerce, law, music, education, the Downtown College of Liberal Arts, the Secretarial School, a downtown high school, and university administrative offices quickly filled the newly built structure.

The building was located in the heart of the "Loop," Chicago's central business district and shopping and entertainment area. This offered students a wide array of opportunities for learning, work, and leisure activities. Its accessibility, from virtually any and every part of the city by efficient public transportation, made its programs particularly convenient, especially to many students from neighborhoods and parishes on the south and west sides of Chicago. The range of the morning, late afternoon, and evening classes provided students the flexibility to accommodate work, study, and other needs and responsibilities.

When he completed two years of study on DePaul's uptown campus, Tom Joyce entered the downtown law school in 1930, two years after the new building was built. His most memorable recollections of the physical structure and his own daily activities at 64 E. Lake Street concerned the de facto cafeteria and hangout familiar to students who attended downtown DePaul during that era: Pixley and Ehlers Restaurant, the principal leased facility on the building's ground floor. In fact, this place represented a major element of the university's extended campus, the unofficial spaces and places that complemented or augmented a student's experience of DePaul (to be discussed in greater detail below).

Beyond Pixley and Ehlers, Tom Joyce recalled the quality of the law library facility at Lake Street. This was particularly important for him, in contrast to the relatively meager library facilities that he had encountered on the uptown campus:

*W*ell, the contrast, of course [with uptown campus], the building on Lake Street was in a business area . . . And we had excellent library facilities . . . excellent, excellent . . . And you know, many, many days I spent there in the library until it closed at ten o'clock . . . DePaul has such an excellent law library, there was no need to go any place else. (43)

Rita Barr (COM 1939) remembered especially the informal dances, "sock hops" or "mixers," that were held on the 4th floor of the building about once a month. She also recalled the Phi Gamma Nu sorority meetings that were held in empty classrooms in the afternoons, when there was a lull in the class schedule. (44) With a shortage of space for student activities, much socializing took place in Pixley and Ehlers, unused classroom space in the afternoon, and in the space on the top floor of the building which functioned as a lounge (in addition to the hallways and stairwells).

Marie Brahm Cogan (COM 1936) similarly remembered that in 1932 and 1933, sororities and fraternities anchored many student experiences on the downtown campus. Along with Rita Barr, Marie particularly recalled what it was like being among the few women in the College of Commerce at the time. In classes with forty to forty-five students there would be six or seven women, she declared. Commenting on the large male to female ratio in the mid to late 1930s, Marie pointed out that there were few options for socializing:

I was a serious student, but I truly enjoyed all the attention because naturally a few girls in a large class got quite a bit of attention. [In response to a question on whether this led to a fair amount of dating] . . . There was an active social life, not right in the school, you know. You'd have your friends that you'd meet downstairs, but you couldn't do much in the corridor between classes and things . . . you'd go downstairs only if you had a break in your schedule . . . But the free period, you know, people would go down to Pixley's. That was it. There was no place else. There were no lounges around or anything. (45)

Bernard Carney (COM 1942) had different memories of Lake Street in the late 1930s and early 1940s. Carney recalled that the classrooms reminded him of the Catholic high school classes he was familiar with and that "we wouldn't have expected anything different." He recalled the lounge on the top floor of the building and vividly remembered the juke box and the informal dances that were held there on Friday afternoons and on Saturdays. Carney also remembered the colorful elevator operators who worked the manual elevators in the building: *"There were some characters . . . I just remember that there was very entertaining elevator operation. And they were young, and not so fast, particularly on the way down."* Bernie was a student worker in the commerce offices while he was an undergraduate, and he mentioned that while the physical space of the building was not that particularly notable, a friendly spirit pervaded the place.

> *I* think it was the relationships [that were significant]. I had made friends from the first day I got there. In fact, I was looking for another student to share a locker with, and I met a young man who became my best friend in time. We were the best of friends until he died, a couple of years back. (46)

Nick Valenziano started his music school studies at DePaul in 1954. His first reaction to the School's facilities at the Lake Street building also was memorable:

> [It was] . . . kind of a shock. And it was just a stark building, elevator up and the foyer there by the music school was just some windows and it was rather cold, you know, unattractive kind of place . . . Not much there. I was a kid. I didn't really know the difference. But now that I think back, it was rather unattractive. To me it was kind of cold. This just seemed like this is a place where you are really going to work . . . And nothing really decorative or colorful or anything like that. Just looked like a hard working place . . . I just remember it being rather sparse.

Nick mentioned that students would often make fun of the facilities, the holes in the practice hall walls, the barely adequate equipment, the bad lighting, but also points out that "we knew we had work to do. We knew what we were doing. Why we were there." (47) And, ostensibly, that was to make-do with what they had and get as good an education as possible. All of the alumni I interviewed from this period believed that this was, in fact, what they accomplished.

A Sense of Place: Limitations and Adaptations

These comments and reminiscences of DePaul alumni, attending either one of DePaul's campuses during the 1928–1955 period, reflected a number of common themes. These individuals seem to have shared a retrospective sense of having attended an urban campus of limited physical means, and they realized that such limitations were not particularly troublesome at the time. For most, just being able to attend a college or university was the key, and any shortcomings were accepted as natural, understandable, and, more important, surmountable. By and large, the school's characteristics were associated with a relatively affordable and accessible education of reasonably good quality. On balance, the importance of the opportunity and education they were receiving far outweighed these sensed limitations of the institution. They were, essentially, among the first generation of working and middle class urban residents to receive such an education in a period of socio-economic bust and boom; an era that spanned the Great Depression, the Second World War, and the postwar recovery period. They were not about to complain about the facilities.

Additionally, DePaul was perceived as an extended part of the urban environment. It was a city school for city students, perhaps not that different from the high schools they had attended, in environments perceived as "familiar" and not unlike their own home neighborhoods. DePaul was, in this sense, perceived as "local," "convenient" and, perhaps, "safe." It was a good educational value, despite its physical deficiencies. In this regard, its character as a private "commuter school" in an urban setting defined the student experience at DePaul. The enthusiasm that the alumni felt as students was rooted in the urban environment surrounding both campuses, and was accompanied by and built on an array of opportunities that augmented their DePaul experience.

The Extended Campus

Adaptation is a natural evolutionary process that affects all forms of life. The limits of immediate structures and environments are conditioned or mediated by the richness of alternative sources of opportunity in the broader environment. Cities provide a concentration of alternative opportunities to resident populations and institutions. Chicago provided DePaul students with just such an array of alternative sources and resources. These conditions augmented or counteracted whatever academic, economic, or other social and cultural shortcomings, deficits, or limits the institution might have had.

The second quarter century of DePaul's history has been characterized as one of physical stability (without a great deal of physical development or expansion). In many instances, alumni have noted that within the available campus spaces at DePaul downtown, there were significant limitations, particularly regarding the library, space for social activities (no official cafeteria until the post-World War II period), and limited athletic or recreation facilities. Many DePaul students also needed to work to help pay for their university education. While perceived by many as quite an affordable education, this was a period in which DePaul students could not depend on scholarships or on-campus work/study or loan programs to help pay their tuition. For these students, the city of Chicago and surrounding neighborhood institutions became significant resources for both work and play.

First there was the question of social gatherings. Prior to the building of Wangler Hall in the post-World War II period, students on DePaul's uptown campus at midday would commonly either wait to eat lunch when they returned home, eat on their way to work, or stop at

Coeds in front of "Eddie's" diner at the corner of Webster and Kenmore. Eddie's was a popular student hang-out and part of the "extended campus." Circa late 1940s, Lorraine Bond private collection.

Interior view of "Eddie's," a diner popular with students before DePaul had an "official" cafeteria. Eddie's was, along with The Roma and Kelly's, part of DePaul's "extended campus." Circa late 1940s, Lorraine Bond private collection.

one of the local food shops near campus. These cafés were located, for the most part, on a two-block-long strip along Webster Avenue straddling both sides of Sheffield Avenue, within a block or two of the uptown campus. Not only did they provide food services to students, but they also became social "hangouts," as much as their proprietors and the schedules of students would allow. In this way, they soon became DePaul "institutions," extended or unofficial facilities that DePaul students would use with some regularity.

Principal among these establishments on Webster Street during this period were The Roma Restaurant (in business until 1995); Kelly's Tavern and Restaurant (still in business), Friendly's Bar, Eddie's Diner, The Varsity Restaurant, the Falzone Pizzeria, and the Marquis on Lincoln Avenue, just south of Fullerton. There were also several small specialty shops on Webster, such as an ice cream parlor whose name had slipped from the memories of former students. These were the neighborhood places that virtually all DePaul students knew about as part of the unofficial campus.

Fran (Armstrong) Kevin recalled that in the mid- to late-1930s, Kelly's Tavern was primarily a male-dominated environment:

Girls did not go in Kelly's. I . . . was never in Kelly's and I was pretty easy going about most things. . . . And they had a book in there, and you could bet on a horse for a quarter. Well, I'm one of these . . . anti-gambling people, you know . . . but I always had money. So, there would always be these football players, "Fran, lend me a quarter, lend me . . ." you know. And I'd lend out about four or five quarters and they'd all go over there. But, I have to say, they all paid me back. . . . The girls didn't really go over there, they'd give it to somebody else, [to place the quarter bet].

The Roma Restaurant served as the principal hangout and de facto cafeteria for generations of DePaul students. Fran (Armstrong) Kevin recalled that the menu did not offer much variation.

I think I lived on chili, barbecued beef or pork, and tuna on Friday. That was the menu. That was it. Once in a while, they'd have fried ham. You know, [it] was just so limited. (48)

Although there was a limited number of places to go, other alumni recalled—depending on the exact period—frequenting different places for sandwiches, hot dogs, hamburgers, ice cream, and other items. Most of these spots were within a block or two of one another near the intersection of Sheffield and Webster. In many cases, the owners of the food shops were from the neighborhood and/or had close relationships to the academy or university. Edwin Schillinger recalled that, in the late 1930s, Eddie's Diner, a competitor of The Roma at the corner of Webster and Kenmore (where Schillinger worked as a student waiting tables for twenty-five cents and lunch), had a definite link to the institution.

> *[It] was run by Eddie Kolker, who was also the athletic trainer during the war, when our good trainer . . . went into the defense industry. . . . But, the person that ran it was his wife Martha. She later worked at our cafeteria in the Alumni Hall . . . and she did all the cooking, and she ran it.* (49)

Tony Behof remembered that Falzone's Pizzeria, located at Kenmore and Webster, also had a DePaul connection.

> *[It] was owned by Pete Falzone [LAS 1948]. Pete worked there, but Pete taught me chemistry in high school [DePaul Academy]. And he had a brother Frank, I think. . . . For a while they owned the place.* (50)

On occasion, students would go elsewhere for a bite to eat, particularly the Marquis Restaurant on Lincoln Avenue. But establishments such as this were not as commonly patronized as the handful of places on Webster Street. In fact, for the vast majority of uptown alumni I interviewed, the immediate everyday campus experience was bounded by the few blocks of the official campus and the two block strip near Sheffield and Webster. Students seldom seemed to have gone farther west than Racine Avenue, farther south than Webster, or farther north than Fullerton. And most would only go farther east than Lincoln Avenue when they headed toward the lakefront to visit the park or zoo, usually in warmer weather. The "campus" of everyday use was a compact, two square block area.

CHAPTER FOUR

Fran (Armstrong) Kevin remembered other unusual establishments in that two-block-square area in the mid- to late-1930s.

> *There was a place down at the other corner, the block west of Sheffield, and . . . they made cigars in there . . . they'd all be in there, and they'd be sitting at these wooden benches, and they'd have, like a little table, in front of them, and baskets of leaves. And they'd be rolling these cigars. (51)*

Edwin Schillinger recalled the significance of the Monte Carlo Bowling Alley on Lincoln just south of Belmont. It became a recreational hangout for students in the late 1930s, when bowling was very popular. But he remembered that it was rare that students wandered this far away from the immediate campus area. (52)

This was not the case for other social events that were a part of DePaul student life. This is particularly true of the major, formal dances held during the school year, where the city of Chicago's vast array of hotels and many ballrooms became the extended social venues for student events. Here, the entire city became a source for recreational and entertainment possibilities.

Alumni recalled attending formal dances in such widely dispersed sites as the Knickerbocker Hotel, The Belden Stratford, The Edgewater Beach Hotel, The Bismarck Hotel, The Aragon Ballroom, The Hamilton Hotel, The Congress Hotel, The Conrad Hilton, The Morrison Hotel, The Drake Hotel, The Sherman House Hotel, The

Religious service at the dedication of the Alumni Hall, 1956.

Melody Mill Ballroom, The Holiday Ballrooms (on the north and south sides), and The Milford Ballroom, among others. These were located in the downtown area, the near and far north side of the city, the near and far south side and various points in between. The city of Chicago truly offered students a dazzling array of entertainment possibilities.

The full meaning and significance of an "extended campus" is driven home when considered in the lives of DePaul students attending the 64 E. Lake Street campus in this same period. And any discussion of this particular extended or "unofficial" campus would have to begin with the most commonly mentioned non-DePaul institution: Pixley and Ehlers Restaurant. No former student failed to mention this historical establishment. It functioned as the de facto downtown cafeteria and social gathering place for tens of thousands of DePaul students for a quarter century.

Pixley and Ehlers Restaurant leased the prime space on the first floor of the 64 E. Lake building. While not particularly noted for its cuisine (Carole Nolan noted that it was often referred to as "Pixley and Ulcers"), former students seemed to have fond memories of particular items on its menu. Rita Barr (COM 1939) recalled the wonderful 5 cent pork tenderloin sandwiches that she and her sister would order on a regular basis. Bernard Carney (COM 1942) remembered that they had "great hot dogs and the soup was good". Nick Deleonardis (COM 1951) remembers the 5 cent cup of coffee and the fact that you could bring a sandwich from home for lunch and complement it with a wonderful bowl of Pixley and Ehler's soup. This aptly denotes the accommodating nature of the establishment to the circumstances of DePaul students and the times. Rita Barr described Pixley's as indispensable.

> [It was our] student Union . . . Well, that was the place you would go to the minute your classes were over. And the tables were high, marble topped, and had high stools and tables for four. There may have been other types at the back of this long, narrow restaurant, but what I remember is these tall tables . . . Most people, because of the times again [1935–39], would go home right after the last class and have their lunch at home. But if you had a break in between classes, you'd go down to Pixley's as well. (53)

Nick Valenziano added that, for some students, Pixley was more a morning rendezvous point than anything else:

Pixley was important because it was where we'd congregate. Generally, we'd bring our lunch. We were brown baggers in those days, but we didn't go down for lunch usually. Usually for a breakfast, maybe, we'd go for a sweet roll or I remember their big Danishes or big sweet rolls and their English muffins. And then in the evening often when we stayed for a class, we might have a rehearsal, whatever, three or four o'clock. So we'd have to stay then for a six o'clock academic class and so we'd go down to Pixley's, grab a bowl of soup or something and always, of course, jaw about the food because it wasn't the greatest. But that's what it was. And even when I see people today that were with me in those [years] . . . they remember Pixley's so much. (54)

Pixley and Ehler's, as important as it was in the everyday routine of students, was only the very beginning of a long list of Chicago Loop places and spaces that were important to downtown DePaul students. Depending on personal interests, schedules and disposable incomes, students took advantage of the resources of the central business district and its exciting social and cultural opportunities.

Nick Valenziano (MUS 1958) recalled frequenting places like "Browns," a tavern and sandwich shop on Wabash, The Elm on Van Buren and across the street, pizzeria Mario's. He pointed out that there was a lot for a music major to see and hear downtown.

We were down here all the time . . . it became our second home, really . . . we became acquainted with some of the jazz spots. The Preview Lounge was over on, Randolph, I believe . . . There was the Brass Rail, which was right down there . . . on Clark and Randolph or Dearborn . . . near the Oriental . . . and the Blue Note . . . absolutely . . . I can remember hearing Count Basie there, Duke Ellington. I think there was a place right across the alley there from the Chicago Theater . . . There was another couple of smaller joints but those couple I remember well. Also for us music students downtown involved a yearly convention over at what was the Sherman House, Sherman Hotel, which is now the Illinois Center.

Nick also recalled walking a few blocks to Orchestra Hall for Friday afternoon performances and seeing the conductor Fritz Reiner for the first time. The Civic Opera House, The Chicago Lyric Opera Company, the Art Institute, also became part of the extended campus, of particular interest to students drawn to the arts and culture scene.

For Music students like Nick Valenziano, "jobbing," or being picked up by local bands that needed a musician here or there, was made possible through his DePaul University connections—teachers, other students, and the university's reputation. Conveniently, the musician's union local offices were located not far from the Loop campus. Nick played with big bands like Dan Belloc's and Ralph Marterie's at such places as the Holiday Ballroom on the south side, the Old Melody Mill Ballroom and The Milford Ballroom. "This was part of our education," he declared. (55)

Rita Barr (COM 1939) remembered the Chicago Theater a few blocks from 64 E. Lake.

> On nice days we had Michigan Avenue . . . but the Chicago Theater was the better outlet when the weather wasn't good . . . we wouldn't cut classes, of course, although sometimes it happened.

Bernard Carney (COM 1942) also frequented the Chicago Theater and recalled that it was quite accessible.

> [It] was a part of the campus too, for that matter. It was right around the corner. In those days there were stage shows. Yeah, I think I saw Sinatra and [Perry] Como . . ., there was live entertainment. (56)

A frequently mentioned Chicago sports and recreation facility was the Chicago Stadium. For many years, DePaul's basketball team played most of its games in the barn (and later in Alumni Hall), but played many Saturday night games and double-headers—along with Loyola University or Northwestern—at the Stadium. These were extremely popular events, and, evidently were well attended by DePaul students and other fans alike.

Other students of the era remembered such colorful details as the bookie joint on the lower level of Michigan at Lake Street. In fact, the lower level of Michigan Avenue and the area adjacent to it contained a number of eating and entertainment establishments frequented by DePaul students, faculty and staff. This included the Ye Olde Cellar and a bar, Gaffers. Nick Deleonardis (COM 1951) remembered Gaffers as the unofficial fraternity house of Delta Chi, where meetings would be held in a room on the second floor. Gerry Radice (COM 1949) recalled other students hanging out in the famous Billy Goat Inn. Other rendezvous places for DePaul students were Demet's and Stouffer's Restaurants, The Blackhawk Restaurant, and, especially, a Chinese restaurant directly across the street from 64 E. Lake Street.

Finally, a discussion of social and recreational facilities available to downtown DePaul students would be incomplete if it did not mention Grant Park (Chicago's very expansive downtown lakefront public park) with its softball diamonds and other park facilities within walking distance of the campus. Former students routinely mentioned utilizing this public space for a wide variety of recreational and social activities.

A list of other entertainment and recreation facilities and venues mentioned by DePaul Alumni would include numerous movie theaters, burlesque houses, and other common downtown attractions. Other well known Chicago attractions such as Riverview Park (a popular amusement park), The Chicago Cubs and Wrigley Field, The White Sox and Comiskey Park, and The Chicago Bears and football Cardinals, were also mentioned frequently. As noted earlier, the city of Chicago was very rich in social, cultural, and entertainment activities, and many DePaul students availed themselves of these opportunities during their collegiate years.

Of course, there was more to the extended campus than simply entertainment occasions. The city environment offered academic resources as well. One particular shared reality united DePaul students on both campuses and for at least half of the institution's history. Asked what library they went to when they needed research material for a class paper or project, most mentioned "The Downtown Chicago Public Library" on Michigan Avenue (today, the Chicago Cultural Center). The building was located just two blocks from the 64 E. Lake Street facility and hence was quite convenient. Only DePaul's law library, which served a particular group of students, may have been regarded as more useful. Karen Stark (COM 1963) was emphatic on this point.

Any research, good or heavy research that we had to do that our library just didn't support [we did] . . . at the Chicago Public Library. That was our library. In fact, in the early 60s, they [DePaul] had a brochure that the Public Relations Department put out, that may still exist somewhere . . . The

> *publication was to entice people to DePaul . . . So we had pictures taken throughout the city and one of them I remember, because I happened to be in it, [chuckles] so, I remember it very well, was at the library, the Chicago Public Library. And I remember walking up and down those aisles, interminably, until . . . until they got just what they considered the right picture . . . this was considered something that would draw students here . . . see what you have access to. (57)*

Although it was somewhat unusual for an academic institution to publicize or feature a public library—and not its own—as an inducement to prospective students, it probably was the facility actually used most frequently by DePaul students.

Additional academic resources used by students that were not "officially" a part of DePaul included the Art Institute of Chicago, The Field Museum of Natural History, the John Crerar Library (on science and technology, located one block from 64 E. Lake Street), The Museum of Science and Industry, and the Newbury Library. The teachers of applied music were often members of the Chicago Symphony Orchestra, and students had their individual lessons in The Fine Arts Building on Michigan Avenue, where these instructors had their private studios. (58) Law students had access to several law courts in or near the downtown area and commerce students were blocks away from the Board of Trade, Federal Reserve Bank, and the very center of commercial life in the midwestern United States. In all, the Loop provided a most impressive "extended campus" within walking distance or a very short ride by public transportation from the "official" DePaul campus.

The "extended campus" for many uptown and downtown students included a wide variety of sites where they held part-time, or, in some instances, full-time jobs. Paying fully for one's own education was not the challenge that it has become today; on the contrary, many DePaul students were able to defray a significant amount of their tuition by even working at part-time jobs. This was particularly the case for students on the downtown campus, although evidence allowing for a comparison with uptown students is not available. Both uptown and downtown alumni seemed to agree, however, that proportionately more downtown than uptown students held jobs while attending school.

Two principal factors contributed to this situation. First and foremost, the location of the school in the heart of the business and commercial district meant that jobs were available in a very wide variety of businesses. This included banks, insurance companies, restaurants, department stores, law and business service offices of many kinds, and government offices—among others; the variety was actually quite astounding. Former students who were interviewed had worked during college at such places as the Chicago Sun-Times, Chicago Tribune, the Continental Bank, Marshal Field's, Carson Pirie Scott and Company, Mandel Brothers, Goldblatt's and Wieboldt's Department Stores, Railway Express, Standard Asbestos Company, a downtown dentist's office, and a telephone switchboard for a utility company. Still others had part-time jobs at the university. Indeed, most of the jobs students held were part time. This seems to have been the case during the Depression, as well as during the 1940s and early 1950s. Evidently, part-time jobs were especially easy to come by since employers could pay lower wages to these workers, and also because part-time college students were probably considered very good temporary help.

Many downtown alumni specifically mentioned DePaul's very helpful job placement service for such part-time employment opportunities. Nick Deleonardis (COM 1951) remembered this as quite important.

They did have a fairly active placement [service] for part-time jobs . . . and employers would call and say, "We have availability for somebody . . . We called it the Placement Office . . . that was where the big demand was. These guys were always coming in . . . is there a job? And pull out a sheet and this is what I've got . . . I worked for Liberty Mutual Insurance in their proofreading department. (58)

Not all the money earned at such part-time jobs went to cover tuition, of course. Tony Behof, who had a scholarship, worked at the Chicago Sun-Times newspaper in his senior year. Tony described this income as being quite important.

It was a way of . . . getting some supplementary funds. I didn't have to pay tuition. But you know, in those days what would happen, my brother and I worked, the check would go to my mother just to run the household. So it got to be in my senior year where I didn't think I was contributing enough at home. (59)

Tony Behof's experience was a common one at the time. Students would often work to help pay their tuition but also to help support the household. Family obligations weighed heavily on DePaul's commuter students who remained integral members of their respective families during their college days. Several alumni indicated that these years were circumscribed by these responsibilities, and structured by such other family rituals as being home at a specific time for family dinner.

Another useful source for student employment was the informal network supplied by word of mouth from other students who knew about and/or worked at various part-time jobs around the city. Bud Kevin told of a special but nonetheless characteristic opportunity for DePaul students at the time.

> *I'll tell you another thing that I think brought a lot of us together, was Andy Frain ushers . . . Andy Frain was from the Back of the Yards [a poorer neighborhood near the Chicago Stock Yards] . . . [H]e went to William Wrigley, who owned the Cubs, and was still alive, and sold him on the idea of having ushers in a regular uniform, and to get young guys. And he sold him on the idea that college kids were always looking for part-time work . . . When we were at school [DePaul], I'd say seventy percent of our group became Andy Frain ushers . . . We'd get four dollars for ushering and five dollars if you had a gate . . . you could work when it was convenient for you. And lots of times, it would be evenings, basketball games, fights, hockey, ice-skating, . . . the Kentucky Derby [went down to Louisville, KY.] . . . It was a terrific thing . . . because a lot of guys were making that side money who may not have been able to afford to go to school. (60)*

Bud indicated that such jobs sustained a great many DePaul students that he knew. With classes largely in the mornings, college students (Frain, a Roman Catholic, was said to be particularly partial to students from DePaul and Loyola) were ideal for the afternoon and evening ushering assignments that were available all year long.

In any case, the inclusion of work and an off-campus worksite into a student's daily routine was an extremely common DePaul student experience. It integrated students into the life of the city in a way that was particularly significant. Coming from a Chicago neighborhood, ties to family and friends, the daily negotiation of public transportation, classes on campus, the frequenting of "extended campus" facilities for academic, social, and work-related activities, were to many alumni a mark of their "urban" DePaul University education. When asked to define what they perceived to be the "urban" character of DePaul, former students frequently pointed out that this integration into the very fabric of Chicago through their DePaul years made their experience "urban." If by "campus" we mean the physical, geographical, environmental location or space that defines "official" university activities, then "extended campus" might be considered the sum total of space and place that defines the everyday activities of college students, regardless of its relationship to the institution. In this case, it could truly be said that "Chicago" became the "extended campus" for many DePaul students.

DePaul's Campus Experience, 1956–1967

The period from 1956 to 1967 was a transitional period for DePaul. Though new facilities were added on both the downtown and uptown campuses, many of these changes simply involved replacing old structures with new ones to provide increased space for the expansion of academic programs and development of new student services. The "little university under the El" was, however, still that; these changes did not transform DePaul, as did the developments that occurred between 1968 and 1980. The modifications of 1956–67 were designed for a commuter student population, to provide more of the essential services and spaces that had previously been lacking.

The growth of the Lincold Park campus allowed students space to run and play.

The period was marked by the first structure to be added to the uptown campus since the building of the Hall of Science in 1938. For decades, the barn or College Theater had been the principal site for student activities and athletic events on that campus. There was no "official" student cafeteria or social center and there was a growing realization that such a facility was needed by the growing numbers of students, faculty, and staff alike. As noted in other chapters, Alumni Hall opened its doors in 1956. Aside from being the new site for athletic events and physical education classes, it also housed the first "official" uptown campus cafeteria in its basement. It thus became the heart of student social activity for a period of fifteen years, until the Stuart Center was built.

Within two years of the opening of Alumni Hall, a major downtown move—from the north end of the Loop to the south—took place when DePaul opened the Frank J. Lewis Center at 25 E. Jackson Boulevard. The building, formerly known as the Kimball Building, had been acquired in 1955 as a gift from Mr. Lewis and his family. The new Lewis Center also included expanded space for classrooms and a fourth floor cafeteria—which became the primary downtown social gathering point for a period of 35 years—as well as a faculty dining room. Both campuses thus acquired much needed space for basic student services that had formerly been available only through the "extended campus," unofficial facilities, or temporary structures.

Jack Dickman (LAS 1959) was a junior undergraduate sociology major when Alumni Hall was built and opened for use. He remembered it as the "showcase building" at the time; a *"beautiful basketball complex . . . you didn't sit on top of the floor like you did in the old barn . . . and [it was] the hub of social activity."* But, most important, the Alumni Hall basement cafeteria became the hub of social life on the uptown campus.

For Jack Dickman and others, this was mediated and facilitated through the fraternity and sorority areas or tables that became a standard feature of the cafeteria scene in Alumni Hall. Dickman described what became a familiar scene.

The tables were kind of pushed together. You didn't have a fraternity "house"; you had a fraternity area. It was always kind of in the same place. I could have put a blindfold on, walked in to the cafeteria and gone to this area. And if I was the only one there, that was where Lambda Tau always was. And right next to us is where the Alpha Delts always were. And the Alpha Omega sorority was a little bit to our left. And if there was nobody there, nobody else would sit there. I mean, it was kind of your—our [place] not charted out, but that's how it was. (61)

Paul Rettberg (LAS 1966), in describing a typical day on campus, pointed out that social gatherings were a part of the daily routine.

> *I'd get the CTA to school. I would generally get there, oh, somewhere between a half hour and forty-five minutes before class, go directly to Alumni Hall, you know, buy a cup of coffee, head directly to your fraternity table, sit down, and shoot the breeze. And there were always people, I mean, the fraternity tables and I suppose even the independent's areas, I mean, those were the dormitories and fraternity houses for us . . . I usually would try to bunch my classes together, so that I'd have an hour for lunch and sit at the fraternity table. (62)*

Rettberg and Dickman both remembered the cafeteria as a "smoke-filled" room, every one, student and faculty alike, seemed to be smoking at the same time. Rettberg said that there was a constant commotion as well.

> *There was always a humm and a buzz and . . . whatever promotion was going on at the time, be it for a dance and people touting it . . . politicking for the Liberal Arts Council (Student Activity Council), . . . that went on there. (63)*

Tony Behof (LAS 1959) also remembered the cafeteria as "close and confining, almost to the point of being uncomfortable, although I spent a lot of time down there." In a similar fashion, Tom Paetsch (LAS 1966) recalled the somewhat claustrophobic atmosphere of the place, largely he feels, due to the lack of windows and "exposure to the outside world". Alumni I interviewed felt uncomfortable in the new structure in other ways, as well. It seems that the university and the athletic department were highly protective of the new structure. Paetsch remembered this clearly.

> *I*t was funny the way that the new structure was zealously guarded. I mean you literally had to have a purpose for going anywhere in Alumni Hall other than in the cafeteria. Otherwise somebody would stop you because this was a brand new building and [the university] didn't necessarily want it to be spoiled . . . if somebody walked through it. (64)

Others also remembered feeling like interlopers if they wandered any distance from a direct pathway to and from the basement cafeteria. Despite this, alumni I interviewed from the period agree that the small size of the new cafeteria facility had a positive effect in making people interact with one another and, as Tom Paetsch put it, "helped to build relationships with people." My own experience, as a student during this period at DePaul, resonates with this view. By spending an hour or so every day during the week in the cafeteria for one year, I could see, meet, and/or interact with a considerable portion of the student and faculty body.

The lively social environment of the new Alumni Hall cafeteria assumes additional significance when considered in light of changes taking place in the immediate neighborhood around DePaul's uptown campus. From the immediate post war period on through the 1950s and 60s, as Thomas Croak notes in chapter 7, the area around the university underwent a significant population shift, along with physical deterioration of residential properties and urban infrastructure. Many factors contributed to a changed "sense of place" regarding DePaul's more immediate neighborhood and campus environment. Suburban-

The Frank J. Lewis Center (formerly the Kimball Building), acquired in 1955, at the corner of Jackson and Wabash.

ization and the movement of large numbers of families out of the neighborhood had a significant impact on its family-based, religious, ethnic and racial character. The arrival of large groups of poorer white, Latino and African American residents into the neighborhood, the beginnings of urban renewal, and the abandonment or decay of commercial and industrial property to the west and south of the university also had an impact on the neighborhood. The net effect of this, for the alumni I interviewed from this period, was a marked contraction of the campus's dimensions, both as perceived and as experienced by students at the time.

Alumni expressed this as a feeling that large parts of the immediate neighborhood were believed to be "unsafe" at this time. Jack Dickman (LAS 1959) recalled that *"this could be a pretty dangerous area around here. When you came to the University [you] stayed within a couple of block radius and then you went home."* (65) Many former students remembered being warned by the university not to linger after classes, and being cautioned not to wander too far from the few buildings that comprised the campus. As a result, the campus often seemed deserted after two o'clock in the afternoon. I personally can recall female students in the mid-1960s being warned not to go south of Webster Avenue, only one block from the center campus. Whether such fears were warranted or not, they had the effect of concentrating students into the few buildings of the university and limiting the amount of time that students spent in the area.

This did not mean that the concept of the extended campus for students was eliminated. In many respects, students in the 1960s, like those in the 30s, 40s, and early 50s, still frequented Webster Avenue establishments like Kelly's and Roma's, but they rarely ventured very far from the limited campus buildings. By the 1960s, in that case, a clear psychological and social sense of safe neighborhood boundaries and limits had become part of students' awareness of the immediate area surrounding the uptown DePaul campus.

The early 1960s, however, also marked the beginning of the transformation of Lincoln Park, the larger neighborhood that included DePaul. Lincoln Park was (and still is) the area bounded by North Avenue on the south, Diversey Avenue on the north, the lakefront on the east and the Chicago River on the west. Changes began in the "Old Town" section of the area, in the southeastern corner of the neighborhood near Wells Street, at some distance from campus. The development of an entertainment district in this neighborhood (restaurants, cafes, art galleries, shops of all sorts, and theaters) began to make Lincoln Park into an attractive evening and weekend venue, particularly for younger college-age students from around the city and suburbs. For many DePaul students, this provided another reason for coming back to this part of the city, even after the usual hours of classroom and academic activity.

The "Old Town" phenomenon sparked the eventual redevelopment and gentrification of the entire Lincoln Park area, producing one of the most significant urban redevelopment stories of any urban area in the entire nation. For DePaul and its students the most important consequence was the added incentive it gave students to remain in the neighborhood. In the 1950s, prior to the beginning of these transformations, the institution had, at one point, seriously considered moving out of the area. DePaul's decision to stay in Lincoln Park, however, turned out to be quite fortuitous, as the neighborhood now serves as an attraction to students.

For DePaul students, these developments rejuvenated the notion of the extended campus. Students would go to "Old Town" and adjacent areas on dates, or just to hang out. Paul Rettberg (LAS 1966) remembered the early 1960s as a special time there:

> *O*ld Town was developed . . . at the time [as the place] for entertainment . . . It was the place, I would say that, on weekends, when you came back down toward the campus, that sure, you'd go there . . . It was a little bit [inaudible], but I could go to Second City, and places like that. That was the "in" area. (66)

In addition to these earliest changes to the neighborhood, Alumni Hall's expansive seating capacity brought more students, alumni, and others to campus during the basketball season, although DePaul still had big games scheduled at the Chicago Stadium.

Despite some increases in gang activity and crime in the neighborhood during this period, signs of community change were already apparent in certain areas of Lincoln Park. As Thomas Croak notes, neighborhood organizations like the Lincoln Park Conservation Association (LPCA) were active in tackling community problems of crime and safety, infrastructure improvement, zoning issues, and so forth. DePaul became an active contributor to these discussions of community improvement and change, and this laid some of the groundwork for a significant expansion of DePaul's physical presence in the neighborhood in the years to come.

When DePaul's downtown campus moved from Lake Street to the Lewis Center in 1957–58, it marked the end of a thirty year presence at that particular address, and approximately a half century presence in the north Loop. The new building offered greater classroom and administrative space for what was still DePaul's largest set of academic programs and student population. The enrollment of the College of Commerce, the music school, The College of Law, The School of Education and Evening Division programs combined, was nearly three times the size of uptown's College of Liberal Arts and Sciences.

Nick Valenziano (MUS, 1958) vividly remembered the move to Lewis Center during his senior year at DePaul.

The move then to 25 E. Jackson . . . was just terrific because now we had new desks, and, you know, everything was new. It had been renovated, of course, but we had practice rooms that were decent. They had a nice rehearsal hall. The new hall [2nd floor, Center Theater] we used for concerts, for recitals . . . was twice as big as the [64 E. Lake St.] Little Theater. It was just so much nicer. But the facilities for the Music School itself expanded tremendously, teaching facilities, studios for teachers, the classrooms, all of that, the practice rooms. Also, we had, I recall then using the library more extensively . . . And the cafeteria there was more in use by the music students. . . . There was [also] a little restaurant in what is now the bookstore . . . We called it "Ulcer Gulch." It was a real dump. But we would . . . congregate there, now and then, for a cup of coffee. (67)

Karen Stark (COM 1963) also recalled the early years of Lewis Center. The building, it appears, had some commercial tenants. Stark said that the sub-basement housed the Fisher Music Company offices. The upper floors (16th and 17th) contained other commercial offices, including a rather unusual tenant for a university building on the 17th floor, a full men's barber shop. She also fondly remembered the unusual elevator stops on the fifth floor, when the doors would open to the blasts of horns playing, piano music, woodwind instruments, and pounding drums—the home of the School of Music. But, far and away the most memorable part of the newly renovated facility was the 4th floor cafeteria. Stark described it as "an enormous melting-pot." The mix of commerce, music, law, and evening division students made for a diverse group indeed, yet the cafeteria appeared to have had a somewhat college-specific organization and seating pattern:

But people still . . . demanded their own space. So, it was an unspoken rule that the law students sat at this side of the cafeteria, and the music students were over here . . . and the area on the left when you walked in, was kind of no man's land, anybody could sit there. Then, when you walked into

> *the main cafeteria, up against the wall, all along the windows, were all the sororities and fraternities . . . they had actual tables with the insignia of whatever organization they were. And in the middle, was kind of, the business students would kind of hang around there. But, people did mix together, when it got very, very crowded at lunch time, to the point where you really had to hunt for a place to sit. (68)*

Stark described the cafeteria as the social axis of Lewis Center. On a typical day it would have three major waves of usage. First there were many early morning students grabbing a cup of coffee before classes. Then the very busy lunch time, when the room was at capacity before it would empty by 1:00 or 1:30 p.m. It would remain nearly empty until about 4:00 p.m., when the last wave of late afternoon and evening students would begin arriving for classes.

The new building and its classrooms were, however, described by alumni of this period as quite "Spartan." Karen Stark mentioned that the facility was not always conducive to learning.

> *The windows opened, and on hot days no air conditioning, at all, and you could really, literally die from the heat. When you opened the window, though, then you got the El going by. And it was quite loud, so you had to pick. Sometimes it would be the beginning of the class in the summer. You would say, "Well, which do you want? Do you want to hear the lecture, or do you want to have a little breeze come in?" The window shades would erratically pop up at various times, and startle people, especially those that were sleeping in the back of the class. So, the physical facilities were really quite Spartan. But, we didn't know any differently. We thought they were fine . . . I don't think people expected anything else. There was virtually no discussion of the facilities, as there is today. (69)*

The initial lack of air conditioning forced students onto the streets on Jackson and Wabash Avenues in between classes and the commonly heard joke was that "the sidewalk was our campus." If students had a significant break between classes under such conditions, many would wander over to Grant Park for some of the lake breezes. In these terms, students thus

Alumni Hall, the university's athletic facility and the location of student cafeteria, was opened in 1956 on the Lincoln Park campus.

generally accepted what most agreed was an "office building" environment for college: a vertical campus in a purely functional structure, often lacking in creature comforts. Still, it was certainly a major step up from DePaul's previous downtown location.

These few drawbacks did not place any damper on the social atmosphere within the new facility. On the contrary, most former students described it as a very friendly campus environment. As one noted, students from a variety of backgrounds, and from many different colleges and programs, *"had to live and work together, we mingled in the cafeteria . . . people got to know each other much more so, than today. We rubbed elbows with each other all the time."* Much of the camaraderie and friendliness was attributed to what was perceived as a welcoming and open social milieu where WASP, Jewish, Italian, Irish, Polish, and students of many other ethnic backgrounds, all largely from Chicago's working- and middle-class neighborhoods, came together for an education. Alumni frequently described the cafeteria, especially, as the clearest reflection of this. Student groups, such as fraternities and sororities, each had a particular ethnic and/or religious character, and each had—to turn the familiar saying inside out—"a table at the place." This perception of a diverse and welcoming environment may not have been quite true for all groups: African American students were not very well represented on the downtown campus, and did not form a student organization until the beginning of the following decade. But apparently this was a popular conception of the place at that time.

The move from the north to south Loop did not signify a major change in the already rich extended campus that had, for more than thirty years, existed for downtown students. At the time, the south Loop had not yet experienced the downturn in fortunes that would soon beset it with the advent of suburban shopping malls, the development of North Michigan Avenue commercial competition, and the departure of major businesses and service establishments from that part of downtown.

Students at the new Lewis Center facility still had access to the downtown Public Library, museums, Grant Park, and such cultural institutions as Orchestra Hall, the Civic Opera, and The Chicago Theater. The area was filled with cafes and restaurants, with new names appearing: The Yacht Club, a popular pizzeria on Wabash Avenue near Roosevelt University, and Charlie's, a bar on Jackson, across the street from Lewis Center. When added to other popular places such as Stouffer's Restaurant, Brown's sandwich shop, Mario's Pizzeria, and an array of night spots still functioning in the area, downtown offered a rich extended campus indeed. This included the venues for the many dances that still were held during this period: the Axeman Swing, the Praetorian Ball, The Inter-fraternity Council Ball, The Military Ball, and the many fraternity and sorority dances that filled the social calendar. Added to the traditional venues for such events were such posh hotels such as The Palmer House, The Conrad Hilton, and The Sheraton Hotel.

A lot of the dating that was common at the time involved groups of male and female students doing things together, especially on a Friday night. The city, again, became the extended site for such outings. As it was for students at the Lincoln Park campus, the popular areas were the new "Old Town" area along Wells Street. Other popular restaurants and hang-

DePaul University Lyceum demolition, Lincoln Park campus, July 1987.

outs for college students included Hamilton's near Loyola University, Eduardo's, Uno's and Due's for Chicago style pizza, The East End Restaurant, as well as a host of other places.

Students continued to work either part-time or full-time jobs at local downtown commercial establishments. The Lewis Center students had available to them, as had generations of downtown students before them, the rich opportunities and resources of the downtown business district to augment their financial resources. Karen Stark (COM 1963) described the part-time job market for DePaul students in an interesting way: as an informal, but highly effective network where jobs were often circulated.

> *A lot of people in the Loop environment knew DePaul students . . . and many of those students ended up working full time for the employers that they worked for part time. [But] oftentimes, you passed on your job when you were graduating, if it was a good job. And you respected your employer, and you wanted him to have somebody good. So you would seek out somebody, and say, "Okay, I'm graduating, now, here's the job, you can have it . . . Networking was constant, I worked for a theatrical agency. How did I get the job? Another DePaul student worked there, and they liked DePaul students."*
> (71)

Again, the city of Chicago offered DePaul downtown students an extraordinary array of opportunities that extended their everyday environment. The city augmented, complemented, and filled in social, academic, economic, and cultural gaps in the student's experience in qualitative ways that could not have been possible anywhere but in a large metropolitan setting like Chicago.

Conclusion

The period of "the little university under the El" ended in 1967–68 with the opening of the Arthur J. Schmitt Academic Center (1968), the first student residency hall, Clifton Hall (1970—later renamed Munroe Hall), and the Harold L. Stuart Student Activity Center (1971). These buildings, collectively, marked the beginning of a new era for DePaul University: a thirty-year period in which significant physical and academic changes, growth, and development took place radically transforming the institution into the second largest Catholic university in the United States.

The seventy years leading up to DePaul's most recent transformation were, indeed, marked by its modest physical size and limited physical facilities, and consequent limitations in student and academic services. This did not mean that students necessarily received an inferior education, nor unduly suffered a truncated college experience.

What stood out most clearly in the many interviews conducted with alumni was a "sense of place" and "place attachment" that generally reflected their sincere gratitude to DePaul for the opportunity it gave them to get a college education. The school's physical limitations seldom threatened the "place attachment" most students felt, and were hardly ever seen as anything more than the reality imposed by this private urban institution's meager funds and lean endowments. Yes, terms like "Spartan," "functional," "bare-bones," "basic," were used to describe DePaul, but they were always combined with caveats like " . . . but you came out with a good education and people were successful" or "it's not anything that anybody has to apologize about," or, "you knew what you were getting and you didn't expect anything different." A number of significant factors protected the institution, despite its limited size and facilities, from suffering any serious erosion of confidence, morale, or sense of place attachment.

First, DePaul was, for most of this entire period, a very attainable and affordable entry point to higher education for many first-generation college-age students. Its tuition remained quite affordable for working-class and middle-class students and families throughout the period under discussion. It also had, from the beginning, a very diverse student body for a private Catholic institution, and this brought to its doors not only Catholics, but also students who would not normally have elected for a private education.

Secondly, it was eminently accessible from most points in the city, because of its proximity to the El and other forms of public transportation. The affectionate title "little university under the El" has not always been understood for its multiple implications, but the institution's location helped to sustain it through hard times and good.

A third factor that served as counterweight to the limitations of size, facility, and service was the spirit and sense of common identification and solidarity produced by the intimacy of this small commuter institution. The tight physical spaces, the rubbing of shoulders in hallways, elevators, stairwells, classrooms, and the shared experiences of negotiating school, home, work, and public transportation to and from Chicago neighborhoods and parishes, created greater identification with the institution than is commonly recognized. The physical and structural limitations encouraged interaction and the development of relationships between students. The anonymity usually associated with a commuter student existence and experience was offset by greater familiarity, an environment of personalism and friendliness among students, and an identification with perceived urban and social class commonalities that were felt to exist between them. Membership in student organizations, such as sororities and fraternities, which were more common then, as well as in a variety of college organizations, also served to reinforce such institutional identifications.

Finally, the ability of DePaul students to adapt to the extended campus opportunities offered by the immediate environment of Chicago, the Lincoln Park neighborhood, and the downtown Loop to satisfy social, educational, cultural, and economic needs, offset the many limitations that were noted in the institution itself. The extended campus offered significant support and nurturance for the development of place attachment to DePaul, despite such limitations. The city provided an unusually rich set of alternative and complementary resources to make a student's DePaul years full, interesting, manageable, affordable and satisfying. It is not surprising, therefore, that with nostalgia, pride, and fondness, alumni, through the many decades when DePaul was "the little university under the El," remembered their alma mater.

Chapter Four Notes

Author's Note: *The author wishes to acknowledge funding support for this project from the DePaul University Research Council.*

1. The transcribed interviews with alumni are available in the DePaul University Archive, John T. Richardson Library. They are accessible by the name Centennial Alumni Interviews-Suchar, and the name of the interviewee. The interviews, unless noted otherwise, were conducted by myself.

2. The earliest presence on campus by any of the alumni I interviewed for this essay was 1928. It is for this reason that a quick tour of DePaul from its birth as St. Vincent's College in 1898 to the period around 1928 is in order.

3. Irwin Altman and Setha M. Low, editors, *Place Attachment* (New York and London, 1992) 1–12.

4. David M. Hummon, "Community Attachment" in *Place Attachment*, Altman and Low, eds. 253–278.

5 Information for this preliminary section is largely taken from histories of the early years of DePaul by the Rev. Daniel J. McHugh, C.M. "The Background and First Year" The DePaul University News 1935, and the Very Rev. Michael J. O'Connell's "History of DePaul Buildings", Jan. 15, 1945, and other historical documents. Documents available in the DePaul University Archives, John T. Richardson Library. The document box "Buildings"—Box 1 1875–1909 and Box 2, Accession Numbers 1990.40, 1995.28 contained items particularly helpful in providing information on DePaul's early structures.

6. McHugh, "The Background and First Year," 5.

7. O'Connell, "History of DePaul Buildings," pages unnumbered.

8. Several documents in Box 1: "Byrne Hall 1906–07" by Rev. Patrick Mullins and "Byrne Hall 1907."

9. O'Connell, "History of DePaul Buildings."

10. College Theater, Newspaper clippings, Box 1, "Buildings," DePaul University Archives (DPUA).

11. Documents in file "College Theater 1907—Newspaper clippings," Box 1, "Buildings," DPUA.

12. Documents: "Lyceum Building 1906–07" by Rev. Patrick Mullins and miscellaneous documents in Box 1, "Buildings," DPUA.

13. McHugh, "The Background and First Year," 4–5.

14. Lyceum Building documents in Box 1, "Buildings," DPUA.

15. The *1906–07 DePaul University Bulletin*, Series II No. 1. (Chicago, 1906) 15–16.

16. O'Connell, "History of DePaul Buildings."

17. This applied equally to almost all students until the mid- to late 1970s and the vast majority of students up to the present.

18. DeLeonardis interview, September 1996.

19. Nolan interview, April 1996.

20. Kevin interview (with John Rury) September 1996.

21. Carney interview, July 1996.

22. Schillinger interview, August 1996.

23. Barr interview (with John Rury), July 1996.

24. Radice interview September, 1996.

25. Joyce interview, August 1996.

26. Nolan interview April, 1996.

27. Behof interview, July 1996.

28. Joyce interview, August, 1996.

29. Kevin interview, September 1996.

30. Carney interview, July 1996.

31. Edwin Schillinger returned to DePaul upon receiving his Ph.D. in Physics from Notre Dame to become, eventually, the chair of the physics dept. and dean of the College of Liberal Arts and Sciences.

32. Behof interview, July 1996.

33. Dickman interview, May 1996.

34. Behof interview, July 1996.

35. Nolan interview, April, 1996.

36. Kevin interview, September 1996.

37. Nolan interview April, 1996.

38. Kevin Interview, September 1996.
39. Nolan interview, April 1996.
40. Behof interview, July 1996.
41. Nolan interview, April 1996.
42. 64 E. Lake Building documents, Box 2 "Buildings", DPUA. See documents by Rev. Patrick Mullins.
43. Joyce interview, August 1996.
44. Barr interview, July 1996.
45. Cogan interview [with John Rury], August 1996.
46. Carney interview, July 1996.
47. Valenziano interview, April 1996.
48. Kevin interview, September 1996.
49. Schillinger interview, August 1996.
50. Behof interview, July 1996.
51. Kevin interview, September 1996.
52. Schillinger interview, August 1996.
53. Barr interview, July 1996.
54. Valenziano interview, April 1996.
55. *Ibid.*
56. Barr interview, July 1996; Carney interview, July 1996.
57. Stark interview, August 1996.
58. DeLeonardis interview, September 1996.
59. Behof interview, July 1996.
60. Kevin interview, September 1996.
61. Dickman interview, May 1996.
62. Rettberg interview, August 1996.
63. *Ibid.*
64. Paetsch interview, April 1996.
65. Dickman interview, May 1996.
66. Rettberg interview, August 1996.
67. Valenziano interview, April 1996.
68. Stark interview, August 1996.
69. *Ibid.*
70. *Ibid.*
71. *Ibid.*

CHAPTER FIVE

STUDENT LIFE AND CAMPUS CULTURE AT DEPAUL

A Hundred Year History

John L. Rury

Throughout DePaul's history, its students have contributed to the institution's distinctive character. Since 1898, as the university has changed and the campus has grown, a vibrant student culture has evolved. This was hardly unique to DePaul. In many respects, the university's students have reflected national trends in their activities and interests. But as an urban institution, DePaul's location and programs have affected the character of its students and their activities.

Historically, Chicago has been a city of immigrants, and over the years DePaul has served the city's principal immigrant groups. It has ministered to Chicago's Roman Catholic population, to be sure, but it has also provided educational opportunities for others. As constituents of an urban university, DePaul's students have reflected the diversity and vitality one would expect of a major Chicago institution of higher learning. This is an important part of the university's heritage.

In coming together at DePaul, these students created a distinctive social world of their own that changed over time, often mirroring broader tendencies in student life. Still, certain features of the DePaul student experience were quite durable and helped to define an institutional identity. While in many respects its students were similar to their counterparts at other institutions, there were aspects of life at DePaul that were unique. In part this was simply structural. Campus life at DePaul has long been divided between its downtown and uptown (or Lincoln Park) locations, with each site acquiring its own atmosphere. But there were other factors operating that endowed the two campuses with a common set of traditions and social expectations. One was coeducation, which long made DePaul unique among Catholic institutions. Another was sports, particularly DePaul's identification with basketball. To the extent that it was possible, athletic events and social activities helped to bind the university's diverse student body together. (1)

As noted in other chapters, DePaul expanded rapidly in the years immediately following World War Two, and in the following decade the university became even more diverse as new ethnic and racial minority groups appeared in the student population. During the 1960s students began expressing concern over the major social and political issues of the day. Although DePaul certainly was not a hotbed of student activism, there were occasional signs of unrest as some students protested university policies or responded to such national issues as the Vietnam War. In the years that followed, growing numbers of DePaul's students came from outside of the city. In the 1970s and eighties, as the university built dormitories to accommodate them, the Lincoln Park campus expanded. DePaul diversified yet again, as students from across the country came to study in Chicago. And it became more cosmopolitan also, as the university forged a growing national and international reputation in the 1990s.

In many respects, however, DePaul's student traditions have remained constant through all of these changes. DePaul has continued to be an institution marked by openness, and even in the face of the university's growth it has managed to preserve an element of the intimacy that characterized earlier periods of student life. Much of the university's student body is still made up of adults seeking further professional training. Even these students, however, have managed to create a social life within the institution. If DePaul today is no longer the "little school under the El," and the Greek-letter organizations no longer dominate the campus social life, it is still possible to know a large number of one's classmates and to identify a distinctive DePaul culture in the late twentieth century.

Origins

DePaul's beginnings were modest, and its first students appear to have come from the neighborhoods surrounding its near north side location. From the beginning, DePaul served an urban clientele who attended college for a variety of reasons. It was from this array of constituents that the distinctive student culture of the institution was born. It is important to consider the backgrounds of these students. If DePaul offered an urban and Catholic variant of mainstream American college culture, it was rooted in the lives of the individuals who first came to this particular institution to study.

When Saint Vincent's College was established, the student body was predominantly Catholic, and like the faculty, entirely male. It served students preparing for collegiate studies, most of these in what was called the Academy, and a smaller number of bona fide undergraduates. The largest group, however, was enrolled in the "commercial" course to obtain certification of competence in accounting, record keeping or other business fields. Much of the student population was quite young, at least by today's standards, and probably attended Saint Vincent's for a variety of reasons. Even in the beginning, DePaul students represented a diverse range of interests. (2)

If there was one characteristic that these early DePaul students shared, it was their immigrant backgrounds. The first generation of students at the university consisted largely of the sons and grandsons of Chicago's Irish and German immigrants. An analysis of the backgrounds of students enrolled during the first ten years of the institution's existence reveals that nearly half were from Irish households, while roughly another third were German. The others included representatives of an array of other immigrant groups, including British, Canadians and Italians. Fewer than 8 percent had grandfathers born in the United States. Tables 1 and 2 summarize the statistical profile of the institution's earliest students and show that there can be little doubt that DePaul started as a school for the city's principal Catholic immigrant groups. (3)

The Irish made up the largest group of Catholic immigrants in the city at the turn of the century, and they had long dominated the local Catholic community. The Irish also were native speakers of English, and generally enrolled in college at higher rates than other Catholic

Table 1 *Enrollment in Various Courses of Study, St. Ignatius College and St. Vincent's College, 1897–1909 (averages across the entire period)*

	Academy	*Commercial*	*Collegiate*	*Other*
St. Ignatius	51%	18%	20%	9%
St Vincent's	35%	34%	12%	19%

Note: Figures for St. Ignatius are based on the years 1897 to 1909, while those for St. Vincent's are for the years 1898 to 1903 and 1905 to 1908. The latter should be interpreted as general estimates rather than precise indicators for the period in question. Source: L. Goodchild, "The Mission of the Catholic University in the Midwest, 1842–1980: A Comparative Case Study of the Effects of Strategic Policy Decisions Upon the Mission of the University of Notre Dame, Loyola University of Chicago, and DePaul University" (Unpublished Ph.D. dissertation, University of Chicago, 1986) Volume 1, pp. 191 and 229.

Table 2 *Ethnic Backgrounds of Students Enrolled in Various Curricula at St. Vincent's College, 1898–1908 (grandfather's nativity) From Sample of Students (N=172)*

	College Course	*Commercial Course*	*Academy*	*Other*
Irish	30	24	22	10
German	5	17	15	13
U.S.	4	2	3	6
Other	1	2	1	2

Source: John L. Rury, "The Urban Catholic University in the Early Twentieth Century: A Social Profile of DePaul, 1898–1940" *History of Higher Education Annual* 17 (1997) pp. 6–8.

immigrant groups. It is little wonder, given this, that the Irish were the largest segment of St Vincent's students in the decade following 1898. Though the Germans were also an important immigrant group at this time, even more numerous than the Irish, only a minority of the Germans in Chicago were Catholic. Even so, they represented a considerable presence in the institution. Like the local Church itself, tiny Saint Vincent's was a cross-section of much of the city's immigrant population. (4)

In other respects, however, the backgrounds of this first generation of DePaul students were quite different from the backgrounds of the city's other immigrants. Chicago was an industrial city at this time. The bulk of its immigrant labor force worked in shops and factories, many of them as unskilled or semiskilled laborers. Others were skilled workers or small-scale proprietors, often struggling to make ends meet. Surveys conducted at the start of the twentieth century found that many immigrant families sent their children into the labor force to contribute to household income, or adopted such alternative ways of making money as taking in boarders or performing home-work of various sorts. While the families of DePaul students appear to have utilized some of these strategies, particularly those with no father present, the others represented something of an elite among the city's ethnic population. Two-thirds of these students' fathers held white-collar or proprietary jobs. They included lawyers, merchants, wholesalers, and a wide variety of clerks, contractors, city employees and managers. The rest worked in blue-collar jobs, but only 12 percent were unskilled or semiskilled laborers. This occupational profile was dramatically different from that of the city's larger immigrant community. Furthermore, about two-thirds of the families that sent their sons to Saint Vincent's owned their homes; and this rate was about double that of the city as a whole (this was true of blue-collar student families as well as others). Even if Saint Vincent's students offered a picture of ethnic diversity, as a group they also represented a rather select social stratum of Chicago's Catholics. (5)

Saint Vincent's was not a residential college, and the majority of its early students lived close by. Over half of the students from the first ten classes lived in the three wards adjacent to the school in 1900. Many lived in other north-side neighborhoods and a significant minority came from the wards around the city's center. For the most part, Saint Vincent's was a neighborhood school, although it seems to have attracted some students from a considerable distance as well. Even though its student body consisted of the sons of well-to-do Catholic immigrants, at the beginning DePaul was a local institution, drawing its clientele from Chicago's largely Catholic north side. (6)

Early Student Activities

From the beginning, students at Saint Vincent's engaged in a variety of activities. Athletics were an important element of life at the institution, and the large field behind the college's principal building was emblematic of the significance sports held for the all-male student population of the time. It was here that the various college teams competed with other institutions and where most of the student body played in intramural games. But like other colleges of the time, Saint Vincent's (and DePaul) provided students a range of options for expressing particular interests and abilities away from the classroom.

Saint Vincent's fielded teams in football and baseball, and eventually added basketball as well. While a relatively small number of students participated in these activities, they had great symbolic significance for the entire institution. As was the case at other schools, athletics was seen as an outlet for the school's all-male constituency and as an inducement to young stalwarts to enroll, attracted by the opportunity to compete on the athletic field. The space behind the College's main building and Saint Vincent's Church, a vast playing field, constituted the largest part of its campus at the time. It was here that the institution's various teams practiced and competed against opponents from a wide variety of organizations, including businesses, ethnic clubs and independent athletic groups, as well as other colleges. (7)

DePaul students walking along "The Wall" on Kenmore Avenue, October, 1937, DPU magazine.

It is difficult to gauge the extent to which these events became centerpieces of public attention outside of the college, but they clearly were important within it. Few contemporary reports are available, but storied contests were recalled by later generations of DePaul students and became a part of the institution's lore. Such events included the 1906 and 1907 football games against Notre Dame, one of which DePaul reportedly won, though it lost the other by a narrow margin. In the second decade of the century, college athletics became a focal point of the earliest student journal or newspaper, *The Minerval*, which reported the fortunes of DePaul's teams assiduously. Eventually, the university became a member of an informal network of local and regional institutions, most of them Catholic, competing against one another in various sports. By the twenties traditional rivalries had been established with such schools as Loyola, Saint Viator's College, the University of Detroit and, of course, Notre Dame. The result was a regular schedule of athletic events that provided an altogether new dimension to student life. The various games became a point of pride and identification for the entire university, an affirmation of DePaul's status among peer institutions, and each athletic event became an opportunity for students to gather outside of their normal class routines. In time, athletics became a major feature of student life at DePaul, just as it did at other universities across the country. (8)

There was more to student life than athletics, of course. From the very start students at Saint Vincent's—and later DePaul—engaged in a variety of other activities, ranging from literary societies and science clubs to professional organizations and fraternities and sororities. In the Saint Vincent's College years, such activities appear to have been limited to participation in groups organized for the discussion of literature and other subjects, supervised by the faculty. In this respect Saint Vincent's was similar to other nineteenth-century colleges, where adult guidance of such clubs was commonplace. Given the low numbers enrolled in the college in these years, institutional sponsorship of such activities was probably essential to their vitality. (9)

In later years student activities proliferated as the institution grew and its population became more diverse. The appearance of *The Minerval* in 1912, an outlet for student compositions and short stories, was a critical step in providing students with a forum for the expression of ideas and opinions. At roughly the same time, the first independent student organizations began to appear, fraternities and professional groups for students in law and business. The opening of the College Theater in 1907 provided a stage for campus speakers and theatrical productions (it would later be called the auditorium, gym, or "the barn"). By 1917 the university had established a standing student theater company. At the same time the first general fraternities began to appear on the uptown campus. (10) Even though DePaul was a small institution, and the student body was largely male and constituted entirely of day-student commuters, a limited range of extracurricular activities was available to students. This was a feature of DePaul's social environment that became even more important as the institution expanded in the years ahead.

Years of Growth and Diversification

As noted in earlier chapters, in 1913 DePaul established a second "campus" in offices rented in the Loop for its business education program and a newly acquired law school. As was the case at other urban, denominational schools, enrollments grew quickly at this downtown site, soon surpassing those uptown. The students in these professional programs were different from their counterparts at the uptown location. They often had a more utilitarian view of university study, and many of them were older. The downtown campus developed a somewhat different ethnic profile as well, enrolling a significant population of non-Catholic (mainly Jewish) students. The addition of the downtown programs made the university significantly more diverse. In time, the "downtown campus" acquired its own distinctive identity. For the time being, however, the campus uptown on Webster Avenue remained the center of student culture at DePaul.

Student activities evolved slowly at the uptown campus, and enrollments remained low, despite new programs in engineering and summer courses for teachers. The university's theater was used by the community for the first decade of its existence, although student theatrical productions also were offered on occasion. *The Minerval* apparently served as literary journal and campus newspaper combined until about 1922, ten years after it was founded. DePaul thus offered the essential trappings of collegiate life in these years, but enrollments rarely exceeded two hundred full-time students in the College of Liberal Arts and Sciences. The event that appears to have changed this was the university's decision to admit women as regular students just before the start of the First World War. (11)

DePaul was among the first coeducational Catholic universities in the country. Beginning in 1911, female students attended occasional teacher training institutes, conducted primarily for teachers in the parochial schools—most of whom were members of religious teaching orders. There is also evidence that a small number of women enrolled in the College of Commerce and the law school in this period. Coeducation became a question of university policy, however, in 1916. (12)

Most Catholic educators at this time were opposed to coeducation, but DePaul's Vincentian administration was willing to try it. The first full-time female students were admitted to the College of Arts and Science (LA&S) in the 1916–17 academic year. It was in the wake of these enrollments that university President Francis McCabe, C.M. wrote to Archbishop Mundelein about the idea of establishing coeducation at DePaul. The Archbishop's reply was not favorable, but the university went forward with plans to allow more women to enroll as full-time students. The 1917 catalogue first described the new policy of coeducation. That year six women registered in the college, along with thirteen in law, sixteen in commerce, and more than 200 in the teachers' institutes. Over the next five years the number of full-time LA&S women students grew to 78, or about 40 percent of the total student body uptown. Women were also enrolled in the other colleges, but in smaller numbers. Once the decision was made to admit women as full-time day students, coeducation developed quite rapidly at DePaul. (13)

By the 1920s, DePaul was becoming a complex institution, with two separate and distinct campuses serving a diverse student population. The university began to expand rapidly, exceeding several thousand students by the end of the twenties. Student activities at this time assumed the form familiar at other institutions, with football, fraternities and sororities, dances, yearbooks and other traditional collegiate functions predominating. In many respects this was the "college spirit" era of DePaul's history, and it extended into the early 1930s.

A Diverse Student Body

The university's growth brought greater diversity, but it poses the question of who attended DePaul in the years following World War I. Unfortunately, there are no individual records for later generations of students. But there are sources of information on student backgrounds that suggest what types of students came to DePaul in the 1920s and thirties.

The first university yearbooks appeared in the 1920s, listing the names of seniors (and sometimes other classes) and students involved in various activities. Using a dictionary of names, it is possible to group the surnames into broad ethnic classifications, and to obtain a general picture of the institution's ethnic profile at a particular time. The university collected information on the religious backgrounds of students, beginning in the early 1930s, and it occasionally conducted surveys on the occupations of students' parents and where they lived in the city. It is possible to extrapolate from these data a fairly detailed picture of DePaul's student body in the 1920s and thirties. (14)

DePaul coeds along "The Wall" on Kenmore Avenue in the late 1940s, Lorraine Bond private collection.

To begin with, surnames listed in the yearbooks offer valuable clues about the ethnic composition of the student body. In 1925, for instance, more than half of the seniors in all branches of the university had last names that could be classified as being Irish or English in origin. On the other hand, slightly over one-quarter of the seniors had surnames that could be described as German or Jewish. Roughly 10 percent had surnames that were clearly eastern European (mostly Polish) or Mediterranean (mainly Italian) in origin. Similar patterns appeared in 1930. Last names, of course, are notoriously inexact indicators of ethnic origin. Still, if the broad groupings identified from the yearbooks are generally accurate, it would suggest that the number of DePaul students with Irish backgrounds remained significant, and that the city's German neighborhoods continued to be an important source of students as well. This was a pattern at other Catholic institutions of higher education in the twentieth century, where the Irish also tended to be the dominant group. At that time, there were relatively small numbers of applicants to DePaul from Chicago's other principal Catholic ethnic communities, particularly Poles and Italians; but evidently these groups were not sending large numbers of their sons and daughters to college during that period. The Irish and the Germans continued to be the city's wealthiest and most influential Catholics, and it was their sons and daughters who appeared at DePaul in the largest numbers in these years. (15)

The presence of many surnames identifiable as "English" and "Jewish," raises the question of religious background. In its promotional literature DePaul clearly declared itself open to students of all religious backgrounds, and pointed to the presence of non-Catholic students throughout the university. Like many other institutions, the university grew rapidly in the years following 1920. And there is indeed evidence of a significant non-Catholic minority among DePaul's students at this time. The largest number of these non-Catholic students were Jewish.

DePaul was an urban institution, and like other universities in large cities at this time it attracted Jewish students interested in its professional programs. Data on the religious backgrounds of DePaul students, collected by the university in the 1930s, permit a more precise examination of this issue than the yearbooks. At the Loop campus, for instance, Catholics constituted a majority, but as much as one-quarter of the student body was Jewish. The program with the greatest concentration of non-Catholics was the law school, where Catholics numbered slightly fewer than half the students and Jewish students constituted as many as 40 percent in the mid-thirties. Other schools had fewer Jewish students, although they were still an important minority. In the College of Commerce, nearly three quarters (74 percent) of the day students were Catholic in 1936, while some 15 percent were Jewish. Commerce and law, of course, enrolled the largest numbers of full-time day students at the downtown location. In the Downtown College of Liberal Arts, which chiefly served teachers seeking extra credits and college degrees in evening classes, fully 80 percent of the lay students were Catholic, and only 4 percent were Jewish. But the vast majority of these students attended in the late afternoon or evening and did not participate much in the social life of the school. Among full-time students at the Loop campus, Jewish students may have constituted about 30 percent altogether, the largest proportion of these being enrolled in the law school. (16)

At DePaul's uptown campus, on the other hand, the picture was quite different. There, fully 85 percent of the students in the College of Liberal Arts and Sciences reported their religious affiliation as Catholic. The remainder were about evenly divided between Protestant and Jewish. Analysis of surnames in the 1925 and 1930 yearbooks, moreover, indicates that more than two-thirds of the students uptown had Irish or English surnames. Combined with the information on religious backgrounds, this suggests a good deal of cultural homogeneity on DePaul's Webster Avenue campus. And the vast majority of these students attended full time. Thus it is likely that the ethnic quality of the university's two principal campuses in this period was quite different. If the uptown campus was somewhat Irish Catholic in flavor, there certainly was greater diversity in the Loop.

DePaul students and an unidentified Vincentian priest outside the Liberal Arts Building, circa the late 1940s, Lorraine Bond private collection.

By and large, in that case, it appears that DePaul remained a largely Catholic institution in the years following 1920, but it also educated a sizable group of other students. In the university as a whole, given the figures above, Catholics probably numbered about 70 percent of all full-time students. Jewish students represented a little less than 20 percent, with the largest concentration being at the Loop campus. This means that Protestant students were the smallest group at the university, at least among the full-time students—those most active in student affairs. The patterns of representation were quite different at DePaul's two campuses, as the Jewish presence was certainly most clearly evident in the Loop. But on both campuses, the majority of the university's students continued to be drawn from the city's immigrant communities. Despite the number of apparently "English" last names (or German ones, for that matter) evident in the yearbooks, there were relatively few WASP students at DePaul in these years.

In addition to data on students' religious backgrounds, the university also recorded information on where students lived and other aspects of their social status in the mid-1930s. In fall 1936, the College of Liberal Arts and Sciences asked its freshmen about their fathers' occupations, a strong correlate of social standing. By and large, the results do not appear to have been much different from the occupational profile for the university's very first students. About 80 percent of the students reporting such data indicated that their fathers worked in white-collar occupations of one sort or another. Relatively few, about 7 percent, were employed in traditional professions requiring college-level education. Most of the others were small businessmen, managers, salesmen, clerks or government employees. Only one in five reported that their fathers were blue-collar workers, and a slight majority of these were skilled. As in the labor force at large, the number of blue-collar households represented among DePaul students dropped in the decades following 1900. This trend may have been exacerbated by the Depression, of course. But it also reflected the largely middle-class constituency for institutions such as DePaul. Judging from the data provided by this particular survey, DePaul's uptown campus continued to serve the city's Catholic middle class throughout this period. (17)

If the occupational profile of many DePaul students did not change, however, other things did. Chicago had grown considerably since the turn of the century, and it also possessed a well-developed and complex transportation system. As commuters, DePaul's students were undoubtedly sensitive to questions of the college's location. And there is evidence of this in the geographic distribution of students' homes. Among students at the uptown campus, fully 45 percent came from the north and northwest sides of the city in 1936, the area of closest proximity and the location of Chicago's largest German communities and many Irish neighborhoods as well. For these students, the college's location may well have been an attraction. But this was also a much lower proportion of the university's student body than formerly, when the vast majority of students came from these neighborhoods. By the mid-1930s, another 45 percent of the students uptown came to school from other Chicago neighborhoods, including large contingents from the southeast and southwest sides (over 25 percent combined). These areas represented important and growing Irish Catholic neighborhoods in these years. Another 10 percent came from nearby suburban communities. The majority of DePaul's full-time liberal arts students commuted a considerable distance to attend college. While the university's Webster Avenue location continued to be important for some of DePaul's students, it probably was not an inducement for most of them, apart from its accessibility to public transportation. (18)

In the Loop, proximity was less an issue for most students, since all of the major public transportation lines fed into the downtown area. A student survey there indicates that they came from all parts of the city. In early 1936 some 637 commerce students were more or less evenly divided between five major regions of the city (north, northwest, west, southwest and south). Indeed, the area with the largest absolute number was the city's south side, home to 149 students. This was hardly a traditional source of students for DePaul, and the numbers certainly cannot be attributed to the consequences of proximity to the university. Rather, the geographic distribution of students in the College of Commerce appears to reflect the central location of DePaul's Loop campus, and the well-developed system of public transportation, particularly elevated trains and busses, in Chicago at the time. By the mid 1930s DePaul drew students from all over the city. (19)

Important changes occurred at DePaul between 1900 and 1940. Clearly, it was no longer a neighborhood institution but now served all of Chicago. At the same time the student body became more diverse, although it continued to consist largely of the descendants of recent immigrants. Judging from the data on the occupations of LA&S freshmen's parents, the university also continued to serve a largely middle-class constituency. But the new ethno-religious diversity was significant indeed. While Catholics remained the largest group of students, and the Irish apparently the largest body of Catholics, a sizable number of Jewish students also commuted to the university's downtown campus. Others attended DePaul, but it was undoubtedly these larger groups that dominated the social and cultural life of the university. On the eve of the Second World War DePaul remained an urban institution representing several of the major ethnic groups of its city. Examination of the social and extracurricular activities of its student body is revealing, therefore.

The Collegiate Era at DePaul

The period following 1920 was a time of heady optimism at DePaul, as it was at most other colleges and universities. Enrollments approached six hundred at the uptown campus by mid-decade, and more than a thousand downtown. Despite the fact that all of these students were commuters, telltale signs of collegiate culture began appearing at this time. An array of student organizations emerged at both campuses, along with activities ranging from forums on various topics to homecoming celebrations and a busy annual schedule of dances and other social events. The 1924 yearbook, the first such publication in the university's history, listed more than a dozen student groups. Most of them were fraternities or sororities of one sort or another, but there was also a French Club, a Biology Club, a group called "The Scribes" for future writers, and "the Merrie Club," which aimed to foster "happy relations among women." The number of groups increased in the years that followed, as DePaul's students—like their counterparts elsewhere—became absorbed in the increasingly complex collegiate culture of the day. By the end of the decade, students at DePaul could boast the same assortment of campus activities as college students at larger residential institutions elsewhere in the country. (20)

Then, as now, some college students were more active than others, of course. At DePaul, membership in most organizations appears to have ranged from twenty to forty, with some numbering as few as fifteen and others as many as fifty. In the twenties the most active groups were located on the uptown campus. Judging from activities reported by graduating seniors and recorded in the yearbooks, there was a high level of participation in such organizations. In 1924 and 1925 more than half the graduating seniors reported belonging to at least one organization or participating in a college-sponsored extracurricular activity during their collegiate career. A smaller number, about 15–20 percent, reported taking part in two or more. The latter group no doubt represented the most animated cadre of students in campus activities, and its size corresponds to the most active group of students at other colleges at this time. But DePaul boasted an unusually large number of students involved in at least one activity, especially among urban, nonresidential campuses. In this respect DePaul provided a well-integrated campus experience for its relatively small enrollment of full-time students, or at least for those at the uptown campus. (21)

There were several reasons for this. The uptown students were overwhelmingly Catholic and they all attended the same college, liberal arts and sciences. The Webster Avenue campus was also the location of the university's principal athletic field and its auditorium/gym (in the old theater building), places where many important athletic and social events occurred each year. Significantly, most of the organized student groups were housed on this campus as well. The main office of the *DePaulia*, the student newspaper, was there, as was the editorial office of the yearbook, the *DePaulian*. Given this concentration of resources and enterprises, it is not surprising to discover a high degree of participation in student activities there. One coed wrote in the student newspaper in 1932 that there was greater "zest" at the uptown campus, and more involvement in a variety of extracurricular activities. Remarks such as this were commonplace in these years. (22)

The Webster Avenue campus was also the site of one of the university's most enduring student traditions, an annual competition between freshmen and sophomore males over small green hats the freshmen were expected to wear. This also was a common practice at other institutions. It appears that the institution of a "green beanie" rule at DePaul occurred in the twenties, and when aggressive upperclassmen started to enforce it by "ducking" violators in the nearby Lincoln Park lagoon, a veritable war broke out. To avoid spontaneous fights between members of these classes, university administrators arranged a "rush" to decide whether the freshmen should be required to wear the beanies until homecoming. The first of these occurred in 1928, and for a number of years they were little more than organized brawls, as the sophomores attempted to stop the freshmen from placing a flag atop a pole placed in the athletic field. In the thirties, however, this practice was replaced by a "pushball" contest, in which the two groups vied to propel a giant inflated rubber ball to one side of the field or another. This struggle, usually conducted in mud, continued annually in the early fall for more than forty years at DePaul, long after the beanies and the hazing of freshmen had disappeared.

Although the number of students directly involved was usually fairly small, the pushball contest became an event which reinforced class loyalties and helped stimulate camaraderie. The hazing of first-year students was a long-standing practice at American colleges, dating from the nineteenth century, when most students were men. For DePaul's freshmen, it often served as a way of forging new friendships and relating to upperclassmen in a spirit of good-natured rivalry. And for upper-class students, particularly sophomores, it affirmed a role of helping to introduce first-year students to the norms and social expectations of university life. For many students, particularly the men, it was a potent rite of socialization. And it primarily involved students from the uptown campus. (23)

For students in the College of Liberal Arts and Sciences in the late 1920s, DePaul offered a campus culture that closely resembled that of other American colleges in this period. This collegiate atmosphere was cultivated in spite of the institution's wholly commuter student body. But there was a good deal of cultural homogeneity on the uptown campus. The vast majority of the students were Catholic, most, apparently, of Irish descent. Because non-Catholics were a small minority, the social composition of the student body posed few obstacles to the development of extracurricular student activities.

The social scene at the Loop campus was quite different. There were several colleges downtown, large numbers of part-time students, and a significant group of Jewish students attending the colleges of law and commerce. It was often suggested that downtown students exhibited less "college spirit" than their counterparts uptown. Loop campus students sometimes complained that they were too often left out of extracurricular activities, or that uptown students thought themselves the natural leaders of student activities. Former students remember this clearly. Rita Barr, a commerce student in the thirties and the downtown editor of the student paper, noted that the uptown students "felt they were the university, and we were something put together." (24) Tensions between the two campuses were a constant theme in student commentaries. Yet it is hard to gauge whether important differences distinguished student life at either location.

It is difficult to determine, for instance, the extent to which students from a particular campus were involved in a given activity, even for those housed on one campus or the other. But by using college yearbooks, it is possible to link students enrolled in particular DePaul colleges to various student organizations. Altogether, some 272 students were identified by the yearbook as participating in student activities in 1930 (aside from membership in fraternities or sororities). It is possible to link 217 of these names to students listed under class photos, which indicated the college and class. Interestingly, a clear majority of these students attended colleges on the Loop campus, some 117, or 54 percent. This dispels to some extent the notion that the students who attended the various schools of DePaul in downtown Chicago were not involved in extracurricular activities. Indeed, a higher proportion of Loop students than uptown students participated in more than one activity. But the majority of all DePaul students attended the Loop campus in this period, and the students listed in the various group and activity photos included those attending part time. At the uptown campus, on the other hand, the 100 students identified as participating in such activities represented about one-fifth of the entire student body, a very high level of participation for a single year. Thus, while it is true that many downtown students did engage in various student activities, the degree of such participation was considerably higher at DePaul's Webster Avenue campus. It was there that the collegiate model was most firmly established, and where students had the time and inclination, after all, to pursue the collegiate lifestyle. (25)

The fraternities and sororities, the "Greek" world that flourished at American colleges and universities in this period, constituted yet another important area of student activity. Although there was much variation across the country, historians suggest that as many as half the students at some schools joined such organizations, with participation highest in the east. (26) Judging from the evidence in the 1930 yearbook, the appeal of Greek societies seems to have been just as strong at DePaul as elsewhere. The 1930 yearbook listed more than 450 members of fraternities and sororities on both campuses, in seventeen different organizations (ten fraternities and seven sororities). This was less than one-fifth of all the students at DePaul but it was a much larger fraction of the day or full-time student population. While many fraternities and sororities included evening and part-time students as members, the clear majority were full-time day students. If this were the case, these organizations probably involved about one-third of DePaul's full-time students. This level of participation was comparable to many of the residential campuses other historians have described, and as such it is striking in light of DePaul's wholly commuter student body. For students at this Catholic, urban institution, the period's traditional forms of campus life as embodied in student organizations appear to have been quite alluring.

Some of DePaul's fraternities and sororities were affiliated with national groups and others were exclusive to the institution. Whatever their origin, however, the organization of DePaul Greek societies reflected the peculiar structure of the university. Having developed in an urban setting, these groups did not have houses or property of their own. Some of them rented office space or even apartments, and others used university space for meetings and social events. (27) The Greek organizations were very active in the social life of the university, but most of the social activities they sponsored occurred away from the campus. DePaul was neither large nor generously endowed and space in an urban environment was always at a premium. Student groups made do with whatever resources were available to them.

The fraternity population on the Loop campus was the larger one, undoubtedly because of the predominantly male student body in the colleges of law and commerce. Indeed, it was these colleges that supplied the vast majority of part-time and evening students to the fraternities, along with large numbers of day students. Further, the principal professional fraternities and sororities appeared in the Loop colleges, especially at the law school. Conversely, at the Webster Avenue campus, which had the larger number of full-time women students, there were more sorority members. There was at least one "fraternity" which included both men and women in 1930, and which appears to have spanned the two campuses. But for the most part the organization of Greek life at DePaul was divided quite clearly along gender lines and differentiated by colleges and campuses.

There were yet other ways that the organization of the Greek system may have reflected social distinctions in the university. Historians have noted that fraternities and sororities in this period often engaged in exclusionary behavior along ethnic and religious lines. Jewish students especially were subject to such practices when they began to appear in relatively large numbers on college campuses. At many schools Jewish students were excluded from the Greek world altogether, or they were obliged to form their own organizations. And there is clear evidence of the latter at DePaul in these years. (28)

Many DePaul fraternities and sororities included a mixture of students from a variety of backgrounds, although others seem to have been dominated by students from particular groups. Using the 1925 and 1930 yearbooks in which fraternity and sorority photos list the names of students, it is possible to identify ethnic categories tentatively, based on analysis of surnames, and to draw conjectural conclusions about the ethnic backgrounds of the fraternity and sorority members. It is not surprising that most of the Greek society groups, particularly at DePaul's uptown campus, were headed by students with English or Irish names. Members appear to have been mainly Irish, although there were German, Scotch and Welsh names also. Occasionally there were Polish, Norwegian or Czech names, but these were relatively rare. If there was a dominant group of students in Greek society at this time, its members were the children of English-speaking immigrant groups.

But what about "other" students? The greatest concentration of these students was at the Loop campus, and it is there that they were most evident in DePaul's Greek system. Jewish students made up the largest group of non-Catholics, and they were especially active in the law school. DePaul had a number of law fraternities and at least two legal sororities between

1925 and 1930. Among the three major law fraternities in 1925, there was considerable variation in membership. One was composed almost entirely of students with Irish and English names. A second fraternity was populated largely by students with names which were Jewish in origin. The third law fraternity in 1925 had a mixture of Jewish, English and German names, but included no Irish names. In the law school, with its large Jewish enrollment, there was a clear pattern of ethnic affiliation with particular Greek organizations, especially for Irish and Jewish students. These patterns continued to be evident in the 1930 yearbook. Although the names of the fraternities had changed, there were still organizations dominated by Irish and Jewish students. In some respects the severity of the ethnic segregation had diminished, as each fraternity included at least several members of the formerly excluded group. And the third fraternity counted almost equal numbers of Irish/English and German/Jewish students in its membership.

It is difficult to say just why this manner of fraternity organization existed. There is no mention of these issues in student publications or university documents. Interviews with former students reveal little conflict between students from different ethnic backgrounds. Bud Kevin, an Irish student who attended the law school briefly in the late 1930s, recalled that he and others were aware of the different ethnic profiles of the two campuses. "There used to be a joke," he said, "that when came the (Jewish) holidays, the law school would be half empty." Kevin did remember "teasing" the Jewish students but said it was done in good fun and without animosity. Other students who attended the Loop campus during these years were also aware of diversity in the student body, but it was not an issue they remember as being important at the time. (29)

Separate fraternities might have been formed to compensate for hidden discrimination against Jewish students, but they might also have reflected a desire on the part of those students to belong to an organization that was sympathetic to their religious and cultural heritage. The fact that so few Jewish students were members of fraternities with predominantly Irish memberships may indicate the existence of subtle tensions between these groups. There can be little doubt that DePaul students were aware of their differing ethnic identities. Thomas Joyce, a student born in Ireland who first enrolled in the College of Liberal Arts and Sciences in 1928, became a member of an all-Irish social club and recalled similar Jewish organizations in the law school when he was a student there in the early thirties. But he did not remember conflict between these groups, either. (30)

If ethnic competition existed at DePaul, it did not surface in other observable ways. Jewish students were involved in a variety of student activities and organizations, albeit in somewhat smaller numbers than others, particularly the Irish. In 1925 a student with a Jewish name was one of four leaders elected to the university's Student Council, and in 1930 a Jewish student, the head of a law fraternity, served as president of the Student Activity Council. (31) Clearly, some Jewish students were prominent participants in student activities. But there also may have been a subtle practice of exclusion, which kept Jewish students out of certain orga-nizations and activities (very few Jewish women were involved in sororities or other student groups). If this were the case, DePaul was similar to most other colleges in this period. This may have been simply one more way in which the student experiences at this Catholic, urban institution mirrored those of students elsewhere.

By the 1920s, the elements of a fully developed campus culture were beginning to appear at DePaul, particularly at the Webster Avenue campus. DePaul was still a small institution: its two campuses together had fewer than fifteen hundred full-time students; somewhat more than two thousand were enrolled part time in one program or another. Still, large segments of the student body were quite absorbed in various aspects of college life, exhibiting a degree of involvement in campus activities comparable to many residential schools in this period. This may be explained partly by the emergence of collegiate athletics as a point of interest and identification for students across the institution, as well as by the development of fraternities, sororities, professional groups and other organizations. Traditions such as freshman hazing and the rush and pushball contests helped as well. But there may have been other factors besides. One of these was the unusual policy of coeducation instituted at DePaul during these years. In mixing young Catholic men and women together, the university may have unwit-tingly created the conditions for an unusually high level of campus social activity.

Coeducation and the Social Scene

While the "spirit" phase of student life at DePaul faded with the demise of football (in the late 1930s) and the activities that went with it, a host of other functions sustained a vital campus culture. At the center of student life was a well-attended series of dances and other social events that took place throughout the school year, providing opportunities for dating and other forms of collegiate conviviality. Fraternities and sororities flourished in this atmosphere, and students from both campuses participated in similar activities. All of this helped to define a distinctive and closely knit student culture for several decades after the mid-thirties.

The key to the social life of most DePaul students was the university's policy of coeduca-tion. This, of course, was quite unusual for Catholic universities at the time. DePaul was the only large commuter school on Chicago's north side with a coeducational student population. By the late 1920s and into the thirties, between 30 and 40 percent of the students on the Webster Avenue campus were women. On the Loop campus there were some women in com-merce and a small but consistent presence in the law school as well. The establishment in 1922 of a "Shorthand School" within the College of Commerce boosted the number of women on the Loop campus considerably, even though they generally did not take classes with stu-dents in other departments. When programs in music and theater were added in the twenties, they also attracted a significant number of female students. Almost 70 percent of the students in the Downtown College of Liberal Arts, which served mainly teachers in evening classes,

DePaul students organizing donated canned food for distribution to the needy, circa late 1940s

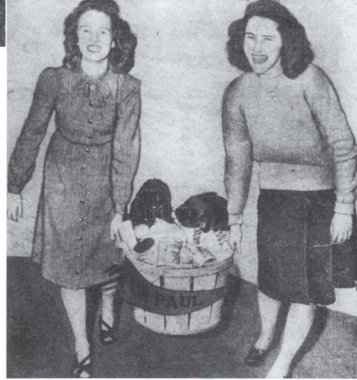

were women. By the 1930s, in that case, DePaul may very well have been the most thoroughly coeducational Catholic university in the country. (32)

For many students, enrollment at DePaul represented more than simply an opportunity for collegiate instruction; it also afforded the unique prospect of a social life in a coeducational environment. Like coeducation itself, the new milieu took time to develop. But the eventual result was a busy calendar of social events that involved a significant portion of the student body. Dances, the most important of these events, were held with great regularity and became very significant in the social scene. With attendance at athletic events also involving large numbers of students, DePaul offered its largely Catholic, second- or third-generation immigrant students a vibrant collegiate social life.

In this respect DePaul was also similar to many other colleges and universities around the country. Historians have noted that a new atmosphere of playful sexuality and potential romance began to permeate college life in the 1920s. (33) This was no less true at DePaul's Webster Avenue campus than in such college towns as Bloomington and Ann Arbor. Although DePaul's campuses were not large and offered few places for undergraduates to congregate, certain scenes became invested with meaning for young men and women. Referring to the sidewalk on the east side of Kenmore Avenue, along "the wall" surrounding the university athletic field, the 1932 yearbook noted that it was "a contrast to the formal promenade" but nevertheless a "practice course where the eds and coeds stroll to luncheon." In the context of the new coeducational college, even the most mundane daily routines assumed amorous overtones. (34)

Central to most of these concerns was a social custom just beginning to emerge as a significant institution among American youth: the date. At coeducational DePaul, dating became a nearly ubiquitous form of interaction between students. This was not unusual, of course, at least at larger nondenominational residential institutions: historians have noted that dating became a widespread practice in these years. But it might have been particularly important at DePaul. Social functions there gave young, middle-class Catholic men and women the opportunity to explore a selective marketplace for potential future partners. The social events also offered a place at which to entertain prospects from outside the university, no doubt contributing to the vitality of the school's social life. (35)

The custom of arranging dates between young men and women at DePaul seems to have evolved gradually, and certainly was not a corollary to coeducation in the eyes of the university's administration. In the twenties most student social activities revolved around the intercollegiate athletic schedule, and events such as the homecoming football game and various booster affairs were high points on the social calendar. There were also May "Carnivals" in the spring and other university-wide events scheduled throughout the year. Yet there can be little doubt that there was a high level of student interest in campus activities staged in conjunction with athletic events, particularly football.

At first there was little sign that student social life would revolve around events designed specifically to bring young men and women together. (36) While there were other alternatives to the athletic schedule, the most popular were dancing and related activities, which induced young men and women to assemble in an implicitly sexual context. Dating was still a controversial topic in the twenties, and DePaul, of course, was a Catholic institution under the supervision of Vincentian fathers. In 1928 the *DePaulia* ran an editorial titled "Should Coeds Date," which argued that it was "the question that today faces every college student in the United States." Noting the potential loss of study time and the distractions dating might present, the editorial also declared that "not to date means a loss of friends and recreation." Given these dire possibilities, the paper advised that coeds should indeed date, "wisely and in moderation," to round out their education. The appearance of this editorial undoubtedly signaled the openness of university administrators to the idea of dating, which, after all, was a growing practice on campuses across the country. Even at Catholic universities, it appears, the new collegiate interest in romance and sexuality could not be denied altogether. In fact, it was a notion that the men and women at DePaul were quite ready to receive. (37)

In DePaul's coeducational setting there were ample opportunities for young men and women to develop interests in one another. The classes were not large, so students quickly came to know each other, and romantic liaisons often resulted. There was evidence of this shortly after coeducation was instituted. In 1921 the student paper noted the work of "Daniel Cupid" at the Lincoln Park campus, and suggested that "he is shooting sure and straight," with several "bulls eyes to his credit . . . and the most appreciative audience you ever heard of." With time the interest in romantic affairs grew more widespread. In 1924 a *DePaulia* editorial lamented the growing interest in social events, worrying that it would prove a distraction from studies and a drain on "school spirit." This was a theme often revisited, and there was little doubt about the nature of these distractions. But eventually student journalists accepted this facet of college life, and even celebrated it. In 1928 another editorial made joking reference to the "universal art of whispering 'sweet little nothings into shell pink ears'" that preoccupied college men as Valentine's Day approached. (38) In time the culture of dating, organized around most student activities but particularly the dances, became a cardinal feature of the collegiate lifestyle at DePaul.

Coeducation made this dimension of college life easier to achieve at DePaul than at all-male Catholic universities (such as local rival Loyola). The advantages of coeducation for the university's social life were routinely acknowledged in student publications. Indeed, while there was a growing debate about coeducation elsewhere in Catholic educational circles at this time, it was barely evident at DePaul. And when the question did arise, support for coeducation was downright enthusiastic. *DePaulia* editorials occasionally deplored the backward thinking on other Catholic campuses, and the paper disapprovingly reprinted articles from Catholic college newspapers in which coeducation was ridiculed. For students and the administration alike, the policy of coeducation at DePaul was worn as a badge of honor, a sign of the university's forward thinking and its enlightened campus atmosphere. (39)

This celebration of coeducation does not mean that tensions did not exist, however, and they were most evident with respect to the question of dating. In 1928 a coed complained in the *DePaulia* that DePaul men too often preferred to bring other women to dances and other social events, leaving the college women without dates. In the same issue another declared that "even if the boys do not care to ask the DePaul girls to a dance they might at least notice them at dances." Other women complained about the "cliquishness" and "coldness" of other students, problems that may have been aggravated by the growth of Greek societies at this time. For their part, the men countered that college women were too demanding when asked for dates, and that entertaining them was expensive. "Too many fellows have to work for all the money they have," one wrote in response, "why go into debt just to please some coed who will probably tell her friends that the fellow is afraid to go places and do things?"

But the women, it appears, had the last word. In 1930 another coed noted the complaints that the men did not ask college women on dates but suggested that their motives were not pecuniary. "We can see, where, in some instances," she declared, "college men flatter themselves by displaying the little education they have for the benefit of the less educated shop girl, ribbon counter clerk, or what have you." College women, she felt, need not worry about men who were challenged by female intellectual abilities. To such men she wrote: "you are merely incidentals in the coed's day, a diversion in an otherwise tedious world of books." (40)

Such banter revealed some of the underlying potential for misunderstanding and conflict that accompanied coeducation and the rise of the dating system. But it also pointed to the importance these questions held for most undergraduates. Dating was becoming more widespread at the same time as the expansion of the Greek system, and it inevitably became tied to questions of social standing in particular college circles. As other historians have noted, membership in certain groups, the friends one associated with, and the choice of dates one made all became measures of social status in the relatively cloistered world of undergraduates.

This was no less true at DePaul than elsewhere. One female correspondent to the *DePaulia* complained about male "big shots" who were appealing and "nice," but who devoted attention to "only the most popular coeds." "You can just imagine," she wrote, "their embarrassment if they were seen at any (social) affairs with one of the hoi polloi." The problem, she believed, was that becoming popular meant having money and "being cut from the same exact pattern as Miss Everybody." Even at an urban, Catholic university, it appears, undergraduates established a system of social status that defined success in terms quite similar to those at larger nonsectarian residential campuses across the country. At a smaller institution there also were considerable pressures to conform to the norms established by one's peers. The emergence of a distinctive adolescent society—which other scholars have suggested accompanied the rise of the dating system—was very much in evidence at DePaul. (41)

The Dance Era

At the center of this new collegiate world were the dances, and they eventually became the most popular feature of student life at DePaul. Dancing had become a favored activity for urban youth some years earlier and quickly caught on at other campuses in this period. In the late twenties an annual schedule of university-wide dance events developed and provided a structure around which other such social events were organized by particular groups. Highlights of the fall schedule were the DePaulia Dance, a fund-raiser for the student newspaper, and Homecoming. Winter brought the Frosh-Soph Cotillion, and Spring the Junior Prom and the Senior Ball. In between these events were other dances, such as the annual Halloween Dance, the Saint Valentine's Day Dance and the All-DePaul Dance, each traditionally held at the university's auditorium. These were major events on the university's social calendar and drew participants from both campuses.

In addition to these university-wide dances, specific Greek organizations and other groups held social events, sometimes to raise money, other times just to provide an opportunity to dance and mingle. Most of these dances appealed to groups on one campus or the other, although some of them attracted a broader constituency. It is not surprising that scheduling conflicts often arose. Indeed, many of the rules the university promulgated to govern the Greek societies (through the Inter-Fraternity and Inter-Sorority Councils) were intended to regulate the scheduling of dances and other social events to prevent such conflicts. As if this were not enough, the student government (or "Activities Council") occasionally sponsored afternoon dances, just to provide a time for students to relax. All told, this made for a robust social scene at an institution as small as DePaul.

Though the dance era in DePaul's campus culture developed gradually, it was already evident in the early twenties. At the outset, some students apparently worried that the popular preoccupation with dances was hurting other student activities or proving a drain on "school spirit." In a 1924 editorial that may have reflected concerns of the Vincentian fathers, the *DePaulia* called for greater involvement in such traditional student activities as literary societies, drama clubs and athletic events. "While we have been planning dances, we have neglected these organizations," the editorial declared. Wondering whether the university was appealing to students' "baser natures," it asked, "is a college considered seriously by those who really want an education because of its social calendar alone?" In time the question was moot, however, and even the Vincentians appear to have accepted the importance of the dances, along with dating, as vital elements of the new collegiate culture that emerged in the 1920s. Despite its student body of commuters divided between two campuses, dances at DePaul were for everyone and provided a social event to look forward to in the immediate future. They became a highlight of social life for DePaul's Chicago college students. (42)

Dancing necessarily involved both young men and women, and thus was well suited to the rise of dating as an accepted form of behavior. Indeed, the regularity of scheduled dances at many colleges in these years undoubtedly contributed to what historian John Modell has described as the development of the date as a distinctive adolescent institution. Some of the dances were formal and required elaborate preparation. Marie Cogan referred to these as "date dances." Fran Armstrong, a student at the uptown campus in the late thirties, recalled "going to a lot of trouble, getting a formal for this dance and that dance." Even though there were fewer women at the Loop campus, much of the social life revolved around the dances there also. Rita Barr, attending school in the Loop, remembered that "all the dances seemed to be formal, and there was always a rack of formals in the house." Most of the these affairs were held in hotels around the city, usually downtown or on the north side, but sometimes elsewhere as well. Bud Kevin recalled the glass floor at the grand ballroom of the Knickerbocker Hotel, one of the more popular venues. Rita Barr echoed the sentiments of other former students when she declared the formal dance a "big deal," and "held at a big hotel." These were occasions that loomed large in the lives of many DePaul students. (44)

Many of the dances were informal too, and these often drew the largest crowds. It was not unusual in the late twenties for the Halloween or Valentines "gym" dances to draw as many as a thousand students and visitors, a very large proportion of the full-time student body at the time, perhaps 70 percent. These dances were often viewed as informal get-togethers rather than dating affairs, a venue for meeting other students and enjoying the company of friends. Thomas Joyce remembered the gym dances, and the "very beautiful girls" in attendance. These gatherings were also places to meet potential dating partners and initiate fresh romantic liaisons. It is little wonder, therefore, that these informal university-wide dances drew the biggest attendance. Though other dances, especially formals, also attracted large crowds, they rarely drew more than four or five hundred. More typically, the Frosh-Soph Cotillion or the Senior Ball numbered 200–300 participants, also a very large proportion of the class groups. Even a dance with four hundred represented a significant portion of DePaul's total student body. (45)

It is impossible to tell where the participants in these various functions came from. If DePaul men dated mainly DePaul women, students from the uptown campus—where more coeds were available—may have outnumbered those from the Loop. Ethnic, religious and other cultural factors may have played a role as well. It is a question whether many of the university's Jewish students participated in the various social functions. While it is clear that some did, it seems unlikely that their rate of participation was as high as it was for other groups, particularly the Irish. Concentrated in the university's principal professional schools, with largely male student bodies, and often isolated in separate Greek organizations, the Jewish students may not have experienced the emerging collegiate dating culture quite as intensively as DePaul's Irish Catholic students.

DePaul's whirlwind social calendar apparently slowed but certainly did not stop in the 1930s as the Depression reduced enrollments and left students with less money to spend on their social lives. Enrollments at the Lincoln Park campus fell by nearly 50 percent between 1928 and 1936. Judging by attendance, interest in athletic events had also dropped conspicuously by the mid-thirties. Like many other urban Catholic institutions, the university discontinued its football program in 1938. At the same time, participation in dances of all sorts fell only slightly, though the number of dances diminished a little too. In 1935, after attendance at football games had started to fall, a crowd of more than five hundred attended the Junior Prom, the largest to date. Other university-wide formal events continued to draw big throngs and informal dances were still held in the gym and at the downtown campus, but attendance of more than a thousand was a thing of the past. The dances continued to be held regularly, however, and former students remember one "almost every weekend." Although the numbers reported attending dances continued to fluctuate from one event to another, there continued to be a very high level of student participation in such activities. (46)

Dating, which was essential for dances to succeed, particularly the important formal ones, was a nearly universal activity by the end of the thirties. In a survey of uptown students in 1939 the *DePaulia* reported that most dated on a regular basis. The fact that men outnumbered women may have accounted for differences in dating patterns. Men averaged one date per week, with some ("a few") having as many as three. Women, on the other hand, averaged

Formal dance in a hotel, circa 1950s.

Semiformal dance in "The Barn," circa 1950.

Students dance in the 1950s. Note integrated crowd.

Semiformal dance, 1940s.

Everyone is having a good time at the Inter-fraternity dance in 1951.

two dates per week, "with many of them having as many as four." Women on the Loop campus, where there was a greater disparity in male-female enrollments, had an even greater advantage. Marie Cogan, an accounting major in the mid-thirties, noted that there were many potential dates to choose from. Significantly, Saturday was reportedly the favorite date night for both groups in the *DePaulia* survey. This meant that many—perhaps most—of the dates probably occurred away from the campus. In this respect the university functioned as something of a dating exchange for young men and women, offering opportunities to find a partner for a longer-term relationship. DePaul was not unusual in this regard, and most coed residential schools probably served a similar function at this time. It was uncommon, however, for an urban Catholic institution to fill this role, as most Catholic high schools and colleges were not coeducational. (47)

The date, of course, also presented an opportunity to test the degree to which a couple were compatible and enjoyed one another's company. A large number of DePaul students married fellow students. Fran Armstrong noted that her own children "thought you always married who you went to school with, because so many of our friends from DePaul married other students from DePaul." Thomas Joyce made a similar observation, and Bernard Carey, a student at the Loop campus in the late thirties, noted the same phenomenon downtown. In this respect, the university also served as something of an informal marriage market for children of the city's Catholic middle class. (48)

The fact that young men and women attended classes together, participated in the various student activities and had a busy schedule of dances made dating quite commonplace at DePaul. And this helped to put questions of romance and implied sexuality at the very center of students' lives. Even though DePaul was a commuter school, its students experienced a very rich social life. Like students at other institutions, many of their activities revolved around meeting and spending time with members of the opposite sex. The campus was small—indeed, downtown it was just one building—but for the young men and women attending DePaul, the city was the setting in which they pursued their social lives. And this tradition changed little in the decades that followed.

The Second World War and Beyond

The social system that had evolved at DePaul by the 1930s remained largely intact for the next several decades. Some changes occurred, but fraternities and sororities continued to constitute the center of much campus life, and dating and dancing remained very popular. After the university discontinued its football program, the arrival of Ray Meyer as the men's basketball coach in the early forties marked the start of big-time collegiate basketball at DePaul. Meyer's teams experienced almost immediate success, and basketball games soon became important social events for students at both campuses. (49) Following a brief hiatus during the war, the annual cycle of dances, parties and other social occasions resumed in the late 1940s and changed little in the years that followed. For many DePaul students, the forties and fifties were a time characterized by well-established campus traditions that continued to provide DePaul with its own special brand of collegiate culture.

As noted in other chapters, the university grew substantially in the years following the war, and its student body became even more diverse. Returning war veterans made up the biggest immediate source of new students. With tuition benefits provided by the government under the G.I. Bill, adult veteran students swelled the enrollments of colleges and universities across the country. At DePaul, however, the influx was unusually large, and within a few years the university's enrollment more than doubled, to nearly ten thousand students. The largest number of these students enrolled in the College of Commerce at the Loop campus, but enrollments increased significantly uptown also. (50)

The veterans at DePaul, as at other institutions, were unusually serious students. Nationally, adult student veterans received higher grades than traditional college students and were less interested in extracurricular activities. At DePaul the veterans were especially concerned with getting a practical education that could be helpful in securing a job or a higher salary. Nick DeLeonardis, who attended the College of Commerce in the late forties, remembered the veterans adding a degree of seriousness to his classes. "I think the professors had to change," he recalled, to a "less theoretical, perhaps more practical process in their approaches." Historians have made the same observation about veterans at other campuses.

Because space was at a premium on DePaul's campuses, particularly downtown, veterans crowded into small classrooms; some reportedly even attended classes held in hallways. But these older students did not mind. Jerry Radice, a veteran who enrolled DePaul during those years, recalled that "all we were concerned about was learning and putting our energies, thoughts and minds to do what we had to do, to get a degree, to learn." By and large, these students did not partake of the rich campus culture that had evolved at DePaul over the preceding decades. They added a practical, mature note to life at the university, and left the extracurricular activities to the new generation of college-age students then beginning to appear on campus. (51)

Even though the number of students at DePaul fell gradually over the following decade as the veterans left, the postwar period marked a new era of prosperity for the university. It was a time when more young people wanted to attend college, and a wider cross-section of families could aspire to send their sons and daughters to DePaul. The university became even more culturally diverse as a consequence, and new wrinkles began to appear in its rather secure and well defined campus culture.

With expansion, the composition of the student body began to change in subtle ways. The largest single group of students continued to be those from Irish backgrounds, but growing numbers of students from Chicago's other large Catholic immigrant groups began to appear as well. An analysis of graduates in the mid-1950s reveals that more than 20 percent of students at the uptown campus had names that were identifiably Italian or Polish, groups that had not been well represented at DePaul in the prewar years. Ten years later, the number of Poles and Italians combined had increased and constituted nearly one-third of the graduates in the College of Liberal Arts and Sciences. Jewish students continued to be a significant group also, particularly on the Loop campus, where they made up as much as one-third of the student population in commerce and in law. Ethnic differences in the backgrounds of students at DePaul's two campuses continued to be a facet of university life. But new groups of students began appearing at both campuses in the postwar years, suggesting that greater access to higher education was leading to a more representative student body for institutions such as DePaul. (52)

African American students, who also began to attend DePaul in sizable numbers in the forties and fifties, represented one such group. As Albert Erlebacher has pointed out in Chapter 6, DePaul did not always welcome Black students, but university policies to discourage Black enrollment were dropped in the postwar period, and as the university expanded, it grew more racially diverse.

DePaul was one of many colleges and universities that experienced an increase in African American enrollments following World War Two, as veterans came to campus. In fall 1949, the university conducted a survey of its various schools and colleges to determine the number of Black students. Well over 100, the largest number, were enrolled in the evening graduate

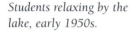

Students relaxing by the lake, early 1950s.

school (serving mainly teachers) and the College of Commerce. These schools were located in the Loop and served many of the university's student veterans. In the College of Liberal Arts and Sciences uptown, which enrolled primarily younger students, there were just 28 African Americans out of a total enrollment that approached one thousand. Black students were a small minority at DePaul, and many were adult veterans enrolled at the university's Lake Street campus. Still, their numbers were increasing. Three years later, in 1952, the university reported nearly three hundred African American students, all but 34 of whom attended school in the Loop. Again, the bulk of these students were adult veterans, most of them men, attending class in the evening. (53)

Although they were not prominent participants in campus social life, there is evidence that African American students were welcomed by many staff members and students in these years. This was the beginning of the civil rights era, and some Black students were self-conscious about being among the first generation of African Americans to attend predominantly white colleges. In 1948 Bernice DePass, a recent graduate of the College of Liberal Arts and Sciences, wrote to President O'Malley to thank DePaul for helping her finish college. Hinting that not all white students were supportive, she described some Catholic students as being "more conscious of their race than their religion." But the campus mood regarding race and civil rights was decidedly liberal, at least uptown. Support for the sentiment, if not necessarily the substance of civil rights reform, was evident in the *DePaulia*, as it ran articles highlighting Black athletes in the mid-1950s. The *DePaulia* also condemned racist attacks on a Black family in Cicero, and editorialized about the need for greater support for racial integration, suggesting that integrated athletics was an important step in the struggle against segregation and discrimination. As hopeful as these signs were, however, they did not address the possibility that African American students might confront discrimination at DePaul itself. This issue emerged forcefully in the following decade. (54)

In spite of this new level of diversity, many features of student life at DePaul remained unchanged during the postwar years. Established campus rituals, such as freshman beanies and the annual pushball contest, remained as vital as ever. Fraternity and sorority membership remained substantial, even though it had declined in proportion to the entire student body. In 1955 there were some 363 members of Greek organizations and honor societies pictured in the yearbook, slightly fewer than in the 1930s. This may have been due in part to the influx of veterans, many of whom cared little for campus activities and student organizations. But the fraternities and sororities provided an ongoing stream of campus-related activities that formed the core of college social life for a significant segment of the student body, and membership in Greek organizations grew in the years that followed. Fraternities and sororities were the largest organizers of dances and other social events that brought young men and women together in potentially romantic circumstances. They also provided a point of day-to-day contact and camaraderie that helped to personalize and enliven the collegiate experiences of

DePaul's commuter student body. For many students during these years, the Greek societies remained at the very center of DePaul's culture at both campuses. (55)

Like DePaul itself, student organizations—Greek and otherwise—continued to be distinguishable by campus and clientele. As in earlier years, the law and business societies were on the Loop campus and most of the purely social organizations were uptown, although there also were groups with members on both campuses. There continued to be evidence of some ethnic differences in the composition of student groups. In the 1950s Alpha Phi Delta, a national Italian fraternity, appeared at DePaul. And as in earlier years, there were a number of organizations with few or no Jewish members, and at least one with a predominantly Jewish membership. Relatively few African American students were pictured in yearbook photos of student groups, although there were a number of organizations with one or two Black members. Even though there was a substantial number of Black students at DePaul in the 1950s, there is relatively little evidence of African American participation in many student activities at the time. As was the case at many other predominantly White institutions in this period, African American students generally were not included in the mainstream campus culture. (56)

As in earlier years, the principal activity of fraternities and sororities at DePaul involved arranging dances and other social events. Jack Dickman, the social director of a fraternity in the late fifties, noted that dance admission fees were the Greek organizations' principal source of income at this time. These events were staged at hotels downtown or elsewhere in the city, just as they were in the 1930s. Each organization had a preferred location for much of the period. For Dickman's fraternity it was the Belden Stratford Hotel. Carol Nolan, who graduated in 1954, recalls that her sorority always held its dances, teas and receptions at the Edgewater Beach Hotel. The business of arranging these events was complicated, yet for the cadre of dedicated organizers it was valuable experience for the real world of commerce. It was also a source of great enjoyment, and for many DePaul students in the 1950s these dances and other organized affairs were among the principal features of collegiate culture. (57)

Dating continued to be a focal point of student life in the postwar era, and at DePaul there were numerous occasions for young men and women to get together. Formal dances required dates, of course, but students also made dating opportunities out of a number of other social events. One was DePaul's continuing tradition of Friday night dances in the university auditorium, popularly known as "the barn" by this time. When Alumni Hall was built in the mid-fifties, the old auditorium became the site of a variety of activities, but to most students it was known primarily as a setting for informal dances and other social get-togethers. Going to DePaul basketball games, either at Alumni Hall or the Chicago Stadium, was another popular social event for students from both campuses. Games held at the Stadium were considered especially important, as DePaul was often paired with a nationally recognized opponent in a double header featuring either Loyola or Northwestern. Attending such a game was

A car, particulary a convertible, was a sign of status, and a cause for celebration, early 1950s.

an exciting way to share in school spirit and go "out" with other students at the same time. Public events such as these provided ideal vehicles for young men and women to enjoy one another's company, whether watching a sports event together or informally dancing and having fun with friends. And because these occasions happened so frequently, dating was often a weekly event. (58)

For some students, of course, dating led directly to romance and eventually to marriage. This tradition began in the 1920s and 30s, but there were new wrinkles to dating in the 1950s. One was the heightened possibility of forming long-term dating partnerships. "Steady" dating partners formed relationships that were recognized and upheld in student circles, often wearing pins or rings to signify commitment to one another. Such bonds became quite commonplace in the fifties, and represented a new step in the dating culture of American youth. At DePaul as elsewhere, the collegiate social scene was particularly important to the development of such relationships. Mutual commitments required some measure of public recognition, after all, and Greek societies often provided pins, rings and other symbols of membership used to signify these bonds. "Pinned" partners were expected to attend social events together and provided a measure of stability or predictability to the collegiate social world. As a preparation for marriage, these relationships often helped to cultivate greater maturity in college students. And their ubiquity helped to sustain DePaul's reputation as a school where young Catholic men and women (and non-Catholics too) could find a mate for life. (59)

Despite its growth, DePaul continued to be a small school serving a wholly commuter student body. With roughly one thousand students on the uptown campus through the 1950s, it continued to be a place where friendships were made easily and students could become as involved in social activities as they wanted. The vast majority of uptown students were from the city, although a growing minority came from neighboring suburbs, and more than 80 percent were Catholic. The annual cycle of social events instituted in the twenties and thirties continued, including the fervent pushball competition between freshmen and upperclassmen. At the downtown campus the atmosphere was a bit more cosmopolitan, and there were large numbers of adult students seeking professional certification of one sort or another. Located in the newly acquired Kimball Building by the late 1950s, the Loop campus was also divided between four separate colleges which shared few faculty members or facilities. But even there it was possible to make acquaintances and become involved in the school's social life. On both campuses DePaul remained an institution characterized by a high degree of familiarity among students and staff, and for the most part this extended to the peculiar student culture that had evolved over the preceding three decades. It was an urban variant of the collegiate culture existing on other American campuses at this time. But it also was distinctively Chicago's and DePaul's.

DePaul Students in the Sixties

Like their counterparts at other institutions, DePaul's students changed in the 1960s. Some of these changes were subtle and others were dramatic, but altogether the decade was a watershed in the history of the peculiar campus culture that had been developing at DePaul since the 1920s. Participation in dances and other traditional student activities dropped later in the decade, and new interests found expression in issues ranging from civil rights and the emerging youth culture to political activism. Student strikes and demonstrations in the late 1960s and early seventies marked a new era in student life at DePaul, one that, in some respects, has continued into the present.

The decade of the sixties brought a new generation of students to DePaul and other colleges and universities. These were young men and women born in the postwar era, for whom attendance at college or university was less a privilege than a certainty. Theirs was a generation that confronted racial injustice and protested American military involvement abroad. Even if only a vocal minority expressed these sentiments forcefully in public, the majority of American students shared their views. (60) This was also true at DePaul, although the university's peculiar dual campus structure highlighted deep divisions in the student body. As DePaul's students became more politically liberal and were increasingly concerned with events and issues off the campus, the traditional elements of student culture began to fade in significance, especially in the uptown colleges. By the mid-1970s the transition was complete, and a new campus ethos of liberal individualism had supplanted the older collegiate culture of fraterni-

Membership of the Black Student Union, 1968

ties and sororities, dancing and dating. Gone too was the old system of ethnic differentiation, and in its place there emerged a heightened awareness of racial identity and socioeconomic status.

The issue of racial equality had a more powerful effect on DePaul in the 1960s than other questions of the day. This was partly a matter of context. On the national scene, the decade of the sixties was characterized by growing tensions over racial issues as the Civil Rights Movement gained momentum. Chicago was an important center of protest activity connected to a variety of issues. This was a period marked by increased Black concern over educational equality in particular, with large-scale protests over school segregation and access to higher education. In Chicago there were massive demonstrations in the early 1960s over the segregationist policies of public school superintendent Benjamin Willis. Active chapters of the NAACP, CORE, the Urban League and other civil rights organizations were working in the city, and more militant organizations such as the Black Panther Party were also active in Chicago. The generation of students that came to DePaul in the 1960s was acutely aware of the major issues of the day. Many of them were prepared to examine these questions intensively at the university. (61)

This was also a time of continuing change in the composition of DePaul's student body. In 1960 the university counted about one hundred and fifty Black students at both campuses. In fall 1969, when the administration conducted a census of black students, it counted nearly five hundred, more than a 300 percent increase. Although the report did not provide a breakdown by college, much of this growth probably occurred on the uptown campus, where most of the university's full-time students took classes. If the number of Black students in the College of Liberal Arts and Sciences increased at about the same rate as the rest of the Black student population, African American students at the uptown campus probably numbered about 150 at the end of the decade. Because overall enrollments in the college remained relatively constant over this period, an increase of this magnitude pushed the proportion of Black students on the uptown campus to roughly one in ten. This alone was a big change in the composition of the traditional student body of the university. (62)

The rest of DePaul's student body was changing as well. The number of Jewish students declined somewhat in these years, and more students from historically underserved Catholic groups, particularly Poles and Italians, appeared on campus. Even more significant, however, was the growth in the number of students commuting from the suburbs, for whom ethnicity may have been less important than other forms of identification, particularly race and economic status. In 1960 more than 80 percent of the undergraduate population at the uptown campus was from the city of Chicago. By the mid 1970s the figure had fallen to less than 70 percent. A new type of student was appearing in the College of Liberal Arts and Sciences: the children of Chicago Catholics who had moved to the suburbs, especially to communities northwest of the city. This group grew in significance and in numbers in the years ahead. (63)

The attitude of American college students changed in the sixties as these young men and women displayed greater willingness to challenge traditional practices and to question familiar maxims. But change did not occur overnight, and it took a while to reach DePaul. In the mid-1960s Greek membership at DePaul was still above 450, and dancing and dating continued to be popular among students at both campuses. Beanies and the pushball contest remained important campus traditions. Participation in these activities may have involved a smaller percentage of the student body, however, as the university's various colleges expanded in this period. With more than two thousand undergraduates on both campuses, only about one-quarter of the university's full-time students participated in the Greek system at any given time. This was the core of students who continued to value the traditional forms of collegiate social life throughout the decade, at DePaul and elsewhere. But change was evident, especially later in the decade. (64)

Even with substantial student involvement in traditional campus activities, there was a new atmosphere uptown (now called the Lincoln Park campus) by the late sixties. Students were interested in a variety of issues, and the campus newspaper, the *DePaulia*, urged greater activism and debate in the student body. Eloy Burciaga, a freshman in 1968, recalls that DePaul students were aware of protests on other campuses, and that a few began to develop interests in the key political issues of the day. Nineteen sixty-eight was a critical year around the world as students in Europe and North America mobilized against war in Southeast Asia, and especially against inequality and discrimination in the United States. There were signs of this new level of activity at DePaul. Forums on race relations and the Vietnam War in the opening months of 1968 were well attended and sparked discussion of national affairs. DePaul's first antiwar demonstrations were inspired by the presidential "peace" candidacy of Eugene McCarthy in March, and in April McCarthy won a campus poll of student preferences among leading candidates, defeating Robert Kennedy and Richard Nixon. Support for McCarthy was strongest at the uptown campus (Nixon won the general election vote the following fall, with heavy support at the Loop campus). A growing number of DePaul's students were closely attuned to events on the national stage, and some of them sought ways to bring these debates to the campus. (65)

For African American students, however, the issues of equity and fairness were immediate concerns. Late in the decade, a survey of DePaul's African American students revealed a good deal of dissatisfaction with their experiences at DePaul. Respondents complained about feeling isolated from other Black and minority students, about the lack of attention to Black history in the curriculum, and about the way certain faculty members treated them. "There are constant reminders of minorities not being on the same level as whites," wrote one African American student, "so they must put forth extra effort." Isolation was another factor. A number complained that there was too little for Black and other minority students to do outside of classes, and the vast majority said they would welcome the opportunity to meet more minority students. (66)

It is difficult to say exactly when DePaul's Black students began to organize, but in the years following 1965 there was a new level of concern about questions of social justice on the campus. In 1967 DePaul's African American students established the university's first student organization that represented Black concerns on campus: the Black Student Union (BSU). This was a critical step, and it mirrored similar groups on other campuses across the country. Chief among the issues they were interested in was the university itself, and the way it treated students from minority group backgrounds—particularly African Americans, but other groups as well.

In spring 1968, a series of events began to unfold which eventually pulled DePaul into the growing national controversy over equal rights and racial discrimination. The university's Black student activists, dissatisfied with many aspects of the university, organized diligently to draw attention to their cause. And this marked a new era in the history of student life at DePaul.

On May 1, 1968, Liberal Arts and Sciences Dean Edward Schillinger met with a delegation of "about twenty" Black students, led by James Hammonds. The group demanded that representatives from the Black Student Union be appointed to university committees that made policy recommendations regarding students and faculty. Not accustomed to being confronted by students, Schillinger was taken aback by the term "demand," but several days later he expressed interest in finding a way for the BSU to be represented on student committees. It is not clear how this response was communicated to the students, but it marked the beginning of a long dialogue between the BSU and the university administration. (67)

To respond to BSU demands and any others that might arise, the university established a Committee on Human Relations (CHR). Chaired by Dean Schillinger, it included representatives from BSU and other minority student groups and was supposed to look into the various issues raised by the BSU and others and to make recommendations to the President. In September the CHR issued a report listing a series of courses, old and new, that had been developed to address these concerns. The report also noted efforts in the various departments to recruit Black and other minority faculty members, although it was difficult to find eligible candidates. In addition to this, the CHR investigated charges that Black and Hispanic students experienced discrimination when seeking housing in neighborhoods adjacent to the university. And it looked into ways of offering more extracurricular activities for minority students. (68)

The pace of change was uneven, and not everyone was satisfied with the university's response. Members of the BSU complained about resistance to change encountered among certain faculty members and in various departments. The BSU—along with others in the university community—also protested DePaul's lack of communication with community groups concerned about the university's expansion. This had become a heated issue with the demolition of housing to allow for construction of the Schmitt Academic Center in 1967. Even though the university had opened a dialogue with its students, the potential for misunderstanding remained significant.

In the opening months of 1969 members of the BSU were becoming frustrated. After working closely with the CHR, little seemed to be happening. The BSU also had not been assigned office space by the university, like other student groups. In the 1968 and 1969

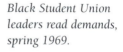

Black Student Union leaders read demands, spring 1969.

DePaulian yearbooks, the BSU had not been listed as an official student organization. Many wondered whether most faculty, administrators and students at DePaul even cared about the issues the BSU had raised.

On Wednesday, May 7, members of the BSU staged a small rally in the SAC pit—at high noon—to read a new set of "demands" being presented to the university. This time the list went well beyond the curriculum and touched on many of the issues then becoming points of controversy among students across the country, including access to the university for the disadvantaged and the university's relationship to its immediate neighborhood. The atmosphere on campus became highly charged in the wake of these demands, and the university administration answered the charges and demands issued by the BSU promptly. On the following day (May 8) after the BSU had received the response, it held another meeting in the SAC pit to consider it. The university agreed to discuss most of the new points but noted that a number of them would be difficult or impossible to address.

At this juncture, the crisis escalated quickly. Later that afternoon, members of the BSU went to Dean Schillinger's office and asked to see university President John Cortelyou, C.M. At 8:30 that evening members of the BSU and students supporting them "secured" the fifth floor of the building, and after classes had ended, they took possession of the rest of the building, blocking or barricading doors so that students and university personnel could not enter. Within barely two days of seeing the new demands issued by the BSU, DePaul had joined the growing list of institutions experiencing disruptions related to student unrest.

Fortunately, the confrontation precipitated by the takeover of SAC did not last long. Although there was a tense standoff as students attempted to gain access to the building on the morning of May 9 and the university threatened to seek an injunction to open the building by force, the BSU abandoned the takeover shortly after noon that day and held another rally. There was great interest across the campus in the issues raised by the BSU, and hundreds of students came to find out what was going on. Representatives from the Black Panthers and Young Lords (a Puerto Rican group), concerned about the university's impact on the neighborhood, also attended and spoke. If the goal of the takeover was to draw attention to the BSU's position, it had clearly succeeded. (69)

Campus opinion was divided regarding the BSU's demands and actions, but most students supported the call for greater curricular focus on problems of discrimination and inequality. Support was clearly strongest on the uptown campus. On the following Tuesday the Student Activity Council, the principal student governance body at the time, voted to support the BSU demands for curricular changes and for establishing special programs for minority youth. For its part, the Committee on Human Relations resumed its dialogue with the BSU and determined to look into inequities in the curriculum and school policies. Even though there had been some heated moments, it appeared that a resolution to the conflict was at hand. (70)

Just when the situation seemed to be stabilized, however, a new crisis erupted. Late on the afternoon of May 14, a week after the BSU had publicly issued its demands, arsonists struck the old Lyceum building (the former library), which contained the university bookstore and the BSU offices. Although no one was harmed and it was never determined who set the fire, the BSU declared it a racist attack, and at a rally two days later the BSU and other student groups called for a general student strike across the university.

For two days a small group of students at the Lincoln Park campus did not attend classes, and pickets circled the entrances to SAC and other university buildings. Even though most students did not observe the strike, many went to workshops on institutional racism conducted by the BSU on the following Monday and to a rally held at noon. Many students supported the quest to improve conditions for Black and other minority students at the university, and a resolution signed by several dozen faculty members also expressed support. There can be little doubt that the arson attack on university property, and the BSU office in particular, helped to build sympathy for Black students and contributed to broad endorsement of the BSU position. In the space of a little more than two weeks, DePaul's African American students had mobilized a significant portion of the university community behind their concerns. (71)

As short as it was, the BSU building seizure and strike of 1969 had a major impact on DePaul. It opened lines of communication between the university and minority students and established the BSU as a major factor in campus life, at least for a time. Shortly after the events of May 1969, the BSU reported a membership of nearly one hundred, about one in five Black students at DePaul, making it one of the largest student organizations. Students also continued to express interest in the Vietnam war, and a chapter of Students for a Democratic Society (SDS) was formed at DePaul. It was a time of rising social consciousness, and at DePaul's Lincoln Park campus students confronted the issues that defined the period. Even though DePaul was not a major center of student protest at this time, it certainly was not isolated from the activism and unrest that marked the times. The institution no longer asserted that students did not have a say in the curriculum—and other areas of university policy making—as had been the case in the past. (72)

The student protest era lasted only a short time, but its impact was significant. The Black Student Union remained active for several years, but by the early seventies it numbered only a handful of active members and was no longer a major force on the campus. The Vietnam war was an issue for some students, and there were lively demonstrations in spring 1970 (at the time of the Kent State shootings) and later (around the bombing of Cambodia). In 1970 a small band of protestors disrupted the university's commencement exercises in an antiwar protest. The notion that the university was exempt from political activism and that the Vincentian priests who administered DePaul were above reproach was clearly out of date. (73) To many students at this time, the university was perceived as just another seat of power and privilege; as such it was linked to a host of social problems. Even after the protest era had passed, DePaul students continued to hold two simultaneous and opposing views of the institution: it posed problems for them to solve at the same time it was offering them the skills and knowledge—and credentials—necessary for success in life.

The Seventies and Beyond

As DePaul has grown in the years following 1970, its students have continued to be diverse and politically and socially sophisticated. Conflicts continue to punctuate the regular course of university life, but the tenor was considerably less strident and confrontational than in the late sixties. While DePaul still served the children of the Chicago ethnics it educated in the past, significant new groups appeared on the Lincoln Park campus, including a growing number of students from outside of the Chicago area.

As a consequence of these changes, DePaul today has a markedly different student culture. The university's traditionally college-age student body has become more cosmopolitan, while at the same time DePaul has been expanding its role as educator of adults in the Loop and in some suburban locations. The university has become a considerably more complex and sophisticated purveyor of educational services, addressing a broad range of constituencies. The close-knit campus life of the past, with its familiar traditions and cohesive social life has rapidly faded in the wake of these changes. In its place a new and highly differentiated campus culture has emerged, one that allows students freedom to forge their own associations amid the myriad possibilities offered by a large and complex institution. Informality has become the rule of the day, and individual friendships have replaced the old activities of the past as a new generation of students works to shape its own distinctive social world.

The traditional campus activities and organizations that had characterized student life at DePaul for several decades declined quickly in the 1970s. The previous decade had brought a new critical attitude to campuses across the country, one that questioned the value of dances,

Anti-war graffiti, SAC, 1970.

dating, and even such long-standing campus traditions as homecoming. In a telling commentary, the 1969 *DePaulian* yearbook described the spring dances as "opaque, smoke filled rooms" where a student becomes acquainted "with the people he is never in class enough to meet." In the same yearbook, homecoming is referred to as a form of "university chauvinism," comparable, at least in spirit, to other forms of status consciousness which had become anathema to many students. The rebels of the sixties had wielded enormous influence, and by the end of the decade even the college yearbook was casting aspersions on the familiar elements of the collegiate culture of past years. (74)

The shift to a new campus ethos came quickly. By the mid-seventies a veritable sea change had occurred in student life. Membership in the Greek organizations declined so precipitously that by 1974 it totaled barely 250. The annual pushball contest between the freshmen and sophomores, a campus tradition since the late twenties, was discontinued after 1975. And even though it was revived for a time in the early 1980s, it never regained its significance as an acculturating experience for successive generations of students coming to the campus each fall. Needless to say, the assignment of green beanies for freshmen, and everything it signified, ended in the early seventies as well. The traditional Friday night dances became less frequent and attendance was smaller. And eventually even the larger, formal dances drew fewer students. Although the basketball team experienced great success in the late seventies, homecoming events drew smaller crowds. Finally, in the eighties the annual homecoming dance was discontinued because of lack of interest. By that time a new student culture had established itself at DePaul's uptown campus, one that, while it eschewed the old organizations and activities, offered its own values and norms. (75)

The university's student body was changing. In 1975 almost two-thirds of DePaul's full time students came from the city of Chicago. By 1983 that number had dropped to less than half, a decline attributable to the increase in the number of students who commuted from the Chicago suburbs, principally the west and northwest regions of the metropolitan area. This trend continued as time went on, and by the mid-nineties students from the city represented barely one-third of the university's total enrollment, while those from the suburbs constituted almost half. At the same time, the number of students from outside of the Chicago area altogether rose, albeit less quickly. In 1975, fewer than 8 percent of the student body came from outside of Chicagoland; ten years later, this number had increased to nearly ten percent, with most coming from out of state. By the middle of the 1990s, however, those coming from outside the metropolitan area constituted nearly one out of five DePaul students and were almost one-third of all freshmen on the Lincoln Park campus. At that time the university's student body looked quite different than it had just two decades earlier. DePaul was no longer an institution serving primarily the city of Chicago. It had become an important regional university, drawing larger numbers of students from greater distances.

At the same time that DePaul drew more students from outside Chicago, it also continued to have a racially and culturally diverse student population. While the proportion of students from the city declined, more Black, Hispanic and other minority-group students came to DePaul from Chicago, a reflection of changes in the city's schools, which graduated relatively few white students after the 1970s. This increase in minority representation at DePaul contributed to the diversity of students' backgrounds and experiences on campus. By the mid 1990s about 10 percent of the university's students were African American and another 8 percent were Hispanic. Asian students represented about 7 percent of the student body, and students from an array of other ethnic minority backgrounds constituted smaller percentages. Added to this was a growing number of foreign students, attracted by programs in computer science and related disciplines. While the Catholic student population at DePaul peaked in the sixties at nearly 80 percent, it gradually fell in the years afterward. By the late eighties only about 60 percent of the student body was Catholic, and by the late nineties it had fallen to half. Taken all together, these changes contributed to the creation of a highly diverse student body at DePaul, considerably more varied than in the past. (76)

These changes held important implications for student life, apart from the underlying modifications in American youth culture associated with the 1960s and 1970s. First, the shift to a suburban clientele meant that many commuter students traveled longer distances to attend DePaul, often driving into the city from distant suburbs. This might have made it more difficult for some students to consider such campus-based social commitments as participation in traditional collegiate activities: Greek societies and formal dances. Although most students still came from the Chicago area, enough were from beyond the city to diminish the geographic cohesion in the student body, a big change from the time when a large number of uptown students lived on the city's north side. As the student population at the Lincoln Park campus expanded, DePaul was no longer "the little school under the El," and this no doubt made it difficult for the old-time collegiate organizations to maintain their dominant roles on the campus.

Finally, recognition that students were coming from outside the city in increasing numbers led to the university's decision to make it possible for students to live on or near the DePaul campus. This meant acquiring dormitories and building new ones in the sixties and the years following 1970. While DePaul had a limited number of resident students in the sixties, the acquisition of the McCormick Seminary campus in 1978 enabled hundreds of students to live in the dormitories the seminary had constructed. New dorms were built in the years that followed, and by the mid-nineties the number of resident students at Lincoln Park had climbed to nearly two thousand. Larger numbers of students, particularly upperclassmen, also rented nearby apartments, adding substantially to the resident student population. This meant that suddenly there was a large group of students living on DePaul's Lincoln Park campus, an altogether new development. This too altered the shape of student culture on the uptown campus. (77)

For DePaul's increasingly diverse student body, campus life has become highly differentiated and personalized in the years following 1970. Other scholars of student life have observed a similar tendency across the country. Following the tumultuous sixties, students did not return to the familiar campus activities. Instead, they were more serious about their studies and engaged in activities associated with their academic interests or other issues they personally were concerned with.

At DePaul today the old organizational forms of student life no longer command the loyalty or the attention of most students. Instead, groups of friends get together and select specific activities on which to focus. Dating, once the mainstay of DePaul collegiate culture, has fallen out of fashion with late 20th-century undergraduates. So, too, have the formal dances at downtown hotels and the elaborate preparations for a night on the town. Rather, informality is the order of the day. This is in part a legacy of the sixties and the revolt against formality in so many spheres of life in that era. And it is also the hallmark of a new period in the history of student culture, one marked by a new attention to personal tastes and interests.

The post-1960s students valued spontaneity and authenticity, and this meant doing things with friends, often without much planning or preparation. Kieran Conrad, a student in the

Students picket SAC following Kent State shootings, May 1970.

late eighties, noted that she never remembered going out on an actual date, although she—like so many DePaul students before her—met her husband while they were both students at the university. Her memories of campus life feature time spent with friends in the music school (where her future husband was a student), spontaneous events like a massive snowball fight in the middle of a winter night during her freshman year, and her relationships with professors. She was active in a number of campus organizations and worked as a desk assistant in the dormitories, but these organizational forms of campus life were less important to her than the friends she associated with. Extracurricular activity meant something quite different to her: less an element of a unified student culture she experienced than just another organizational dimension of the university—like classes—in which she chose to participate. In this respect her experience was quite different from earlier generations of DePaul students, for whom the Greek societies and other organizations were central features of campus life. Kieran, like many other DePaul students in the years following 1975, had a personal DePaul experience that was shared by other students but also was uniquely her own. (78)

The new era in campus life was evident in the types of organizations that were established by students at DePaul's two principal campuses. The directory of student organizations published in 1988 featured a dozen Greek-letter societies, but several were really professional associations restricted to students majoring in certain subjects, and only a few of the "social" groups had more than two dozen members. Five years later the number of Greek societies had fallen to nine, even though there was a national revival of these groups at that time. By the mid-1990s Greek membership at the university was less then five percent of the student body. At DePaul, it appears, a different form of student organization predominated, reflecting the diversity of student interests. The largest number of groups were those representing academic or other special interests linked to individual skills or talents (ranging from the artistic to the athletic). More than a dozen community or social service groups, and twelve different "ethnic" student groups, each representing a different cultural or racial minority were also active. In addition, there were politically oriented special interest groups with specific constituencies, such as women or gay and lesbian students. While the members of these groups engaged in an assortment of social activities, they existed so that students could pursue a wide range of individual interests. The extra curriculum was no longer dominated by the largely convivial agenda of the Greek societies and the dating culture. Rather, it had become another avenue for students to pursue personal development and potential career advancement. (79)

Like students elsewhere, DePaul students—particularly those on the uptown campus—continued to harbor a certain irreverence and exhibited a willingness to undertake protest as a strategy to advance causes they were interested in. This, too, was a legacy of the sixties, although the issues changed with time. In the early seventies, for example, DePaul students conducted small-scale protests over the university's treatment of popular professors. In the 1980s there was a major controversy over the university's decision to withdraw support for

NOW president Eleanor Smeal as a campus speaker, an issue about which many students felt strongly (and one that mobilized various student constituency groups). In the 1990s again there was a crisis on the campus over the treatment of African American students, and a host of related issues quite similar to those raised by the BSU some twenty years earlier. Even if the war in Vietnam had ended, and the Civil Rights Movement was a distant memory, the new tradition of students demanding changes in the way the university was run was alive and well at DePaul. This was hardly an old tradition, as earlier generations of DePaul students virtually never questioned the university administration. But students voicing their opinions about a wide range of issues was an important carryover from the student protest era. While Black student complaints and confrontations such as the one over Smeal were not everyday occurrences, they happened frequently enough to keep alive the prospect of student mobilization—a vital element of the new DePaul student culture of the late twentieth century. (80)

DePaul students in the post-1970s era resembled their counterparts on other campuses across the country. For many, especially the students on the Lincoln Park campus, college was the means to a secure middle-class career, and a lifestyle similar to that enjoyed by their parents. They were serious about school and chose not to embrace the traditional collegiate organizational forms. DePaul continued to educate many first-generation students also, and it remained a major center for adult higher education in the Chicago area. But even for these students, college was less an occasion for shared socialization than an avenue to personal and professional development. While the Greek associations and dances dominated the lives of previous students, college for the latest generations of DePaul students is a largely personal experience. These students can organize protests and express a common viewpoint when motivated by a particular interest, but they do not share the distinctive unitary student culture of their predecessors. Though today's students may be somewhat more sophisticated than those of the past, they may also have lost something. (81)

Conclusion

DePaul has served a wide array of students over the past century. The very first were the sons of Catholic Irish and German immigrant families. Starting largely as a north side institution, DePaul's students became more diverse as the university expanded, particularly in the years following World War I. For decades after that, DePaul educated the sons and daughters of Chicago's major immigrant ethnic groups. And in the 1960s and beyond it served growing numbers of Chicago's newest minority groups: Blacks, Hispanics, Asian Americans and others. In this respect the university has represented its urban setting well. Its student body has been a reflection of much of Chicago and the larger metropolitan area and the changes it has undergone since the turn of the century.

Over the course of this period DePaul's students have strived to create their own distinctive campus culture. To a very large extent this culture has mirrored national trends in student tastes and behavior. But DePaul has always featured its own style of student life. Even though they were virtually all commuters in the twenties and thirties, for instance, DePaul students embraced the trappings of collegiate life with gusto. While football and such traditional social events as homecoming were important, DePaul's students were swept up in the dance craze then popular among urban youth. As a coed Catholic institution, a rarity for much of the twentieth century, DePaul offered its students the opportunity to place dating and the potential for romance at the very center of their activities. The result was an urban Catholic variant of the coed dating culture that was taking shape on campuses across the country at that time. At DePaul much of the social activity occurred off campus in the larger world of entertainment and conviviality presented by the city. The university offered collegiate culture, Chicago style.

Even though they were commuters, DePaul's students were active in a wide range of campus activities. For the better part of five decades membership in fraternities and sororities was high, and a vast assortment of other groups helped to focus students' energies on a variety of issues. The university's students contributed to their own education as they organized themselves to have fun and to learn more about the world outside of the classroom. Athletics were also important, as DePaul's various teams provided students with many occasions to cheer and celebrate, and a reason to take extra pride in their alma mater. Altogether, DePaul showered a rich array of activities on its students, and out of this they fashioned a unique social and cultural identity, with athletics, students' organizations, dances and other activities forming its major components. It was an identity that sustained many generations of DePaul students, and one that continues to live in the hearts of its alumni.

This distinctive student culture changed profoundly in the years following the 1960s. Once again, DePaul was following national trends. The student protest era did not last very long at DePaul, but by the mid-1970s there was clear evidence that the traditional forms of collegiate culture were in decline. At the same time, DePaul began drawing more students from the suburbs, and eventually students from across the country started coming to the Lincoln Park campus. In a sense it is ironic that the old unitary student culture disappeared just when the university acquired a sizable residential population. Yet DePaul was no different in this regard from many other institutions. Students everywhere in the eighties and nineties viewed college as a place to develop their personal interests and abilities, not as a venue for collective socialization. In this respect also, DePaul is right in step with the national mood.

Regardless of these changes, however, DePaul today retains much of the openness and intimacy it gave to earlier generations. Students in the eighties and nineties have found it easy to make friends, and the city continues to offer a wide field for diversions of all sorts. The university still sponsors activities that allow students to learn about themselves and the larger world outside of the classroom. And the various elements of the traditional collegiate lifestyle, athletics, Greek societies and the rest, are available for those who wish to pursue them. But the unitary core of student life that existed in the past has vanished. Today, diversity is the watchword, and personal choice. At DePaul this is not as forbidding a development as it would be on a larger, more impersonal campus. DePaul has kept its atmosphere of personalism, and that is the connection to the past, the core of student life at the university that ties the present generation to those that came before.

Chapter Five Notes

Author's note: *I would like to acknowledge the excellent research assistance of Christopher Glidden, Laura Voulo, and Dawn Zaphron. I would also like to acknowledge assistance from DePaul's University Research Council.*

1. On student life at other institutions, see Helen Lefkowitz Horowitz, *Campus Life: Undergraduate Cultures from the End of the Eighteenth Century to the Present* (Chicago, 1987) , Chs. 5 & 6. Paula Fass, *The Damned and the Beautiful: American Youth in the 1920's* (New York, 1977), Chs. 3 & 4.

2. The best overview of the early years of St. Vincent's College can be found in Lester Goodchild, "The Mission of the Catholic University in the Midwest, 1842-1980: A Comparative Case Study of the Effects of Strategic Policy Decisions Upon the Mission of the University of Notre Dame, Loyola University Chicago and DePaul University" (Unpublished Ph.D. dissertation, University of Chicago, 1986), Ch. 6. Goodchild also provides a description of the founding of St. Ignatius College in Chapter 5.

3. For a more complete discussion of the characteristics of early DePaul students, see John L. Rury, "The Urban Catholic University in the Early Twentieth Century: A Social Profile of DePaul, 1898–1940," *History of Higher Education Annual* (17: 1997): 5–32.

4. On this point, see Charles Shanabruch, *Chicago's Catholics: The Evolution of an American Identity* (South Bend, IN, 1981), Ch. 2; also see Eileen M. McMahon, *What Parish are You From? A Chicago Irish Community and Race Relations* (Lexington, KY, 1995), 18.

5. For discussion of the occupations and earnings of industrial workers in Chicago at this time, see Eric L. Hirsch, *Urban Revolt: Ethnic Politics in the Nineteenth Century Chicago Labor Movement* (Berkeley, CA, 1990), 8–9. On Irish and German immigrants in Chicago and other major cities, see Nora Faires, "Occupational Patterns of German Americans in Nineteenth Century Cities" in Hartmut Keil and John Jentz, eds., *German Workers in Industrial Chicago, 1850–1910: A Comparative Perspective* (DeKalb, IL, 1983), 37–51. For a discussion of the Lincoln Park neighborhood, see Christaine Harzig, "Chicago's German North Side, 1880–1900: The Structure of a Guilded Age Ethnic Neighborhood" in the same volume, 127–144. Also see Dominic A. Pacyga, *Polish Immigrants and Industrial Chicago: Workers on the South Side* (Columbus, OH, 1991), Ch. 1; and David John Hogan, *Class and Reform: School and Society in Chicago, 1880–1930* (Philadelphia, 1984), Ch. 3. For statistics on the occupational structure of Chicago in this period, see Hogan, 149. On the occupational status of Catholic immigrants, see Harold J. Abramson, *Ethnic Diversity in Catholic America* (New York, 1973), 38. On the occupational backgrounds of early DePaul students, see Rury, "The Urban Catholic University in the Early Twentieth Century," 7.

6. Rury, "The Urban Catholic University in the Early Twentieth Century," 8.

7. On this point the 1908 bulletin offered that "with a view to encourage physical training as an inestimable aid to the intellectual and moral development of the students, the faculty allows and approves of a reasonable interest in athletics." *Bulletin of DePaul University, 1908–1909* (Chicago, 1908), 30. On the use of athletics for attracting boys to school, see John C. Maxwell, "Should the Education of Boys and Girls Differ? A Half Century of Debate" (Unpublished Ph.D. dissertation, University of Wisconsin, 1966) *passim*.

8. Evidence on early opponents can be found in *The Minerval*, "Christmas Number Vol. 1, No. 1 (December 1912): 56. Also see individual season schedules preserved in the Sports Memorabilia Collection, DePaul University Archives (DPUA). On the early contest with Notre Dame, see the "Silver Jubilee" yearbook of 1932, *DePaulian*, 1932 (Chicago, 1932): X. On early student sports coverage, see *The Minerval*, Vol. 4, No. 2 (December 1915): 53–66. For a later perspective, see the discussion of the 1924 football season in the university yearbook, The *DePaulian*, 1925 (Chicago, 1925): 82–85.

9. Both St. Vincent's College and DePaul University featured student clubs by describing them in early bulletins. In the 1908 bulletin, it was noted that participation in such activities "enlivens the ordinary dull, monotonous work of the classroom." *Bulletin of DePaul University, 1908–1909* (Chicago, 1908) 30.

10. An early informal accounting of campus organizations associated with the various colleges can be found in *The Minerval*, Vol. 3, No. 4 (June,1915) *passim*. On fraternities, the theater company and other student activities, see *The Minerval*, Vol. 9, No. 5 (June 1921): 438–447.

11. For an overview of enrollments in this period, see Goodchild, "Mission of the Catholic University in the Midwest," p. 271. On the early years of DePaul's College of Law, see Lester Goodchild, "The College of Law's First Thirty Years," *DePaul University Magazine* (Summer 1987): 14–30. On the College of Commerce, see Lester Goodchild, "DePaul Means Business: From the Founding of the College of Commerce to the Present," *DePaul Diamond Jubilee Publication*, 1988, 6–16.

12. Unfortunately, there is no single comprehensive source on the development of coeducation at DePaul. For useful overviews, see Goodchild, "Mission of the Catholic University in the Midwest," Ch. 10; and Sandra Averitt Cook, "The Origins and Development of Evening Undergraduate Education in Chicago: 1891–1939" (Unpublished Ph.D dissertation, Loyola University Chicago, 1993) Ch. 2.

13. On enrollments at DePaul, see Goodchild, "Mission of the Catholic University in the Midwest," Ch. 10. On Catholic opposition to coeducation and DePaul's role, see Philip Gleason, *Contending with Modernity: Catholic Higher Education in the Twentieth Century* (New York, 1995), 179–185. On Catholic opposition also see John L. Rury, *Education and Women's Work: Female Schooling and the Division of Labor in Urban America, 1870–1930* (Albany, NY, 1991) Ch. 4. On high schools sending students to DePaul, see "Academic Enrollment: Statistics, Comparative and Summary," 1898–1939/40" 1932–33 File, DPUA. A survey of Chicago college students conducted in 1932 shows about two-thirds of DePaul freshmen that year came from parochial schools, the vast majority of which were single sex institutions.

14. The information for the analysis which follows is drawn from two yearbooks: *The DePaulian, 1925*, passim, and *The DePaulian, 1930* (Chicago, 1930) *passim*. Names were located in at least one of two dictionaries: Patrick Hanks and Flavia Hodges, *A Dictionary of Surnames* (New York, 1988) *passim*; or H. Amanda Robb and Andrew Chesler, *Encyclopedia of American Family Names: The Definative Guide to the 5000 Most Common Surnames in the United States* (New York, 1995) *passim*.

This analysis was based on names linked to photographs in each yearbook. Thus it should not be considered a scientific survey of the student body. There also were names which could not be identified with the dictionaries used for this study, although the numbers were not great. In 1930, for instance, only the names of five seniors could not be identified, out of a total of 153. For the freshmen the numbers were somewhat higher: 69 out of 466 could not be identified with an ethnic group (fifteen percent). While the patterns identified with these data can be revealing, in that case, particular numbers should not be taken as accurate counts of students enrolled. It is noteworthy, however, that none of the students pictured in yearbooks during this period were African American.

Beginning in 1931, data on the religious affiliation of DePaul Students can be found in "Academic Enrollment, Statistics Comparative and Summary, 1898–1939/40," DPUA.

15. Andrew Greeley has noted the historic predominance of the Irish in American Catholic higher education. See Andrew M. Greeley, *The Changing Catholic College* (Chicago, 1967) 34–35. On the relatively low educational attainment levels among Italian and Polish immigrant families, see Joel Perlmann, *Ethnic Differences: Schooling and Social Structure Among the Irish, Italians, Jews and Blacks in an American City, 1880–1935* (New York, 1988) 118–121.

16. Comparative data on the religious backgrounds of DePaul students in the various colleges is drawn from "Academic Enrollment, Statistics Comparative and Summary, 1898–1939/40," Fall 1936 File, DPUA.

17. The results of this survey, but not the individual level data themselves, are available in "Academic Enrollment, Statistics Comparative and Summary, 1898–1939/40" 1937–38 File, DPUA.

18. The survey about place of residence is located in "Academic Enrollment, Statistics Comparative and Summary, 1898–1939/40" 1935–36 File, DPUA. On the development of these areas of Chicago and Irish settlement patterns, see McMahon, *What Parish are You From?*, Chs. 1–4; also see Irving Cutler, *Chicago: Metropolis of the Mid-Continent*, Third Edition (Dubuque, IA, 1982), 50–52.

19. For the survey of commerce students' places of residence "Academic Enrollment, Statistics Comparative and Summary, 1898–1939/40" 1936–37 File, DPUA.

20. *The DePaulian, 1924*, pp. 110–118. On students at other institutions at this time, see Helen Lefkowitz Horowitz, *Campus Life*, Chs. 5 & 6.

21. The names of group members were listed under photos in the 1924 yearbook. *DePaulian, 1924*, pp. 110–118. Figures calculated from senior photographs and accompanying data in the 1924 and 1925 *DePaulian* yearbooks.

22. *DePaulia*, 17 March 1930.

23. To document the evolution of this custom, see *DePaulia*, 18 October 1929; 3 November 1932; 23 November 1932; and 9 November 1933. By the latter date, the annual frosh-soph contest was described as a "combination boxing tournament, wrestling match, track meet and jiu jitsu free for all." For a description of perhaps the first push-ball contest, see the *DePaulian, 1940* (Chicago, 1940) p. 104. For initiation rites on other campuses, see Horowitz, *Campus Life*, 42–45.

24. John Rury interview with Rita Barr, July 1996. See the lengthy discussion of this issue in the *DePaulia*, 17 March 1932. Also see the commentary in *DePaulia*, 4 May 1933, which declares that "one half of DePaul is hardly aware that the other half exists." It concludes that "between the sky-scraper school and the uptown college there is a breach far wider than the few intervening miles can satisfactorily explain." The 1934 yearbook declared Webster Avenue "the 'home' campus and its student body the nucleus of student activity." *DePaulian 1934* (Chicago, 1934). In the *DePaulia*, 3 November 1938, the uptown campus is described as "reputedly more 'collegiate'."

25. Horowitz suggests that the numbers of students involved in multiple activities at most institutions was relatively small in this period, particularly at commuter campuses. See *Campus Life*, Ch. 8.

26. For a discussion of Greek society membership in Horowitz, see *Campus Life*, 146.

27. This is evident in interviews with former student members of DePaul's fraternities and sororities. John Rury interview with Rita Barr, July 1996; John Rury interview with Marie Cogan, August 1996; John Rury interview with Fran Armstrong and Bud Kevin, September 1996; Chuck Suchar Interview with Thomas Joyce, June 1996.

28. On discrimination against Jewish students in this period, see Daniel Levine, *The American College and the Culture of Aspiration, 1900–1940* (Ithaca, NY, 1986) Ch. 7. Horowitz suggests that Greek societies were more discriminatory in the years preceding World War Two than afterwards. "The fraternity," she writes, "turned out to be an all too effective school for prejudice." *Campus Life*, 146.

29. John Rury interview with Fran Armstrong and Bud Kevin, September 1996; Chuck Suchar Interview with Thomas Joyce, June 1996.

30. Chuck Suchar Interview with Thomas Joyce, June 1996.

31. The 1925 student was Michael Perlman. See *The Depaulian, 1925*, passim. The 1930 student was Joseph Westermeyer. See the *DePaulia, 1930*, passim. A good number of other students with Jewish names also held offices in student organizations in these years, on both campuses.

32. Gleason, *Contending with Modernity*, 179.

33. Horowitz, *Campus Life*, Ch. 4.

34. *The DePaulian, 1932* (Chicago, 1932), 98.

35. Horowitz, *Campus Life*, Ch. 4 John Modell, *Into One's Own: From Youth to Adulthood in the United States, 1920–1975* (Berkeley, CA, 1989), 85–97

36. See, for instance, *The DePaulian, 1929* (Chicago, 1929), 138; *DePaulian 1930*, 142–3; *DePaulian 1931*, 140.

37. *DePaulia*, 2 March 1928

38. See *Minerval*, Vol. 9, No. 5 (June, 1921): 421; *DePaulia*, 8 October 1925; or *DePaulia*, 10 February 1928.

39. See, for instance, *DePaulia*, 8 December 1927, or 18 April 1929. In the latter instance, the editors characterized their counterparts at Marquette as "old fashioned and misinformed."

40. *DePaulia*, 19 April 1928; or the *DePaulia*, 20 October or 17 March 1932. The former was an editorial decrying cliquishness.

41. See the discussion of this point in Fass, *The Damned and the Beautiful*, Ch.s 3 & 4; and Horowitz, *Campus Life*, Ch. 4.

42. "Constitution and Rules for the Inter Fraternity Council, 1936." Student Affairs Collection, Box 1, DPUA.

43. *DePaulia*, 21 May 1924.

44. John Rury interview with Rita Barr, July 1996; John Rury interview with Marie Cogan, August 1996; John Rury interview with Fran Armstrong and Bud Kevin, September 1996. On the formality of the "hotel" dances, see *DePaulia*, 1 May 1930. On the growing expense of these affairs, and the difficulty of sustaining them during the depression, see *DePaulia*, 26 April 1933.

45. Chuck Suchar Interview with Thomas Joyce, June 1996. For an account of the social nature of the gym dances, see the *DePaulia*, 13 February 1930. Similar observations were frequently offered in other articles. In the 1931 yearbook, for instance, one gym dance is described as lasting until 1 a.m., when "the dancers departed rather reluctantly, but with a large number of newly made aquaintances." See *The DePaulian, 1931* (Chicago, 1931), 123.

46. *DePaulian, 1935* (Chicago, 1935), 112; The numbers at the gym dances, probably the most telling in terms of broad participation by students, fell to around 500 by the mid thirties, but this was still a rather large portion of the full time student body—more than a third. See *DePaulia*, 19 May, 1932 for a discussion of the drop in attendance. John Rury interview with Fran Armstrong and Bud Kevin, September 1996.

47. *DePaulia*, 19 January, 1939. John Rury interview with Marie Cogan, August 1996.

48. John Rury interview with Fran Armstrong and Bud Kevin, September 1996; Chuck Suchar Interview with Thomas Joyce, June 1996.

49. For details on Ray Meyer's early career at DePaul, see his autobiographical account: Ray Meyer, with Ray Sons, *Coach* (Chicago: 1987), Chs. 1–5.

50. For an overview of DePaul's enrollment in this period and an assessment of the impact of veteran students, see Goodchild, "Mission of the Catholic University in the Midwest," pp. 478–480. For enrollments of specific colleges, see "Academic Enrollment, Statistics Comparative and Summary," 1948–49 File, DPUA.

51. On veteran students nationally, see J. Hillis Miller and John S. Allen, *Veterans Challenge the Colleges* (New York: Kings Crown Press, 1947) passim, and Horowitz, *Campus Life*, 185. Chuck Suchar Interview with Nick Delonardis, July 1996; and Chuck Suchar Interview with Jerry Radice, August 1996.

52. This analysis was performed with the 1955 and 1965 *DePaulian* yearbooks, using the method described in note 14 above.

53. The results of this survey can be found in "Academic Enrollment, Statistics Comparative and Summary," 1947–48 File, DPUA. On Black students at other Catholic institutions during these years, see Gleason, *Contending with Modernity*, 235–40.

54. The DePass letter is printed in the *DePaulia*, 19 October 1951. DePass graduated in 1948 and worked as a librarian at the uptown campus until 1951, when she left to enter a convent. The editorial regarding the Cicero riots appeared on 28 September 1951. The editorial on athletics and race appeared 28 September 1956.

55. Greek membership was derived by counting names linked to pictures in the 1955 yearbook, *The DePaulian, 1955* (Chicago, 1955) passim. On the role of these groups in campus life, see Chuck Suchar Interview with Jack Dickman, May 1996.

56. These observations are made from an examination of photos and names listed in the 1955 *DePaulian* (see previous note).

57. Chuck Suchar Interview with Jack Dickman, May 1996; Chuck Suchar Interview with Carol Nolan, April 1996.

58. Chuck Suchar Interview with Tony Behoff, July 1996; Chuck Suchar Interview with Jack Dickman, May 1996.

59. Chuck Suchar Interview with Karen Stark, August 1996; Chuck Suchar Interview with Jack Dickman, May 1996.

60. For discussion of this, see Horowitz, *Campus Life*, Ch. 10.

61. For an account of this period in Chicago, see A. B. Anderson and G. W. Pickering, *Confronting the Color Line: The Broken Promise of the Civil Rights Movement in Chicago* (Athens, GA, 1986) passim.

62. On Black enrollments at the end of the fifties, see "Academic Enrollment, Statistics Comparative and Summary," 1959–60 File, DPUA. The results of the survey of Black students is in the "Black Student Union", Student Affairs Collection, DPUA.

63. These data are available in "Geographic Profiles of Students (Day)," Student Affairs Collection, Box 1, DPUA.

64. These figures have been calculated from an analysis of pictures and names in the 1965 yearbook, *The DePaulian, 1965* (Chicago, 1965) passim.

65. The race relations forum is reported in *DePaulia*, 18 January, 1968; on "Peace Days" at the uptown campus, see *DePaulia*, 4 April, 1968; the McCarthy victory is announced in the *DePaulia*, 2 May 1968; on Nixon's victory, see *DePaulia*, 31 October, 1968. John Rury Interview with Eloy Burciaga, July 1996.

66. Survey of Black Students, "Black Student Union," Student Affairs Collection, DPUA.

67. These events are described in documents contained in the "Black Student Union," Student Affairs Collection, DPUA. On the BSU demands, see *DePaulia*, 24 May 1968.

68. "Committee on Human Relations, 1968–69," Student Affairs Collection, DPUA.

69. "Black Student Union," Student Affairs Collection, DPUA; John Rury Interview with Francine Salounis, October 1996.

70. For discussion of these events, see *DePaulia*, 19 May 1969.

71. *DePaulia*, 22 May 1968; "Black Student Union," Student Affairs Collection, DPUA.

72. See, for instance, the university reponses to demands in "Committee on Human Relations," Student Affairs Collection, DPUA; and report of the committee's deliberations in *DePaulia*, 21 November, 1968.

73. *DePaulian, 1970*; John Rury Interview with Eloy Burciaga, July 1996; John Rury Interview with Francine Salounis, October 1996.

74. *DePaulian, 1969* (Chicago, 1969), 27. Horowitz, *Campus Life*, Ch. 10.

75. Estimates of greek letter memberships is taken from the 1974 yearbook, the last to feature pictures and lists of group memberships: *The DePaulian, 1974* (Chicago, 1974) passim. On pushball, see *DePaulia*, September 18, 1981; on doing away with homecoming, see *DePaulia*, 14 March 1983.

76. Figures on the origins of students are taken from "Enrollment Statistics, Comparative and Summary" various years, DPUA; also see "A Snapshot of DePaul, 1995–96" DePaul University informational pamphlet.

77. On the decision to build dormitories, see chapter one in this volume.

78. Chuck Suchar Interview with Kieran Zastrow, April 1996.

79. Lists and brief descriptions of student organizations in the 1980s can be found in Student Affairs Collection, Box 2, DPUA. See the directories of student organizations published each year.

80. An ongoing series of student protests, of varying intensity, is evident from the mid seventies forward. See *DePaulia*, 18 April 1975 (Hispanic students charge discrimination); *DePaulia*, 21 November 1979 ("Iran controversy brews here."); *DePaulia*, 11 April, 9 May 1986 (controversy over Smeal); *DePaulia*, April 1995 ("Black students protest DePaulia, conditions at DePaul").

81. For discussion of student culture in the post-sixties era, see Helen Lefkowitz Horowitz, "The Changing Student Culture: A Retrospective" *Education Week* (Summer/Fall 1989), 25–29.

Adult Students in the Loop—and Elsewhere

For most of its existence DePaul has been divided between its uptown (or Lincoln Park) campus and its various downtown (or Loop) locations. As suggested in chapter 5, the student culture at each of these campuses was quite different. While both were frequented by commuter students through most of the university's history, the downtown students were enrolled in professional schools and most of those attending in the evening were adults.

Adult students generally have not participated in the various activities that defined the culture of DePaul's traditional-age student body. By and large, they did not join the Greek societies in nearly the same numbers; nor did they participate in the dances and dating that preoccupied so many DePaul undergraduates in the years between 1920 and 1970. Most adult students worked during the day, and for them school was tied directly to career advancement. Their social lives did not revolve around the campus. Like the veterans whom Nick DeLeonardis described in the latter forties, they were serious students who wanted a practical education. And DePaul's various evening programs offered the very sort of no-nonsense education they sought, without social attachments.

This does not mean, however, that there was no social life among DePaul's adult evening students. From almost the very start of the university's various evening programs there were organizations representing student interests, many related to the professions they studied. There also were student government representatives. And at points in time social organizations and even Greek societies existed for the evening students of one college or another. But these activities did not touch the lives of most adult students. For the majority of DePaul's evening clientele, the social life associated with school occurred in the hallways and classrooms of the university's Loop facilities. There many of them met other students with similar backgrounds and interests, and made friends while completing their programs of study. In some cases lifelong relationships were started, in others the social life of the hallways and the sidewalks around the Loop campus provided a friendly environment for coping with the challenges of school. If it was not the convivial social milieu of the day students, it was one of mutual support and comaradarie regarding school questions.

As the university developed a residential campus at Lincoln Park in the seventies and eighties, differences between the experiences of day and evening students widened. While such student organs as the *DePaulia* and the yearbooks (*DePaulian*) had long focused on the undergraduate day population, the growing numbers of residential students and their activities drew even more coverage in the years following 1980. Many adult students, particularly in the large M.B.A., Computer Science and School for New Learning programs, came to believe that activities and services were concentrated disproportionally at the Lincoln Park campus. The development of satellite campuses to serve adult students from the suburbs, first near O'Hare airport and then in Westchester, Oak Forest and Naperville, sharpened such perceptions. Adult students at these locations, while feeling strong connections with their particular programs and classmates, often reported little sense of attachment to the university as a whole. Student support systems and conventional campus amenities were sparse at these sites, and the world of campus activities reported in the DePaulia and other university publications seemed quite remote. In this respect, the experiences of DePaul students continued to vary widely.

As DePaul approaches its centennial, it continues to contend with the challenges associated with its diverse student population. Maintaining a sizeable residential campus and serving a growing population of adult students across the metropolitan area, the university could never claim to have a single, unitary student culture. Instead, it has had multiple campus cultures, just as it has employed several campuses, each with a distinctive clientele. The adults who utilize DePaul's professional and continuing education programs, consequently, have defined their own degree of involvement with the institution and with each other. And in doing this, they continue to help shape the peculiar mix of student experiences that has long characterized DePaul.

John L. Rury

DeP

PART III

MAKING

THE

MODERN

UNIVERSITY

CHAPTER SIX

DePaul University 1920–1945

Years of Growth and Crisis

Albert Erlebacher

Between the sudden departure of Rev. Francis X. McCabe, C.M., early in 1920 and the resignation of Rev. Michael J. O'Connell, C.M., in autumn 1944, DePaul wrestled with issues that profoundly influenced its future. Fathers O'Connell, Levan and Corcoran, the three men who led the university during that quarter century, faced some fundamental questions. First, could the university continue to increase its student enrollment? Second, could the institution improve and expand its curriculum with new programs that would respond to the needs of the time? Third, if the first two took place, would the quality of these programs be recognized by the national and professional accrediting agencies without whose imprimatur DePaul's student population could not possibly continue growing? Finally, could the university meet the challenge to find new economic resources that would keep the institution moving forward?

At the same time that DePaul was struggling to get ahead, its leaders were placing new emphasis on its Catholic and Vincentian heritage. Religious instruction became more important, and the university looked for ways to express its religious identity more clearly. At the same time, its leaders confronted some difficult ethical issues.

The end of this period coincided with the Second World War, and that national crisis brought many changes to the university, as DePaul first demonstrated its support for the war and then was pressed into service as a center for military and technical training. By the end of the conflict, the university was entering a new era wherein growth and challenges would bring further changes.

DePaul in the 1920s

In the 1920s, every segment of the higher education enterprise in the United States expanded. The number of public universities and colleges not only increased but they also offered a greater variety of programs. Cities established municipally financed four-year public institutions in which graduate work and professional degrees soon complemented undergraduate programs (Chicago had no four-year public university at the time, however). The private sector experienced a similar expansion as professional programs proliferated and improved in response to increasingly stringent accreditation criteria applied by such professional associations as the American Bar Association and the Association of Colleges of Business Schools. Universities in general faced increasingly rigorous surveillance from the North Central Association and similar regional accrediting groups. And a new type of institution, the junior college (now called the community college), began to appear on the educational scene. In general, the 1920s was a decade in which students enjoyed a greater variety of institutions of higher education as well as expanded and improved curricula. The United States had become far more complex than the society of earlier generations, and changes in higher education reflected this.

DePaul's search for recognition and growth in the next quarter century is set in this context. The university's most intractable obstacle was the precarious state of its finances. Lacking any endowment other than the teaching and administrative duties contributed by the Vincentian fathers, the school remained almost wholly dependent on tuition for its revenue. In addition, the university was still burdened by the unfortunate legacy of Father Byrne's and Father McCabe's ambitious but problem-plagued plans, a debt in excess of $500,000, a sum almost equal to the annual operating budget of the early 1920s. (1)

As Anna Waring notes in her chapter, a highly decentralized administration characterized this period: each academic dean was closely involved with the issues of his own college or school. Consequently, each of these units viewed the growth of the university as a question of its own prosperity or lack thereof. This made it difficult for administrators to institute university-wide changes. Further, the American public expected continuing improvement in higher education, and Catholic parents and educators harbored the same expectations.

These issues were so interrelated at DePaul in the 1920s that none could be solved in isolation from any of the others. The ability to attract more students depended on providing them with additional choices of courses and programs. DePaul's challenge was a complex one, as it sought to serve both its full-time day students and also an increasing number of individuals who came in the late afternoon, at night and on Saturdays to complete their degree programs or begin graduate or professional courses. Had it not been for this large afternoon and evening student body, DePaul would have remained a very small liberal arts institution. But as the higher education enterprise expanded, the matter of quality became more important. Students who had completed their undergraduate education and wanted to do graduate work or enter professional schools needed the assurance that their baccalaureate degrees would be recognized by the schools to which they applied. Further, they needed to know that their credentials would be accepted by employers and professional peers. The university had to address questions of quality while attracting additional students, even though resources were scarce.

The constituency served by the university was not wealthy and was historically limited to lower middle-class and middle-class households, primarily first and second generation sons and daughters of European immigrants. The part-time students who took classes on the downtown campus worked in Loop commercial and financial enterprises and came from neighborhoods throughout the city. But the majority of the university's full-time students on the uptown campus continued to come from the city's north side. DePaul was a commuter school and the vast majority of its students were from the city.

The university had provided liberal arts, business and law education in the Loop, always in rented quarters. By the mid-1920s, the administration was convinced that to accommodate its growing downtown operation, the institution needed its own building. Moreover, no new facilities had been built on the Webster Avenue campus since the early years of the century. Though DePaul had never engaged in large-scale fund raising in metropolitan Chicago, it attempted to address the needs of both campuses during the 1920s. As a result two major projects were taken on: one uptown and the other in the Loop. The first large-scale fund-raising campaign also was begun in the mid-1920s. This effort produced a new classroom building, now named Levan Hall, on the uptown campus and a seventeen-story tower at 64 E. Lake Street, the northeast corner of the Loop.

Eagerness to achieve accreditation for its academic programs spurred the university to improve the quality of its programs. This required hiring more instructors, many in professional fields in which the traditionally trained Vincentian priests had little expertise. These newly hired professors had to have stronger academic preparation in their disciplines than their counterparts in the past. This forced the university to raise salaries to attract and hold an experienced teaching staff and to provide improved library facilities and more flexible teaching schedules.

The Struggle for External Recognition

Perhaps the most serious problem faced by the three presidents of the 1920–45 period was winning and keeping accreditation. This task was complicated by the constant need to increase the number of students and add to the programs offered by the university, for growth was an absolute necessity if DePaul was to continue as a viable institution. Growth had been rapid during Father McCabe's tenure as president. A School of Commerce had been established and the Illinois College of Law had been acquired and renamed DePaul University College of Law. Probably the most important educational innovation of Father McCabe's administration was opening DePaul to women. In summer 1911, for the first time, nuns were admitted to the university during the summer session. Six years later, despite clear opposition from Archbishop Mundelein, female students were admitted to all undergraduate and graduate divisions of the university. (2) This boosted enrollments considerably, as John Rury has noted. By the start of the twenties between 30 and 40 percent of full-time uptown students were women. At the end of the decade they constituted a large fraction of the part-time students in the Loop as well.

Accreditation was important for a number of reasons. Only students who graduated from an accredited institution were admitted to graduate and professional schools. Those who planned to teach in public schools found that coming from an accredited school made it easier to obtain certification. But winning accreditation from the University of Illinois and later from the North Central Association of Schools and Colleges posed a huge challenge for Fathers Levan and Corcoran during the 1920s because the accrediting bodies set criteria that tested the university's frail financial standing. Furthermore, accreditation from the University of Illinois, the North Central Association and several professional groups had to be won almost simultaneously. This was a time when such measures of institutional quality became widespread.

All these issues converged in the mid-1920s. During the previous decade accreditation had been granted on a virtually ad hoc basis, through correspondence between DePaul presidents and University of Illinois officials. In the absence of a comprehensive regional accrediting system, flagship state universities often served as informal agencies for the certification of program quality at other institutions. DePaul's leaders wrote to these individuals to assure them of the preparation of specific students, or to gain certification for students who had applied to work in the Chicago public schools. Early in 1923 the university petitioned the University of Illinois to grant DePaul's School of Commerce a comprehensive review. A team was sent to inspect DePaul's program. The report was less than laudatory. The College of Commerce was

Coach Ray Meyer and the DePaul Blue Demon basketball team upon winning the NIT championship in 1945. George Mikan, one of the all-time great basketball players, is standing behind Meyer.

urged to revise its admission standards to reduce the number of students with poor pre-college preparation, to increase the number of highly trained faculty members, to improve its pre-professional liberal arts courses, to seek more financial support, and to create a good working library of its own. (3) In the past DePaul had always relied on the Chicago Public Library and the John Crerar Library to serve its students. An earlier report had commented favorably on the improvements DePaul had made, such as maintaining a maximum of eighteen hours of teaching per week for its professors. (4) The visitation team concluded that while specific DePaul students could have individual commerce courses approved, the university would have to put more improvements in place before its commerce college could be granted blanket approval.

On the heels of his effort to gain approval from the University of Illinois, Father Levan tried to win accreditation from the American Association of Law Schools (AALS) and the North Central Association (NCA). The university promised to increase the law school curriculum to three years for day students and four years for the night school in order to get AALS accreditation. It also pledged to improve the library facilities for law students. Levan felt that these promises might win approval for DePaul in time for the 1924–25 school year. (5) Next, Levan tried to leverage this tentative approval into full accreditation from the NCA for all of DePaul's programs. The NCA was just becoming the region's principal agency for accrediting secondary schools and colleges, and like many Catholic institutions, DePaul was eager to gain its approval. The NCA application had been pending for some time, and Levan was anxious to bring it to a successful conclusion at the earliest possible moment, for he realized that without accreditation, the university's ability to continue attracting students would be threatened. Yet early in 1924 he sensed that the NCA might not move as quickly as he had hoped. In his argument to that body's Commission on Accreditation, Levan argued that the forthcoming approval of the law school ought to convince them that DePaul had made all the improvements demanded of it. Levan claimed further that the university had completed all the changes requested earlier by the NCA, and now he asked for a speed-up of the procedure. If the NCA's hesitation had been based on AASL's inaction, that obstacle had been removed, according to Father Levan. (6)

By 1925 Levan had completed the task of winning accreditation from the three prestigious organizations he had approached over the previous several years. Winning this recognition was one thing, but keeping it would prove to be equally difficult. As Anna Waring notes, a number of times during the late 1920s and into the 1930s DePaul's newly won academic status was challenged. Just before stepping down from the presidency in 1930 Levan was faced with the prospect of yet another visit from the NCA. The association criticized DePaul's relationship with its High School for Girls in the Loop and DePaul Academy on the north side, and the university was also accused of giving too many athletic scholarships. Dissatisfaction was expressed because it still did not have a separate library building (a problem that was finally remedied when the John T. Richardson Library was completed in the early 1990s). Although Levan understood that he would have to address these criticisms he pleaded with NCA leadership that DePaul had been given insufficient notice for another full visit, and he successfully petitioned for more time. (7)

When Father Francis C. Corcoran, C.M., succeeded Levan in 1930, he inherited these issues. The harsh financial conditions imposed by the Depression did not make it any easier for Corcoran or his successor, Michael J. O'Connell, C.M., to continue to make the steady progress that had been the hallmark of Levan's administration. By the time Levan resigned in 1930 (owing to serious illness and exhaustion at least in part from the accreditation battles), the struggle to maintain accreditation was less onerous for his immediate successors. The desperate financial conditions of the early 1930s probably affected all higher education institutions and might have made accrediting associations a bit more accommodating. When the University of Illinois completed its inspection of DePaul in 1937 it continued to identify a number of concerns. Among them was the library, which, though it was an attractive place for students to study, was hamstrung by its limited schedule. The various classroom visits by the team showed that the quality of teaching varied from fair to good. (8) The credentials of the faculty had improved from earlier years, but too many professors still did not have terminal degrees in their disciplines. Criticism was leveled at DePaul professors for offering so many off-campus courses, especially at religious houses in the Chicago area. (9)

Father O'Connell gave serious thought to increasing the university's graduate offerings by the late 1930s. To prepare for the accreditation team's scrutiny that would precede NCA approval of DePaul's new graduate programs, he consulted Dr. Roy J. Deferrari, graduate dean at the Catholic University of America, a man highly respected by both Catholic educators and accrediting associations. Deferrari came to Chicago and made a personal survey for Father O'Connell. His report was not as favorable as O'Connell might have wished. While Deferrari observed many positive features, he noted that at least four departments in the liberal arts college were not led by individuals holding terminal degrees. The library, Deferrari commented, needed to expand its collections, especially its scholarly journals. Besides urging a separate library building, Deferrari also noted that the physics and chemistry departments had no laboratories, although he was impressed by the biology labs and facilities. Finally, Deferrari told O'Connell that DePaul had to centralize its administrative functions such as registration and record keeping and that professors should set more rigorous standards for grading students. (10) It appears that Deferrari felt DePaul still had a long way to go before its graduate offerings could be approved. Ironically, many of Deferrari's comments in 1937 were the same as NCA's criticisms in 1949, when the university found itself in a serious accreditation crisis.

During World War II accreditation standards were relaxed slightly to compensate for the departure of a number of young academics from many institutions, including DePaul, for government service or the military. The accrediting associations were more willing to let schools make adjustments in schedules in order to make better use of their facilities and their remaining faculty.

The accreditation process at DePaul was complicated by the university's careless financial record keeping, which was due in part to its highly decentralized administration, but also to the personality and methods of its treasurer, Father Daniel J. McHugh, C.M. McHugh had been a member of the very first group of Vincentian priests at DePaul. A hard-working scholar, an able astronomical researcher and a member of the Royal Society of Astronomers, McHugh had guided the university in the construction of its telescope on the roof the main academic building. (11) Despite his interest in science, attention to detail and order did not carry over into his duties as the university's financial book-keeper, and the financial records were often both messy and unintelligible. The inability of DePaul's leaders to understand where the university stood financially was made more troublesome because the accounting methods followed by McHugh merged the funds of the university, the academy, St. Vincent's parish, and the Vincentian community. Since 1897, the individual who was DePaul's president also served as pastor of the parish and religious head of the community. There were years when the income of the entire Vincentian enterprise in Chicago was used to cover whatever deficits might have occurred in any particular constituent institution, which made it very difficult to determine the university's financial status at any particular time.

DePaul's confused financial records—as well as its chronic shortage of funds—worsened during the Great Depression. Outsiders might have suspected that the university did not have a secure financial foundation on which to build its educational structure. By 1932 the situation was serious enough to force President Corcoran to make a major change in the financial management of the university. He appointed Dave Sharer, an accounting teacher on the commerce faculty, to be comptroller. Apart from the presidents under whom he served, Sharer became the single most important voice on disbursement of DePaul's money. Corcoran kept McHugh on as treasurer, but the real financial authority was transferred to Sharer, the first layperson to hold such an important administrative position. From then until his retirement in the early 1960s Sharer carried the burden of this responsibility. The rise of Sharer as a major policy maker at the university improved its record keeping considerably, raised the community's confidence in the university and allowed the institution's leaders to gain a clearer understanding of its financial status. Thus presidents could begin to spend more time and energy on educational planning for the future. (12)

By the early 1940s DePaul had accomplished a great deal. It had managed to secure and maintain accreditation from a variety of organizations. It had also avoided financial collapse, although its fiscal status remained shaky. Most importantly, however, it continued to draw students from Chicago's many ethnic communities, Catholic and non-Catholic alike. And this allowed it to continue pursuing its mission of Catholic and Vincentian education with new vigor.

DePaul's Religious Identity in a Time of Change

DePaul's commitment to its Roman Catholic heritage during this quarter century originated in its combination of certainty within itself and its increasing sense of security within the larger American community. In its first quarter century the university assumed but did not seriously examine its commitment to the teachings of the Roman Catholic faith. It stated its allegiance to Catholicism, while at the same time reminding prospective students that its charter required it to admit students of all religions and ethnic groups. (13) The Very Reverend George Cardinal Mundelein, Archbishop of Chicago during the 1920s, had struggled hard to diminish the influence of ethnicity among Chicago Catholics ever since his arrival in 1915. (14) To feature a consistent standard of religious instruction was one way to accomplish this. As historian Phillip Gleason has noted, other Catholic institutions began placing greater emphasis on religious instruction in the late twenties, partly in response to the perception that they were losing their distinctive religious character. These developments were undoubtedly positive inducements to make the teaching of religion at DePaul a higher priority.

There were other reasons as well. In 1920 when Father McCabe was removed as president by his superior at Perryville, Missouri, the reason cited was carelessness in his duties as the head of the Vincentian community in Chicago. There was little doubt that his personally relaxed attitude toward religious discipline was seen as a poor model for the Vincentian community. That he had become "persona non grata" to Archbishop Mundelein, leader of Chicago's Roman Catholics, was also a factor in forcing his superiors to remove him. McCabe and Mundelein had diametrically opposed views on the question of higher education for Catholic women. When McCabe ignored Mundelein's instructions not to admit women, surely it must have irked the strong-willed archdiocesan leader. It is also possible that McCabe's behavior as an activist spokesman for the cause of Irish independence in Chicago made him unpopular with a bishop who was trying very hard to suppress ethnic loyalties among his followers. (15) After McCabe's departure, it appeared that the university would have some fences to mend with the local Catholic leadership. (16)

Change did not occur immediately, however. It was not until the end of the 1920s that DePaul began formal classroom teaching of religion. Prior to that, attendance at religious services was required only for full-time Catholic students; attendance was strictly optional for the growing number of non-Catholics who came to DePaul in the 1920s and 1930s. Even after religion became part of the formal curriculum, religion courses earned fewer credits for students than other liberal arts courses. (17) Ellamay Horan, an instructor in the religion department as well as in education, argued that Father O'Connell should go to the National Catholic Education Association (NCEA) to argue that religion courses be given comparable academic credit. Horan thought that religion courses would achieve academic respectability if they were rigorous and were accorded sufficient academic value. Administrators should not be surprised, she maintained, if Catholic students did not take seriously religion courses offering only one credit hour compared to the three credits students earned in other classes. (18)

Horan was a leader in the effort to institute religious education at DePaul during these years. She devoted her career to improving the teaching of religion at the grammar and high school level through her editorship of the *Journal of Religious Instruction*, which DePaul sponsored from its inception in 1930 until 1942, when it was transferred to a commercial religious publishing house in the east. The offerings in religion were quite limited in the 1920s. It was not until the mid to late 1930s that the number of such courses began rising, but by that time there was a significant increase in offerings in many other disciplines. In the 1932–33 academic year students in the College of Liberal Arts and Sciences could elect from a menu of five religion courses including "Christ and His Church," "Life Problems," "Moral and Religious Problems of the Present Day" and two courses dealing with the teaching of religion in grade and high schools. The religion department originally consisted of only two teachers, a Vincentian and Dr. Horan. (19)

During the 1930s the university's leaders began advocating a stronger Catholic educational position, which they hoped would make DePaul stand out among other institutions of higher education. Throughout the 1930s Presidents Francis Corcoran, C.M., and Michael J. O'Connell, C.M., made it a practice to publicly proclaim these beliefs within and outside of

Adult students meeting at the downtown campus, 1970s.

the university. In his annual address to a general faculty meeting in September 1933 Father Corcoran reviewed DePaul's experience as a Catholic university, and quoted Pope Pius XI's definition of the purpose of such an institution: "to cooperate with divine grace in forming the true and perfect Christian, that is to form Christ himself in those regenerated by baptism." Corcoran noted the pope's argument that the true product of Catholic education was the supernatural person who thinks, judges and acts in accord with reason illumined by the supernatural light. Father Corcoran thought that this goal, if properly pursued, would not narrow a person's mind but would give him or her a positive and inclusive outlook. For Father Corcoran this Catholic definition did not close the university's door to people of other religious faiths, and he proudly proclaimed that "none . . . ever found it necessary to sever his or her connection with the university on religious grounds." (20)

The university's leaders did more than advance DePaul's religious identity through statements, however. Its Catholic and Vincentian identity also obligated it to reach out to the greater Chicago community. In 1933 Father Corcoran initiated the DePaul Art League which, in his view, would promote a strong relationship between art and Christianity. The league sponsored art shows and lectures, and it undertook a citywide effort to bring the work of Catholic artists to the attention of the larger community. There were precedents for other forms of community outreach as well. Years earlier Father McCabe had avidly supported the DePaul Settlement House on Halsted Street, actively promoting its children's nursery. (21)

At his inaugural address in 1935 the Very Reverend Michael J. O'Connell, C.M., expanded on some of his predecessor's themes. He reminded his audience that DePaul had been established to give "to the people of Chicago a center of higher learning under Catholic auspices, and the proof of its need lies in the fact of its phenomenal growth." He felt the need neither to defend nor apologize for DePaul's Catholicism, since this philosophy had stood the test of time for almost two millennia. For DePaul, according to O'Connell, knowledge was not an end in itself but a means to bring wisdom to society. As far as its programs were concerned, DePaul needed only to infuse this spirit into all of its courses and curricula. If knowledge did not bring wisdom with it and define the true meaning of life, he asserted, it was not worth much. If DePaul did not teach its students the art of right living, which could come only from right thinking, it was not worth its place in the firmament of society. DePaul must stand for its conviction that it was "essential to a proper education to have given to each of those whom it forms the mental and spiritual moorings which enable them to ride out safely and serenely the storms of life." (22) A similar theme was struck by Father Walter Case, C.M., head of the English department, who delivered a sermon on the occasion of O'Connell's installation, reminding him and the entire community that DePaul had played an exceptional role in the educational life of Chicago.

Some students reflected this more overt advocacy of a distinctly Roman Catholic philosophy of education in their burgeoning interest in religious activities. A student organization known as the Chicago Inter-Student Catholic Association (CISCA) promoted student attendance at mass on the first Friday of each month, and some of its members undertook a special discipline of spending fifteen minutes each Friday in devotion to the Blessed Sacrament. Members of another student organization, the Women's League, marched in the League of Decency parade and did charity work. (23) The university also organized a sodality organization among the predominantly female students in the Secretarial School. They were encouraged to attend services, even if that meant they had to go to the uptown campus to do so. The university's full schedule of student dances, usually held off-campus, was suspended during the Lenten season; a restriction lifted only for St. Patrick's Day. By the mid-1930s the faculty and deans were urged to encourage students to attend the annual religious retreat. (24)

The religious atmosphere which Presidents Corcoran and O'Connell promoted was balanced by the sensitivity these leaders exhibited toward non-Catholics. From its earliest days DePaul's leaders had proudly proclaimed the lack of a religious affiliation requirement for its students and faculty. For American Jews, who found entrance into many institutions limited by artificial quotas, the openness of DePaul was particularly welcome. Many prospective Jewish law students could enter DePaul even if they were barred from other institutions. Alex J. Goldman, later a practicing rabbi as well as an attorney, recalled that his father, an Orthodox rabbi, encouraged him to attend DePaul and told him to respect its traditions by attending graduation baccalaureate services, even if he could not participate in the religious aspects of the ceremonies. The elder Goldman became a great admirer of Dean William Clarke of the law school, "a devout Catholic and gentle Irishman," and the two often sought each other's advice. (25) DePaul helped to forge bonds such as these.

While DePaul's leaders took pride in the aura of tolerance under which they operated, it had limits. In 1937 the university informed the National Catholic Education Association (NCEA) that non-Catholics were excluded from teaching in the religion, philosophy, history, biology and education Departments, and that all department heads were Roman Catholics. Such provisions were common at Catholic institutions during these years. Further, the university reported that "non-Catholic teachers are interviewed about their views on Catholic doctrinal issues and are visited by the department heads and the dean of instruction." This religious defensiveness occurred more characteristically in the College of Liberal Arts and Sciences than in the professional schools, which enrolled proportionally fewer Catholic students. (26)

By the late 1930s unabashed expressions of its Catholic philosophy appeared in some of DePaul's official literature. The 1935–36 Bulletin of the College of Commerce proclaimed that its curriculum was designed "to train young men and women for business careers . . .in accordance with a Catholic philosophy and ethics . . . designed to present a broad perspective." (27) The philosophy curriculum offered to students in the Colleges of Liberal Arts and Sciences and Commerce reflected a standard scholastic philosophy approach, with courses in logic, cosmology, metaphysics, epistemology and the psychology of education. (28)

Groundbreaking for Alumni Hall. Father Comerford J. O'Malley, president of DePaul, at the controls of the crane with dignitaries and students, 1955.

Such lofty statements of purpose contrasted with the university's conduct during those years with respect to certain ethical issues. Two incidents which put application of these principles in question occurred in the 1930s. The first was a case in which an instructor, John B. Fuller, had been hired to teach German at DePaul in 1935 at a salary of $2,000. President O'Connell had assumed that Fuller was a practicing Catholic. Between the time he was hired in the spring of 1935 and the start of school that September, O'Connell discovered that Fuller was a former priest who had left his religious community and married. O'Connell fired Fuller before the term began. As a result Fuller sued the university and confronted Father O'Connell in Cook County court. The conflict was resolved when Fuller received a financial settlement from the appellate court. (29)

The second situation concerned DePaul's policy toward admitting African American students. Like other Catholic institutions at that time, from parochial schools to hospitals, DePaul had a policy that discriminated against Black students. From time to time in earlier years, there had been Black students at DePaul, and in the twenties there had been a number of nonwhite students from the Philippines and China. But the university had not encouraged them to attend, even when they were Roman Catholic. In 1934 the University Council, the most important advisory body to the President, considered the issue. While it was clear that the university would not adopt an outright "no Negro students" policy, it advocated the use of various academic and administrative devices to limit the number of African American admissions. Black students who applied to DePaul were required to submit complete transcripts and pay their tuition in full before being admitted to the university. If African American applicants met all the stringent requirements, they were still discouraged by being informed that since they were likely to be the only "colored student" they might "encounter an uncongenial atmosphere" for which the institution would not like to assume responsibility. The statement assumed that if such students understood that they were "persona non grata" they might not pursue the matter further. (30)

These informal policies apparently had not kept all African Americans from coming to DePaul and the council was asked to adopt a more formal policy. One issue faced by the council, the majority of whose members were Vincentian priests, was the reaction to the presence of African American students by White students and their parents. A variety of views were expressed by members of the council. Some were concerned about the effect that African Americans might have on the rest of the student body, some of whom might not "be educated to accustoming themselves to the presence of the colored students . . . or parents might raise objections to mixed classes." Because of these concerns, the council concluded that non-Catholic Black students should not be admitted, while Catholics would be admitted if they met a literal application of the admission requirements. The council recommended to President Corcoran that he announce a formal policy based on considerations of religion "and secondarily on numerical restriction, scholastic selectivity and favorable qualifications of personality." (31)

Discussions such as these reveal the pervasiveness and power of racial discrimination at that time. It is possible that the university's leadership worried that the institution's historic core constituency, ethnic Whites, might leave DePaul if Blacks were admitted in significant numbers. If that fear had any basis in fact, it changed with time. By the late 1940s DePaul was admitting African American students, particularly veterans, and highlighting their success in school. As John Rury notes, however, the question of race continued to be an important issue at DePaul for years to come.

These incidents reveal the sometimes contradictory nature of DePaul's emphasis on religious education in these years. In certain respects the policies of Presidents O'Connell and Corcoran were formal responses to the suggestions of Catholic educational leaders and perhaps also to the provincial Vincentian leadership. As noted earlier, many Catholic institutions placed greater emphasis on their religious identity during this time. Most Catholic students and faculty members undoubtedly welcomed greater attention to matters relating to religion. But this was also a period of exclusion, when the university barred certain groups of people from faculty positions, and discouraged other groups from enrolling as students. In attempting to pursue the university's Catholic and Vincentian mission zealously, DePaul appears to have violated some of its self-proclaimed principles. This too made the interwar years a particularly troubling time in the university's history.

DePaul During the War Years

Following the Japanese attack on Pearl Harbor on December 7, 1941, DePaul faced a new set of institutional challenges. For more than a year Father O'Connell and his administrative team had had some indication that DePaul's survival, tenuous during the financially dark years of the Great Depression, might now be threatened in a different way. In the late summer of 1940 the U.S. Congress passed the first peacetime draft in American history. This legislation threatened to move young college-age men from the classroom into the armed services for one year. Shortly before the law expired in late summer 1941, the world situation had worsened. Congress renewed the legislation, even though the measure squeezed through the House of Representatives by only a single vote. Meanwhile, Germany had attacked the Soviet Union in June and the diplomatic maneuvering between the United States and Japan had reached a critical stage. Most of President Franklin Roosevelt's advisors—as well as knowledgeable citizens—understood that the entry of the United States into the Second World War was not in question, only when and under what circumstances it would occur were not foregone conclusions.

The university had already noted a small drop in male enrollments in the day divisions of commerce and law in autumn 1940. These declines were partially compensated for by rising enrollments in the night divisions of those schools. Among those who left in the first draft calls of 1940 was the basketball coach, Thomas Hagerty, although he was expected to return for the 1941–42 season. (32) One problem facing the university was how to handle students who received their draft notices in the midst of a semester. One suggestion allowed them to get academic credit if they had passed a certain point in the term. Most of the early draft regulations gave college students time to finish their current term before reporting for duty. Later in the war the university experimented with new rules that gave students additional time to finish incomplete courses after they returned.

Another device used by the university to keep its student population from falling disastrously was to create additional programs to attract new students. The University Council recommended that the secretarial department initiate a new two-year course to train men to serve as executive secretaries for the top managers, who would be needed as defense manufacturing expanded rapidly in the Chicago area. (33)

The attack on Pearl Harbor—and the Declarations of War against Japan, Germany and Italy which followed in the next few days—were probably a surprise to many students and faculty. Chicago and the middle west had been the center of isolationist opinion throughout the 1930s, a mind-set to which the large German and Italian ethnic communities living here had subscribed, influenced no doubt by Colonel Robert McCormick, editor-publisher of the *Chicago Tribune*, one of the major voices opposing American involvement in the war. But the suddenness of the Japanese attack made isolationist thinking inconceivable after the "day of infamy."

Lieutenant Bob Booth USAC as pictured in the 1942 DePaulian. During the war years, much of the uptown campus was used by the military.

The DePaul community joined the wave of patriotism and desire for revenge that swept the nation. At the first meeting of the University Council, which took place in the week immediately following Pearl Harbor, deans estimated the drops in enrollment their colleges might experience if full mobilization took place. The forecasts ranged from 20 percent to as high as 60 percent with commerce and law deans reporting the highest percentages. Not only would the draft and enlistments deplete the student body, but the lure of high paying jobs in the expanding defense industry might also draw off additional students. The council decided to limit extracurricular activities to a minimum and suggested that the national anthem be sung at all university convocations. It also urged President O'Connell to offer the university's facilities to the federal government. A month earlier, Father O'Connell had reported that the university's quota for the Civilian Pilot Training Corps had been filled. (34)

In subsequent weeks Father O'Connell ordered a sharp decrease in the number of bulletins published. The council had also suggested that the time to degree be accelerated by increasing the number of hours in each semester and by shortening the break between terms, although administrators feared that such unilateral actions might be criticized by accrediting associations. Father O'Connell was relieved when the North Central Association authorized its member schools to make any calendar changes that did not endanger educational quality. (35) By late 1942 the university abandoned the publication of the *DePaulia*.

While in publication, *DePaulia* editorials challenged any residual prewar isolationist sentiment by urging that the true duty of Catholics was "submission to recognized authority, and . . . for a revival of faith, for a new birth in the spirit of patriotism." The student editor regretted that war had come, stating, "we are fighting a war, and war in this world has come to mean hate . . . but for us there can be only love, and greater love which lies in Christ." (36)

Students responded to the challenges immediately. They were urged to report for civil defense work as air raid wardens and to assist the Red Cross. The December 18, 1941 edition of the *DePaulia* included detailed instructions to students who wished to enlist for a civilian pilot training program starting the following February at Glenview Naval Air Station, northwest of the city. (37) The newspaper began a "War Notes" column in January containing information about students and faculty who joined the military so that their friends at home might correspond with them. Later in February, the editor advised students to look over a recent issue of *Life* magazine that ran graphic pictures of German atrocities against civilians if they wanted to understand what Americans were fighting about. (38)

The 1942 *DePaulian* sarcastically commented that although the war had brought many changes to college life it had not done away with "homework—the bugaboo of the undergraduate." Oddly, anti-German hysteria had not yet overcome good sense, as the *DePaulia* reported on December 18, 1941 that the Christmas party of the German Club had been the most popular of all campus Christmas social events. (39)

As the war continued, social activities were modified to remind students that the war

*Military recruiters visit
DePaul in the 1940s.*

effort had to continue. Formal dress would not be required at the 1943 Junior-Senior Ball. Many fraternities and sororities maintained their schedule of social events, especially dances, although in 1943 Phi Kappa Alpha announced that it intended to suspend activities during the war, no doubt because so many of its members were in the service. Red Cross units were organized at both campuses and its members, mostly women, knitted socks, rolled bandages and also sold war bonds and stamps. (40) By the fall of 1942 a student reporter observed that there was some complaining among students, perhaps about the idea that their draft notices might remove them from school before the end of the term. The editor remonstrated that such complaints were uncalled for and that "students should realize that Uncle Sam doesn't owe them a college degree." (41)

When the larger contingents of young men in various military training units arrived at DePaul in the spring and autumn of 1943 there was an active attempt by student organizations to involve them in the various social activities of the campus, although these student-soldiers had relatively little time to participate because of their long schedule (see the discussion of such programs below). By the end of the 1943–44 academic year most of the special programs for soldiers and civilians had been completed, and the university began to give serious thought to the postwar problems that it would face.

Early in 1942 the university had established a large number of noncredit courses to train civilians to work in war defense plants. These courses were taught by the university's regular faculty and some experts drawn from Chicago's defense plants during the late afternoons and evenings. Men and women who took them paid no tuition, and their study materials were furnished. The university kept close track of the costs associated with these courses, and it was reimbursed for all direct and indirect costs by the federal government through the office of the Commissioner of Education. (42) The curriculum covered such topics as production supervision, business organization, industrial personnel management, cost and budget accounting and statistical analysis. Each class met for four hours per week. In addition, on the uptown campus there was instruction in techniques for chemical analysis and control. To help preserve the integrity of the regular curriculum, DePaul's regular students were not eligible for these classes, nor was college credit offered to the adults who took them. (43) No doubt these courses, which introduced DePaul to many Chicagoans who would otherwise not have had the opportunity, could also have served as models for various forms of postwar adult education. This program attracted thousands of students to DePaul for short but intensive courses of study.

School spirit was not ignored during wartime. Fred Waring, the noted popular band leader and choral director, had written a new anthem for the university which was aired on the NBC Red Network on March 6, 1942. In autumn 1942, the editor of *DePaulia* urged students to make a fuller contribution to the war effort by donating blood to the Red Cross, participating in drives to collect paper, metal and cooking fats for the government and volunteering at the U.S.O., an organization that provided recreational and social activities for soldiers and sailors on leave; this activity must have been especially attractive to female students because two large basic training facilities, Fort Sheridan and Great Lakes Naval Training Station, were located just north of Chicago, and tens of thousands of servicemen spent their precious weekend passes in Chicago's Loop, seeking a brief respite from the rigors of training and heartaches of homesickness. (44)

Student enthusiasm for the cause continued to grow throughout 1942 and 1943. Clubs, fraternities and sororities made the war cause a fundamental part of their activities. The 1943 *DePaulian*, the last to be published during the war, proudly announced that DePaul students dared not ignore the fact that three-fourths of the universe was involved in a "struggle for life and death" and that DePaul's proclamation to seek "Eternal Truth" and "the saving of man's soul" had to stand in defiance of those "which seeks to destroy it." (45) The Amazons, a girls' social group, hosted many U.S.O. dances. By spring 1943, when a full contingent of soldiers had arrived at the university, its members were brought into the social activities whenever possible. When Ray Meyer was hired as the new basketball coach in 1942, he made playing against the service teams at Great Lakes and Fort Sheridan a part of his rigorous schedule.

The entire university played a role in the war effort. Father O'Connell never considered closing DePaul, but instead sought ways to keep it viable. Between the start of the 1942–43 school year and the beginning of academic year 1943–44, the student population dropped from about 6,600 to 4,200. Fortunately the university did not have to dismiss any faculty because a considerable number of instructors either joined the military, served in various civilian and wartime agencies or went into private industry. A number of Vincentian priests left for the service to become military chaplains.

In order to keep the institution going and absorb the loss of students and faculty during the war, the university collaborated with military and civilian agencies on various wartime programs (some of which have been discussed above). The most difficult years were 1942–43 and 1943–44. By the end of the 1943–44 academic year the tide of war had swung to the side of the Allies. The invasion of France in June 1944 and the steady progress of American naval and military forces on two parallel fronts in the Pacific made the outcome of the war certain. Some observers in the U.S. had already called 1944–45 the year of victory. (46) The challenges facing the university involved changes in student demographics, relocation of some classes, and efforts to conserve human and material resources. The major wartime activities of the university had served complementary goals. They had satisfied DePaul's desire to be part of the great national effort to win the war and they had provided the means to help the university survive this stressful period. The presence of contingents from the Army Signal Corps and two full contingents from the Army Specialized Training Program (ASTP) as well as the training programs for civilians in war industry (discussed earlier) were the university's major wartime academic contributions.

The most marked effect on campus life came from ASTP, a program DePaul participated in from fall 1943 through spring 1944. Each ASTP contingent consisted of almost 600 men. For a university that had never had a residential student body, this produced some novel challenges, for the students had to be housed, fed and given physical and military training as well as classroom instruction. Up to this time DePaul's clientele had been overwhelmingly commuter students, and except for snack bars the university provided no food service. Most social activities, with the exception of intercollegiate and intramural sports, had always been off campus. The arrival of ASTP students in fall 1943 dramatically changed all this.

The university virtually closed the uptown campus to civilian students and quickly made necessary renovations to serve the student-soldiers. Part of the academy building was converted into residential quarters with soldiers sleeping on double-deck cots. The cafeteria was transformed into a military style mess hall, and students ate standard Army food served on regulation aluminum trays. Classes were held in the Science Building (now O'Connell Hall) and on the first floor of the academy building (now Bryne Hall). The athletic field, which extends north of the academy building to Belden Avenue, was used for physical education and military drill. In case of inclement weather these activities were moved into the auditorium. An extensive program of intramural sports was planned for these soldiers. (47)

ROTC cadets drill on the floor of "The Barn," late 1960s.

The *DePaulia* devoted one page in each issue to the activities of its military students. Student meals consisted of as many non-rationed foods as possible. In order to make the DePaul experience as similar as possible to life on a regular Army installation, the students had only twenty minutes to eat. Classes were held from eleven to noon each morning and from two to four each afternoon. Regular DePaul faculty taught chemistry, physics, mathematics, English, and history while Army instructors taught those courses more directly related to military training. In addition to the academic classes the soldier-students drilled six hours a week and also had six hours of physical training. The remaining time was devoted to required study halls. The semester began on August 9, 1943 and lasted twelve weeks. It concluded with two separate sets of examinations. The first consisted of the regular course exams given by university instructors while the second was a series of standardized Army examinations administered to all ASTP students nationwide. The threat that those who failed would "be returned to their outfits to await further orders," placed a serious psychological stress on the students. (48)

Following the end of the exam period the soldiers were invited to relax at an on-campus dance hosted by coeds. The experience of these student-soldiers was characterized by one of them as their first contact with college life; he assured the civilian students that these soldiers had enjoyed the halls of academe as well as the sincere friendship of DePaul students and faculty who made them "feel that we belong." (49) It is possible that some of these young men who might have recalled their DePaul experience after the war, were motivated to return to colleges and universities under the sponsorship of the G.I. Bill.

A second group of ASTP students arrived in January 1944. By early spring 1944 almost 10,000 men a month were completing the program throughout the country. It was a major resource for highly trained technicians needed by the Army to serve as noncommissioned and commissioned officers. In late spring 1944, General George C. Marshall, U. S. Army Chief of Staff, suddenly ended the program. Rapid advances by American forces in Europe and in the Pacific had produced higher casualties than expected, and the existing infantry divisions needed more personnel. (50) Thus, although the ASTP had to be sacrificed for more pressing require-ments, it provided the U.S. Army with a source of highly skilled technical personnel. For DePaul, as well as for many other universities throughout the nation, it was a way to help keep the doors open during a critical period.

Encouraged by the successful spring and summer 1944 offensives in both the European and Pacific theaters of the conflict, many DePaulites felt that the year 1944–45 would be the year of victory. (51) The D-Day invasion of France in June 1944, only a day after Rome was liberated, combined with rapid advances of the American naval and military forces in the Pacific, which began the liberation of the Philippine Islands in November and the daily air attacks on the Japanese home islands in late autumn 1944, made such hopes reasonable. At DePaul im-portant changes took place that year, too. In mid-1944 Father Michael O'Connell announced his forthcoming retirement after serving as DePaul's sixth president since 1935. Father Comerford J. O'Malley was appointed his successor. (52) In the previous few years O'Malley had played an increasingly important role as the number two man on the administrative team. Not only had he served as dean of the College of Commerce, he also had responsibility for carrying out many of the war-related activities in which the university had been involved.

Conclusion: DePaul Looks Forward to a New Era

The war years had forced the university's leadership to consider many basic questions. One of these was the makeup and function of the board of trustees which had been unchanged ever since St. Vincent's College had been incorporated in 1898. As Richard Meister has noted, in spring 1944 Father O'Connell had commissioned a management study by a layman, Stanley P. Farewell. The report contained some fundamental recommendations. One was to broaden the representation on the board of trustees by including more laymen, even if one or more might not be Roman Catholic. Another recommendation was to create some sort of advisory board composed of laymen prominent in the commercial, financial and industrial sectors of Chi-cago, whose knowledge and connections might bring additional resources to the university. The other recommendations included an effort by the university to reach out to its alumni and the establishment of a permanent university public relations program to strengthen the institution's ties and influence in many sectors of the Chicago community. In the past DePaul had not communicated with its alumni very consistently, other than to ask them for money. Farewell felt that alumni must be listened to as well as solicited for funds. Finally, the report urged the university to consider establishing new educational programs that would attract more students to the university.

Thus with the war ending and the university approaching its half-century mark, the Farewell report presented DePaul's leaders with a number of fundamental challenges to look for new directions. (53) The timing of this report together with the beginning of Father O'Malley's long presidency (it was to last from 1944–1963, the longest of any DePaul president) was an ideal confluence of factors. In the Farewell report, for the first time, the university leadership looked outside itself and the accrediting associations for guidance. The tone of the report suggested looking beyond day-to-day issues to examine fundamental trends and challenges the university had to face. DePaul's first fifty years were coming to a close; it had achieved much, but the world was changing even more rapidly than before, and American Catholicism was reaching a new level of maturity.

The war was coming to an end, Father O'Connell had retired, the resources of the university had been stretched thin by fifteen years of depression and war, and thousands of new students were getting ready to enter or return to school as soon as the war ended, to complete or begin their educations and careers. One fortunate change had not gone unnoticed by DePaul's leaders. That was that by the end of the war they had virtually eliminated the last of the debt, some of which had been incurred during the very first years of DePaul's existence. Thus Father O'Malley and his new team of administrators could begin to think about the implications in the Farewell report and to consider how DePaul might take advantage of the new opportunities the postwar world presented. The university entered this era in an optimistic frame of mind. Before it realized the benefits of this renewed energy, however, it faced one more crisis—perhaps the most important of its existence.

The Rev. Comerford J. O'Malley, C.M., president 1944–1964.

Chapter Six Notes

1. It is quite difficult to get exact figures about DePaul's finances before the 1930s. The debt referred to was incurred between 1898 and 1907 to pay for the construction of several buildings on the uptown campus. In the 1920s it was still between $500,000 and $700,000. The budget of the university was probably in the area of $250,000 to $300,000 in the mid-twenties. In examining the available figures one must keep in mind that both the income and expense side of the budget also include the costs of operating DePaul Academy. Consistently accurate bookkeeping did not exist at DePaul until the 1930s.

2. There is no question that the Archbishop and Fr. McCabe had opposite ideas about Catholic lay-women entering a male college or university. Francis X. McCabe, C.M. to Archbishop George Mundelein, 14 September 1917 and George Mundelein to Francis X. McCabe, 17 September 1917, Daniel J. McHugh Papers, DePaul University Archives (DPUA). Mundelein stated "I do not desire DePaul University to accept any young women in your college of Liberal Arts and Sciences." The author is indebted to Rev. Patrick Mullins, C.M., for sharing his unpublished manuscript "Recognizing the Ladies," DPUA. Also see memo from Rev. John T. Richardson, C.M., to Patrick Mullins, C.M., 19 September 1979, DPUA. Richardson characterized McCabe's administrative style as "running the university almost single-handed." Richardson thought that Mundelein favored separate colleges for women.

3. "Report on College of Commerce," 11 April 1923, Comerford O'Malley Papers, DPUA.

4. *Ibid.*

5. Thomas F. Levan, C.M., to Members of the Committee on Higher Education of the North Central Association of Colleges and Secondary Schools, 14 March 1924, O'Malley Papers, DPUA. North Central Association will hereafter be referred to as NCA.

6. *Ibid.*, and Ralph W. Aigler to P.M. Hughes, 19 February 1924, O'Malley Papers, DPUA.

7. Levan to Committee on Review of NCA, 17 March 1930, O'Malley Papers, DPUA. Fr. Levan frequently asked for and sometimes received additional time to meet the issues which NCA inspectors had raised.

8. "Report of University of Illinois Committee on Admissions on DePaul University," 31 March 1937, O'Malley Papers, DPUA.

9. *Ibid.*

10. Roy J. Deferrari to Rev. M.J. O'Connell, 8 January 1937, O'Connell Papers, DeAndreis-Rosati Memorial Archives located in Perryville, Missouri. Hereafter referred to as DRMA. Deferrari, a layman, was Dean of the Graduate School at Catholic University of America and was considered to have an astute ability to gauge when new graduate programs might be accredited.

11. Based on information from Rev. Patrick Mullins, C.M.

12. Comerford J. O'Malley, C.M., to Dave Sharer, 8 September 1960, O'Malley Papers, DPUA. Fr. O'Malley said that much of the stability and improvement that DePaul had made "can be traced to the wholesome influence you exercise. . . . "

13. *DePaul University Bulletin, Downtown College of Liberal Arts and Sciences, 1933–34* (Chicago, 1934) *passim.* Throughout the 1930s and 1940s bulletins carried similar statements.

14. The best study of Mundelein's work in Chicago is Edward J. Kantowicz, *Corporation Sole: Cardinal Mundelein and Chicago Catholicism* (Notre Dame, Indiana, 1983). One of Mundelein's major ambitions was to build a gigantic "Catholic University of the West" on a plot of land in Libertyville, Illinois. This institution would match Catholic University of America. Therefore Mundelein could not have been an enthusiastic supporter of such existing Catholic universities as Loyola and DePaul.

15. Thomas Finney, C.M., to Superior General, 13 February 1920, DRMA. Letter translated by Judith Ross.

16. This is the author's conclusion based on a letter from Rev. Joseph Donovan, C.M., to Rev. Francis X. McCabe, 8 June 1946 a copy of which is in the author's possession. Fr. Donovan told McCabe " . . . and I imagine the present rulers of the Irish Free State put your name and energies second to none among all their helpers outside of Ireland." McCabe was very active in Chicago's Irish community speaking and raising funds for the cause of Irish independence. See *Vincentian Weekly* 15 December 1918 and 8 February 1920, DRMA.

17. Most bulletins of the university during the 1920s, 1930s and 1940s carried a statement excusing non-Catholic students from attending compulsory religious services. This was quite reassuring to the many Protestant and Jewish students who attended DePaul, especially in the law and commerce colleges.

18. Ellamay Horan to Rev. Michael J. O'Connell, 10 December 1936, O'Connell Papers, at DRMA.

19. *DePaul University Bulletin for Downtown College of Liberal Arts and Sciences for 1932–33* (Chicago, 1932) *passim.*

20. "Address of Rev. Francis C. Corcoran to General Faculty Meeting," September, 1933, Francis C. Corcoran Papers, DRMA.

21. When Fr. McCabe was forced to retire a number of letters appeared lauding McCabe's leadership. See *Chicago Herald-Examiner*, 25 March 1920. His defenders urged Mundelein to use his influence to retain McCabe at DePaul. Telegram, Jay J. McCarthy to Archbishop Mundelein, 25 March 1920, McCabe Papers, DRMA. Such pleas may have fallen on deaf ears since Mundelein was probably happy to see McCabe leave; one could speculate that perhaps he had urged the Vincentian provincial to remove McCabe.

22. "Inaugural address of Michael J. O'Connell, C.M.," 9 December 1935, NCA Papers, DPUA. "Sermon of Rev. Walter E. Case, C.M." 9 December 1935 in *DePaul University News* (December 1935), O'Connell Papers, DRMA.

23. *Ibid.* Another social action group active at DePaul in the 1930s was CISCA, the Chicago Inter-Student Catholic Association; Andrew Greeley, *The Catholic Experience: An Interpretation of the History of American Catholicism* (Garden City, New York, 1967), see pp. 247–274 for an excellent discussion of Catholic social movement in the 1930–60 period. Greeley suggests that Chicago was the center of these reform movements.

24. "Constitution of DePaul University Student Activities Council," 9 December 1935, DPUA.

25. Alex J. Goldman, *My Father, Myself: A Son's Memoir of His Father, Rabbi Yehudah N. Goldman, America's Oldest Practicing Rabbi* (Chicago, 1997), 30 and 33–34.

26. "Survey of DePaul University to National Catholic Education Association" (1937), DPUA.

27. *DePaul University Bulletin of Downtown College, 1935–36* (Chicago, 1935) *passim,* reflects Fr. O'Connell's more pro-active attitude identifying DePaul as a Catholic institution. This quote remained in the bulletins for many years.

28. There were very few changes in the wording of the statements about the purpose of teaching philosophy or religion in the 1930s.

29. See John B. Fuller vs. DePaul University, Abstracts, Briefs and Arguments, 1937–1938, 293 Ill. App. 261. The author is indebted to Theodore G. Zervas for his unpublished paper "History of DePaul University vs. John B. Fuller" (1997).

30. "University Council Minutes," 12 January 1934, DPUA.

31. *Ibid.*

32. "University Council Minutes" 3 December 1940; 8 February, 8 May and 7 October 1941, DPUA includes a discussion of some of the issues relating to DePaul's reaction to the problems resulting from the enactment of the military draft.

33. "University Council Minutes" 18 February 1941, DPUA.

34. *Ibid.*, 7 October and 18 November 1941, DPUA.

35. *Ibid.*, 9 December 1941 and 14 April 1942, DPUA.

36. *DePaulia*, 11 December 1941.

37. *Ibid.*, 18 December 1942.

38. *Ibid.*, 26 February 1942.

39. *Ibid.*, 18 December 1941.

40. See 1942 and 1943 *DePaulian* in DPUA. The student annual was not published in 1944 and 1945 probably as a war-time conservation measure and probably because there were not enough students available to work on it.

41. "Editorial", *DePaulia*, 15 October 1942.

42. "Audit by Wolfe and Company of ESM Training Program from October 1, 1943 to August 13, 1944," DPUA. ESM stood for Engineering, Science and Management, the program in which civilians were trained to work in local war industries.

43. Interview with Edwin Schillinger, 2 March 1993. Schillinger, later a physics professor and dean of the College of Liberal Arts and Sciences, was an undergraduate student at DePaul during the war and worked as an assistant in the ESM Program. He recalled that these programs included women.

44. *Chicago New World*, 27 October 1943 and *DePaulia*, 29 October 1943.

45. *1943 DePaulian* (Chicago, 1943) passim.

46. The 7 January 1944 issue of the *DePaulia* referred to 1944 as the "Year of Victory."

47. *Chicago New World*, 27 August 1943 carried a long article describing the academic schedule, military training and recreational opportunities which the student soldiers in the ASTP program had. Autumn and winter issues of the 1943–44 *DePaulia* devoted many articles to the educational and social activities of these soldiers.

48. *DePaulia*, 15 October 1943.

49. *Ibid.*, 29 October 1943. ASTP stood for Army Specialized Training Program. Two contingents came to DePaul in the autumn and winter terms of 1943–44. Each contained about 600 men. Smaller groups had come to DePaul in Programs sponsored by the U.S. Army Signal Corps.

50. Louis E. Keefer, "Exceptional Young Americans: Soldiers and Sailors on College Campuses in world War II," *Prologue* 24 (Winter 1992): 374–383. The manpower situation in the spring of 1944 was so serious that Gen. Marshall ordered all men in ASTP units returned to their divisions; the navy, however, maintained its program to the end of the war.

51. *DePaulia*, 7 January 1944.

52. Fr. O'Malley, a native Chicagoan from Saint Vincent's parish had been at DePaul since the 1930's. He had been a philosophy professor, dean of the College of Commerce and had major responsibilities in running many of the war-time activities in which DePaul was involved. A man of some reserve, he was considered extremely close to hundreds of students who he knew by name, especially his outreach to many of the non-Catholic students in the Colleges of Commerce and Law. The idea of a lay board of trustees was originally suggested by Britton Budd to Rev. Michael J. O'Connell, 14 January 1944, O'Malley Papers, DPUA. The present author speculates that the idea was informally discussed by members of the board of trustees. O'Connell wanted to implement the idea, but by this time his resignation had already been announced. Therefore the implementation of the idea was left to Fr. O'Malley and the board of trustees. See Michael J. O'Connell to Britton Budd, 15 July 1944, O'Malley Papers, DPUA.

53. Stanley P. Farewell to Rev. Michael J. O'Connell, 26 May 1944, O'Malley Papers, DPUA.

CHAPTER SEVEN

TOWARDS THE COMPREHENSIVE UNIVERSITY

The Teaching-Research Debate at DePaul and Developing the Lincoln Park Campus

Thomas Croak, C.M.

DePaul's transition from "the little school under the El" to major urban university has been a long process. Earlier chapters in this volume have pointed to some of the key events in this transformation, particularly the accreditation crisis in the 1950s. In this chapter I will trace the development of doctoral programs and research, major factors in the university's effort to define itself, and DePaul's continuing commitment to the growth of the Lincoln Park community. These two developments, though conceptually different, are connected in time and space: both span the decades immediately following World War Two, and it was on the Lincoln Park campus that the university's doctoral programs of study were developed. Indeed, the appearance of these programs influenced demands for additional facilities that dictated campus expansion there. Though much of the university's commitment to research and to the development of the Lincoln Park campus took place in the quarter-century immediately after the war, progress and expansion in both of these fields is evident to this day, continuing to shape today's comprehensive urban university.

Prelude: Postwar Expansion and the Accreditation Crisis of 1950

DePaul's enrollments exploded at the conclusion of World War Two, in the late 1940s, as throngs of students arrived to pursue their college educations under the auspices of the Servicemen's Readjustment Act of 1944, popularly known as the G.I. Bill. (1) Though enrollments at some schools grew by 10% to 20% over pre-war figures, DePaul's student population doubled in the 1946–1947 academic year (from 4,817 to 9,485). (2) Few institutions were more profoundly affected by this whole generation of students than DePaul. In characteristic entrepreneurial fashion, the university adjusted its programs and operations to provide services and classroom opportunities for the masses of men and women returning from the armed services. (3)

The adjustment was not always smooth, however. The influx of students highlighted long-standing contrasts between the university's two campuses: the large, bustling Loop operation, where fully 93 percent of the student population attended classes in three distinct shifts—morning, afternoon and evening—almost in lock-step fashion, and the Lincoln Park campus, "the other DePaul," still "the little school under the El." DePaul lacked the residential campus found at most universities and did not offer the kinds of services required by a residential student body. (4) But Lincoln Park enrollments expanded too, though with little of the crowding and chaos of the Loop campus (where some classes had to be held in hallways).

Both academically and socially, DePaul was a maelstrom of activity in these years. The exponential growth generated revenues used to reduce the university's debt, but came at a cost: academic program quality deteriorated and the institution's standing and reputation were put at risk. With students having to sit on the floors of some classrooms (primarily in the Loop), being taught in shifts by an overwrought faculty, and with a library perilously short of materials, resources were stretched to the breaking point. (5) But in spite of conflicts, inadequacies and other drawbacks, by 1947 DePaul had become the largest Catholic university in the United States. (6)

Then came one of the first institutional shocks. As other chapter authors have noted, the postwar pattern of entrepreneurial growth came under the scrutiny of the North Central As-

Schmitt Academic Center groundbreaking 1967. The Vincentian fathers flank mayor Richard Daley, second from right, a DePaul Law School alumnus.

sociation (NCA) during its accreditation visit in 1949. When its 1947–1948 financial study placed DePaul in the bottom category of universities granting the master of arts degree, the NCA Board of Review asked the university to prepare a special report on the faculty, the library, and DePaul's finances for the 1948 academic year. (7) Its deficiencies were shockingly evident in this report, and the NCA team, appalled at the state of academic and administrative resources and services available to students at both campuses, recommended that accreditation be withdrawn. (8) DePaul had failed to maintain even minimum standards that could be classified as "university-quality," the team contended. (9)

This "wake-up call" galvanized the university into reexamining its commitments and resources. The administration began making it a priority to use funds generated in the post-war years to recruit an able and scholarly faculty, postponing changes to the physical layout of the university, particularly in Lincoln Park. To attract a high quality faculty meant committing resources not only to salaries and benefits but also to faculty development. In American higher education at this time, this entailed a dedication to research.

The Teaching Versus Research Debate

DePaul's traditional commitment to teaching complicated the university's ability to accept research as a basic faculty activity. In the eyes of some university leaders, the seemingly irreconcilable conflict between teaching and research made any attempt to support research problematic. Despite the NCA report, there continued to be resistance to faculty engagement in scholarly inquiry and the pursuit of consistently high academic standards. Institutional resentment of the negative NCA evaluation and threatened withdrawal of accreditation did not die easily, and neither did DePaul's reluctance to reconsider long standing suspicion of faculty research. At the opening University Council meeting of 1950 this was pointedly addressed in the minutes, which noted that "attention was again called to the fact that DePaul's essential objective is teaching and training rather than productive research." (10) At the same meeting Rev. Joseph Phoenix, C.M., argued that the "education department need not be held to the standards of the strictly academic departments." (11) But DePaul's redefinition of itself as an institution of higher education, which had to begin with the recruitment of a professionally trained faculty, demanded wholehearted university support of a faculty dedicated to both teaching and research.

DePaul's *Faculty Handbook* for 1950 stated that in order to be considered for promotion, a faculty member would be required to achieve the Ph.D. within an unspecified "reasonable length of time." (12) The composition of the faculty at the time suggested that it would have been difficult to attract faculty members at this level of proficiency without institutional support for scholarly activity. Among the full-time faculty, only one in four (48 or 25.4%) held terminal degrees in academic year 1950–1951. (13) University president Father Comerford O'Malley, C.M., reported to the University Council at its March meeting that year that new faculty members included "three doctorates in Sacred Theology, one doctorate in Political Science and one doctorate in Law (Professor Karasz of the university of Budapest)." (14) In order to be reinstated as an accredited institution, O'Malley asserted, "DePaul needs Ph.D.s and the faculty needs to participate in learned societies." (15) Since existing policies had not allowed the faculty to meet NCA standards, changes were in order.

The debate within the university on research versus teaching continued, however. At that same March council meeting, opponents argued that DePaul was "a Group III type of institution" (in the NCA ranking system, a school that granted no degree above the master's degree level) and "different from distinctly Ph.D. and research institutions." (16) Even though the council apparently preferred that DePaul remain an institution devoted primarily to teaching, its members admitted that "there is an acknowledged weakness in Ph.D.s." (17) The NCA's unfavorable evaluation and the potential threat to accreditation continued to haunt DePaul's administration throughout the next two decades.

Father O'Malley and the administration mounted a three-pronged response to the North Central Association's recommendation to withdraw accreditation. First, O'Malley filed an immediate appeal with the North Central Executive Committee and in spring 1950, and he followed up with an institutional report requesting a delay in the actual revocation of DePaul's accreditation. (18) Next, he enlisted Dr. George Works, president and secretary emeritus of NCA to conduct a complete survey of the university. Finally, DePaul committed some of the money accumulated during the hectic growth days of the G.I. Bill to recruiting new faculty members with terminal degrees or nearly completed terminal degrees. The results were gratifying: by the start of the 1952 academic year, two out of five (78 or 43.3%) of the full-time faculty held terminal degrees. (19)

These advanced-degree faculty members expected and lobbied the university administration for improved library facilities for research and a reduction in teaching loads to expedite their pursuit of scholarly activities. They applied for research grants both from within and outside the university. DePaul supported these efforts by granting some financial assistance and by providing release-time from teaching. (20) The decline in enrollments during the Korean War (1950–1953) made it easier to meet these expectations, especially with respect to teaching release-time.

Administrators were sometimes suspicious when it came to faculty leaves of absence for research, however. As late as 1957, questions were raised about whether faculty interest in research was merely a ploy to escape teaching responsibilities. At a University Council meeting in spring 1957 Father Edward Kammer, C.M., vice president and dean of faculties, asked, "how far do you want to go in supporting faculty research?" (21) As Kammer saw it, the matter was "a dollars and cents issue" and turned on the question, "who will pay the man who takes time off for research?" (21) He also added that "the public normally will expect the university to foster such research as one of its functions." (23) This created something of a dilemma. The cost in both time and money inherent in the pursuit of scholarly research helped to keep the debate alive over who should be given release-time for research and how to pay for it.

The question of offering advanced graduate programs was one that certain faculty members and administrators believed DePaul should examine. (24) The university's experience in the NCA accreditation crisis led some to suggest that offering doctoral degrees was another way of raising the institution's academic prestige. This view gained a strong supporter in Father John T. Richardson, C.M., who was appointed graduate dean in 1954. Father Richardson's arrival was even more significant, given the attitude of then President O'Malley, who remained convinced that the university should adhere to "an educational philosophy consistent with DePaul's undergraduate, graduate, and professional teaching tradition." (25) He had expressed this view in a *Report on the State of the University* to the University Council:

> *D*ePaul University is not a research institution, it has sought to maintain a sound and thorough-going teaching standard supported by a high philosophy of education; if we are to continue to maintain that standard, the teaching must be on the highest level. It must be kept in mind that the University should prove a vital force in education—academic and professional—in Chicago. (26)

Shortly after Father Richardson's arrival, events in the wider world conspired to propel DePaul toward viewing research as a legitimate component of its mission. When the Soviet Union launched the Sputnik satellite in 1957, it elevated national anxiety about the quality of American higher education. At the same time, the eminent Catholic historian Monsignor John Tracy Ellis was raising questions about American Catholicism and intellectual life. And in this atmosphere of academic and learned ferment, a new and inquiring spirit began to manifest itself at DePaul. (27) In 1955 Father Richardson, who as graduate dean had already begun changing the graduate programs, received probationary approval from NCA to offer a Specialist Degree in Education and a Certificate of Mathematics Specialist, credentials in the field of education beyond the master's degree. Richardson's report to the university board of trustees in that year noted that "most of the faculty in the departments in question already held their doctorate degrees." (28) Over the next eight years (1955–1964) DePaul awarded sixty-one education specialist degrees and three mathematics specialist degrees. Father Richardson's leadership in the graduate program demonstrated to the North Central Association, other administrators in the university, and the Vincentian community, both locally and province-wide, that DePaul could offer graduate programs beyond the master's degree and perhaps even at the doctoral level. (29)

Father O'Malley, almost reluctantly, asked Father Richardson for specific recommendations that would foster graduate research. (30) As the university accepted the new direction that events and personnel changes warranted, questions asked repeatedly in meetings of the Graduate Council and the University Council over the next two years concerned DePaul's contribution to the urgent needs of the nation in the fields of mathematics and the sciences. (31) The final motivation to develop a doctoral program with its accompanying research apparatus was the recognition by the University Council and the Graduate Council that, according to the terms of the National Defense Education Act, only institutions that granted doctorates were eligible to receive its financial support. It was quite apparent that if DePaul were to share in post-Sputnik federal dollars, it would have to offer doctoral degrees. (32) Although DePaul's Charter of Establishment did not prohibit this step, NCA approval was also required. The organization that had reprimanded DePaul a scant few years before, was now to determine if the university was ready to offer the highest research degrees. The first step in the process of obtaining NCA approval called for the University Council and the Graduate Council to authorize a comprehensive three-year (1958–60) self-survey to evaluate the university's readiness to offer a doctoral program. (33)

The lack of unanimity on the advanced-degree question made for continuing lively debate in the University Council during the mid-1950s. At its October 1955 meeting, Father John R. Cortelyou, C.M., chair of the biology department (and future president of the university), suggested that faculty conducting research be given a reduced teaching load. (34) Father Kammer responded that "service to the university [in all forms] is included in salary increases." (35) At the same meeting Father O'Malley reiterated his view that "the success of any educational institution depends primarily on the teaching staff," pointedly avoiding any mention of research in the entire course of his speech marking the opening of the academic year. (36) At the council meeting in December, Father Kammer noted that the *Faculty Handbook* called for a teaching load that "normally is 30 hours per academic year. The load is reduced only in particular circumstances for doing such things as doing research, directing theses, pursuing graduate study and the like." (37) As for the reduction of teaching load in return for directing graduate courses or to provide faculty the time necessary to publish their research, Kammer stated emphatically that "the dean is the best judge of such a reduction; he would consult with the department chairs but no quantitative measures are possible." (38) Indeed, Kammer pointed out that "the problem with a reduced load in teaching for research work is fewer classes for faculty members and this necessitates hiring additional teachers to make up the deficiency." (39) Again, research was seen as a costly distraction from the university's central role of teaching.

Some faculty showed little interest in research. The council noted that "a number of faculty prefer extra teaching to research" (presumably for additional salary). (40) Father Kammer suggested that productive research was already going on at DePaul in 1955 and referred to a faculty research survey he had conducted from December 1952 to December 1953. He urged the council to study that survey for data on project outcomes (though he apparently did not complete it). (41) A closer look at Kammer's study, however, reveals that prior to Father Richardson's arrival and the impetus of Sputnik, DePaul faculty members had a rather limited research agenda. According to Kammer's survey, there were 120 authors on the faculty, who had completed 110 works, of which six were books, (one of them a textbook and one just submitted for publication). Of 188 works in progress, most were articles, though there was a significant number of Ph.D. dissertations as well. Academic divisions showing highest scholarly activity were law (21 authors), music (11 authors) and English (9 authors). (42) While this kind of academic involvement in scholarship represented a start, it was not enough to sustain advanced graduate degree programs.

The university's academic leaders, joining in the national debate on this subject, expressed ambivalence over the merits of scholarly research. Three DePaul deans, who reported to the University Council in January 1956 on a meeting of academic deans held in St. Louis earlier that month, said that Tracey Strevey of the University of Southern California had commented "that the emphasis on Ph.D.s had reduced the number of good teachers." (43) Strevey had recommended that "contract research be limited to summer programs so that more teaching would occur during the academic year." (44) Throughout 1956 the council wrestled with the problem of criteria for faculty promotion, and the role of research was only one issue among many at these discussions. (45) The lengthy debates on qualifications for rank and promotion covered several pages of the council's minutes at the May meeting but they made no mention of either research or scholarship. (46)

The issue could not be overlooked, however. When the council composed the *Faculty Handbook* for 1956, research was cited as a criterion for promotion as well as the reason why "teaching loads may be reduced." (47) The following April, the relation of research to teaching load surfaced once again in discussions surrounding the *Faculty Handbook*. (48) A research section was added to the handbook indicating that the university would provide support for faculty research in the form of secretarial and staff help as well as teaching load reductions. (49) Department chairs were "to encourage membership in learned societies, research and publication," the handbook further stated. (50) With respect to academic leaves to pursue research, the *Faculty Handbook* spelled out the university's requirement: "it must be demonstrated that the leave will clearly add to the teaching effectiveness, research, and improving the professional status of the faculty." (51) These statements marked the dawn of a new era in the university's history: the expectation—stated in print—that DePaul's faculty would engage in professional activities outside the institution.

Nonetheless, ambivalence about scholarly activities persisted, and publication remained "less important than teaching" in the revised handbook's criteria for evaluating faculty members. (52) Since DePaul could ill afford release-time from teaching that did not lead to productive research, moreover, the council, which was still suspicious of faculty interest in research, required that the "results of research should be publication." (53) The rationale was straightforward, echoing earlier concerns: "this is a protection against faculty who claim to do research but do not and is a means to look out for faculty making use of research to take time off." (54) The debate over establishing doctoral programs had a similar thrust: the cost to the institution, not only in dollars but also in energy diverted from the institution's core teaching mission, lent the discussions a tone of both anxiety and suspicion.

The Decision to Establish Doctoral Programs of Study

Once DePaul had clarified its expectations for scholarly research by the faculty, it had taken the first important step toward supporting advanced graduate study. Many administrators and faculty members believed that the momentum to inaugurate a doctoral program would be deterred neither by administrative suspicion of faculty motives for conducting research nor by indecision on the part of the university and graduate councils. But other decision-making bodies still needed to be won over, and university administrators and faculty members continued to press the case for advanced graduate study. In 1960, Father Richardson's report to the board of trustees explained why DePaul should have a doctoral study program:

> *The offering of graduate work on the Ph.D. level would certainly not only appeal to our present faculty members—but would also attract good professors to DePaul. It would also appeal to our own graduate students who in turn would feed our Ph.D. program. Furthermore, there would be greater participation in research programs, as well as government and other grants.* (55)

The trustees were crucial to the decision-making process, and a change as significant as adding a new level of study required their approval. Though they listened to Richardson's arguments, the trustees decided that DePaul needed to raise the quality of its programs and its undergraduate population first, and they shelved for the moment the idea of advanced degree education at DePaul. (56) Even though Father Richardson remained committed to the notion of doctoral studies, he had to proceed with caution. It was not clear whether either the university or graduate councils shared his convictions about the importance of doctoral programs at DePaul; nor did his thinking enjoy widespread support in the Western Province of the Vincentian community. In 1960 the Vincentians were engaged primarily in educating and organizing Roman Catholic clergy for the U.S. dioceses west of the Mississippi River. If DePaul instituted a program of doctoral studies, the Vincentian community might well have to reconsider its relationship to the university.

Father Richardson wrote Father O'Malley in 1961 expressing little hope about the prospects for advanced graduate study at DePaul, pointing out that the university could not support its current operations and a doctoral program as a solely tuition-driven institution. Furthermore, the university's mission statement seemed to him to be outdated and inconsistent with the level and quality of research that a doctoral program demanded. Finally, he worried about the effect that a doctoral program would have on the religious and philosophical foundations of DePaul. (57) The despair Richardson experienced in 1961 was lifted by two events in 1962 that revitalized the drive for doctoral education and the research to accompany it.

Dr. Julius Hupert of the university's physics department sent a memo to Father Richardson, Father John Cortelyou and Father William Cortelyou (who had been appointed graduate dean) in January 1962. Hupert, an old world scholar from Poland who had served in the British Admiralty during World War II, had come to DePaul in 1947. He helped to develop the graduate program in the field of electrophysics, which he described as "an area of interdisciplinary interest bordering on physics, electric engineering and applied mathematics." (58) Dr. Hupert wrote the three Vincentians to argue for a modification in the *Faculty Handbook* for the following year. (59) In his memo he advanced a powerful argument in support of research as a vital university activity:

> *A university is not, in my opinion, a center of TEACHING. It is a center of STUDY, by faculty and students alike. This is what distinguishes universities from schools. We have all known demonstrably ineffective teachers who were great scholars and who contributed to the accomplishment of their universities. By contrast, I could not name a demonstrably ineffective scholar who could be even a passable "teacher" at a college level. Scholarship is in my opinion an all-embracing term which includes research, lecturing, review articles, textbook writing, conduction of courses and seminars, laboratory demonstrations and exercises, in fact all academic activities. They are all equally important and they can all be conducted at various levels of endeavor and also, let us remember, at various levels of quality. (60)*

Hupert's memo inspired an enthusiastic response in the three Vincentians, all of whom were committed to the pursuit of scholarly research and advanced graduate study, including doctoral programs.

The second development was the appointment of a new provincial for the Western Province of the Vincentians. In summer 1962 Father James Fischer, C.M., was named to succeed Father James Stakelum, C.M., as leader of the province. Father Fischer, a scholar of the sacred scriptures, had spent his entire career in seminary work and was presumed to be sympathetic to the view that research might divert DePaul from its traditional teaching role. From the beginning of his tenure as provincial, however, Father Fischer called on DePaul to define its academic aims and to delineate the role it anticipated for research. Recognizing the critical choices that DePaul and similar institutions were facing in the years ahead, he urged the university to explore its options carefully.

So the question is: What does DePaul want to be? A great research university—or a high grade junior college—I mention the two extremes. A school which will espouse scholarship to the hilt, or a school which is merely interested in educating men to a "college level" and leaving it at that. (61)

The Rev. John Cortelyou, president of DePaul, awards an honorary degree to the renouned American singer Mahalia Jackson, at the June 1971 convocation.

Fischer's statements left little doubt that he viewed support for research as a critical task of a university. This position represented a basic change in the attitude of the Vincentian provincial leadership and created a climate in which doctoral programs could be developed at DePaul. Hupert's memo and Fischer's declaration gave Richardson the support and the rationale to start laying the groundwork for advanced degree scholarship at the university.

Father Richardson, who was asked to prepare a proposal for an executive committee meeting of the board of trustees in November 1963, urged that "a definite commitment to a doctoral program be agreed upon as an ultimate objective of the university, an objective to be accomplished at a time when we will be in a position to see our way clear to support it." (62) Richardson, emphasizing the need for the board to make an immediate decision on the issue of the doctorate (63), offered the following reasons:

1. *The Program for Greatness (DePaul's strategic plan) requires the University to make a decision about the direction of its academic program toward the expansion of either of the teaching or the research function;*

2. *The doctoral program will attract competent faculty—DePaul has been losing good faculty to doctoral granting universities;*

3. *The doctoral program will attract the most talented students;*

4. *There is a national trend toward doctoral programs because of the government support of programs to produce degreed graduate faculty. (64)*

With board sanction of Richardson's proposal DePaul embarked on an untrodden path with respect to its academic philosophy and the design of its graduate programs. (65) Although tension persisted between teaching and research at DePaul, the university's commitment to the principle of academic research as an institutional mission could no longer be questioned.

It took four years to implement the board's decision and actually put a doctoral studies program in place, however. During this interval, a further change, the inauguration of DePaul's eighth president, improved the prospects of advanced degree studies even more. As Father O'Malley neared retirement, he changed his position and endorsed the idea of research as a vital aspect of academic experience at DePaul. In choosing a successor to O'Malley, it was essential to find a president who would be a forceful spokesperson for this fledgling commitment to a research agenda, whose energy and vision would move the doctoral proposal ahead. Though Father Richardson seemed the logical choice, Father Fischer recognized that in Father John Robert Cortelyou, C.M., a research biologist and chair of the biological sciences department at DePaul, the university had an individual endowed with the kind of academic pedigree that would provide both luster and credibility. Father Richardson held a doctorate in theology from a Roman church-related institution; Father Cortelyou had earned his doctorate in biology from Northwestern University, a respected research institution. While Father Richardson fostered the developments that made research a vital component of the DePaul experience, Father Cortelyou's scientific credentials and enthusiasm for the doctoral agenda provided the affirmation essential to its pursuit. In January 1964 Father Fischer nominated Father Cortelyou to be president of DePaul and the board of trustees confirmed the nomination. (66)

Father Cortelyou believed that graduate studies leading to a doctorate "represented the primary function of a university," and he supported the modern idea of the university, with scholarship and inquiry at its very core. (67) On the other hand, Father Richardson's interest in developing research at DePaul was based on the pragmatic notion that promoting research would professionalize DePaul's faculty and its programs. (68) The idea that doctoral studies might be an outgrowth of research activity was, in Richardson's view, an important but secondary consideration. But like Father Fischer, Father Richardson ardently believed that the pursuit of research at DePaul was essential to the continued development of the institution. In his report to the trustees in 1963 he declared that "educational institutions like DePaul either grow or atrophy." (69) Father Richardson's principal contribution to the development of research at DePaul lay in his ability, as executive vice-president, to promote research without endangering other programs at the university. (70) Cortelyou and Richardson joined forces to move DePaul into the world of research and scholarship and to associate the university's mission with the ideals of twentieth century American higher education.

Though interest in developing a research agenda and a program of doctoral studies at DePaul was high, the type of support that O'Malley, Richardson and Cortelyou had anticipated did not materialize. Doctoral studies grew very slowly and remained isolated from other programs, but the university's advanced degree programs and its increased hospitality toward research activities brought new prestige and status to DePaul. After NCA approval of the university's application for startup of its doctoral programs in August 1967, the board of trustees agreed to implementation and enhancement of advanced degree curricula in the biological sciences, philosophy, and psychology. (71) As a consequence, eleven new faculty members were hired, the library increased books and periodicals in these fields by 100 and 200 percent respectively, and the biology department underwent a $150,000 expansion and renovation. (72) Modest funding that came through the Higher Education Act of 1965 helped support educational-opportunity grants, college work-study programs, and national direct student loans for doctoral students. (73) In the end, the university also received government assistance to build academic and residence buildings, which benefited the entire student body.

DePaul's move toward research helped redefine the university and its mission. First, the university reevaluated the role research might play in its rehabilitation following the accreditation crisis. The influx of professionally competent faculty members with agendas and standards that differed from the traditional DePaul model pressured the administration into reconsidering DePaul's mission and purpose. Doctoral studies, a logical outgrowth of the research being initiated, transformed DePaul into a comprehensive university. Yet DePaul still cherished its traditional teaching role. Despite his clear commitment to research, Father Cortelyou expressed to a trustee his Vincentian devotion to teaching: "The Mission of DePaul University is principally as an instructional institution with such research goals as will enable it to make a modest but persistent contribution toward the advancement of knowledge and toward the support of learning research." (74) Father Richardson was even more emphatic:

For its own distinctive purposes DePaul places the highest priority on its programs of instruction and learning. The University shall have the depth of scholarship and the other resources to offer the doctorate in a few academic disciplines, but programs at the bachelor's and master's levels shall predominate.

Research, although in a position secondary to instruction, shall play a significant role in the University. Pluralistically conceived, research entails not only the creation of new knowledge, but the application of learning to the solution of practical problems, creative activities in the fine arts, and innovative processes for transmitting knowledge. Particularly encouraged and supported is that type of research which is directly tied to programs of instruction and indirectly benefits students. (75)

Nonetheless, with the introduction of research as an essential element in DePaul's academic life, the university entered the mainstream of American higher education. The university established the Office of Sponsored Programs in 1965 to assist faculty in their research pursuits. By committing both personnel and finances to this office, the university demonstrated its continuing pursuit of Father Peter Vincent Byrne's 1907 goal of establishing a modern American Catholic university. It turned out that research became an indispensable aspect of that goal, and in the thirty years since doctoral studies began and the Office of Sponsored Programs opened, the university has never wavered from its determination to realize Father Byrne's vision by reaching toward his goal. (76)

Development of the Lincoln Park Campus

At the same time that DePaul was making significant changes to its academic programs through the introduction and encouragement of faculty research, it embarked on a policy of physical development and curricular improvement in Lincoln Park. A response to growing enrollments and a corresponding need for new facilities which took more than two decades to unfold, this entailed an extended planning process and more than a little good fortune. The university's relationship to the surrounding neighborhood was profoundly altered, and DePaul's Lincoln Park campus was changed forever—and with it the face of the university.

The pattern of physical deterioration in the Lincoln Park neighborhood that had started with the Great Depression accelerated during World War II. Residences were converted into small apartments to accommodate the population increase resulting from the war industry boom in Chicago. At the same time, government-caused shortages in building materials caused a virtual halt to new construction, and even to maintenance and repairs. (77) The conversion of larger spaces to smaller apartments was practically the only construction activity in the area from the mid-1930s until the end of World War II. (78) By 1940, 15 percent of all the residential properties in Lincoln Park had been subdivided and another 10 percent needed major repairs or were deemed unfit for habitation. (79) It was a neighborhood in transition, one

Interior view of the John R. Cortelyou Commons Building, acquired in 1976.

becoming more crowded and less appealing to the middle class constituency of institutions such as DePaul.

This deterioration drove the more affluent residents, particularly those with families, either to other parts of the city or to the rapidly growing suburbs. By 1950 there was not a single block of family homes in Lincoln Park that had not undergone at least one conversion to a small apartment-type residence. Failure to maintain these residences along with lack of maintenance in the unconverted buildings meant that fully 25 percent of the residential units in Lincoln Park were classified as "substandard or dilapidated" by 1950. (80)

Though the changing character of the Lincoln Park neighborhood posed a challenge to the university, it was hardly the only one. In addition to the problems associated with a decaying neighborhood, DePaul faced hordes of returning World War II veterans determined to acquire an education. Most of these adult students headed for DePaul's Loop campus, but there was a significant increase in enrollments uptown as well. The bonanza that the "G.I. Bill of Rights" represented for returning servicemen and women was both an opportunity and a crisis for universities like DePaul, whose limited facilities and poor locations strained their resources and ingenuity. This was reflected in a DePaul report issued in 1947 by the architectural firm Skidmore, Owings and Merrill.

The Board of Trustees of DePaul University is faced with the problem of providing additional classrooms and laboratory spaces both for their Uptown College and their Downtown College and Graduate Schools. Present facilities in both branches of the University are taxed beyond capacity and any opportunity for increasing the post war enrollments is impossible. (81)

Unless the university could expand its facilities significantly, it would be unable to take advantage of its rapid enrollment growth at the end of the war. DePaul was operating in three distinct locations which could hardly be called "campuses"—a downtown school in the Loop at 64 E. Lake Street; an uptown division in Lincoln Park in an area bounded by Sheffield to the east, Kenmore to the west and Fullerton Avenue to the north; and the Department of Physical Education housed in the Lincoln-Turner Gymnasium at 1019 W. Diversey, a mile north of the uptown campus. (82) The institution's leadership, anticipating the increased demand on DePaul's limited resources, commissioned the architectural firm of Skidmore, Owings & Merrill to study the university's location and environment and develop a long-range building program to handle the increase in student population that had materialized by 1947. (83) The study made a dramatic recommendation:

> *That DePaul University physically integrate the Uptown [including the College of Physical Education] and the Downtown divisions in a new building to be situated in or adjacent to the Loop. The consolidation of these two divisions . . . in a downtown building would benefit the greatest number of students and would result in increased administrative and teaching efficiency, as well as in greater prestige for the University. (84)*

The Skidmore study characterized the uptown campus as "deteriorating" and argued that it was "best and safest" to move the entire institution downtown. (85) Further, the Loop campus already served the vast majority of students and was by far the most accessible site for the greatest number. At the close of the 1947 academic year, only about 15 percent of DePaul's nearly 10,000 students, including those in the physical education program, attended classes at the uptown campus. (86)

But the architectural firm, acknowledging DePaul's historic presence on the city's north side, submitted an alternative proposal calling for two campuses—one in the Loop and the other on the north side, presumably in Lincoln Park. It proposed that the uptown campus house the College of Liberal Arts and Sciences and the physical education department. However, the proposal assumed that there would be significant increases in enrollments in each program—1,500 additional students in liberal arts and sciences (a 37% increase) and as many as 500 students in physical education (a 100% increase). (87) The plan mandated only a few physical changes. The Liberal Arts Building (currently Levan Hall) would get an additional 7,800 square feet of space for classrooms and office space. The science building (currently O'Connell Hall) would have 3,800 square feet of additional space for classrooms, laboratories and offices. (88)

The plan, at a total cost of $2,244,340, also called for construction of two new buildings: a 27,000 square foot library with book stack space for a minimum of 200,000 volumes and an on-campus gymnasium/auditorium (36,000 square feet) to accommodate not only the physical education program but also a student lounge, a swimming pool, locker facilities and office space for faculty and staff. (89) The difficulty of finding enough space on the Lincoln Park campus to build these two buildings may explain the Skidmore report's strong support of the single Loop campus proposal. If the university had chosen Skidmore's alternative, however, the plan called for the two new facilities to be located on Belden Avenue west of the science building, or at the very least, connecting the science building and the liberal arts building to provide additional space. In any case, the two-story residence that stood between the science and the liberal arts buildings had to be acquired and demolished. (90) Alternatively, the new library and the new gym/auditorium could conceivably have been built on Sheffield Avenue after the Lyceum and the auditorium buildings, which still stood there, were razed. Removal of both these buildings was part of the alternative plan. (91)

While the university pondered the Skidmore recommendations, President O'Malley found himself facing the 1949 North Central Association evaluation that signaled possible de-accreditation of DePaul as a university. The administration immediately committed itself to bolstering academic resources as a first priority, redirecting energy, time and money to the restoration of its academic credibility by hiring more doctorally trained faculty members and promoting research. Plans for improving DePaul's physical infrastructure were postponed, but the university retained the Skidmore, Owings & Merrill proposals, and the call to invest university resources in Lincoln Park became the basis for development plans in the 1950's. (92)

Before these plans were articulated, however, DePaul engaged the Business Research Corporation (BRC) to survey space problems on both campuses and evaluate existing facilities. In its report BRC noted that the North Central Association had drawn attention to DePaul's failures in the following areas:

> *The provision of an adequate university plant is one of the major problems which confronts DePaul University. . . . The buildings owned by the university itself are 15 in number and have a present value of $1,117,500. These buildings would for the most part rate low as facilities for a modern metropolitan university.* (93)

After analyzing what was essentially a restatement of the Skidmore, Owings & Merrill recommendations, DePaul found itself with two options: either continue operating on a business-as-usual basis or expand both of the university's two divisions—Loop and Lincoln Park—by renovating and/or adding new facilities by either building or leasing. (94)

While DePaul was considering these alternatives, events were taking place in the Lincoln Park community that might have influenced the university's ultimate decision. Neighborhood organizations, including the Lincoln Park Community Council, the Old Town Triangle Association and the Mid-North Association, met at the North Park Hotel in June 1953 with John C. Downs, housing and redevelopment coordinator for the city of Chicago. Downs reminded the assembled citizens of Lincoln Park's undeniable advantages: its gracious sweep of lakefront, ready access to public transportation and its proximity to the city's business, financial, recreational and cultural centers. Lincoln Park should not be classified as "a slum," Downs argued, because slums were to be leveled and replaced with new construction. Rather, he claimed,

Lincoln Park should be designated "a conservation area" in which land clearance, renovation and rehabilitation were to be the hallmark activities. (95)

The city had created the Interim Commission on Neighborhood Conservation in the previous year, with Downs as chair, to coordinate the federal government's urban renewal program. Four areas of the city had already been certified as "conservation areas," and Downs considered Lincoln Park a strong candidate for certification as a fifth. An umbrella organization was needed to coordinate the efforts of Lincoln Park's disparate neighborhood groups, including institutions such as DePaul. (96) The Lincoln Park Community Council appointed a committee, the Lincoln Park Conservation Association (LPCA), to serve "as a representative vehicle by which many people living in a particular geographical area can adapt the city to themselves and themselves to the city." (97)

Things were beginning to look up in Lincoln Park, and for better or worse, DePaul was going to be part of its future. In its expansion program entitled "New Horizons for DePaul and You," released in 1953, the university announced its decision to remain in Lincoln Park. Outlining its goals for the next decade, DePaul made capital improvements the centerpiece of its plan. It had to raise "capital structure funds to expand the university's physical facilities so that the educational program may be more adequately housed and more services made available to students, alumni and the general public." (98) DePaul was to make a major contribution to the physical transformation of the neighborhood.

The university's plans were ambitious, embracing all the features of Skidmore, Owings & Merrill's alternative proposal. The construction firm of Naess and Murphy furnished the technical specifications for the university's two major construction projects: an all-purpose auditorium for academic and extracurricular activities and a new library to house the rapidly growing collection of books and periodicals and provide services to students and the faculty. Naess and Murphy also drew up plans for renovations to the science building to accommodate the projected demands for research in the sciences, and to the liberal arts building for more classrooms and faculty offices. The master plan also detailed expansion and improvement of facilities for the colleges at the Loop campus. (99)

Naess and Murphy estimated a total cost of $5.5 million, but the question of site location for the proposed buildings was as critical an issue as the projected expenditures. The auditorium, at $1.2 million, was to be built on the site of the DePaul Athletic Field between Sheffield and Kenmore avenues, with the main entrance on Belden. The library, planned for Belden Avenue between Kenmore and Seminary, was to be built on land west of the science building. Additions were planned for both the science building (to be renamed Science Research Laboratory) and the Liberal Arts Building. With the exception of the athletic field and the two-story residential building (slated for demolition) between the science and the liberal arts buildings, there was little vacant land. (100) A further obstacle to the university's long-range planning was the fact that DePaul owned no other property in the area, which was largely residential.

The Hayes-Healy Athletic Center, acquired by DePaul in 1976.

Ironically, the university's major acquisition of property during this period was not in Lincoln Park but in the south Loop where, in October 1955, the Frank J. Lewis Foundation gave DePaul the eighteen-story Kimball Building—and the land on which it stood—at 25 E. Jackson Blvd. (101) It was the largest gift to the university to date, and though it helped to stabilize the Loop campus it relieved some of the urgency from DePaul's plans for Lincoln Park. Only one of the four objectives in the Naess and Murphy plan for the uptown campus got under way as the university broke ground for its proposed auditorium/gymnasium on the DePaul athletic field. Named Alumni Hall in honor of the graduates and former students who had donated most of the money to build it, the new facility was dedicated on Sunday, December 16, 1956, the first major building project on the uptown campus in eighteen years. (102) It provided a home for university events, for the physical education program and for student

The Concert Hall, acquired in 1977 with the purchase of the McCormick Theological Seminary property.

extracurricular and recreational activities. Besides classrooms, faculty offices, exercise rooms, a student cafeteria and lounge, Alumni Hall housed a 5,200 seat gymnasium for intercollegiate basketball games. Frank McGrath, the director of athletics, declared, "Alumni Hall is a beehive, not only satisfying the needs of the DePaul family, but also providing for many outside organizations." (103)

DePaul did not abandon its proposed expansion plans in the 1950s, however; it modified them instead. Recognizing an opportunity in the conservation concept developed by the Lincoln Park neighborhood organizations, the university chose to participate. Beginning in 1959, the university council openly discussed the allocation of urban renewal funds for Lincoln Park and expressed the belief that DePaul was in a very favorable position to take advantage of such an opportunity. The board of trustees gave Father O'Malley authority to appoint a committee and have a professional planner facilitate the university's involvement in the development of Lincoln Park. (104) This time DePaul employed a planning firm, Real Estate Research Corporation (RERC), whose investigation confirmed the assessments made in 1947 by Skidmore, Owings & Merrill and in 1950 by Business Research Corporation: DePaul's Lincoln Park campus had too few buildings and too little land to accommodate even the modest population of 1,200 students it enrolled at that time. If the number of students were to grow to 2,000 over the next ten years as anticipated, the university would have to expand its Lincoln Park holdings three-fold, from 5.4 acres to 18 acres. (105) Growth continued to pose the most intractable challenges for DePaul's uptown campus.

The university realized that Lincoln Park in 1960 was not the neighborhood Skidmore, Owings & Merrill had evaluated in 1947. Vigorous neighborhood organizations had learned how to take advantage of government investment in urban renewal and renovation and their expertise encouraged DePaul to work in partnership with them, out of self-interest as well as community-mindedness. At a meeting of the Board of Directors of the Lincoln Park Conservation Association on May 15, 1961, DePaul laid out its plans for its neighbors. Father Theodore Wangler, C.M., vice president for student affairs and point-man for future university development in the neighborhood, read a prepared statement expressing DePaul's intention to involve itself in the renewal of Lincoln Park. He told the association that "the university was prepared to spend over $10 million within the next ten years and become the anchor of an academic community in Lincoln Park in which people will be proud to live." (106) Further, Father Wangler pointed out that if DePaul was to be a player in the renewal of Lincoln Park "we must have room to expand." (107) Father Wangler requested DePaul's inclusion in Phase I of the Lincoln Park Urban Renewal Project. The university's property lay outside the urban renewal project boundaries but its proposed expansion required that it acquire land near the campus that would fall within these boundaries, the cost of which could be written down as part of the planned rehabilitation of the neighborhood through urban renewal. This request, which appeared self-serving, was not unusual since Section 112 of the 1959 Housing Act provided that "preferential treatment be given residential and urban universities." (108) Wangler was simply putting the Lincoln Park neighborhood on notice that DePaul intended to remain in the area either in cooperation with its neighbors or on its own terms. In any case, Father Wangler's plea fell on deaf ears and DePaul was excluded from Phase I of the Lincoln Park Urban Renewal Project.

The RERC report was highly critical of DePaul's Lincoln Park facilities with the exception of Alumni Hall, which it recommended should become the hub for the university's future land-use planning. (109) It pointed to the overcrowded classrooms and antiquated buildings that limited the prospects for improvements. The university needed not only land on which to construct new facilities but also well integrated open space, and its holdings in the neighborhood were woefully inadequate. They consisted of the Lyceum and the old auditorium/theater (known popularly as "The Barn"), the Reserve Officer Training Corps (ROTC) building just west of the liberal arts building and the small facility immediately north of the science building which served as a combination science storage facility and faculty office space. Other property on the Lincoln Park campus technically belonging to the Vincentian community was not available to the university at this time. It consisted of the priests' residence, known as Faculty Hall, DePaul Academy and St. Vincent de Paul Parish Church, School, Convent and Rectory.

The campus that the university envisioned would need considerably more land than the 171,633 square feet earlier reports had estimated. Necessary space as determined in the RERC report exceeded 260,000 square feet. The planned campus would have to be 3.3 times the size the existing campus, with 22 percent of this added space committed to the construction of new buildings, 24.8 percent to parking, 13.7 percent to athletic fields and drill areas and 39.5 percent undesignated open space. The projected Lincoln Park campus would encompass 774,000 square feet or 22 acres. (110) Finally, the plan was to embody a new feature, student housing, a first in the history of DePaul. The first residence hall was to be situated near the intersection of Belden and Clifton avenues, well west of the existing university property. (111) With this blueprint of DePaul's intentions made public, residents of Lincoln Park witnessed the opening salvo in the university's ten-year "Program For Greatness," a $22.4 million development program.

To begin implementing its plan, in 1962 DePaul made its first attempts to purchase land in Lincoln Park for the construction of new buildings. Father O'Malley felt that time was of the essence, with "the pressing need for additional buildings, and by reason of the pending legislation in Washington which would make federal funds available for part of the improvements." (112) This action was a corollary to the development program, "make a good university great!," which consisted of two five-year phases timed to culminate in 1973 with DePaul's 75th anniversary. Phase I targeted the arts & sciences as the focus of development and called for a science research center, a library and a new classroom building. Phase II addressed student services with plans for a new student union, an auditorium (distinct from Alumni Hall) and resident halls for 700 students. Costs were estimated at $5.5 million for Phase I and $5.8 million for Phase II. The rest of the $22.4 million was targeted for faculty and academic resource development. (113)

Estimating that it would have to acquire at least two-thirds of a square block for the science building, library and classroom buildings, DePaul considered several sites in the immediate area before finally settling on the block bordered by Fullerton (north), Belden (south), Kenmore (east) and Seminary Avenues (west). (114) Though it needed only 2/3 of the square block for its planned construction, the university opted to purchase the entire section. (115)

Initially the university tried to keep its land acquisitions secret, to prevent prices from rising artificially high. Though Father Wangler had openly expressed the institution's intentions in his statement in May 1961, DePaul hoped to disguise its plans by using escrow accounts set up with the Chicago Title and Trust Company. Purchases would be made through the law firm of Mitchell & Conway and title would be held in the name of one of the firm's employees. (116) This method of land acquisition was both unwieldy and a public relations disaster when the university's plans were posted in the LPCA's offices. (117) To forestall further rumors and to mend whatever damage had been done to relations with the Lincoln Park

Munroe Hall, formerly Clifton Hall, was DePaul's first residence hall, opened in 1970. Harold Stuart Center in background opened in 1971.

community, Father O'Malley sent a letter to all the resident owners of property in the area targeted by the university for purchase, inviting the addressees to a meeting at which the institution would lay out its plans. Father O'Malley assured his correspondents that DePaul was willing to pay fair market value in cash for their property; at the same time he encouraged them to consider DePaul's offers, to consult with their own real estate advisors and be prepared to ask any questions of the university they might have. (118)

From November 1962 to April 1964 with the help of two realtors, L.J. Sheridan Corporation and Burke & Lynn, DePaul negotiated the purchase of the property for Phase I: nineteen buildings—five single family houses, six double flats, six triple flats and two large non-residential buildings. The property closest to the university, on Kenmore Avenue, turned out to be the most difficult to obtain. (119) With the acquisition of these properties the Program For Greatness was up and running. Although DePaul experienced little difficulty acquiring the needed properties, Phase II was not accomplished without controversy. Neighborhood organizations, especially those representing renters in the residential buildings DePaul had targeted for purchase, vigorously protested the university's actions. The Concerned Citizens of Lincoln Park (CCLP) and the Young Lords, a Puerto Rican street gang that became a national civil rights organization, contended that DePaul was pushing the poor out of the neighborhood "like animals being transferred from one zoo to another." (120) While these organizations accused DePaul of being "a racist institution . . . which only cares about moving people out so they can expand their property and their power," older organizations such as the LPCA continued to work with the university. (121)

This cooperation became quite apparent in 1966 when Phase II of the Neighborhood Renewal Program was being proposed and DePaul again asked to be included—not only on the basis of Section 112 of the 1959 Housing Act, but also because the university had invested over $930,000 in the acquisition of property for its Program For Greatness. This expenditure made the area eligible for almost $3 million in federal credits, and whatever the rationale, this time DePaul was included in the renewal program. (122) It acquired the entire block bounded by Fullerton (north), Belden (south), Seminary (east) and Clifton Avenues (west) during this phase. It also purchased the southern half of the block bounded by Fullerton (north), Belden (south), Clifton (east) and Racine (west). Munroe Hall and the Stuart Center Student Union were built on this land in 1970 and 1971, respectively, during the second phase of the Program For Greatness. (123)

DePaul's expansion was not without its human costs, however. The CCLP estimated that DePaul was responsible for removing 300 families in 84 buildings in the course of its expansion. Indeed, the CCLP condemned the university's ten-year Program For Greatness, claiming that it was "based upon the destruction of a sizeable portion of the neighborhood as it is now . . . driving large numbers of people from their community and thus helping to destroy the cultural and economic diversity we Lincoln Parkers are so proud of." (124)

The Schmitt Academic Center, the first new academic building on the uptown campus since before the Second World War, was built during the first phase of the Program For Greatness and opened in fall 1968. Providing 67 percent more classroom space than had previously existed on the campus, SAC, as it came to be known, used its third and fourth floors as the new, 250,000 volume library. Five seminar rooms and a faculty lounge, as well as college offices for liberal arts and sciences, the School of Education, the graduate program and 100 faculty offices took up the fifth floor. The second floor housed classrooms primarily, and a few administrative offices, and building services facilities were located in the SAC penthouse. (125)

The rest of the planned first phase of the Program For Greatness failed to be realized. The much needed science research building did not materialize, nor did a free-standing library building. The university did relieve some of the pressure on its old science building in 1965 by leasing a one-story factory structure a block west of the campus on Fullerton Avenue. Popularly known as "Science West," this facility housed the physics and research psychology departments. In 1969 the old science building underwent a massive renovation at a cost of $330,000, which created space for some new laboratories, equipment and facilities for biology and chemistry. (126) When DePaul Academy shut its doors in 1968, the Vincentians made that facility available to the university. The sturdy six-story Bedford-stone building was extensively renovated, after which it was occupied by the physics and psychology programs as well as an expanded Community Mental Health Clinic. (127)

The Arthur J. Schmitt Academic Center under construction. The building was opened in 1968. C.F. Murphy and Associates, architects.

The Arthur J. Schmitt Academic Center opened in 1968.

The entrance to DePaul's O'Hare Campus, 3166 River Road, Des Plains, Illinois.

DePaul announced the completion of its Program For Greatness at its 75th anniversary celebration in 1973, at which time the Lincoln Park campus consisted of eleven buildings owned by the university and one (Science West) leased from Alexian Brothers' Hospital. Though DePaul had spent $27 million, well above its estimate of $22.4 million, not all the program's goals had been achieved. (128) No land had been acquired for either the planned Science Center or the Fine Arts Center. Only one of several residence halls called for by the Program for Greatness had been built. Father Wangler had warned that DePaul must expand if it were to survive, but the university was short of both money and land. Fate interceded, however, and gave the university the means to heed Father Wangler's admonition.

In May 1974 DePaul's neighbor to the east, the McCormick Theological Seminary, announced that it planned to move its entire school to the Hyde Park area on Chicago's south side. McCormick was joining several other seminaries to form the Chicago Cluster of Theological Schools. (129) The proximity of the McCormick property to the Lincoln Park campus made it extremely attractive to DePaul. But a number of other organizations and institutions coveted this choice site. Children's Memorial Hospital, the Moody Bible Institute, Columbia Business College, Grant Hospital, Northwestern University, the People and Land Center, Inc. (a charitable organization) and the city of Chicago all expressed interest. (130) The Lincoln Park Conservation Association, which hoped to keep the open spaces and the campus character of the McCormick land and to control any new construction, attempted to lay down guidelines and principles that would govern future use of the McCormick property. (131) On the Seminary's land there were 56 single family homes, three recently constructed academic buildings, two residence halls, a gymnasium, a large dining hall/cafeteria, tennis courts used by the Fullerton Avenue Tennis Club on a long-term lease, land leased to the city for $1 per year on which a branch of the Chicago Public Library was situated, and a chapel. (132)

The residents of the rental properties were especially concerned about the McCormick move, and they formed an organization, the Seminary Town House Association, under whose auspices they proposed to buy the residential properties from McCormick. The association would then re-sell the properties to the tenants. The seminary accepted the association's offer, and on June 21, 1975, the association purchased the 56 residential units from McCormick for $3 million. (133) The significance of this sale lay in the fact that it effectively split the seminary property into two distinct sections: an eastern portion, bordered by Fullerton on the north, Belden on the south, Halsted to the east and the town houses on the west, and a western portion, which was a much larger parcel, bordered by Fullerton, Belden, and Sheffield on its western side and the town houses on the east.

Though DePaul was interested primarily in the western portion of the seminary's property, it included the tennis courts and the public library space which the university did not plan to use. (134) The cost associated with the purchase of the entire west end section concerned the university's leadership, which had no stomach for adding to its debt after the cost overruns of the Program For Greatness. McCormick was asking $1.2 million for the entire west end section with a down payment of $250,000, the balance to be paid off over five years at 8 percent quarterly interest. DePaul preferred the section east of the El that did not include the library or tennis courts, and for this McCormick was asking $950,000. (135)

The Rev. John R. Cortelyou, C.M. president 1964–1981.

Urging the administration not to pass up such an opportunity, the university's advisors recommended that they accept McCormick's first proposal for the entire west end of the seminary campus. (136) In February 1976, after the purchase agreement was concluded, Father John Cortelyou, C.M., university president, announced that DePaul had purchased approximately eleven acres of land with five buildings, tennis courts, and a gymnasium from the McCormick Seminary. (137) Now the university had to devise strategies to pay for this property.

Within a month Father Cortelyou had mailed a request to alumni, friends and donors of the university for contributions to meet the $250,000 down payment. In his letter he recalled how Skidmore, Owings & Merrill's sweeping blueprint for DePaul's future had inspired the university's presidents to hope and to work for an expanded campus, and he suggested that the hope might be nearing fulfillment. Father Cortelyou, who had witnessed and participated in all the struggles of the past two decades, eloquently summed up his and the university's feelings.

*A*fter having experienced the tantalizingly slow piece-by-piece acquisition of land in the environs of our neighborhood-locked campus during the years of the Program For Greatness, I cannot adequately convey the sentiments I feel at having the McCormick property dropped all at once into our laps—seven acres of land and five principal buildings. (138)

Aspects of the Program for Greatness that had seemed unattainable were now possible, and the much needed and yearned for residence halls and open space finally became a major part of the Lincoln Park campus. The wholehearted response to Father Cortelyou's appeal easily covered the down payment.

The university leadership, possibly emboldened by this response or recognizing that even with the acquisition of McCormick's entire west campus DePaul's expansion was incomplete, discussed the possibility of acquiring the remainder of the McCormick property during the summer of 1976. In November the university board of trustees unanimously endorsed the concept of buying all the remaining McCormick land and buildings, and in December, after six weeks of negotiations, McCormick's board of directors approved the final sale. DePaul obtained title to the buildings and the 4.3 acres of land that comprised the east campus of the seminary on March 1, 1977. (139)

DePaul won something else, something less tangible than 11.3 acres of land, eight buildings, parking space and revenue sources when it bought the McCormick property. It concluded

John T. Richardson Library interior study hall on the third and fourth floors. The building opened in 1992.

a process that had begun at the end of World War Two, and by reasserting the entrepreneurial attitude that accepted growth as a legitimate strategy, the university rediscovered the philosophy that would guide its leadership in the last quarter of this century. DePaul continued to acquire property during the 1980s and 1990s, both in Lincoln Park and elsewhere. When the Art Institute of Chicago discontinued the Goodman School of Drama, DePaul stepped in and took on the program. It acquired the grade school and convent of St. Vincent's Parish, both of which had been closed previously, in order to create a home for the Theater School. Faced with ever increasing demands for space, DePaul found itself moving into a number of older facilities and converting them to new purposes.

Lincoln Park experienced another transformation in the years following 1980, as a new generation of migrants to the city began to take up residence there. These newcomers were different from the poor and working class residents who had crowded into the area in the forties and fifties. These were young urban professionals, drawn to the city by new employment opportunities in business and the professions, and they valued the neighborhood for its proximity to the Loop and its lakeshore ambience. Property values escalated, and once again Lincoln Park became a desirable place to live. The university's land became increasingly valuable, and DePaul began to attract students who were drawn to the city's most rapidly developing residential community. By the late eighties the area immediately around the university, known as "DePaul," had become one of Chicago's wealthiest neighborhoods, and being in Lincoln Park clearly worked to the university's benefit.

DePaul continued to grow, and as it attracted students from outside the Chicago area and its residential student population expanded to nearly two thousand, the university began building a campus infrastructure to support this new group of students in residence. In the 1990s the library finally materialized after being a featured structure in the succession of planning documents from Skidmore to Aschman. The John T. Richardson Library was built, appropriately enough, on the site that had been set aside for the first expansion of the Lincoln Park campus. As this is being written, a new biological sciences center (McGowan Biological and Environmental Sciences Center) is under construction next to the Stuart Center, fulfilling another long postponed dream of improved science research facilities at DePaul. By expanding its physical presence on the north side of the city, the university has changed itself irrevocably.

Research and Physical Expansion: The Emergence of a New DePaul

When it took on research activity and a program of aggressive expansion, DePaul stopped being "the little school under the El" and—as Richard Meister has noted—became the new American university. It expanded in the Loop, too, of course, acquiring buildings adjacent to or near the Lewis Center at the corner of Wabash and Jackson. DePaul became a major presence downtown with the purchase of the Blackstone Theater (renamed the Merle Reskin Theater) in 1989 and its acquisition and remodeling of the former Goldblatt Department Store building (renamed the DePaul Center) in 1991. But it was the development of the Lincoln Park campus that made the expansion of the College of Liberal Arts and Sciences, the School of Education, and the music and theater schools a reality. And as others have noted, it was these programs specifically that drove DePaul's transformation from a university dominated by evening and professional schools to one with a balance of programs serving students of all ages. The movement toward faculty professionalization, and university support for research, also helped move DePaul into the mainstream of American higher education and gained recognition for the university. A nationally recognized faculty, essential to the expansion of the institution, made its physical growth a reciprocal necessity. In this respect, research and physical expansion have been two sides of the same coin: institutional growth and development. Both helped transform DePaul into the modern comprehensive university it has become at the end of its first century.

Clockwise: *Ramsey Lewis appears at DePaul, 1968. Peter, Paul and Mary perform, 1966. The rock group Chicago plays at DePaul, 1971.*

285

Chapter Seven Notes

1. "Comparative Report on Enrollment for Autumn Quarter & First Semester 1948" Office of the President, Academic Files Box 5 DePaul University Archives (DPUA): Lester Goodchild, Chapter 12 "The Inauguration of the Doctorate at DePaul University, 1963–1967," in "The Mission of the Catholic University in the Midwest, 1842–1980: A Comparative Case Study of the Effects of Strategic Policy Decisions Upon the Mission of the University of Notre Dame, Loyola University Chicago and DePaul University" (Unpublished Ph.D. dissertation, University of Chicago, 1986) 478.

2. "Comparative Report on Enrollment For Autumn Quarter & First Semester 1948" Office of the President, Academic Files Box 5 DPUA: Goodchild, "The Mission of the Catholic University in the Midwest," 479.

3. "Interview with Arthur Schaefer, Vice-President for Development & Public Relations 1955–1979, Chicago, Illinois, 4/20/82" and "Interview with Dr. Robert Fries, Park Ridge, Illinois, 4/16/82," in Goodchild, "The Mission of the Catholic University in the Midwest," 479.

4. "Interview with Schaefer and Fries," Goodchild, "The Mission of the Catholic University in the Midwest", 479.

5. "Interview with Fries," Goodchild, "The Mission of the Catholic University in the Midwest", 479.

6. "Report on the State of the University," Rev. Comerford J. O'Malley, C.M., 10 September 1946, University Council Minutes, and "Minutes of the Lay Board of Trustees," 18 December 1946 Board of Trustees File Box 1, DPUA: Goodchild, "The Mission of the Catholic University in the Midwest,"479.

7. Goodchild, "The Mission of the Catholic University in the Midwest" p. 480.

8. North Central Accreditation Report, 1949, NCA Files, Box 5, DPUA.

9. *Ibid.*

10. 18 October 1950 University Council Minutes, 917, DPUA.

11. *Ibid.*

12. *Ibid,* 918.

13. Goodchild, 483; Institutional Papers, 1952 Faculty Reports, Office of the President, Comerford J. O'Malley, C.M., Papers, Box 14, DPUA [terminal degrees included Ph.D.; Ed.D; Mus.D.; S.T.D.; LL.B.; J.S.D.].

14. 16 March 1951 University Council Minutes, 968, DPUA.

15. *Ibid.*

16. *Ibid.*

17. *Ibid.*

18. Goodchild, "The Mission of the Catholic University in the Midwest", 481–482: 20 May 1950 Presentation of DePaul University to Executive Committee of the North Central Association, NCA Files, Box 7, DPUA.

19. Goodchild, 483: 1952 Faculty Reports, Office of the President, O'Malley Papers, Box 14: NCA Files Box 10, DPUA.

20. 13 December 1950 University Council Minutes, 930; 9 April 1952, University Council Minutes, 1037, 1039, DPUA: Goodchild, "The Mission of the Catholic University in the Midwest," 484.

21. 10 April 1957 University Council Minutes, 1379, DPUA.

22. *Ibid.*

23. *Ibid.*

24. Dr. George Works, "Report on DePaul University 8/30/50," 15–16, NCA File, Box 7, DPUA.

25. Goodchild, "The Mission of the Catholic University in the Midwest," 487.

26. 9 October 1946 University Council Minutes, DPUA; Goodchild, "The Mission of the Catholic University in the Midwest," 487.

27. Goodchild, "The Mission of the Catholic University in the Midwest," 485–486.

28. John T. Richardson, C.M., "Report on Specialist Degrees in Education and Mathematics," Subcommittee of the Admissions and Degrees Committee, Board of Trustees Minutes, 1955, Board of Trustees File [BOT], Box 3, DPUA.

29. Goodchild, "The Mission of the Catholic University in the Midwest," 484.

30. Comerford O'Malley, C.M. to John T. Richardson, C.M. 9 December 1957 "On Subject for Graduate Council Meeting," O'Malley Papers, Box 12, DPUA.

31. 1 September 1957 to 1 January 1959 University Council Minutes, DPUA; 17 December 1957; 18 July 1958; 9 December 1958 Graduate Council Minutes, O'Malley File, Box 12, DPUA.

32. 10 December 1957; 14 January 1958 University Council Minutes, DPUA; 9 December 1958 Graduate Council Minutes, O'Malley File, Box 12 DPUA.

33. 10 December 1958 University Council Minutes, DPUA; Goodchild, "The Mission of the Catholic University in the Midwest," 488.

34. 12 October 1955 University Council Minutes, DPUA.

35. *Ibid.*

36. *Ibid.*

37. 14 December 1955 University Council Minutes, DPUA.

38. *Ibid.*

39. *Ibid.*

40. *Ibid.*

41. *Ibid.*

42. Edward Kammer, C.M., "Report on Research and Publication at DePaul December, 1952 to December, 1953," 15 December 1953, O'Malley File, Box 19, DPUA.

43. 18 Janaury 1956 University Council Minutes, DPUA.

44. *Ibid.*

45. 15 February 1956; 14 March 1956; 18 April 1956 University Council Minutes, DPUA.

46. 9 May 1956 University Council Minutes, DPUA.

47. Faculty Handbook 1955–1956, 20, Academic File, Box 4, DPUA: 19 May 1956 University Council Minutes, DPUA.

48. 10 April 1957 University Council Minutes, DPUA.

49. Faculty Handbook 1956–1957, 17, Academic File, Box 4, DPUA.

50. *Ibid*, 20.

51. *Ibid*, 21.

52. *Ibid*, 17.

53. 10 April 1957 University Council Minutes, DPUA.

54. *Ibid*.

55. 22 November 1960 Board of Trustee Minutes, BOT File, Box 3, DPUA.

56. *Ibid*.

57. 1 November 1961 Richardson to O'Malley, O'Malley Papers, Box 20, DPUA; Goodchild, "The Mission of the Catholic University in the Midwest," 489.

58. 15 March 1965 Professional Summary, Department of Physics, 3, Department of Physics Archives through the courtesy of Anthony Behof, Ph.D., Chair of Physics Department.

59. 5 January 1962 Julius J. Hupert to Father John Richardson, C.M., John R. Cortelyou, C.M., William Cortelyou, C.M., Memorandum, Department of Physics Archives, DePaul University.

60. 5 January 1962 Hupert to Richardson, J. Cortelyou, W. Cortelyou, Memorandum, Department of Physics Archives.

61. 14 September 1962 Board of Trustee Minutes, BOT File, Box 3, DPUA.

62. 1 November 1963 Committee on Education of Board of Trustees Minutes, BOT File, Box 3, DPUA.

63. 19 November 1963 Board of Trustee Minutes, BOT File, Box 3, DPUA.

64. 19 November 1963 Board of Trustee Minutes, DPUA: also Goodchild, "The Mission of the Catholic University in the Midwest," 492.

65. *Ibid*, 493.

66. 14 January 1964 Board of Trustee Minutes, BOT File, Box 3, DPUA.

67. Goodchild, "The Mission of the Catholic University in the Midwest," 497.

68. *Ibid*.

69. 1 November 1963 Committee on Education of Board of Trustees Minutes, BOT File, Box 3, DPUA.

70. Goodchild, "The Mission of the Catholic University in the Midwest," 496–497.

71. 9 August 1967 Norman Burns to John R.Cortelyou, C.M., John R. Cortelyou Papers, Box 1, DPUA.

72. 15 November 1967 Board of Trustee Minutes, Report of the Academic Committee, BOT File, Box 3, DPUA.

73. Goodchild, "The Mission of the Catholic University in the Midwest," 495.

74. 23 July 1976 John R. Cortelyou, C.M., to Earnest Wish, Memorandum on the Mission and Scope of the University, Cortelyou Papers, Box 1, DPUA.

75. 10 October 1976 John T. Richardson, C.M., Personal Memorandum, John T. Richardson Papers, Box 19, DPUA.

76. 3 September 1997 History of Office of Sponsored Programs, DePaul University.

77. William Waters, "The Changing Economy of Lincoln Park After World War II to 1980," 2, 1989, Lincoln Park Study Group File, Box 3, DPUA; Ben Spencer, "Lincoln Park Development in the 1960's," 5, 1996, DPUA.

78. Waters, "The Changing Economy of Lincoln Park," 2, DPUA; also Spencer, "Lincoln Park Development in the 1960's," 5, DPUA.

79. Robert Cross, "Big Noise from Lincoln Park," *Chicago Tribune Magazine*, 11/2/69, Lincoln Park Collection File, Box 1, DPUA; Spencer, "Lincoln Park Development in the 1960's," 5, DPUA; Waters, "The Changing Economy of Lincoln Park," 2, DPUA.

80. Waters, "The Changing Economy of Lincoln Park," 2, DPUA; Spencer, "Lincoln Park Development in the 1960's," 5, DPUA.

81. Skidmore, Owings & Merrill, "DePaul University Expansion Program: *A Plan for Development of DePaul University*," 1947, 3, Building File, Box 1, DPUA; Scott Moore, "The Physical Expansion of DePaul University in Lincoln Park, 1950–1975," 1997, 2, DPUA.

82. Moore, "The Physical Expansion of DePaul University 1950–1975," 2; Brian Goodwill, "The Physical Expansion of DePaul University in the Lincoln Park Area from 1947 to 1973," 1997, 3, DPUA.

83. Moore, "The Physical Expansion of DePaul University 1950–1975," 3, DPUA.

84. Skidmore, Owings & Merrill, "DePaul University Expansion Program: *A Plan for Development of DePaul University*," 11, DPUA: Moore, "The Physical Expansion of DePaul University 1950–1975," 3, DPUA.

85. *Ibid*.

86. Moore, "The Physical Expansion of DePaul University 1950–1975," 3–4 DPUA: Skidmore,Owings & Merrill, "DePaul University Expansion Program: *A Plan for Development of DePaul University*," 15, DPUA.

87. Skidmore, Owings & Merrill, "DePaul University Expansion Program: *A Plan for Development of DePaul University*," 47 DPUA: Moore, "The Physical Expansion of DePaul University 1950–1975," 4, DPUA.

88. Skidmore, Owings & Merrill, "DePaul University Expansion Program: *A Plan for Development of DePaul University*," 47–48, DPUA.

89. Skidmore, Owings & Merrill, "DePaul University Expansion Program: *A Plan for Development of DePaul University*," 48–50, DPUA: Moore, "The Physical Expansion of DePaul University 1950–1975," 4–6, DPUA.

90. Skidmore, Owings & Merrill, "DePaul University Expansion Program: *A Plan for Development of DePaul University*," 57–58, DPUA: Moore, "The Physical Expansion of DePaul University 1950–1975," 8, DPUA.

91. *Ibid*.

92. Moore, "The Physical Expansion of DePaul University 1950–1975," 8, DPUA.

93. North Central Accreditation Report, 1949, NCA File, Box 5, DPUA: Business Research Corporation, "DePaul University: Report on Space Requirements," September, 1950, 2, Building File, Box 1, DPUA: Moore, "The Physical Expansion of DePaul University 1950–1975," 9, DPUA.

94. Business Research Corporation, "DePaul University: Report on Space Requirements," 5–7, DPUA; Moore, "The Physical Expansion of DePaul University 1950–1975," 9, DPUA.

95. 18 June 1953 Minutes of Lincoln Park Community Council, **3**, Lincoln Park Conservation Association File, [LPCA] Box 1, DPUA: Jon Lundbom, "The Relationship Between Urban Renewal Legislation, the Lincoln Park Conservation Association, and DePaul University from 1949 to 1970 and Thereafter," 1997, 2–3, DPUA.

96. 18 June 1953 Minutes of Lincoln Park Community Council, 3, DPUA: Lundbom, "The Relationship Between Urban Renewal Legislation," 3, DPUA.

97. Stephan Shamburg, "Statement to the 1969 Annual Meeting of Lincoln Park Conservation Association," LPCA File, Box 3, DPUA: Lundbom, "The Relationship between Urban Renewal Legislation," 3, DPUA.

98. "New Horizons for DePaul and You [1953]," Building Files, Box 1, DPUA; Moore, "The Physical Expansion of DePaul University 1950–1975," 10, DPUA.

99. "New Horizons for DePaul and You [1953]" DPUA: Moore, "The Physical Expansion of DePaul University 1950–1975," 10, DPUA.

100. *Ibid,* 11–12.

101. "DePaul University Chronology," 5, Building Files, Box 4, DPUA: Anthony Bertucci, "The Physical Expansion of DePaul University in Lincoln Park, 1950–1970," 1997, 2, DPUA.

102. "DePaul University General Information Booklet: The DePaul Development Program [1969]," LPCA File, Box 3, DPUA: Moore, "The Physical Expansion of DePaul University 1950–1975," 12, DPUA.

103. Moore, "The Physical Expansion of DePaul University 1950–1975," 12–13, DPUA.

104. 18 November 1959 DePaul University Council Minutes, DPUA: Lundbom, "The Relationship Between Urban Renewal Legislation," 8, DPUA.

105. Real Estate Research Corporation, "Analysis of Future Space Needs—Uptown Campus: DePaul University, 1961," 1–7, Building Files, Box 1, DPUA: Moore, "The Physical Expansion of DePaul University 1950–1975," 13–14, DPUA.

106. Rev. Theodore Wangler, C.M., "Statement to the Board of Directors, Lincoln Park Conservation Association, 11 May 1961," LPCA File, Box 2, DPUA: Lundbom, "The Relationship Between Urban Renewal Legislation," 9, DPUA.

107. Wangler, "Statement to the Board of Directors, LPCA, 11 May 1961," DPUA: Lundbom, "The Relationship Between Urban Renewal Legislation," 9, DPUA.

108. Wangler, "Statement to the Board of Directors, LPCA, 11 May 1961," DPUA: Lundbom, "The Relationship Between Urban Renewal Legislation," 9, DPUA.

109. 10 September 1962 DePaul University Council Minutes," Special Meeting To Determine Procedure for Land Acquisition, 10 September 1962, O'Malley Papers, Box 20, DPUA; Moore, "The Physical Expansion of DePaul University 1950–1975," 14–16, DPUA.

110. Real Estate Research Corporation, "Analysis of Future Space Needs," 1–7, 31, 39, Building File, Box 2, DPUA: Moore, "The Physical Expansion of DePaul University 1950–1975," 14–15, DPUA: Barton-Aschman Associates, Inc., "A General Development Plan for Uptown Campus of DePaul University, Chicago, Illinois, May, 1961," 6–8, Building File, Box 2, DPUA.

111. Barton-Aschman Associates, Inc., "A General Development Plan," 19, DPUA.

112. 27 February 1962 Comerford J. O'Malley to Donald T. Sheridan, Building File, Box 8, DPUA: Brian Goodwill, "The Physical Expansion of DePaul University in the Lincoln Park Area From 1947 to 1973," 1997, 6, DPUA.

113. Barton-Aschman Associates, Inc, "A General Development Plan," 19–20, Building File, Box 2, DPUA: Moore, The Physical Development of DePaul University 1950–1975," 21, DPUA.

114. 5 October 1962 Minutes Property Owners Meeting, Building File, Box 6, DPUA; Goodwill, "The Physical Expansion of DePaul University in Lincoln Park Area from 1947 to 1973," 6, DPUA.

115. 2 April 1962 Frank Lynn to Comerford J. O'Malley, C.M., Minutes Property Owners Meeting, Building File, Box 6, DPUA: Goodwill,""The Physical Expansion of DePaul University in Lincoln Park Area from 1947 to 1973," 6–7, DPUA: 21 March 1962 Donald T. Sheridan to Comerford J. O'Malley, C.M., O'Malley Papers, Box 20, DPUA.

116. 22 March 1962 Rev. Albert Dundas, C.M., to Frank C. Wells, Building Files, Box 6, DPUA: 21 March 1962 Thomas J. Russell to A.J. Dundas, C.M., Building Files, Box 6, DPUA: Goodwill, "The Physical Expansion of DePaul University in Lincoln Park Area from 1947 to 1973," 7, DPUA.

117. 5 October 1962 Minutes Property Owners Meeting, Building Files, Box 6, DPUA: Goodwill, "The Physical Expansion of DePaul University in Lincoln Park Area from 1947 to 1973," 7, DPUA.

118. 5 October 1962 Minutes Property Owners Meeting, Building Files, Box 6, DPUA: 1962 Correspondence, O'Malley Papers, Box 20, DPUA: Goodwill, "The Physical Expansion of DePaul University in Lincoln Park Area from 1947 to 1973," 7, DPUA.

119. 2 April 1962 and 10 April 1962 Frank Lynn to Comerford J. O'Malley, C.M., Building Files, Box 6, DPUA; Goodwill, "The Physical Expansion of DePaul University in Lincoln Park Area from 1947 to 1973," 7, DPUA.

120. 26 January 1964 Concerned Citizens to the General Public, Building Files, Box 8, DPUA: Lundbom, "The Relationship Between Urban Renewal Legislation," 11–12, DPUA.

121. 26 January 1964 Concerned Citizens to the General Public, DPUA: Lundbom, "The Relationship Between Urban Renewal Legislation," 12, DPUA.

122. 30 March 1966 "Presentation in Support of DePaul's Inclusion in Phase II of Neighborhood Renewal Program," Minutes of Lincoln Park Conservation Association, LPCA File, Box 3, DPUA: Lundbom, "The Relationship Between Urban Renewal Legislation," 12, DPUA.

123. Lundbom, "The Relationship Between Urban Renewal Legislation," 12–13, DPUA.

124. 1967 Concerned Citizens "A Real Program of Greatness For DePaul," Building Files, Box 8, DPUA: Lundbom, "The Relationship Between Urban Renewal Legislation," 11, DPUA.

125. 1966 "Academic Center Prospectus," Building Files, Box 8, DPUA: Moore, "The Physical Expansion of DePaul University 1950–1975," 23–24, DPUA.

126. "The DePaul University Program For Greatness: a Nine-Year Program Report 1972–1973," 1–4, Building Plan Files, Box 3, DPUA: Moore, "The Physical Expansion of DePaul University 1950–1975," 24–25, DPUA.

127. "Nine-Year Report 1972–1973," 6–7, DPUA: Moore, "The Physical Expansion of DePaul University 1950–1975," 25, DPUA.

128. "A Prospectus of the DePaul Lincoln Park Campus, 1967," Building File, Box 3, DPUA: "Invest $27 Million in Program For Greatness," DePaul University Magazine, Fall, 1973, 12–15, Building File, Box 3, DPUA: Maureen Berry, "The Program For Greatness and The Acquisition of McCormick Seminary," 1997, 4–5, DPUA.

129. Marshall Scott, *McCormick Theological Seminary: An Informal History,* (Chicago: McCormick Theological Seminary, 1980) 78 LPCA File, Box 6, DPUA: Berry, "The Program For Greatness," 5, DPUA.

130. Elizabeth K. Ware, *The Seminary Townhouse Story* (Chicago: DePaul University, 1994), 22; 17 March 1975 "McCormick Seminary Sub-Committee," Minutes Lincoln Park Conservation Association, LPCA File, Box 2, DPUA: Berry, "The Program For Greatness," 7, DPUA.

131. October, 1974 "Special Subcommittee Formed to Study McCormick Seminary," Lincoln Park Conservation Association Newsletter, LPCA File, Box 1N, DPUA: Berry, "The Program For Greatness," 7, DPUA.

132. April, 1975 "McCormick Theological Seminary," Lincoln Park Conservation Association Newsletter, LPCA File, Box 1N, DPUA: Berry, "The Program For Greatness," 6–7, DPUA.

133. Ware, *The Seminary Townhouse Story*, 20: Berry, "The Program For Greatness," 9, DPUA.

134. 8 April 1976 "Minutes of the Physical Plant Committee," Building Files, Box 8, DPUA: Berry, "The Program For Greatness," 9, DPUA.

135. Berry, "The Program For Greatness," 9, DPUA.

136. 8 January 1976 Robert Drevs to John R. Cortelyou, C.M., Cortelyou Papers, Box 1, DPUA: Berry, "The Program For Greatness," 10., DPUA.

137. 16 February 1976 John R. Cortelyou, C.M., to Faculty, Staff, and Students, Cortelyou Papers, Box 1, DPUA: Berry, "The Program For Greatness," 10, DPUA.

138. 9 March 1976 John R. Cortelyou to Friends of DePaul, Cortelyou Papers, Box 1, DPUA: Berry, "The Program For Greatness," 9, 11, DPUA.

139. "DePaul University Adds McCormick Land to Campus," Sheffield Neighbors Association Newsletter, January, 1977, Vol. 27, No. 7, 6, LPCA File, Box 1N, DPUA: Berry, "The Program For Greatness," 11, DPUA.

We Ourselves Are Plural

Curricular Change at DePaul, 1960–1997

Charles R. Strain

The story of curricular change in American higher education is often a litany of lamentations by the latest Jeremiah to appear in the pages of *Newsweek, Time*, or the *New York Review of Books*. In his best-selling work, *The Closing of the American Mind*, Alan Bloom argued that in the 1960s, when we will begin our story of curricular change at DePaul University, American higher education abandoned its commitment to a liberalizing education, succumbed to the siren song of moral relativism, and turned tail before the influx of the new barbarians. In short, it lost its way. (1) Bloom's lament has a long pedigree, with most variants placing the emphasis on separating the "pursuit of learning" from "preparation for modern professions." Thorstein Veblen gave this vision its classic expression as early as 1918 in *The Higher Learning in America*. Unless the two conflicting aims could be kept separate, Veblen thought the traditional vision of liberal learning would be crushed under the weight of professional training whose aim was self aggrandizement. (2)

A similar chorus of Jeremiahs within Catholic higher education has proclaimed an analogous dualism but one that is heightened by eschatological overtones. Here the pursuit of professional education is linked to the pervasive spread of secularism in American culture. Pitting the sacred against the secular, Catholic Jeremiahs urge Catholic institutions of higher education to resist the process that has eroded the religious character of their Protestant counterparts—institutions such as the University of Chicago, Northwestern University and Illinois Wesleyan—that retain little more than mere shards of their religious foundations. (3) According to David J. O'Brien, those who see Catholic higher education poised on the slippery slope of secularization fail to perceive how purposefully American Catholics in general and Catholic higher education in particular *willed* their own explosive trajectory out of the confines of "ghetto Catholicism" during the period we focus on. (4) The conscious commitment of American Catholic universities to draw their strength from multiple cultural roots burst into prominence in the 1960s. To claim, as I will, that Catholic universities like DePaul have, for a long time, exercised pluralism in both their ideology and curriculum (in fact if not in self-conception) is to dismiss the Jeremiahs as "profoundly misleading." (5)

To another group of commentators—who may be called "pragmatic adapters"—all of this lamentation was beside the point. In the half-century since the end of World War II demographic changes were the driving force behind the transformation in American higher education. In this familiar narrative, the G.I. Bill inaugurated a new era in which higher education welcomed those whom Bloom could only perceive as the barbarians at the gates. Clark Kerr refers to the period from 1960 to 1980 as the "third great transformation" of higher education in America. The first occurred at Harvard and William and Mary in the 17th century, with the founding of the liberal arts college based on a classical curriculum; the second took place in the period from 1870 to 1910, when the German model of a departmentally-based research university became the dominant force in higher education. Over the course of the third transformation, the number of students in higher education rose from 3.5 million in 1960 to 12 million in 1980; the community college swept into prominence and federal money poured into research institutions effectively harnessing them to the political purposes of the Cold War and to the prevailing economic forces. (6) As early as 1964, Kerr coined the phrase "knowledge industry" to signify this integration of higher education into the larger society. "What the railroads did for the second half of the last century and the automobile for the first half of this century may be done for the second half of this century by the knowledge industry: that is, to serve as the focal point for national growth." (7)

The good news, according to Kerr and many others, was that higher education was remarkably flexible in adapting to immense demographic changes at the same time that it responded vigorously to its enhanced role of preparing a professional workforce for the national economy. (8) An unprecedented burst of academic reform accompanied these revolutionary changes, he noted.

Never in the history of the United States, or for that matter any other nation, has there been such a wave of academic innovation . . . with such minuscule results as during the great transformation. There were "cluster" colleges . . . and "without walls" colleges; also "work-study," "field study," and "study abroad;" and every other innovation that the mind could possibly devise. . . . Few of the innovations survived, and these few had little general impact on higher education—everything was tried; nearly everything failed. (9)

In other words, when it came to curricular change, Kerr—a pragmatic adapter with long-range optimism—leaned decidedly in the direction of the Jeremiahs.

Bruce Kimball, a more consistent pragmatist than Kerr, accepts as a given the proposition that extensive changes in student numbers, age, gender, race and ethnicity have been *the* major force shaping the undergraduate experience, and he sees the flurry of experimentation as the triumph of a pragmatic temper in higher education. Viewed collectively, efforts at curricular change, especially in the contested arena of liberal education, affirm a commitment to epistemological pluralism, to the integration of knowledge and value, to tentative and self-correcting constructions of what we know and to the establishment of multiple communities of inquirers, each of which is a trait of the pragmatic spirit. (10)

There is a counterpart to Kimball's view among commentators on Catholic higher education. It has found expression in those who emphasize the movement of Catholic institutions from self-protective marginality to willing involvement at the center of American culture. What this meant in practice was that Catholic universities were transformed when the ethos of professionalism was applied to every aspect of institutional life. O'Brien has pointed out some of the implications of this view.

> *A*lmost everyone agrees that professionalization is a key to understanding contemporary American Catholic higher education. Academic freedom, institutional autonomy, emphasis on research and publication within the disciplines, and problems with general education have all come with this process. So has the demand for structural reform to recognize the faculty's primary responsibility for academic policy. (11)

The proponents of this view interpret this pervasive professionalization not as a form of secularization but as the manifest sign of a willed commitment to carry out the educational mission of Catholic universities from within the heart of the surrounding culture. The G.I. Bill, the post-World War II movement of American Catholics from ethnic enclaves to suburbs, Vatican II and the social and cultural revolutions of the 1960s were among the external and internal processes driving the change. (12) It is important not to overlook, however, how enthusiastically institutions like DePaul have adapted to American culture in the postwar period even when they worked to change it. Later in this chapter, we will see in DePaul's emerging urban mission an example of efforts to embrace and transform the surrounding culture using the mechanism of curricular policy.

At the Threshold of the 1960s: Creating a Context for Innovation

In DePaul's case, movement toward the center of American culture was no easy task. Nor was coping with the huge influx of students in the immediate postwar period. A severe crisis over accreditation, in fact, almost shipwrecked the institution. On March 23, 1950, a Chicago *Sun-Times* front page headline blared: "DePaul U. Standing Periled." The article stated that on March 22 the North Central Association's Commission on Colleges and Universities had recommended dropping DePaul from its list of accredited schools. "Without accreditation," the article continued, in what must be read as either a masterfully diplomatic or a benignly ignorant understatement, "the university would lose prestige in the academic world and DePaul students might have difficulty in getting their scholastic credits accepted by approved schools." (13)

The university was acutely aware of the urgency of its situation. Comerford O'Malley, C.M., president of the university, filed an immediate appeal and a hearing date was set for May 8. (14) The bill of particulars, from an external NCA review of the institution in 1949, was quite detailed. Though it acknowledged that the university had not exploited the G.I. Bill for financial gain, the report suggested that rapid expansion of the student body in the postwar period had precipitated a crisis with respect to the size and competence of DePaul's teaching staff. (15) The report demanded a significant strengthening of the number of Ph.D.s among faculty responsible for graduate instruction. It raised questions about the adequacy of general education requirements for certain departments and programs, characterizing graduate programs in general as overextended, and calling the program of the "secretarial" department more characteristic of a "proprietary business college" than a four-year university. Other criticisms touched on the adequacy of library holdings and the relative lack of control that faculty exercised over academic policy. (16)

The university did not evade these criticisms. In a matter of weeks it developed an action plan to address each concern. It promised to add 20 new Ph.D.s before the beginning of the 1950–51 school year. Seventeen faculty whose progress toward the Ph.D. had been interrupted during the war years indicated that they would earn their degrees within a year. Within the space of two years the university planned to double its Ph.D. faculty. (17) Several under-enrolled graduate programs were dropped. A university faculty curriculum committee was appointed to review general education requirements in the departments and programs that were specific targets of NCA's criticism. The secretarial department was placed under immediate review and a team of external consultants was brought in to make an institutional study. (18)

Immediate and decisive action proved effective. The NCA deferred action that would revoke accreditation pending a review during the 1950–51 school year. (19) The immediate crisis passed but DePaul's efforts to sail into the mainstream of American higher education during this period of unprecedented expansion were hardly off to an auspicious start.

It is not easy to locate the truly auspicious beginning, the turn toward academic excellence at DePaul. My own sense is that in many ways it is connected with the career of one man, Reverend John T. Richardson, C.M., who served the university for over forty years, first as dean of the Graduate School (1954–1966), next as executive vice president and dean of faculties (1960–1981), then as president (1981–1993) and finally as chancellor. While Father Richardson insists that the academic crisis of the early 1950s was resolved by the time he entered the university as dean of the Graduate School in 1954, it is clear that what he saw in the university's graduate programs troubled him. (20) Responding to internal pressures to offer a few doctoral programs, Richardson pointed out in a memo to the graduate faculty in late 1959 that no school is stronger than its weakest link. Frankly recalling what must have been a painful memory, he insisted:

> *Exception is sometimes taken to the regulation of regional accrediting associations which requires a university to reach a degree of excellence in every single department before just one or two departments offer a doctoral program. There is much wisdom in this regulation, for why should shoddy work in some areas be hidden from the public eye or bask in the reflected glory of one or two strong departments? Excellence is being achieved in a few departments or if not actually achieved, this excellence is at least understood and the proper machinery in operation to achieve it. But there is a tremendous gap separating the level of work now being performed in different parts of the Graduate School.* (21)

One sure sign of a broad-spectrum move toward excellence would be "positive evidence that the great majority of the graduate faculty are not only capable of, but actually engaged in, research." Only then could "DePaul be a 'university' in fact as well as in name." (22)

Richardson was afraid that Catholic higher education in general, and DePaul in particular, would remain in an academic backwater—ideas would circulate, changes would occur— but only within the immediate community, not through interaction with the larger currents of American higher education. (23) This sentiment, along with Richardson's criticisms of the graduate school, echoes the views of John Tracy Ellis, then a leading historian of American Catholicism. In his speech to the annual meeting of the Catholic Commission on Intellectual and Cultural Affairs in St. Louis in 1955, Ellis made the most searching examination of Catholic higher education of the 1950s. Where are the Catholic "scholars of distinction?" he asked. Where are the Catholic intellectuals who could influence the larger culture the way renowned nineteenth century converts like Orestes Brownson had? Where were the Catholic scientists, the Catholic Nobel laureates? (24) Though he acknowledged that many cultural and internal forces had hindered development of a vigorous intellectual life within Catholic universities, including most importantly their commitment to educate the masses of Catholic immigrants, Ellis argued that Catholic higher education had fallen prey to the American pursuit of vocational education with its anti-intellectual ethos. Above all, Ellis excoriated his fellow Catholics for their "frequently self-imposed ghetto mentality which prevents them from mingling as they should with their non-Catholic colleagues. . . ." (25)

Ellis's dismissive view of mass education and his advocacy of a pure "intellectual apostolate," put him squarely in the tradition of the Jeremiahs. But this aspect of his thought, this dualistic juxtaposition of the theoretical and the practical, did *not* have an impact at places like DePaul. Rather it was the awareness of being trapped in a self-enclosed and self-perpetuating backwater, of moving without going anywhere, that rankled. When he became executive vice president in 1960, Richardson felt that the time was ripe to lead the university out of that backwater and into the mainstream. Acknowledging the firm support of Comerford O'Malley and, later, John Cortelyou, C.M., the two presidents under whom he served before assuming the presidency, Richardson sees himself in retrospect as the "maverick" among the university's administrative leaders. *"But having had six years as dean [of the Graduate School] . . . I think I*

The Rev. John T. Richardson, C.M. president 1981–1993

296

had . . . gathered enough confidence [from] the other administrators of the university so that when I became executive vice president, dean of faculties [in 1960], I felt I had a strong base from which to move." (26) If this tale of curricular change has within it an auspicious moment when the university turned toward academic excellence, this was it.

DePaul did not wait for the official sanction that Vatican II provided for sweeping changes within all Catholic institutions, nor did it tack to the winds of the social revolution of the 1960s. Curricular modifications were well under way before these external forces made themselves felt. Again and again in my interviews, faculty members recalled the university encouraging autonomous innovation. In contrast to the stereotype of the Catholic university—where someone in robes lurks in the background sniffing out deviation from orthodoxy—DePaul trusted its own faculty and staff to develop sound programs. (27) The 1960s were a watershed in this regard. (28) In fact, Richardson sees it as one of the more important accomplishments of that period that the impetus to change, originally an administrative initiative, was handed to the faculty. (29)

Roberta Garner, a sociology professor and member of the faculty since 1971, notes that while flexibility and a commitment to change came to characterize the institution, the changes themselves were conservative. DePaul's scarce resources meant that there was always a narrow margin for error. Commitment to innovation had to be balanced against a largely first-generation college student body's desire for something "solid," an education relevant to the job market. Conservative change meant "intelligently seeing the match between our goals—our goals as faculty [and] students' goals—and available internal resources. And having some sense of how these fit together." (30) Garner's sense of conservative innovation characterizes most, if not all, of the curriculum changes examined in this chapter. Even when the innovations were decidedly more experimental, their implementation was "conservative in the best sense."

While the desire to escape the academic backwater was a powerful incentive, the confidence that Richardson and others exhibited as they crossed the watershed was remarkable. After all, they could have approached the situation differently: why not assume that what was called a backwater was really a port in the storm? Why not opt, as many other institutions have, for a "sectarian solution?" Why not maintain a Catholic university as an anchor against the inconstant sea, a bulwark against modernity where, in Marx's apt phrase, "all that is solid melts into air?" The first real test of the direction the university was to take occurred in the early 1960s with the decision to open the philosophy department to currents of thought other than scholastic philosophy. The story itself will be told in a later section, but Richardson's comments on the event tell us a great deal about DePaul's openness to curricular change. Given the traditional role of scholastic philosophy in integrating the curricula for Catholic higher education, I suggested in an interview with Richardson that a more common response might be expressed in an analogy: if you open the tent flaps of the university to change, it is very important to have the truth nailed down in at least one corner, have at least one peg of orthodoxy lest the whole tent blow away. Richardson did not let me finish the thought. *"I'd never buy that,"* he interjected. *"No. [I] had no fear that open learning is going to conflict with the tenets of faith. Never had any fear."* (31)

There is a sublime irony here of which Richardson was fully aware. The confidence radiated by Thomistic philosophy ("the only philosophy I ever studied," Richardson said) in the ultimate harmony of reason and faith was the source of inspiration that made it possible to let go of Thomism as *the* peg nailing the university's curriculum to a preconceived orthodoxy. Openness to curricular change stemmed from a religious confidence in the catholicity of truth; that is, the ubiquity of the divinely scattered seeds of knowledge. In practice, this religious confidence meant receptiveness to manifold sources of knowledge and, as William Shea expressed it, referring directly to Catholic higher education, the recognition that "we ourselves are plural." (32) As a matter of theory and hope, Richardson believed that all forms of knowledge would ultimately be in harmony. In actuality, the university would ride the epistemological crosscurrents of higher education's open sea.

First Steps: The Curricular Design of 1964

As Thomas Croak has noted, during the early 60s discussions continued about introducing doctoral programs into the graduate curriculum. Father John Cortelyou, C.M., a researcher in the biological sciences and a future president of the university, was developing plans for expansion in the sciences. A report of the Committee on Education to the Board of Trustees in early 1963 concluded that "the doctoral program appears essential and inevitable at DePaul." (33)

Nevertheless, Richardson had a different set of priorities. Having become dean of faculties in 1960, he set to work reforming *undergraduate* education. The highly decentralized character of university operations meant that each college had set its own policies with respect to both general and specialized education. Recall that the North Central Association had taken issue with widespread inconsistencies in the structure of general education requirements a decade previously. Richardson remembers some "warm discussions," as a clear message was sent to the professional schools: "Look, you controlled all your curricula until now but *no more*." (34) There were occasional confrontations, but Richardson and key leaders among the faculty and administration had a clear vision: *"we wanted a university-wide philosophy of undergraduate education and . . . university-wide standards in basic areas of knowledge."* (35)

The process moved slowly. Initial efforts to formulate the philosophy of undergraduate education began in fall 1962. A progress report and draft were submitted to the board of trustees in spring 1963. Discussion with board members culminated in a decision to develop the philosophy "in relation to the actual educational processes of the university, particularly curricular design." (36) A final version entitled *A Curricular Design for DePaul University* was submitted to the university community on April 13, 1964.

Few DePaul faculty members have ever heard of this document but it is hard to overestimate its significance. Richardson suggested that it *"was the most fundamental and far-reaching curricular policy for as far back as my knowledge of the university goes and for the succeeding decades."* (37) To read this document in autumn 1997, as the university is about to launch a new general education program for undergraduate students, is to be struck by the common threads of issues and goals stretching across three decades. In one sense such continuity should not surprise us. The implied presupposition of the document was the hegemony of specialized and professional education. The *Curricular Design* asserted its principles in dialectical tension with this dominant factor—then and now—in higher education.

The document began by designating the philosophy of "Vincentian personalism" as the religious context and rationale for curricular design. Focusing on the "primacy of the person," this philosophy asserted as its first educational corollary that a person has "the inherent right and the consequent responsibility to develop his own potential in an educational environment that permits him to be involved actively in his own becoming." (38) This emphasis on personal development gave the entire document a student-centered character. The explicit focus of the design is what we call today "learning outcomes." (39) The sections on educational principles and on curricular guidelines both began not by focusing on subject matter but on the potential of the student. Because of this developmental focus the *Curricular Design* stressed the importance of integrating ongoing learning with prior knowledge and experience. Wherever possible, students were to be able to accelerate the learning process. Self-directed study was a sign of "academic maturity," and one of the most important outcomes of the learning process was a habit of life-long learning. "In the university a man only refines the education he must continue in the enterprise of life," the document declared. (40) The *Curricular Design* affirmed that ordinary college-level students possess these central qualities in latent form; they were not seen as the monopoly of an intellectual elite: "The failure to develop the potential of the capable majority may rest with the educational theory and practice of the educators. . . ." (41)

The *Curricular Design* presented other educational goals that DePaul is still struggling to achieve. The university formally committed itself to what had long been practiced, namely, responding to the needs and goals of a diverse student body, particularly one that reflected varied religious commitments. Educating a diverse group for life in a pluralistic society was a central educational goal. *"DePaul believes,"* the document stated, *"that the student's confrontation with diverse value systems [is] beneficial in orienting students to continuing intellectual inquiry and to understanding a variety of defensible values in a pluralistic society."* (42) As part of this endeavor, it called for the study of non-Western cultures and traditions. The curriculum was to "provide exposure to man's religious questionings . . . in all cultures . . . ." (43) To be sure, it was not until the early 1980s that a multicultural, globally focused education became a reality for all DePaul undergraduates—even at a basic level. The university was well ahead of other Catholic schools, however, when it came to articulating this ideal. The *Curricular Design*, in fact, forthrightly presented a new model of the liberally educated person that was an alternative to scholastic philosophy's vision of "man" the rational animal, and that still conformed to the religious mission of the institution.

The *Curricular Design* also proclaimed what has become a major feature of undergraduate education at DePaul only in the 1990s: *"The curricular design shall reflect the student's distinctive opportunities and privileges for education and service that exist in an urban culture and in an urban university"*. (44) Brokering connections between the classroom and Chicago itself as a site of learning received an early formulation in this document: "The curricular design should utilize the resources of the metropolitan area *which, in effect, constitute the total university campus."* (45) But the curricular initiatives to put this educational goal into action were not articulated. The clearest step towards its realization was a firm commitment to the importance of the behavioral and social sciences in investigating the relationship of the human organism to its environment. (46) When DePaul College was created, requirements in philosophy and theology, heretofore seen as the principal agents of curricular integration, were reduced, and space in the undergraduate curriculum was carved out for the social sciences to carry out this role.

In other respects the document reflected changes in the philosophy of general education that were percolating through higher education. A case in point is the emphasis throughout

DePaul University Wish Field dedication November, 1987. Father Richardson, Susan Wish, Ernie Wish and Joan Wish.

the document on "ways of knowing." What the *Curricular Design* mandated for the scientific disciplines—that emphasis was to be placed on direct "experience with the dynamic or exploratory aspect [in contrast to the static or descriptive]"—applied to all areas of inquiry. (47) Integration of knowledge, another battle cry of curricular reformers in the 1960s, was established as an educational goal not in competition with specialized knowledge but as applying to both general and specialized studies. *All* educational offerings were to be assessed using the criterion of "integration of knowledge in a liberally educated person." If the university was "unsuccessful" in its pursuit of this goal, it at least articulated an ideal which did not place liberal and professional education in sterile opposition. (48) The *Curricular Design's* most important accomplishment, however, was that it provided the rationale that enabled the university to develop and retain a solid set of university-wide core requirements in liberal education during the very period of the later 1960s when other institutions were abandoning theirs. (49)

While the work of the Curricular Design Committee went on quietly, another curricular revolution—the effort of the philosophy department to transform the way philosophy was taught at DePaul—received national attention. In October 1964 *Time* magazine trumpeted an event that it considered "probably the most significant attempt to overhaul Catholic philosophy teaching since 1789, when Georgetown . . . opened its doors." (50) But *Time* also quoted one DePaul philosopher who lamented: "It is selling your philosophical birthright for a mess of existential pottage." The controversy roiled over the introduction at DePaul that autumn of "Philosophical Horizons" as an option for students, a program that was to run parallel to the traditional scholastic track.

The effort to transform the philosophy curriculum was led by Gerald Kreyche, the first lay chairman of the Department of Philosophy. It is important to remember that scholastic philosophy was—with few exceptions—regarded as *the* integrating factor in a Catholic college education until the 1960s. Catholic schools claimed to offer a "unified vision of life" as their distinguishing characteristic and the part of the curriculum that expressed this vision was "was not theology or history but scholastic philosophy, which was defined as the only 'Catholic philosophy.'" (51) Prior to the development of DePaul College in the late 1960s, philosophy at DePaul commandeered what Kreyche acknowledged was an "awfully big chunk" of the undergraduate curriculum—18 semester hours in liberal arts and sciences and 12 in commerce. Kreyche, with the enthusiastic backing of Richardson and President Cortelyou, embarked on a different course. (52)

Though DePaul may not have been the first major Catholic university to make radical changes to its philosophy curriculum, Kreyche—despite, or perhaps because of, his status as a layperson—emerged as a national spokesperson for those who shared his vision that a philosophy department in a Catholic university should be fully engaged not only with the multiple currents in contemporary philosophical inquiry but also with the natural and social sciences. Absent this broader involvement, a philosophy department could claim only historical interest for its subject, not contemporary relevance. More bluntly, Kreyche argued that it could not really claim to be involved in philosophical inquiry as such. (53)

In a presentation at a national meeting for Catholic educators, Kreyche characterized the philosophy curriculum in Catholic colleges as simply a diluted version of the seminary model of education for Catholic clergy. No one had paused to consider whether this was appropriate for the masses of lay Catholics, to say nothing of the non-Catholic student. "We have yet to institute a restructured curriculum [in philosophy] which has the needs and desires of the Catholic layman as its primary concern—I mean the layman whose apostolate is *in the world.*" (54) Driving his point home, Kreyche asked, "When will we learn that a college education involves an existential risk?" When it introduced the new, "Philosophical Horizons" track in autumn, 1964, DePaul opened itself and its students to that "existential risk." In 1967, when DePaul College opened, the traditional option was dropped. (55)

The new program, and the notoriety that accompanied it, signified a definitive exodus from Catholic backwaters. DePaul history professor James Krokar recalls that it was the *Time* article that prompted him to enter DePaul as an undergraduate. Coming from a family where ideas were freely exchanged around the dinner table, Krokar concluded that "DePaul seemed to [have] a much more open atmosphere than the competition." (56) Riding the crest of this wave of attention, Kreyche collaborated with a colleague from Georgetown University in 1966 to edit and publish three anthologies of primary sources—*Perspectives on Reality*, *Reflections on Man* and *Approaches to Morality*—which were to be the foundational texts for the new approach. Each book focused on five different currents of philosophical thought: classical and scholastic philosophy, modern continental philosophy, American pragmatism, analytic and positivist philosophy, and existentialism and phenomenology. By 1966 the editors could appeal to the Second Vatican Council's reforms to support new approaches:

> *A*n openness to truth wherever it may be found is revealed in various documents promulgated at the Second Vatican Council . . . . The pluralistic attitude affirmed by the Council has, in recent years, been the direct approach in many Catholic colleges and universities in the United States. The significance of the aggiornamento in philosophy is that the philosophical pluralism initiated by some is now enjoined upon all . . . . Students of philosophy must know the dynamic currents of thought which are expressed in a free society. (57)

Kreyche's and DePaul's own "existential risk" had become a national movement.

From Theory to Practice: The Creation of DePaul College in 1967

Within a few years the ferment in the Department of Philosophy had spread to all of the departments involved with general education for undergraduates. Following publication of the *Curriculum Design*, an implementation committee began translating its principles into a general education curriculum and devising a new administrative structure—to be called DePaul College—to deliver that curriculum to all undergraduate students. (58) Everyone involved in the process remembers this as a time of tremendous excitement. DePaul College was the magnet attracting immense amounts of creative energy. (59) Groups of faculty clustered into four divisions (philosophy and theology; humanities; behavioral and social sciences; and natural sciences and mathematics) met for weekend retreats and extended weekly sessions in the years preceding and immediately following the inauguration of the college in the fall of 1967.

Within the disciplines of each division, the participants undertook a serious search for common ground in modes of inquiry and subject matter. In the humanities division a year-long sequence focused in successive quarters on the classical, romantic and syncretic (or modern) temper in art, literature and music. Faculty from each of the three disciplines shared the course and split the teaching of each section. "Logistically," says Patricia Ewers, then a faculty member in English but eventually vice president for academic affairs at DePaul and now president of Pace University, "it was . . . a nightmare." (60) Shuttling in and out of three sections of a course did not work, but the course sequence remained an ideal, a point where noble reach exceeded practical grasp.

In the history department a more successful experiment was under way. History was converted from a one-year survey course in Western Civilization—"from Adam to the atomic bomb"—to a single course, "Man and History: Ideas and Method," focusing on the nature of historical inquiry and on contending visions of the historical process. (61) To teach the course, faculty who had been trained in traditional graduate history programs had to make a radical shift in their approach. Albert Erlebacher, professor emeritus of history, recalls that those who planned the revisions assumed that high school students who were coming to college would be familiar with the kind of knowledge a survey course offered.

> *Why repeat the same thing that they had already adequately learned in high school[?] So let's . . . teach them about history in terms of a learning experience. . . . [For] me, it was somewhat new, too . . . . Because [in graduate school] . . . you were what they called a carpenter. You learned how to use the tools of history; you built something that was an article or a chapter in a book . . . . You didn't talk too much about why it was you were doing this. . . . And that's what this course was supposed to deal with. (62)*

Ironically, Erlebacher contends that the assumption on which this revision was built turned out to be inaccurate. Students did not have a detailed knowledge of the past to use for testing the validity of historical theories and methods. (63) In fact, the historians found themselves relying on specific case studies of historical events or crises (using such topics as the rise of fascism and the history of the Vietnam war) and examining them in detail to ground their sallies into the philosophy of history. The course worked because of the vitality of this dialectic between concrete cases and theoretical inquiries. (64)

In the Division of Natural Sciences and Mathematics (NSM), turbulence was the order of the day as faculty struggled, in seemingly endless meetings, to create a new science curriculum for general education. "I think that [the inauguration of] DePaul College was the first time," recalls Tony Behof, now chair of the physics department, "that all of the sciences got together and tried to decide . . . just what it is they should be teaching in science courses [for the non-major]." (65) One group, representing several disciplines, sought a complete turnabout in the way science was taught. According to physicist Edwin Schillinger, during the previous two decades, the specialized and technical introductory sequences in many of the departments had been designed with an eye to recruiting science majors. The reformers were convinced that those sequences were not working. (66) Others, however, sought to affirm the hegemony of their particular science or to defend disciplinary boundaries. (67) These battles came to a head over a proposal to develop a year-long integrated sequence for the nonmajor with physics in the first quarter and chemistry and biology in subsequent quarters. This effort in the NSM division soon foundered, as had the design for sweeping integration in the humanities. (68)

The onset of a general crisis in science education in America exacerbated the problems the NSM faculty faced in trying to shape a new curriculum, according to Avrom Blumberg, professor of chemistry and the first person to lead the division. Blumberg argues that the early 1960s represented the apogee of scientific literacy in American college-age students; DePaul College was born on the down slope. In his view, scientific literacy began plunging in the late 1960s and the new NSM program was an effort to resist the ineluctable decline of scientific knowledge among the general populace. The scientists committed to reform saw educating *citizens* to make informed judgments in a scientific and technological age as their goal. *"We wanted to show in each of these courses . . . what it was that scientists did, what are some of the practical applications and utilizations of the sciences, and how does it affect the way man thinks of himself in his own society."* (69) In working toward these goals, Edwin Schillinger argues, DePaul was not following the lead of other institutions but pioneering a new approach. *"[I]n Physics we were coming along with the society-oriented courses three to five years before places like Chicago or Carleton or other places that are well-known for this sort of thing came along."* (70)

Schillinger himself pioneered a course epitomizing these efforts that continued to be offered into the 1990s. Originally entitled "Reason and Unreason in Science," the course applied critical reasoning to the evolution of science itself. It examined how scientific investigators used self-correcting methods to uncover the "unreason" in previously touted "scientific" formulations. (71) The success of this course over the years inspired subsequent efforts to develop what the initial attempt of the NSM faculty had initially failed to do; that is, to present an integrated vision of the nature and accomplishments of the sciences. (72)

The heady ferment of curricular innovation lasted roughly from spring 1966 through the very early years of the 1970s. (73) In many cases it was younger faculty members who were the developers of the new curriculum, another instance of the degree of autonomy DePaul was willing to grant faculty in the field of curricular development. Although Patricia Ewers, when she was dean of the College of Liberal Arts and Sciences in the late 1970s, emerged as the major critic of DePaul College and the instigator of a second wave of reform in general education, she is the first to concede that the *process* of developing the DePaul College curriculum fostered a faculty culture open to curricular innovation.

A lot of the intellectual growth that I had, the broadening of my perspective as a faculty member, arose out of those interactions [in shaping the Humanities core] . . . . I think the experience of DePaul College and working across disciplines for a number of years made [future curricular changes] more possible at DePaul . . . . [I]f you think of the [faculty] who had been meeting together regularly since 1966, you had a foundation of respect and understanding that places that [initiated] these kinds of discussions later just didn't have. (74)

In this specific sense the development of DePaul College was, as Richardson puts it, "transitional and served its purpose well." (75)

Riding the Orbit of Sputnik: Development of the Ph.D. Degree

While the intense and protracted efforts to transform undergraduate general education dominated the institution during the middle years of the 1960s, the earlier discussions about launching the Ph.D. degree at DePaul continued. The post-Sputnik surge in government funding for scientific research was more than enticing: the fox was on the loose and the hounds could not help but pursue. Returning from a trip to the National Science Foundation in 1959, Reverend John R. Cortelyou, C.M., chairman of the biology department, wrote to President O'Malley, "*There is no doubt that academic institutions with reputations for good and continuous research efforts are in the driver's seat with respect to grants . . . . DePaul is hampered with its lack of a*

Ph.D. program in the Sciences and Mathematics." (76) Aspiration turned to exploration in 1962–63 when the Graduate School Council appointed a committee to evaluate the potential of several departments to offer the Ph.D.

The natural sciences, spurred on by John Cortelyou, had jump-started the process. Cortelyou led the committee, and by February 1963 he presented a preliminary report to his brother William Cortelyou, C.M., dean of the Graduate School. Mincing no words, he argued, *"It is perfectly clear that in our existing circumstances, the three [natural science] departments under discussion are, at the present time, in no position to offer the Ph.D. program. This means that certain improvements must be made."* (77) The departments being considered had analyzed the research production and potential of their faculty members closely, and had made assessments of personnel, equipment and library resources that would be needed in order for a successful Ph.D. program to be launched. With a dispassionate objectivity concerning a topic about which he felt most passionately, Cortelyou had measured the difference between the university's reach and its grasp. Clearheadedness about "existing circumstances" did not dampen the aspirations of either Cortelyou or his committee. According to Dolores McWhinnie, a professor of biological sciences, the "idealism" of John Cortelyou and of Professor Mary Ann McWhinnie, his eventual successor as chair of biological sciences, propelled the department toward the Ph.D.— that and the hope for "manna from heaven" that would enable the university to close the equipment gap created by an explosion in the technologies for biological research. (78)

In November 1963, the board of trustees sanctioned the active exploration of the Ph.D. and by spring 1966 the contestants had been reduced to three: biological sciences, psychology and philosophy. These three worked closely with consultants chosen in dialogue with the North Central Association. In November 1966 the board of trustees approved the three proposals, which were then submitted to the North Central Association in January 1967. (79) In August, the NCA indicated to John Cortelyou, then president of the university, that it would extend accreditation to include the Ph.D. in biology, psychology and philosophy. (80)

The NCA review was appropriately cautious about prospects for the Ph.D. in biological sciences. It noted the lack of sufficient funds to support research at the appropriate level and the combined strength and narrowness of the department's focus on physiological endocrinology. Yet it concluded that while the proposed program "is ambitious and may be excessive, . . . the faculty appears to have the maturity to deal with problems as they arise." (81) In fact, the program really never had a chance. The hoped-for manna from heaven evaporated even before the program began as the nation's priorities for funding shifted from science and moon landings to wars on poverty at home and wars against poor people abroad. The hoped for critical mass of students never materialized. The faculty themselves became convinced that the program consumed immense energies without being of real service to its students. (82) After a decade of effort the Ph.D. program was discontinued.

The proposal by the Department of Psychology met a happier fate. As graduate dean,

Rigoberta Menchu Tum, Nobel Peace Prize Laureate receives the honorary doctorate degree, June 1996.

William Cortelyou had recruited the chair of the department, Edwin Zolik, in 1963 with the express intention of exploring the creation of a Ph.D. program. (83) The department carefully prepared for this step by raising admission standards in its M.A. program, building a training program into the work of the Mental Health Center, and reducing the teaching loads of faculty engaged in research, to cite a few of the coordinated endeavors. The program was also responsive to market demands. The proposal cited a report by the American Psychological Association that claimed there were four job openings for every Ph.D. graduate. (84) The NCA agreed: *"The proposed program initially calls for work in clinical psychology, September, 1968, and counseling psychology and general experimental psychology in September, 1969. Clearly, the need for such a program exists in the greater Chicago area as well as in the nation at large. The continuing national demand for Ph.D.s in these areas has been well established."* (85) Here the university's gamble paid off in a program that continues to flourish.

Philosophy, as we have seen, was the symbol and champion of curricular change at DePaul through most of the 1960s. It was only appropriate that it be selected as the humanities entry in the Ph.D. competition. As the NCA noted, Kreyche had recruited a faculty that represented "the best single concentration of existential and phenomenological scholars in America." (86) The philosophy program consciously set out to be different. It made its mark by bucking the main current of Anglo-American analytical traditions, and by "providing graduate training in a . . . field that has only token recognition at other universities." (87) Over the years the program has sustained itself not through the demands of a vigorous market but by a periodic, full-scale renewal of its original mission to be a distinctive voice on the American philosophical scene. Only by means of such renewals could it stay engaged with real cultural concerns, as Kreyche had hoped, and keep from becoming increasingly esoteric. (88)

From today's perspective it is hard to assess the effect on the institution as a whole of this immense, concerted and partially successful effort to create Ph.D. programs. In terms of curricular change, the impact of the new programs was confined to the departments concerned. Claims that the programs would support work in other areas were not upheld by the results. (89) Still, the university was designated "a doctoral granting institution" in the higher education classification schemes then becoming important. We can imagine what that meant to individuals like Richardson, who were determined to move out of the academic backwater. To be a Ph.D. granting institution must have meant becoming a *real* university. Finally the university would be accorded, in Richardson's words, "the status that many of us thought it deserved." (90) Richardson, however, is the first to agree that it was DePaul's *restraint*, its refusal to encourage proliferation of Ph.D. programs—due, no doubt, to fiscal common sense—that freed the university to make its mark through other, less traditional forms of curricular innovation. (91) Having weathered this rite of passage, DePaul would not establish another Ph.D. program for over two decades.

In Pursuit of the Non-Traditional:
Meeting the Needs of Adult Learners Through the School for New Learning

Earlier I quoted Clark Kerr's affirmation that although the "third great transformation" of higher education (1960–1980) did not, in general, have a profound effect on curricula, it was not for want of trying: "[E]verything was tried; nearly everything failed." But Kerr pays scant attention to one group that was part of the demographic revolution he charts: adult learners. Creating DePaul College and establishing a few Ph.D. programs were traditional curricular transformations, firmly anchoring both ends of a well-established educational trajectory. Moving out of academic backwaters, DePaul could have held its course to such well-traveled lanes. But it did not. Soon after completing the push to establish several Ph.D. programs, the university focused on a new issue—the education of adult learners. In this rapidly emerging field it was not a belated follower playing catch-up, but a pioneer.

As early as January 1971, Richardson proposed creating a new unit to be called "The Experimental School of DePaul University." Drawing on recent reports of the Carnegie Commission on Higher Education that called for new ways to meet the needs of those who had "stopped out" of college or who were not traditional-aged students, Richardson wanted to establish a unit that would consciously experiment "with different approaches to learning and different methods for marking achievement in learning."

> *E*stablished course structures and programs leading to degrees [he contin-ued,] have proved their value; new approaches to learning, however, are constantly being developed and there should be the opportunity within the uni-versity to apply these developments or devise ones distinctive of DePaul with-out the restrictions that tradition and outside agencies have imposed on the other units of the university. Well "developed" colleges and universities have relatively fixed patterns for learning and degrees, whereas "developing" insti-tutions are more open and flexible. DePaul would do well to have both the "developed" and "developing" aspects. (92)

This visionary outlook coincided with an evaluation by a group of university administra-tors consisting of DePaul's president and executive vice president and Irma Haftler, an admin-istrator with extensive experience in adult education. They expressed growing dissatisfaction with the way University College—a separate arts and science evening college with its own dean and faculty—was meeting the needs of adult learners. The *Curricular Design*, with its focus on adapting curricula to students' diverse developmental needs, provided the frame-work for change. Cortelyou, Richardson and Haftler were convinced that DePaul could ad-vance to the forefront in higher education by being boldly experimental, by taking account of the rich and complex experiences that adults brought to the learning process. (93) The cur-ricular experiments of the 1960s paved the way for this new endeavor but so did the prevail-ing ethos at DePaul of attentiveness to the individual student, which we call Vincentian per-sonalism. David Justice, former dean of the School for New Learning (SNL) and now vice president for lifelong learning and suburban campuses, argues that this Vincentian personal-ism made DePaul "a naturally comfortable place for an adult program oriented toward indi-vidualized learning to reside." (94)

Opinions were divided among key university leaders about just what action to take. Conflict did not result in paralysis but, rather, in willingness to turn the process of invention over to someone entirely new to DePaul. The university recruited Howard Sulkin from the University of Chicago and soon thereafter Marilyn Stocker to be his assistant. They were given *carte blanche* to develop a new program. To this day, Sulkin shakes his head bemusedly over the extent of the freedom he had. But without that freedom to break with tradition, to discard what others saw as indispensable to higher education, and without the year he had to work on the design, he is convinced that the School for New Learning would never have materialized. (95)

Sulkin set to work in September, 1972. High level academic studies on adult learning were in their infancy. But several principles—"heresies," Sulkin calls them—were emerging and guided the planning process:

> • In developing [a] new curriculum, emphasis had to be placed on the student first and the institution second.
>
> • Learning, particularly for adults, can be legitimately derived from an almost unending variety of sources, and can take place in many settings. If that learning can be responsibly assessed, then it is legitimate to 'give credit' for that learning . . . .
>
> • Everything has to be done to reduce barriers to learning, i.e., time, place, methodology.
>
> • Higher education needed to be reoriented away from credits to a renewed emphasis on competency . . . . (96)

The last of these principles became the integrating factor in the curriculum. "What SNL worked very hard to do," Sulkin argues, *"was to define their bachelor's degree in a new way: . . . it was not to be defined as a compilation of courses, but instead [as] a set of learning outcomes, i.e., competencies. Once this was done and the five-part framework [of required competencies] developed, then **everything** done was based upon this framework."* (97) Although DePaul was not the first institution to develop a competence-based program, it was the first, Sulkin insists, not to hedge its bets. Other institutions assessed adult learners' previous experiences for indications of competency but correlated those experiences within an existing course framework. "We said that was an unacceptable conceptual breakdown for our design." (98)

Sulkin and Stocker developed that design with the aid of focus groups that included faculty, business and community leaders and potential students. (99) Claiming to end the era of the adult learner as the "second class citizen of higher education," the design offered a competence-based program of individualized study, geared to lifelong learning that broke with the "traditional rigidities of campus life such as time, space and systems of academic accounting." (100) Curricula would be organized around five "domains of knowledge," not departmental or disciplinary divisions. (101) In addition to the competence framework most of the structural components of today's SNL curriculum were developed in this original design: (1) an "entrance experience," later named the Discovery Workshop, where "the adult student can confront himself, 'gather himself together,' to assess what skills he has, what his personal goals are, and what educational alternatives are available to him;" (2) an advisory committee including a faculty member and a professional advisor to supervise the student's preparation for the world of work; (3) the use of learning contracts to negotiate the means by which competencies would be demonstrated; (4) a fieldwork experience and a "major piece of work" to consolidate a student's ability to be a self-directed learner; and (5) an "exit experience," later called the Summit Seminar, whose purpose was "to provide closure on this phase of the educational process, to help the student digest, reassess and re-set his sights." (102) Sulkin believes that SNL's subsequent success was due to the strength and soundness of its original curricular design. (103)

In a continuing effort to enhance accessibility, SNL became the first unit in the university to develop a suburban site, which it opened in only its second year of the operation. (104) The competence framework evolved gradually; later revisions were designed to provide both "base-line standards" and greater flexibility for students to meet these standards. Gaps in the area of scientific inquiry were plugged, and more attention was given to the dialectic between theoretical proficiency and the practical ability to apply knowledge. (105) In 1985 SNL proposed a new competency-based Master of Arts degree. A grant from the Fund for the Improvement of Post-Secondary Education allowed SNL to build on David Schon's concept of a "reflective practitioner," defined as a professional who understands the theoretical underpinnings of work, the skills necessary for its conduct, its organizational framework and cultural context, and its ethical challenges. *It is [the] process of reflection-in-action which Schon sees as central to competent and effective practice in the turbulent changing environments of professionals.* The prospectus declared, *"The SNL Master's Program seeks to generate in its practitioner-students the skills of learning by doing, and of thinking about something while doing it."* (106)

David Justice, the third dean of the school, originally thought that a majority of SNL students would be enrolled in the M.A. program. Though the program remained fairly small, it led to a more momentous change: a full-time, tenure-track faculty within the school. Vice president for academic affairs Patricia Ewers believed that a faculty in residence was necessary to ground the graduate program. Justice agreed to move the school in this new direction. The first full-time faculty members were appointed in 1987. (107) The importance of this change can be gauged by the range of conflicting opinions swirling about it. Sulkin saw it as a fall from grace, forsaking an entrepreneurial commitment for the inveterate conservatism of a tenured faculty. Ewers saw it as essential to the establishment of quality control at both the undergraduate and graduate levels. In contrast to both of these senior administrators, Richardson believed that a full-time faculty would give SNL the credibility it needed to function as a leaven within the larger university. (108)

The unequivocal result was a greater professionalization of education within the school. As John Rury, one of the first tenured faculty members in SNL, puts it, professionalization is not to be equated with narrow specialization. In SNL's case it meant just the opposite: moving from the marginality and isolation of a school that saw itself as both experimental and embattled into engagement with the larger academic community. *"Professionalization, in my view, is a dialogue that occurs around questions within a group of people who are doing the same thing,"* Rury argued, *"the very structure of SNL insures a distinctive institutional culture . . . . And professionalization enhances it . . . by things like bringing questions of knowledge . . . into the forefront and entering into those debates . . . . [R]eally looking at the groundwork [in learning theory] and saying, 'Well, did we really do what we say?'"* (109)

This very attentiveness to learning theory, a hallmark of SNL, led to a more complicated process of professionalization. The dialogue and the battles were not just over theories for framing subject matter. In fact, a dialectic ensued between those who brought their scholarship in learning theory and adult development to bear on curricular change and those who upheld particular disciplinary traditions of inquiry. (110) *"[B]oth positions are within the faculty itself . . ."* David Justice comments. *"[T]here's no way to draw a line down the middle of the faculty and say these [are] on one side and these [are] on the other, because on any given issue they will line up somewhat differently . . . . [I]t's an interesting tension."* (111) But Justice is also convinced that this tension reflected the perennial struggle within higher education to stay focused on the learner on the one hand and on what is to be learned on the other, and to negotiate the difference. (112)

The DePaul Center (formerly the Goldblatt Building) was dedicated September 14, 1993.

Despite tensions among the faculty, perhaps because of them, the school successfully passed from the era of charismatic founders through institutional consolidation to a new maturity, and along with this transition came a whole new set of challenges. When he resigned the deanship to take on some of these challenges as vice president for lifelong learning and suburban campuses, Justice told his faculty:

> *I think . . . it was Gandhi who identified . . . the four stages of development of a new organization. In the first stage, you are ignored by everyone. In the second stage, you are reviled by everyone. In the third stage, you are actively attacked by everyone. But then comes the fourth and most dangerous stage . . . , and that is you are emulated by others and complimented. And that is the most dangerous stage because you begin to believe it . . . . I think . . . that the School really does need to take some new risks . . . and challenge itself on some of the assumptions that have crept into our operation that have gone unexamined . . . . One of the hardest things for us as a university is to give up the view that we are anointed to tell people how they should learn and what they should learn . . . and without moving to a totally market-based approach, we need to be able to understand and be responsive to a rapidly changing external environment . . . and I think that has been one of the virtues of DePaul as a whole, but particularly the School for New Learning."* (113)

At age twenty-five SNL had become a seasoned center for continuing experimentation.

A Place for the Fine Arts: Creating a Multidimensional Presence in the Urban Milieu

Each of the innovations of the late 1960s and early 1970s that we have been studying—DePaul College, new Ph.D. programs, the School for New Learning—must be understood against the background of the dominance of professional training especially in law and business. As John Rury and Chuck Suchar have shown, students came to DePaul in search of nuts-and-bolts preparation for the practical world. And the university delivered it.

After launching SNL, Howard Sulkin became vice president for institutional research and planning. Like Richardson, Sulkin was not the type to be confined either philosophically or practically. As Thomas Croak has noted, in 1977 DePaul had broken out of its confined area in the Lincoln Park campus and purchased the adjacent property that had been the McCormick Theological Seminary campus. Now, Sulkin believed, the university had to break out of the

The John T. Richardson Library and quadrangle area, completed in 1992.

confines of the public's perception of it as the nuts-and-bolts university under the El. Frederick Miller, a new dean who had been recruited for the School of Music in 1976, was beginning to turn that college inside out, and the art department was strengthening its role in liberal arts and sciences. "But it wasn't enough," reflects Sulkin—not enough to fashion a new image and reality for DePaul as a "leader of the urban milieu." (114)

In 1978 a rare opportunity presented itself. The Goodman School of Drama, associated with the Art Institute of Chicago for over fifty years, was about to lose its affiliation with that venerable institution. Sulkin and Richardson led the fight to bring the Goodman School to DePaul's recently acquired McCormick campus. They were confident that this prestigious alliance would not only give the university a weightier presence in Chicago's fine and performing arts community, but would also add another dimension to DePaul's complex engagement with its urban milieu. Controversy raged over the wisdom of targeting scarce resources to a unit dedicated to an expensive, conservatory model of education, and even more over this new vision of a multidimensional, multilateral presence in the metropolitan context. (115)

The university's "rescue" came just in the nick of time, in January 1978, just months before the Goodman School was to hold its final convocation. But as dean of the theater school John Watts puts it, in September, when the "small band of nine or ten itinerant gypsies jumped out with their props and their costumes and their file cabinets and their very little bit of resources and hung up their sign and said, 'We're back. We're open for business again,'" they had precious little idea how they would adjust to their new home, and the university was equally at sea about what to do with its new acquisition. (116) The Theater School moved in next door to the music school which was also undergoing a tumultuous transition. Change, it seems, was the order of the day on the old McCormick campus.

"When I accepted the invitation to become dean in 1976," recalls Frederick Miller, who served in that position for 20 years, "I came to DePaul with a clear charge to initiate changes that might lead to overall quality improvements in the school." (117) What Miller found was a school with very few full-time faculty, no selective admission process and a curriculum that was woefully out of date—consisting of a very "narrow repertoire" of Western music and lacking a core program in musicianship. A program designed to fit the needs of the band and choir directors in Chicago's Catholic schools and churches, it provided a set of prescribed exercises for students: workbook or manual-based education. (118) Behind Miller's charge, in effect, to start over, was Richardson's same iron-willed determination that had been evident all along: no remaining in any backwater, no matter how comfortable. What Miller saw was the raw potential of a school of music in the heart of a city, not only a city boasting the Chicago Symphony Orchestra and the Lyric Opera but a city teeming with accomplished musicians. He also recognized the McCormick Seminary campus's potential to provide decent facilities for study and performance. (119)

Within months of Miller's arrival a team from the North Central Association arrived at DePaul for one of its periodic accrediting visits. The NCA report noted the "state of intense activity in the music school and praised the school for the "high level of enthusiasm" with which it was engaging in "extensive self-analysis and long-range planning." (120) Within a year the music school's dean and the faculty had moved to its new home on the Lincoln Park campus, established new admission standards (including an audition), and had instituted a new curriculum built around a "musicianship core." The core would be shared "by all students, whether they aspired to be performers, teachers, [or] composers." Integrating theoretical, historical and analytical studies, the core stressed "the building blocks common in all music: melody, rhythm, texture, architecture;" not "contrived examples and experiences created for texts and workbooks" but the works themselves would teach the students: from Gregorian chants to Broadway tunes, from Bach fugues to Dixieland jazz. "The thought," according to Miller, "was that with a thorough understanding of these fundamental elements, we should be able to approach the music of any genre, any style, period or any culture." (121)

Miller observes that this type of curricular foundation, designed for a new kind of professionally oriented student has, with minor modifications, maintained its integrity for two decades. During that period the School of Music was gaining a national recognition for its performance-oriented programs, and it strengthened its connections with the Chicago Symphony

Orchestra and other musical groups through its part-time faculty. (122) A look at the most recent planning document for the school, however, indicates that new forms of interaction with the musical scene—forms that acknowledge the complexities of the musical industry—are emerging. While the plan calls for reviewing the content of the musicianship core and makes specific recommendations for traditional performance areas, it also moves aggressively into new curricular areas like recording technology and arts management. The document deplores the fact that the study of technological applications in music has been largely restricted to specialized curricula. *"As a consequence,"* it states, *"it is possible that large numbers of undergraduates majoring in performance or music education may be ill-prepared to function effectively in the technological world in which they will live and work. The issue must be addressed in the musicianship core."* (123)

The current emphases are intriguing for two reasons. They indicate that the commitment to a core curriculum as a way to enhance the quality of education persists. Yet the document also spells out the intention to use core-based education as a platform from which to launch a more complex preparation for the world of work. The striking qualitative improvements in the School of Music that began in the late 1970s only intensified the school's and DePaul's concern with education as practical engagement.

When John Watts arrived in August 1979 as the new dean of what eventually would be called The Theater School, he found a faculty trying to adapt a three-year conservatory education to the four-year undergraduate model. During his first year in office, Watts, like Miller in the School of Music, convened his faculty for an intensive review of the curriculum. *"[W]e started,"* Watts says, *"with what it's now fashionable to call outcomes. When someone graduates from here, what should they be able to do and . . . going backwards, what should be the makeup of the last year of their work with us . . . . So we redesigned the whole thing backwards."* (124) The Theater School, like the School of Music, struggled to deal with a rigid set of general education requirements not tailored to its B.F.A. degree or conservatory model. Only when a new liberal studies program was developed in 1981 was the problem alleviated. It was another hard struggle to convince the university Promotion and Tenure Board that costume or set designers' portfolios of photographs were the record of their work and to overcome the incomprehension of colleagues in other colleges who asked "why haven't they *written* anything?" (125)

Unlike the School of Music, the Theater School did not have to struggle to create a national reputation; it had to resurrect it. So far as the world of theater was concerned the Goodman School, in Watts' words, "was dead, was gone. It was closed. It was over." It took a decade to reestablish the reputation of the school. Resurrection also meant reconnecting the students with the profession and revitalizing an alumni network. Each year for the past eighteen years Watts has presented the graduating class in a showcase for casting directors and agents, first in Chicago and then, in more recent years, in New York or Los Angeles as well. "When we did it in Los Angeles [in June 1996], we had two hundred and fifty-six casting directors and agents . . . that came to see the work because of the reputation of the school." (126) Professional preparation meant that students' performance skills had to be *seen*, not simply noted in a résumé. After an event like the Los Angeles showcase, Watts could finally say "We're back."

The integration of the school into the university has taken just as long as the task of reconnecting with the profession—longer, actually, because in a real sense this is unfinished business. The attempt of the university to force the school into structures designed for very different academic programs has largely ended. But the opportunity to use the Theater School faculty with their distinctive pedagogies to invigorate liberal education has yet to be realized. Watts acknowledges that in the early years at DePaul, the Theater School had to keep its attention squarely focused on developing its conservatory training program for its own students. Early efforts to collaborate with departments in the fine arts and humanities soon withered.

University chemistry laboratory, 1938

Yet Watts is the first to insist that experience in the theater, "this most ancient of human forms, the business of being somebody else and the business of not telling but *doing* stories," is a truly liberating art. (127)

The most successful attempt to integrate the pedagogical skills of the Theater School with the academic goals of other programs in the university came in 1995–96 when James Ostholthoff, then chair of performance and one of the original "gypsies" who came from the Goodman School, took a David Mamet play, *Oleanna*, into classrooms in the colleges of liberal arts and sciences, commerce and law. Because *Oleanna* is a highly controversial play, focusing on the issue of sexual harassment, Ostholthoff drew a lot of criticism from people who didn't agree with Mamet's "take" on the subject. Arguing that precisely because the performance highlighted a conflict of values, Ostholthoff insisted that it was more than appropriate for a university context; the *Oleanna* project exemplified DePaul's mission. What surprised even him, however, was that, performed in the intimate setting of a classroom with the opportunity for discussion afterwards, the play revealed something new not only to its student audience but to Ostholthoff himself. "*Which, of course, goes to the essence of what theater is,*" he noted. "*[T]his is not literature that you read; it's meant to be performed . . . . [O]ne of the exciting things about doing this work is you get surprised all the time. You think you've got it figured out and something new happens.*" (128) Expanding on the insights that came out of the *Oleanna* project, Ostholthoff argues that what theater has to offer to a liberal education for DePaul students is visceral learning and a prod toward "visceral maturity."

> *We talk all the time about the life of the intellect in a university. But there is also the life of intuition and the life of the imagination. I think that's what we can teach you . . . . [I]t's helpful to think of how the body educates us as well as the mind because if you think only of the intellect . . . then you get into the mind/body split and acting is all about combining these things with a particular emphasis on the body part of it in terms of training and getting in contact with instinct.* (129)

The very effort—relentlessly demanded of Theater School students—to tap into their own humanity viscerally releases a revelatory power that complements and grounds what the intellect reveals through research and scholarship. (130)

The tinge of frustration in Ostholthoff's plea echoes Miller and Watts when they speak of how the university keeps their schools at arm's length. Conservatory model notwithstanding, Ostholthoff insists that the theater school is categorically different from elite, largely graduate programs in theater that focus on a narrow slice of the talent pie. DePaul is much more will-ing to give a chance to students whose talent may be as raw as it is strong. "It strikes me that that's what DePaul is about and it would strike others . . . that that's what the city of Chicago is about." (131) If we want to think of ourselves as a distinctive Catholic university, Miller suggests that we ask what other Catholic institution has made such a place for the arts. (132) The message from these schools is clear: We may not seem to act the part to you. In our iso-lation we may not think about it as often as we should. But we too express the ethos of this university.

Integrating Professional and Liberal Education: Reforming General Education Once Again

The complaint from the performing arts schools that the university had placed them in a cur-ricular straitjacket focused a spotlight on DePaul College. Faculty in the College of Commerce were particularly concerned about students' inadequate skills development. The creative ener-gies that had established the university-wide general education program in the late 1960s had dwindled by the late 1970s, and faculty new to the College of Liberal Arts and Sciences (LA and S) were genuinely befuddled about what they were supposed to accomplish through DePaul College's often ill-defined courses. The self-study report prepared for the NCA visit in early 1977 echoed these and other concerns. At the same time that it backed up the need for a university-wide program, it bemoaned the one-size-fits-all requirement of the structure. It called for a system of requirements tailored "to serve a heterogeneous group of . . . students with wide variations in academic skills and backgrounds and with significant differences in career choices." The program, the document concluded, lacked "a cohesive and permeating means of transmitting cultural heritage." (133) The critique pointed out that DePaul College was operating on the mistaken assumption that it served a relatively homogeneous student body, "the capable majority," whose elementary and secondary educational background equipped it with adequate skills and knowledge. In reality, it was dealing with a student body at all levels of academic preparedness. Furthermore, each of DePaul's colleges had its own distinctive learn-ing agenda. Plurality had taken on new meaning.

The NCA team confirmed that "dissatisfaction with [DePaul College] is quite high" and that *some* of the criticisms had merit. But it cautioned the university against hasty decisions or quick-fix solutions. Only a careful reexamination of the entire general education program in the context of a continuing commitment to a university-wide program would work. (134) DePaul took the admonition to heart and assembled a new group, the Undergraduate Curric-ulum Revision Committee, shortly after receiving the NCA report. During the next year, the committee developed a "working paper," largely through the efforts of Patricia Ewers, dean of liberal arts and sciences at the time, and L. Edward Allemand, then division head of philoso-phy and religion (and soon to be dean of DePaul College). It provided a framework for a sub-sequent faculty committee which created a new model for general education. The working paper called for attention to both remedial and college-level skills development; it suggested providing a historical foundation to meet the evident lack of cultural literacy and to be a source of curricular cohesion; and it argued for closer integration of general and specialized education. In its most controversial edict it recommended dissolving DePaul College and restoring responsibility for general education offerings to the departments. (135)

Between the time the "Ewers-Allemand working paper" was released and the faculty committee was formed to devise a new model for liberal studies, Harvard University issued a proposal for a new "core" curriculum, stimulating a national wave of curricular reform. DePaul's response to this document was emblematic of its consistent practice of taking into account trends in higher education while hewing to its own course. First, as chair of the committee that was to devise the new program, I remember that we began to look at national reform movements only *after* analyzing our own circumstances and the needs of our own students. The Harvard report, therefore, was interpreted primarily as *legitimizing* our own effort, which was already under way. Second, the report's emphasis on skills development and historical grounding did buttress the arguments of those who, like Ewers and Allemand, wanted to strengthen those aspects of the program. Finally, the report's recommendation to establish a core curriculum was regarded as irrelevant to our circumstances. As Ewers notes, DePaul, unlike many other institutions—including the most prestigious ones—had never given up on the notion of a core curriculum. While other colleges and universities were debating whether or not to follow Harvard's lead in *restoring* a core, DePaul was concentrating on *reforming* its core. (136)

A new liberal studies program was implemented in autumn 1981. Among the new program's principal breaks with the past was the recognition that while all undergraduate students needed to meet university-wide goals, the paths they took would necessarily vary. (137) It addressed the different levels of student preparedness through a skills assessment and skills development program. It also provided distinct models for each college with a requirement structure more closely integrated into the professional programs in each unit. Individual students' needs and the variation among academic units were taken into account, keeping intact such key liberal learning goals as developing the power to communicate, acquiring broad knowledge, integrating many kinds of knowledge, and developing both a reflective cast of mind and an awareness of value issues and conflicts. (138)

This acceptance of plural paths to arrive at common goals subsequently legitimized efforts to meet the special needs of particular groups of students. An example of these efforts was the establishment of an honors program with a distinctive set of liberal studies requirements in L A and S. The university's highly successful "Bridge Program," inaugurated in 1985, helped those students most at risk to make the transition into and through the freshman year of college. Under the charismatic leadership of Janie Isackson, students in this program were soon achieving higher GPAs on average than their non-bridge peers and graduating at similar rates. (139)

The new program also introduced a "Common Studies" requirement that linked a two-course world history sequence with a college-level writing and research class. The planners hoped that Common Studies would be the magnetic core integrating and providing cohesion to work in other divisions, but their hopes were not realized. (140) In fact, the two departments largely responsible for Common Studies, English and history, were not able to establish a long-term cooperative relationship. Common Studies achieved an unforeseen but important triumph, however. The presence of a world history sequence in the new curriculum encouraged several departments to develop a more multicultural, global perspective while avoiding the agonizing "culture wars" that later wrought havoc at such institutions as Stanford. (141) Though the new requirement initially met with resistance from the history department faculty who were trained largely in Western areas, the work of creating a common exam and later, a common text proved to be an incredibly successful retraining experience. In a remarkable display of decentralized leadership, the history faculty created their own version of a graduate seminar in which they took turns as teachers and as students. (142) Both the common exam and the common text soon succumbed to telling criticisms, however, and in a mid-1990s revision of liberal studies, the world history survey itself disappeared. But it had done its job: history faculty members acquired a global perspective that altered their approach to the past. *"So, for example, as someone who is trained in European history,"* argues James Krokar, *" I realize that much of the work that's done [in that area] . . . on the issue of technology is done by people who have no conception of the comparative technological levels of Europe with the rest of the world, and . . . it's just because they've never bothered to look . . . . [W]hile I don't think I'll wind up teaching any kind of world civ survey, I intend to use a world civ perspective in whatever I teach, [and] try to do something cross-cultural."* (143)

The religious studies faculty underwent a similar transformation as they developed a core course in the comparative study of world religions that was consciously designed to complement the Common Studies program. The self-designed retraining of the religious studies faculty occurred when they prepared a common reader for their comparative course. At that time, *no* member of the department specialized in non-Western religious traditions. I recall, as a member of its faculty, recognizing that if we intended to become a religious studies department with a comparative focus in reality as well as in name, we would have to teach ourselves. Grabbing hold of our own bootstraps, we succeeded in making that transition. (144)

The learning goal of integrating different kinds of knowledge has been the will-of-the-wisp of virtually all efforts to reform undergraduate education. Ewers and Allemand set the synthesis of liberal and professional studies as a primary objective for general education reform and the needs of DePaul's largely first-generation college student body made this goal an imperative. *"For DePaul's faculty to attempt to dissuade students from professional careers,"* Ewers argued, *"might be as irresponsible as trying to dissuade them from intellectual ones. Our solu-*

tion . . . was to find a way for the liberal and professional programs to work together to achieve both goals." (145)

A major effort to integrate the liberal studies goals of developing a reflective consciousness and a value consciousness with the goals of professional studies focused on professional ethics. Responding to the demands of its accrediting association, the College of Commerce wanted to set up a required course: "Business Ethics and Society." Much energy went into developing a model syllabus for the course, which was to be taught by faculty from religious studies, philosophy, and eventually, it was hoped, by College of Commerce faculty as well. A new dean of commerce, Brother Leo Ryan, made the course a priority and in the early 1980s the Institute for Business Ethics became the focus of faculty development and supplementary programming. (146) But the hoped-for collaboration between commerce and liberal arts and science faculty members to staff the undergraduate course failed to materialize. Although business ethics became an excellent course, it remained isolated from mainstream professional study. (147) In this regard it met a fate similar to other experiments that yielded such courses as "Science and Ethics," "Biomedical Ethics" and "Computers, Ethics and Society."

At their most utopian, the designers of the new "Liberal Studies" program, as the new general education program came to be called, had hoped that the university might become "a community of moral discourse."

The university is the one institution in our society which can provide a public arena for the interrogation and adjudication of a plurality of value systems and the world views that ground them. In its own faculty it contains the accumulated knowledge, the plurality of outlook, and the habit of reflection which are the conditions . . . for sophisticated discourse about values in an age when any . . . groundings of values in an objective order [have] disappeared. (148)

In the mid 1990s, management professor Laura Pincus, working with a colleague in philosophy, Daryl Koehn, resurrected the virtually defunct Institute for Business and Professional Ethics. Under their leadership the institute began what might be called a series of guerilla operations. Pincus and her associates popped up everywhere with case studies and resources for classes, faculty development seminars, videos and a web site. They looked for the "crossroads" where faculty's own interests might coincide with the possibility of infusing ethical reflection more broadly into the curriculum. Pincus worked with Dean Ronald Patten to promote Ethics Integration Grants among faculty who were interested in developing ethics modules in their courses. (149) While these efforts did not alter the marginality of the whole ethics enterprise and did not establish a single "community of moral discourse," they did create numerous small communal pockets where ethical reflection flourished.

Education for a New Workplace:
Responding to the Cult of the Professional in American Culture

As he prepares to give the keynote address to the State Association of Real Estate Boards, Sinclair Lewis's George Babbitt mulls over the difference between being a "realtor," that is, a professional, and a "real estate man," someone with "a mere trade, business or occupation . . . , a fellow that merely goes out for the jack." (150) Lewis surely meant to satirize George's pretensions but, in fact, he characterized accurately a dominant force for change in the American workplace, one that has supported and affirmed other changes for well over a century, namely, the professionalization of work through, as Babbitt puts it, "trained skill and knowledge" and the claim to be providing a "public service." (151) The cult of professionalism emerged as a practical implication of the eighteenth century Enlightenment and replaced experience-based knowledge and apprenticeship training with an educational process that was formal, theory-based and upheld by certified evaluators. (152) Babbitt, like most twentieth-century Americans, was part of what David Levine calls a "culture of aspiration." Institutions of "higher" learning in the twentieth century have all been profoundly shaped by the fusion of the very practical aspirations of ordinary Americans with the Enlightenment mystique. At DePaul there has always been an acute awareness of this "culture of aspiration."

> *In the United States [argues Margaret Oppenheimer, chair of economics,] there's an historical route into the middle classes through business . . . . [DePaul has] always had people coming whose parents were not middle class, . . . who sacrifice . . . work two jobs or even three . . . to get their students to come here. that business degree is supposed to be their ticket into the middle class. . . . So, I think there is a commitment at the undergraduate level to encourage students like that . . . to get them to see themselves as a successful person in a profession . . . . (153)*

For the first 90 years of its existence, that is, until the mid to late 1980s, DePaul University was dominated by its professional schools, particularly law and commerce. As Richard Meister has noted, even in liberal arts and sciences, the professional preparation programs, nursing and computer science, were the dominant majors in the 1970s and early 1980s. (154)

In this context the turn toward academic excellence which we have been examining throughout this chapter meant a determination to professionalize the training of professionals. Curricular changes in the law school, College of Commerce and School of Education in the 1970s and early 1980s arose largely from this aspiration.

Major external forces affected this internal objective. Changes in various industries influenced the way DePaul trained professionals. But the cultivation of professional*ism* originated in the professions themselves. Accrediting agencies became powerful factors in determining curricular change, especially in the 1980s. As dean of faculties at DePaul during that decade, Patricia Ewers notes that the major thrust of those agencies was to encourage a greater degree of homogeneity in professional education. Though standards of educational quality certainly made a quantum leap during the period, the accrediting agencies deferred to the particular definitions of quality that major research institutions had set. Hence, institutions were rated on how much of their faculty publication was related to the development of new theoretical models rather than applied research. Only in the 1990s, Ewers argues, was there a shift toward more flexible standards that were attuned to a variety of institutional missions. (155) Most faculty in the professional schools, however, were of the opinion that pressures to standardize criteria had a positive outcome by ensuring that students received a high quality education. They also have argued that major components of the "standard model" in areas that linked, for example, legal education and practical training in the profession came from institutions like DePaul. (156) External forces might dictate certain aspects of a curriculum—a focus on ethics or international education, for example—but it was left to local institutions to implement distinctive curricula within a nationally established framework. (157)

At the suggestion of a new dean, Ronald Patten, the College of Commerce began a review of its entire undergraduate curriculum in 1989. After extensive discussions, the new curriculum was finally adopted in 1993. Associate Dean Robert Peters sees the new curriculum as the culmination of a twenty-year shift of focus among faculty from a formulaic, cookbook approach to a theory-laden education. This shift reflected national trends and it brought economic theory into the limelight. "[W]e're all . . . pivoting from economics as far as I can tell," Peters argues. In a parallel development fields like marketing that were less closely related to finance began taking their lead from social scientific research in psychology and sociology. (158)

The new program linked liberal studies and commerce through such "bridge" courses as "Writing for Business" and a quantitative methods course designed to demonstrate the use of mathematical skills in decision-making processes. (159) The new program also required two "Interdisciplinary Senior Seminars" that served as a capstone experience. These seminars were designed to "integrate the societal, political, economic, legal, ethical and other aspects of a world society with the functional areas of business." They established the cultural context within which business decision making occurs, and at the same time, they prepared students to function within a multicultural workplace. (160)

The major departure in the new curriculum was the introduction of an international perspective. Dean Patten initiated this change. Shortly after he arrived at DePaul, following a stint with a multinational corporation, Patten began interviewing Chicago's business leaders about the direction they thought education for business professionals should take. *"I was struck,"* he comments, *"by the number of times internationalization was mentioned. [Typically, CEOs said,] 'our employees must adopt a mind-set which shows they understand there is a world beyond the United States. Our employees must understand that they will be in contact with persons from other countries in the course of their career'."* (161) In the new curriculum, students can choose a foreign study program, instruction in a foreign language, or they can assemble a package of courses in a given cultural area to satisfy the requirement for developing an international perspective. (162)

Building on its reform of the undergraduate curriculum, the College of Commerce established an M.B.A. in "International Marketing and Finance" well ahead of its prestigious competitors. In this program students from the United States do internships in a foreign country while non-U.S. citizens do one in this country. Both undertake a final project working with a Chicago-based multinational corporation. To prepare faculty for this new curricular emphasis in the college, DePaul developed a number of programs with the assistance of the U.S. Information Agency for DePaul faculty to teach abroad, particularly in Eastern Europe.

> *Not only was there an exhilaration effect . . . from being able to play a part . . . in the transformation of these countries from a controlled to a market driven economy but each faculty member had an opportunity to develop personally . . . . This aspect is probably the cornerstone of all of our international work, in that it . . . guaranteed our having at least one-third of our faculty with very current international experience.* (163)

In fact, Patten may have underestimated the number of faculty involved. Margaret Oppenheimer suggests that nothing short of a profound sea change in faculty attitudes and approaches to teaching and research resulted from these experiences. If working on a textbook in history or a reader in religious studies resulted in a new global awareness in those departments, the task of figuring out how to offer condensed versions of Western economic theory and practice to people from a fundamentally different culture had the same effect in commerce. (164)

The law school underwent a process of professionalization similar to the one at commerce and not unlike the pattern at work in the School of Music which began in the mid-

1970s. In the legal profession, however, the pressure for uniformity began around the turn of the century with increased insistence by the American Bar Association (ABA) on conformity to national standards. Under the guise of a push toward professionalization, the ABA was, in fact, defending "the Christian Bar" against schools that were teaching Jewish minorities, of which DePaul was one. In consequence, it was involved in accreditation battles with the ABA through the 1930s. (165)

The shift to theory-based learning coincided with the development of a national market for lawyers and law professors particularly in the early 1970s. The law school had been affected much more profoundly by the social movements of the 1960s than other schools in the university. Politically active law students pushed for greater curricular variety and elective freedom. The school's Legal Clinic was started in 1972 in response to student demands for a more engaged form of instruction. DePaul was ahead of many other institutions in starting an extern program in 1975. The program placed students with "not-for-profit organizations, governmental agencies, and members of the judiciary." In a given semester more than 70 students participate in the program, with well over 1,000 placements since it began, making it one of the largest in the country. This program has provided both public service to the Chicago community and practical training for many more students than the traditional mechanism of a legal clinic could have involved. (166)

A new twist in combining professional preparation with practical engagement was taken in 1990 with the founding of the International Human Rights Law Institute. Doug Cassel, executive director of the institute, asserts, *"By establishing an institute dedicated not only to teaching but also to research, public advocacy, training, technical assistance and litigation support, we were able to offer students not only classroom courses but practical work both in Chicago and overseas."* (167) The president of the Institute, M. Cherif Bassiouni, was appointed by the United Nations Secretary General to investigate war crimes in the former Yugoslavia while Cassel himself was a member of the Truth Commission appointed by the United Nations as part of the peace process in El Salvador. "The case that meant the most to me was solving the murder of Archbishop Romero," Cassel commented. Under the Jeanne and Joseph Sullivan Program for Human Rights in the Americas, DePaul students have served as legal interns in Guatemala, El Salvador, at the Inter-American Court in Costa Rica and with the Canadian Human Rights Commission. While DePaul students interned abroad, lawyers and judges from Spain, Poland and several Central American countries were visiting fellows at the institute. (168) The institute became one of a number of programs, which, in the 1990s invented new approaches to professional education and also expanded the concept of a "learning community" to embrace others besides the degree-seeking student.

The programs developed by the School of Computer Science, Telecommunications and Information Systems (CTI) represent other emerging approaches to professional education.

The university's computer science faculty became a department in 1981 and a separate college in 1995. In quick order it has evolved into one of the largest programs in the university; its Ph.D. program was approved in June 1990 and admitted its first students in 1991.

The computer science program began at a time of declining enrollments at DePaul, and the department played a critical role in reversing the slide. In fact, the key to CTI's success is that it has ridden the crest of the newest wave of technological change in American society, unimpeded for the most part by the constraints that other programs attached to engineering schools have experienced. In 1982 the Department of Computer Science established its Executive Program, the first of a series of certificate programs. Beside producing capital to expand non-degree education, these certificate programs, acutely sensitive to market demands, have put the multiple curricula of the department and later the school on a new footing.

According to David Miller, professor in CTI, the school has learned to keep a sense of balance while institutionalizing a permanent process of review and revision for all programs, something few if any other fields in higher education have managed to do. CTI recognizes that the half-life of any of its programs, degree or non-degree, in an environment of constantly accelerating change is exceedingly brief. Faculty members teaching at present must work with the knowledge that they must prepare to teach new and, in some cases, wholly unforeseen subjects five years down the road. (169) Beyond the quality of its individual programs, it is this ability to be ready for change that is CTI's distinctive contribution to the evolving character of a DePaul education. In the summer of 1997 one of the questions posed at academic planning meetings was how do we adapt CTI's model to all of our professional programs?

The School of Education, more than any other professional school, has had to weather volatile shifts in public attitudes toward teachers as professionals. Precisely during the period we are studying, America put its teachers at the center of a hurricane of problems: racism, poverty, and fractured families. Then it subjected them to "savage inequality" in the distribution of the resources they needed to do their jobs, and finally it decided that teachers must do more than cope—they must prepare children "for life in the twenty-first century," whatever that might possibly mean. The School of Education's fortunes have reflected this volatility. Richardson established education as a separate school in 1962 as part of the overall effort we have been examining to professionalize the training of professionals. (170) In 1988 it was reduced to a department in liberal arts and sciences during a period of extensive public criticism of teacher education, only to be restored as a free standing school in 1990 when enrollments surged once more and the determination "to do something about our schools" was rekindled.

As part and parcel of this volatile environment, curricular reforms have swept through schools of education like so many weather fronts. At DePaul, *three* broad shifts in approach have not passed through but have taken hold: (1) a change in the role of a school of education to focus on meeting the needs of inner city children; (2) development of community-school partnerships to further the education of future teachers; and (3) creation of a new "clinical model" for teacher preparation that connected with those partnerships.

In the early 1980s Patricia Ewers puzzled over DePaul's low enrollment of Latinos, a seemingly natural constituency for a Catholic, urban university. A needs assessment showed that Latino students were applying to DePaul but low SAT/ACT scores kept them from being admitted. DePaul proposed that the Joyce Foundation fund a college preparatory program for Latino students that focused on science and mathematics and business-related subjects. In 1981 the Students, Teachers, Educators and Parents (STEP) program began working with Juarez High School. It deliberately chose students who were middle achievers in a neighborhood high school to participate in the program; not the top achievers siphoned off to one of Chicago's "magnet" high schools. It is still going strong, and involved 267 students in 1996. A number of studies have shown that STEP students' ACT scores are competitive with Illinois averages. The McPrep summer program, funded by the McDonald Corporation, was designed for children in middle schools that are feeder institutions for the STEP high schools. This program tests the effectiveness of early intervention strategies by bringing students to a college campus for intensive study during their grade school years. (171)

Along with STEP and McPrep, the School of Education has launched a number of ambitious interventions to assist the Chicago Public Schools in their system-wide commitment to reform. Some of these programs are led by Barbara Radner, a professor of education, and originate in the Center for Urban Education. In the early 1990s a new dean, Barbara Sizemore, developed a novel form of cooperation with the Chicago Public Schools called the School Achievement Structure (SAS). By 1997, SAS was working with 25 Chicago public schools involving 1,370 teachers and 19,538 students. (172) True to its name, the program emphasizes a highly disciplined approach that is centered on students' learning. The principal sets the tone and communicates through her every action that, as Sizemore puts it, "all children can learn. I expect these children to learn. And it will happen here." (173) An SAS coordinator works with the school to implement "The Routes for High Achievement" that include ongoing assessment of student skills, pacing and accelerating their skills development, developing a coordinated cohesive curriculum and working with the staff to implement it. Discipline and high expectations are the key. "Kids who are from a disorganized community and a disruptive family life need a very structured school life," according to Sizemore. "If they can't get this from their teacher, then they won't get it at all." (174)

While these programs show the School of Education working with Chicago's schools as an agent of change, a partnership with a suburban school district provided the first model for a new type of teacher preparation. In the late 1980s the University of Illinois at Chicago (UIC) collaborated with Glenview School District and designed a clinical, site-based teacher preparation program for college graduates working toward both teacher certification and a graduate

The student residence hall University Hall opened its doors in 1986, Lohan Asociates, architects.

degree. When UIC dropped out of the program, DePaul stepped in as a collaborator with Glenview and actually implemented the model. (175)

Students in the first year of the program begin with a summer of intense academic work. During the regular school year students intern at Glenview going through "rounds," that is, rotating through different levels of instruction working with small groups of students and teacher mentors. DePaul faculty teach classes on-site several evenings a week. In the second and third years students are "residents" with responsibility for their classes though they still work closely with their mentors and prepare a thesis with an applied research focus. Three full years of classroom apprenticeship replace the typical 100 hours of classroom observation and 10–12 weeks of student teaching. Both DePaul faculty and student interns discover whether the theories under discussion in the seminars actually work in the classroom. Mentors, juggling the difficult task of teaching their own students and preparing their interns, realize that both they and their interns experience a transformation. "It is one of the nicest marriages between a university and a public school system that I've seen to date," suggests one principal. (176)

The Glenview model influenced schools in other parts of the state. The Chicago school system, its teachers union, ten universities, including DePaul, and the Golden Apple Foundation banded together to create the "Teachers for Chicago" program. Modifying the Glenview program slightly, Teachers for Chicago works every year with about 100 new students who are spread out among the ten universities. Both programs have influenced the traditional curriculum of the School of Education, especially in the graduate programs, where adult learners have flocked to DePaul in search of new careers in teaching. Faculty members struggle to balance the increasingly intense expectations for traditional research at DePaul with the demands of the clinical model for hands-on involvement. (177) Occasionally in the School of Education, as elsewhere in the university, different models of professional education grind away at each other like massive tectonic plates, while teachers and students alike stand with feet firmly planted on both sides of the rift.

From the Little School Under the El to the New American University

Location. Location. Location. From the late 1980s through the 1990s, the success of the School of Education came from paying careful attention to its urban context. The School was clearly out in front of the rest of the university, but others were not far behind. The *Curricular Design* of 1964, as we saw earlier, called attention to the opportunities for education and service that exist in an urban culture and an urban university. When urban historian Richard Meister arrived as dean of the College of Liberal Arts and Sciences in 1981, he saw a university bobbing in the midst of the energy flows of a very dynamic city, educating a primarily metropolitan constituency as it always had. Though some faculty had an urban focus, the university neither encouraged nor capitalized on their interests. "I felt the need to try to articulate [the urban dimension]," Meister recalls, "to try to bring some substance to that." (178) Others agree that Meister tapped something deeply rooted in DePaul's culture and brought it to the surface. "But it's not totally new," suggests Roberta Garner, "[It's] something that's been organically grown all along. So . . . [while it] appears to be an innovation, it's an innovation that's really rooted in, probably at [the point when Meister arrived,] seventy-five years of reality." (179)

In 1986 Richard Yanikoski, then Associate Vice-President for Academic Affairs, now president of Saint Xavier University, published an article that analyzed a mutation in this organically growing mission. The title of the article, "DePaul University, Urban by Design," captures the shift. "DePaul is an urban institution," Yanikoski argued, "in the obvious sense that it is located within a major city and serves substantial numbers of urban residents." Because it chose to remain accessible to its traditional constituency, the university developed a variety of programs, like the STEP program, to remedy deficiencies in preparation for college among urban populations. To become "urban by design," however, meant more than aiding a new cohort of first-generation college students to succeed at DePaul. Yanikoski discussed a variety of ways through which the university was promoting its urban focus. First, it was increasing the number of courses with an explicitly urban subject matter. Second, a still greater number of courses had begun to use Chicago and its institutions as "a living laboratory." Third, at the pedagogical level more students were encouraged to undertake applied research projects. Focusing on the creative efforts of adult learners in SNL, Yanikoski praised the "police lieutenant [who] developed a physical fitness plan that was put into effect at his station," a student whose assessment manual for future lay ministers was adopted by the Joliet diocese and the student who created "a handbook for judicial aides in the Illinois Appellate Court." Fourth, he noted that some programs, in an effort to mine the knowledge and talents available outside of the university walls, had developed reciprocal relationships with key urban institutions. The associations between the School of Music and members of the Chicago Symphony Orchestra and the Lyric Opera were only the most obvious examples. Finally, Yanikoski cites a wide range of projects, ranging from the Mental Health Clinic to the Theater School's "Playworks" series for Chicago's children, that are integral to the education of DePaul students and provide a service to the larger community. (180) The Small Business Institute established in the early 1970s illustrates this same synergy between traditional research and our Vincentian mission of service—between enhancing the education of our traditional students and reaching new groups of eager learners.

> *I*n 1984–85, it ran five . . . public seminars for aspiring entrepreneurs on how to start a small business effectively . . . . [It] provides individualized counseling and management assistance to approximately fifty small businesses, not-for-profit organizations and Chambers of Commerce. The Institute also . . . conducts research on small business concerns, . . . and serves as a field laboratory for the newly created M.B.A. concentration in entrepreneurship. (181)

Given the length of time that the Small Business Institute had labored in the shadows, Roberta Garner's image of an organic process slowly ripening makes sense. As Yanikoski's phrase "urban by design" indicates, by the mid-1980s there was a new self-consciousness about the whole urban commitment and a multi-pronged effort to expand it into a fuller range of educational activities and educationally related services. At a deeper level we can see that "urban by design" marked a new phase in DePaul's efforts to escape all backwaters. If we can mix our spatial metaphors, the "little school under the El" was by definition a backwater. We have already examined Howard Sulkin's contention that becoming a "place for the arts" repositioned DePaul in Chicago. Yanikoski's "laundry list" of programs and activities reflected a new multilateral determination to redefine the university itself.

Beginning in the mid-80s DePaul also committed itself to a sustained expansion of its undergraduate student body. Enrollment growth enabled the university to add dramatically to its physical plant and create a residential campus in Lincoln Park. Growth sparked a rapid increase in the number of full-time faculty, to more than 500. In liberal arts and sciences the impact on curriculum was immense. Enrollment growth meant that departments that had previously performed service functions through the Liberal Studies Program now had viable majors, and growth in the number of faculty members led to a proliferation of new specialty areas. (182) In many departments new faculty with special knowledge of different parts of the world and different cultures in America created curricula with a decidedly more international and multicultural character.

During this period of rapid expansion, the College of Liberal Arts and Sciences also added a number of interdisciplinary programs: honors, women's studies, American studies, and international studies. A graduate program for adult learners, the Master of Arts in Liberal Studies (MALS), was created in 1981–82. It became an influential model for interdisciplinary education. In the MALS three-stage model a set of team-designed, interdisciplinary core courses form the foundation on which electives selected from different departments across the college build. Students then synthesize their educational experiences in a final seminar or research paper.

It was with women's studies, however, that the integrative vision achieved its fullest expression at DePaul as elsewhere. Here the development of an interdisciplinary program flowed from the theoretical commitment of feminist scholarship, an activist agenda, and individual odysseys of feminist scholars at DePaul from relative isolation within their departments to collaboration within a network of like-minded colleagues. "A breaking down of boundaries between fields was considered a mission of feminist studies," comments Midge Wilson, professor of psychology and a former director of the Women's Studies Program. For feminist studies, crossing boundaries was more than a theoretical exercise, for "in doing that we would be seeking ways to help women, not just study women . . . . So there was a real switch from research *on* women to research *for* women." (183) Jacqueline Taylor, former director of the program and now an associate dean of the college, confirms Wilson's analysis, but adds that the women's studies curriculum was the culmination of initially isolated spiritual journeys whose goal was to connect scholarly inquiry about how we view the world with the central issue of how we live in that world. The efforts of these feminist scholars to create a common core for the Women's Studies Program reflected what the feminist poet Adrienne Rich calls "the dream of a common language." (184) As Wilson and Taylor see it, the program was another way of accomplishing the university's Vincentian mission and, despite the tensions and conflicts inevitable within a Catholic institution, they concur that the university has continued to support divergent interpretations of that mission. (185)

Though women's studies may have tested the limits of pluralism allowable in a Catholic university context, one of the most recently developed interdisciplinary programs is an ironic illustration of the depth to which that pluralistic ethos has penetrated. In winter 1995, a group of eighteen faculty from eleven different areas assembled to create a Catholic Studies Program. This was no rearguard effort to impose orthodoxy. (186) Their report stated bluntly, "Catholicism is not reducible to structures, doctrines or practices." It cannot be adequately understood or conveyed by any one discipline like theology.

> *Catholicism consists of multiple images of experience and meaning centering on the person and message of Jesus Christ. It includes doctrinal, attitudinal, organizational, aesthetic and historical layers. These layers overlap, culminating in a dense body of shared symbols . . . and other elements of shared community. (187)*

The Catholic studies faculty wanted to offer students a "comprehensive analysis" of this multilayered tradition. It created a program unique among comparable programs in other institutions for its curricular diversity and in the range of perspectives these varied offerings represented. Against the Catholic Jeremiahs who decry what they see as the relentless "secularization of the academy," David O'Brien has urged Catholic universities to move away from the polar opposition of the secular versus (orthodoxy's version of) the "sacred" and to hew to what a colleague has referred to as the "radical middle." (188) The Catholic Studies Program epitomizes that commitment with its spirit of openness to a variety of perspectives and interpretations in a manner that reinforces Richardson's earlier confidence in the ultimate harmony of faith and reason.

The faculty collaboration that brought the flowering of interdisciplinary programs in so many areas of the university set the stage for a third round of reform of liberal studies early in the 90s. The centerpiece of the new program, inaugurated in autumn 1996, is a strikingly new kind of course called "Discover Chicago." Offered to incoming freshmen, the course involves a week-long immersion in some aspect of the city's life. Charles Suchar, an associate dean of liberal arts and sciences, remembers that the idea for the course arose while he was attending a conference on experiential education in November, 1994.

> *As a fluke, [I'd] walked in on a round table discussion [with] a professor from Australia, the university of Sydney I think it was, who had [an] outward bound program for their freshmen. Incoming students were sent literally into the outback . . . . After he told us about his program, he . . . challenged people around the table to say what they might do if they had . . . [this] type of program and I indicated I was from a big city. And he got very excited and said "Well what would you do? . . . [T]here must be opportunities out where you are . . . ." [B]y the time I had come back to Chicago, I [was] very excited about . . . an outward bound experience in the city . . . . (189)*

Students focus on topics ranging from Chicago's art community to Latino immigration in Chicago, from violence and hospitality in Chicago's sacred spaces to empowering Chicago's women. During the week all of the participants visit one of seven neighborhoods where local leaders and residents discuss the issues that confront their communities.

Each of these courses signals to students at the very beginning of their college career that the vibrant, complex urban world that surrounds them *is* their classroom. Just as important, every section of "Discover Chicago" requires collaboration among faculty, staff and student mentors, which is breaking down the traditional segregation of roles in the university. The period of immersion concludes with a day of service during which students reciprocate the generosity of the groups and communities that have been their teachers (190) Recall, if you will, the imperative articulated in the *Curricular Design* of 1964: "The curricular design shall reflect the students' distinctive opportunities and privileges for education and service that exist in an urban culture and an urban university." (191)

Incorporating a day of service into the Discover Chicago program was emblematic of another wave of pedagogical innovation that was rolling through the university. Units like the Legal Clinic, the Mental Health Center, the Theater School's "Playworks" and the Small Business Institute had combined service to the community with the education of DePaul students for over 20 years. We have just seen that programs such as women's studies were developing courses that involved applied scholarship or what is sometimes referred to as "action research." Now these scattered endeavors were being replicated all over the university. "Theory is just immeasurably enriched by going out and seeing parts of the real world and, of course, you can do that in a lot of different ways," Roberta Garner argues, focusing on the many ways a "service learning" course can be beneficial to our students and the communities they serve.

I think . . . that [service-learning] is one way that is often very thought-provoking for students and also, and this is important, it gives students a sense that they have something valuable to offer other people . . . . I think there is too much of a sense . . . [that] students are just kids, who are best sitting in the classroom, listening to someone else, or reading things other people have written . . . . [I]n many ways what students at DePaul, or any good four-year institution, have to offer is the fact that they're very good writers; they're very good readers; they're good at math skills. That's one of the reasons why they got in here . . . and those skills have become so important . . . . [P]eople without them are really coming down to the margins . . . and [students] can help other people develop them. (192)

If Garner represents a whole group of faculty and staff seeking to get students connected with various community organizations who ask for their services, Anna Waring, a professor in the Master of Public Services program, is typical of those who introduce the community into the classroom. In her course on the management of not-for-profit institutions, Waring has brought in the leaders of fledgling organizations, people who are "big on energy, big on commitment, big on emotion but still trying to put the nuts and bolts of an organization together." Small groups of students assemble a strategic plan for building an organization after in-depth discussions with the community leader. The students learn how to plan in a real situation and the community leaders walk away with six or seven full-fledged strategic plans that they can plunder for the best and most workable ideas. (193)

The number of courses and programs involving new pedagogies, new forms of engagement with the surrounding urban communities, new patterns of collaborative learning and instruction that Yanikoski had written about in the late 80s had increased exponentially by the mid 90s. Liberal arts and science dean Michael Mezey sees these once isolated efforts as now creating a self-sustaining transformation, fueled by the enthusiasm of both students and faculty. *"When we give students an exciting first year program [through] the [focal point] seminars and Discover Chicago . . . , these students will come to expect [the same] sort of thing in the major areas of study. I think our students will become less tolerant of . . . a passive role, and the faculty . . . will respond to that."* (194)

Even before the new Liberal Studies Program was fully up and running, the university had begun to respond to or, more precisely, to acknowledge that the changes we have documented here were, in fact, transforming the character of the university itself. In spring 1996, Richard Meister, executive vice president for academic affairs, launched a discussion about the future of DePaul whose message continues to percolate through the university.

I believe that DePaul can be the New American University: a model of a university that serves the 'public good' . . . . In this university, teaching and learning are primary; scholarship is broadly defined; interdisciplinary work is encouraged and service to the larger society is part of the mission . . . . [F]aculty, staff and students are representative of the larger society. The definition of faculty is also broadened: faculty are both mentors and the academic leaders of this university, with the responsibility for learning being shared with staff and students. (195)

Clearly Meister was extrapolating from the kinds of programs that we have just been examining. Just as clearly, he was putting a new "spin" on the call of Ernest Boyer, late director of the Carnegie Foundation for the Advancement of Teaching, for the establishment of a "New American College." Boyer, who earlier had led the movement to broaden the meaning of scholarship, now called for a renewal of American higher education's commitment to the common good. "I'm convinced," Boyer argued, "that higher education must respond to the educational and health and urban crises of our day, just as the land grant college responded to the needs of farmers a century ago—a commitment which can be viewed as a dimension of scholarship itself." (196) Boyer's plea recapitulated a long-neglected challenge made by Clark

Kerr over thirty years earlier to create "urban grant" institutions of higher learning. (197) In effect, Meister was suggesting that DePaul should become one of Boyer's pioneer institutions *because* of its Catholic, Vincentian and urban mission and *despite* its limited resources and dependence on tuition revenue.

The ensuing debate brought to the fore all of the complexities, the assorted and conflicting purposes that are so characteristic of DePaul. There were some who contended that this new vision deviated too sharply from the traditional mission of research and teaching—which was what higher education stood for. In a university like DePaul with heavy teaching loads, carrying out a research agenda was taxing enough, without placing the burden of new demands on faculty. (198) Others argued that American higher education, the "knowledge industry" that Clark Kerr had foreseen three decades earlier, was functioning increasingly as a "wedge institution" widening the rift between the haves and the have nots. In such a situation, a Catholic, Vincentian and urban university had no morally defensible choice *but* to transform itself into an agent for healthy social change. (199)

This debate was temporarily suspended in January 1997 when an NCA team was on campus for its periodic accreditation review of the university. Ten years of qualitative change linked to quantitative growth had bred a new degree of self-confidence in DePaul about the value of its academic programs. No backwater nervousness about external inspectors characterized this visit. The NCA team's report was also strikingly different from the one in 1950 that reflected the institution's shaky entrance into a new era. In contrast to the earlier document it praised a faculty that is "well-educated, student-oriented, [and] service-minded." It noted the "broad acceptance" of the university's Catholic, Vincentian and urban mission. Academic programs, it said, "have shown continuous, sometimes, striking improvement." Finally it singled out DePaul's many partnerships with its surrounding urban communities. These partnerships "have strengthened both the educational experience of the students and of the institution. DePaul has become a 'cornerstone for Chicago.'" (200)

Before the NCA team had set pen to paper, Father John Minogue, C.M., president of the university, was working with his leadership team on the next phase of DePaul's academic planning, a phase that would carry it to and through its centennial year. In spring 1997, Minogue, Meister and Kenneth McHugh, executive vice-president for operations, announced three educational goals for the university to consider:

Goal One: To provide all full-time students a holistic education that will foster extraordinary learning opportunities through a highly diverse faculty, staff and student body; extensive use of technology; a wide range of high-quality out-of-classroom learning experiences that engage faculty, staff, and students in the learning process; and an undergraduate curriculum founded on a strong liberal arts core, that enables all students to achieve the ten learning goals.

Goal Two: To be a nationally and internationally recognized provider of the highest quality professional education for adult, part-time students, and to be the dominant provider in the greater Chicago area.

Goal Three: To research, develop, deliver and transfer innovative, educationally related programs and services that have a significant social impact and give concrete expression to the university's Vincentian mission. (201)

The first goal heightened DePaul's commitment to (1) new pedagogies in programs like Discover Chicago, (2) interdisciplinary programs that complemented work in traditional majors and (3) experiential and service learning opportunities in all colleges, not just the School for New Learning. The second goal reflected the quantum leap in the quality of professional programs that we have seen occurring from the 1970s forward. The third goal activated the Boyer-Meister pioneering strategy. As part of being "urban by design," DePaul had created numerous centers, institutes and programs through which the university entered into the partnerships with communities, a process that the NCA had commended. We have already looked at the work of units like The Human Rights Law Institute and the School Achievement Structure Program. Now DePaul was saying that these units would no longer be considered "satellite operations." They would become integral to the whole educational enterprise and be more closely linked to the work of faculty and students while they were pursuing goals one or two. Putting goal three on a par with goals one and two unequivocally announced the birth of a new American university.

Henry David Thoreau said that he left Walden Pond because he "had other lives to live." It is instructive that the one person who has had the greatest impact on DePaul over the past forty years left the university late in the summer of 1997. Sensing that *he* had other lives to live, Reverend John T. Richardson, C.M., chancellor of the university, flew to Kenya to take up a new post as a theology instructor in a Vincentian seminary. Richardson's departure came at precisely the moment when the university—now far removed from any academic backwaters—felt more confident than ever before, secure in its mission to do more than hew to the established sea lanes of traditional higher education. Moving into uncharted seas, DePaul University was declaring that it too had other lives, multiple lives, to live.

Chapter Eight Notes

Author's note: *I am grateful to Paul DeBlase who was my research assistant for this project and to Sister Jane Gerard, C.S.J., and Marianne Morrissey who helped prepare the manuscript. My thanks also go to the fifty current and former faculty and administrators, who provided extensive interviews and supplementary materials for this project.*

1. Alan Bloom, *The Closing of the American Mind*. (New York, 1987) *passim*.

2. David O. Levine, *The American College and the Culture of Aspiration*. (Ithaca, NY, 1986) 90–92.

3. David O'Brien, *From the Heart of the American Church: Catholic Higher Education and American Culture*. (Maryknoll, NY, 1994), 29–31.

4. O'Brien, 11–12, 27.

5. Cf. O'Brien, 31.

6. Clark Kerr, *The Great Transformation in Higher Education: 1960–1980*. (Albany, 1991) XI–XII, 3.

7. *Ibid.*, 120.

8. *Ibid.*, 141–43.

9. *Ibid.*, 279.

10. Bruce A. Kimball, *The Condition of American Liberal Education*. Edited by Robert Orrill (New York, 1995) 56, 87–89.

11. O'Brien, 78.

12. *Ibid.*, 20–22.

13. Chicago *Sun Times*, 23 March 1950, 1, Box 7, North Central Accreditation (NCA) Files, DePaul University Archives (hereafter cited as DPUA).

14. Manning M. Patillo, Jr. to Comerford J. O'Malley, C.M., April 18, 1950, Box 7, NCA Files, DPUA.

15. North Central Accreditation Report, 3, 19, Box 7, NCA Files, DPUA.

16. *Ibid.*, 1–9, 20–21.

17. "Presentation of DePaul University to the Executive Committee of the NCA," 8 May 1950, 14, Box 7, NCA Files, DPUA.

18. *Ibid.*, 6–9, 11, 18.

19. G.W. Rosenhof to Comerford J. O'Malley, C.M., 12 May 1950, Box 7, NCA Files, DPUA.

20. Interview with Reverend John T. Richardson, C.M., chancellor, 17 July 1996. Audio tapes and transcripts of all interviews conducted for this project are available in DPUA.

21. Reverend John T. Richardson, C.M., to Graduate Faculty, 16 December 1959, Box 12, O'Malley Files, DPUA.

22. *Ibid.*

23. Richardson interview, July 1996.

24. John Tracy Ellis, "American Catholics and the Intellectual Life," *Thought* 30 (September 1955): 353, 358, 378–80.

25. *Ibid.*, 355, 363–65, 374–77, 386.

26. Richardson interview, July 1996.

27. Interview with Arthur Thurner, emeritus professor of history, 28 June 1996; interview with Edwin Schillinger, emeritus professor of physics, July 1996.

28. Interview with Richard J. Meister, executive vice president for academic affairs, March 1996.

29. Richardson interview, July 1996.

30. Interview with Roberta Garner, professor of sociology, 1 March 1996.

31. Richardson interview, July 1996.

32. William M. O'Shea, "Catholic Higher Education and the Enlightenment: On Borderlines and Roots," *Horizons* 20,No.1 (1993): 105.

33. Committee on Education to Board of Trustees, 4 March 1963, Box 1, O'Malley Files, DPUA.

34. Richardson interview, July 1996. Emphasis mine.

35. *Ibid.*

36. Report of the Committee on Education to the Board of Trustees, 4 March 1963, Box 1, O'Malley Files, DPUA.

37. Reverend John T. Richardson, C.M., personal communication, 19 December 1995.

38. Reverend John R. Cortelyou, C.M., et al., "A Curricular Design for DePaul University," 13 April 1964, 2, Box 2, College of Liberal Arts and Sciences Files, DPUA.

39. Richardson, personal communication, 19 December 1995.

40. "A Curricular Design," 4–5, 20.

41. *Ibid.*, 8.

42. *Ibid.*, 8, 11.

43. *Ibid.*, 15–16.

44. *Ibid.*, 14.

45. *Ibid.*, 28. Emphasis mine.

46. *Ibid.*, 17. Charles Suchar's discussion of the "extended campus" shows, I believe, how the practice of students in making use of the resources of Chicago as part of the learning process preceded by decades the efforts of a critical mass of faculty to make conscious use of the urban context. An exception to this pattern is the way in which the professional schools have always drawn upon the knowledge and experiences of local practitioners.

47. *Ibid.*, 19.

48. Cf. Richardson, personal communication, 19 December 1995.

49. Meister interview, March 1996.

50. "Departure at DePaul," *Time*. (23 October 1964): 68–69.

51. O'Brien, 42.

52. Interview with Gerald Kreyche, emeritus professor of philosophy, June 1996.

53. Gerald Kreyche, "Is Thomism Relevant to the Twentieth Century," *The Catholic Messenger* (March 1963).

54. *Ibid.*

55. Kreyche interview, June 1996.

56. Interview with James Krokar, associate professor of history, March 1996.

57. Jesse A. Mann and Gerald F. Kreyche, eds., *Perspectives on Reality: Readings in Metaphysics from Classical Philosophy to Existentialism.* (New York, 1966), xi.

58. Schillinger interview, July 1996.

59. Interview with Avrom Blumberg, professor of chemistry, February 1996.

60. Interview with Patricia Ewers, president, Pace University, July 1996.

61. Interview with Cornelius Sippel, emeritus professor of history, March 1996.

62. Interview with Albert Erlebacher, emeritus professor of history, March 1996.

63. *Ibid.*

64. Sippel interview, March 1996; interview with Thomas Croak, C.M., associate professor of history, March 1996.

65. Interview with Tony Behof, associate professor of physics, February 1996.

66. Edwin Schillinger, personal communication, February 1996; Behof interview, February 1996.

67. Interview with Dolores McWhinnie, professor of biological sciences, April 1996.

68. Blumberg interview, February 1996.

69. *Ibid.*; Schillinger interview, July 1996.

70. Schillinger interview, July 1996; Behof interview, February 1996.

71. Schillinger interview, July 1996; cf. "The Nature of Science," Interdisciplinary Studies 100, Syllabus, 1991–92.

72. Behof interview, February 1996.

73. Avrom Blumberg, personal communication, 13 December 1995.

74. Ewers interview, July 1996.

75. In retrospect Father Richardson judged the creation of DePaul College to be a means to an end rather than integral to the end itself—as many advocates in the institution viewed it until the late 1970s. "In my view the organization of DePaul College . . . was only a minor strategy to effect curricular revision. Once the narrow focus and rigid control of the separate colleges and departments over the general education curriculum was removed in favor of a broader University-wide and mission oriented perspective, there was no need for DePaul College. It was transitional and served its purpose well." Richardson, personal communication, 19 December 1995.

76. Reverend John R. Cortelyou, C.M., to Reverend Comerford J. O'Malley, C.M., 25 June 1959, Box 8, O'Malley Files, DPUA.

77. Reverend John R. Cortelyou, C.M. to Reverend William T. Cortelyou, C.M., 25 February 1963, Box 8, O'Malley Files, DPUA.

78. McWhinnie interview, April 1996.

79. "Proposal for the Inauguration of Ph.D. Program in Philosophy," 1–3, Box 15, NCA Files, DPUA.

80. Norman Burns to Reverend John R. Cortelyou, C.M., 9 August 1967, Box 15, NCA Files, DPUA.

81. North Central Association, "Report of a Visit to DePaul University, May 15–18, 1967," 13–17. Box 15, NCA Files, DPUA.

82. McWhinnie interview, April 1996.

83. "Proposal for a Ph.D. in Psychology," 10 January 1967, 13–14, Box 16, NCA Files, DPUA.

84. *Ibid.*, 6, 14–15.

85. "Report of a Visit, 1967," 22–25.

86. *Ibid.*, 17–21.

87. *Ibid.*

88. Interview with David Farrell Krell, professor of philosophy, April 1996.

89. Cf. "Proposal for a Ph.D. in Philosophy," 5. This began to change—in the case of Philosophy—in the late 1980s when Dean Richard Meister brought in David Krell, a noted scholar of Heidegger and Nietzsche, to rejuvenate that department. Meister and Krell agreed that the rejuvenation of the Ph.D. would need to work in tandem with a rejuvenation of the undergraduate curriculum and both would entail a deeper involvement of the department in the life of Liberal Arts and Sciences and with the university's urban mission. Krell interview, April 3, 1996.

90. Richardson, personal communication, 19 December 1995.

91. Richardson interview, July 1996.

92. Reverend John T. Richardson, C.M., "Proposal for a New, Experimental Unit of Study at DePaul University," 21 January 1971, 1–2, Box 5, School for New Learning (SNL) Files, DPUA.

93. Richardson interview, July 1996.

94. Interview with David Justice, vice president for lifelong learning and suburban campuses, July 1996.

95. Interview with Howard Sulkin, president of Spertus Institute for Jewish Studies, July 1996.

96. Howard Sulkin, personal communication, 22 February 1996.

97. *Ibid.*

98. Sulkin interview, July 1996.

99. "A Design for New Learning," 8, Box 5, SNL Files, DPUA.

100. *Ibid.*, 9–10.

101. *Ibid.*, 11–14.

102. *Ibid.*, 24, 27–28, 31–32, 34.

103. Sulkin interview, July 1996.

104. Beverly Firestone, "The School for New Learning: A Time-Tested Model of the Future," 8, Box 1, SNL Files, DPUA.

105. Interview with Catherine Marienau, associate professor in the School for New Learning, June 1996; Justice interview, July 1996.

106. "Prospectus for a Master of Arts Program," April 1985, 3, 13–14, 52, Box 6, SNL Files, DPUA.

107. Justice interview, 1 July 1996; Firestone, p 14.

108. Sulkin interview, 1 July 1996; Ewers interview, 1 July 1996; Richardson interview, 17 July 1996.

109. Interview with John Rury, professor in the School for New Learning, March 1996.

110. Marienau interview, June 1996.

111. Justice interview, July 1996.

112. *Ibid.*

113. *Ibid.*

114. Sulkin interview, July 1996.

115. *Ibid.*

116. Interview with John Watts, dean of the Theater School, September 1996.

117. Frederick Miller, former dean of the School of Music, personal communication, January 1996.

118. *Ibid.*

119. Interview with Frederick Miller, September 1996.

120. North Central Association, "Report of a Visit to DePaul University, Feb. 27–March 2, 1977," 14–15, Box 21, NCA Files, DPUA.

121. Miller, personal communication, 29 January 1996.

122. *Ibid.*; Miller interview, 16 September 1996; interview with Thomas Brown, professor in the School of Music, September 1996.

123. "Thresholds: A Planning Guide for the School of Music, 1992–1997," 5–6.

124. Watts interview, 12 September 1996; interview with James Ostholthoff, professor in the Theater School, May 1996.

125. Watts interview, September 1996.

126. *Ibid.*

127. *Ibid.*

128. Ostholthoff interview, May 1996.

129. *Ibid.*

130. *Ibid.*

131. *Ibid.*

132. Miller interview, September 1996.

133. "Self Study Report for the NCA," January 1977, 41–44, Box 21, NCA Files, DPUA.

134. "Report of a Visit to DePaul University, 1977," 18–21, Box 21, NCA Files, DPUA.

135. "A Report to the Faculty on the Project for the Revision of the Undergraduate Curriculum," Spring 1978, Box 1, College of Liberal Arts and Sciences Files, DPUA; cf. "Undergraduate Curriculum Revision Committee to All Full Time Faculty," May 1, 1978; Ewers interview, July 1996; interview with L. Edward Allemand, emeritus professor of computer science, April 1996.

136. Ewers interview, July 1996; "Harvard Weighs Plan to Reform College Curriculum," and "Harvard's Report on the 'Core Curricula,'" *Chronicle of Higher Education* (6 March 1978).

137. Patricia Ewers, "The Missions of Colleges of Arts and Sciences within Universities," *Liberal Education* 66 (Summer 1980): 157.

138. "The Liberal Studies Program at DePaul University. Report of the General Education and Skills Committees," 15 January 1980, 4–10, 24–33, Box 2, Academic Liberal Studies Files, DPUA.

139. Interview with Janie Isackson, director of the Bridge Program, February 1996.

140. Interview with Charles Suchar, associate dean of liberal arts and sciences, March 1996.

141. Erlebacher interview, March 1996.

142. Croak interview, March 1996; Krokar interview, March 1996; Thurner interview, June 1996; Sippel interview, March 1996.

143. Krokar interview, March 1996.

144. Interview with Paul F. Camenisch, professor of religious studies, March 1996.

145. Ewers, "Missions," 157.

146. Camenisch interview, March 1996.

147. Interview with Dennis P. McCann, professor of religious studies, March 1996.

148. Charles R. Strain, "Personhood, Pluralism and Value Consciousness: DePaul University's New Liberal Studies Curriculum," Association for General and Liberal Studies Annual Meeting, (1980): 13.

149. Interview with Laura Pincus, associate professor of management, May 1996.

150. Sinclair Lewis, *Babbitt*. (New York, 1992), 131.

151. *Ibid.*

152. Laura Thatcher Ulrich presents a telling illustration of this transformation at work in the field of medicine in her *A Midwife's Tale*. (New York, 1990).

153. Interview with Margaret Oppenheimer, associate professor of economics, 30 May 1996; cf. Levine.

154. Meister interview, March 1996.

155. Ewers interview, July 1996.

156. Interview with Mark Weber, professor of law, 9 July 1996; interview with Mark Sullivan, associate professor of accounting, 30 May 1996.

157. Pincus interview, May 1996; interview with Robert Peters, associate dean, College of Commerce, May 1996.

158. Peters interview, May 1996.

159. *Ibid.*

160. College of Commerce Undergraduate Committee, "Proposal for Curriculum Modification," April 1993, 22–23, Box 1a, College of Commerce Dean Files, DPUA.

161. Ronald J. Patten, dean of the College of Commerce, personal communication, April 1997.

162. "Proposal for Curriculum Modification," 7, 16.

163. Patten, personal communication, 8 April 1997.

164. Oppenheimer interview, 30 May 1996; cf. Margaret Oppenheimer, "Teaching Western Economics to Eastern Economists: A Look at Topics, Teaching Methods and Attitudes," *Journal of Teaching in International Business*, 6. No. 4 (1995): 47–64.

165. Weber interview, July 1996.

166. *Ibid.*; interview with John Decker, professor of law, July 1996.

167. Douglas Cassell, director of the International Human Rights Law Institute, personal communication, 15 February 1996.

168. International Human Rights Law Institute, *Annual Report* (1993–94): 2–3, 9, 13, 18.

169. David Miller, associate dean, School of Computer Sciences, Telecommunications and Information Systems, Presentation to the Academic Planning Retreat, July 1997.

170. Richardson interview, July 1996.

171. Interview with Rafaela Weffer, associate vice president for academic affairs, November 1996 .

172. Kymara Chase, personal communication, 26 September 1997.

173. Lenaya Raack, "What Works with City Kids: An Effective School Model," *City Schools* 1 (Fall 1995): 14.

174. Barbara Sizemore, dean of the School of Education, quoted in Raack, 13.

175. Nancy Williams, Kathryn Wiggins, and Barbara Kimes Myers, "The Impact of a Collaborative Teacher Preparation Program on a University and a Public School District," *Critical Issues in Teacher Education* 3 (1993): 13–14.

176. *Ibid.*, 14–16.

177. Interview with Peter Pereira, associate professor of education, April 1997.

178. Meister interview, March 1996.

179. Garner interview, March 1996.

180. Richard Yanikoski, "DePaul University, Urban by Design," *Current Issues in Catholic Education* 6, No. 2 (1986): 5–8.

181. *Ibid.*

182. Meister interview, March 1996; interview with Michael Mezey, dean of the College of Liberal Arts and Sciences, July 1996.

183. Interview with Midge Wilson, professor of psychology, March 1996.

184. Interview with Jacqueline Taylor, associate dean, liberal arts and sciences, August 1996.

185. Wilson interview, March 1996; Taylor interview, August 1996.

186. McCann interview, March 1996.

187. "Proposal for a New Major in Catholic Studies," Winter 1996, 4–5.

188. O'Brien, *passim.*

189. Suchar interview, March 1996.

190. "First Year Students 'Discover Chicago,'" *Insights* (Autumn/Winter 1996): 4–5.

191. "A Curricular Design, 1964," 14.

192. Garner interview, March 1996.

193. Interview with Anna Waring, assistant professor of public services, March 1996.

194. Mezey interview, July 1996.

195. Richard J. Meister, "Expectations and Visions," *Academic Affairs Quarterly*, 2 (Spring 1996): 3.

196. Ernest Boyer, "The New American College," *Chronicle of Higher Education* (4 March 1994): A48.

197. Kerr, Chapter 25.

198. Cf. Meister, "Expectations and Visions," pp 2–3.

199. Charles Strain, "The New American University, Higher Education and Society," *Academic Affairs Quarterly* 2 (Fall 1996): 4–6.

200. North Central Association, "Report of a Visit, May 1997," 50.

201. Richard J. Meister, "Future Directions: 'Make No Little Plans,'" *Academic Affairs Quarterly* 3 (Fall 1997): 1–3.

EPILOGUE

DePaul and the Future of Catholic Higher Education

Richard Meister

As we near the end of the 20th century, Catholic institutions of higher education are struggling with being Catholic and being "universities" in the modern definition of the word. In the past this tension for religiously affiliated universities, founded earlier than their Catholic counterparts, tended to result in either their complete secularization, as they became prestigious institutions, or a narrow sectarianism, as they held fast to the teachings and values of the founding religion. As DePaul begins its centennial year, almost every Catholic college and university is considering what it means to be Catholic. Theodore M. Hesburgh, C.S.C., has edited a volume in which twenty-nine University of Notre Dame faculty members contributed essays on what it means to be a Catholic university. Although Notre Dame sees itself as the national Catholic research university, some of the essayists lament the passing of the old Notre Dame and argue that it is becoming increasingly secularized. In November 1996 a Georgetown University faculty seminar on its Jesuit and Catholic identity issued a report, entitled "Centered Pluralism," that called for the university to renew and articulate its distinctive mission. Yet, a year later, *The Chronicle of Higher Education* featured Georgetown in an article headlined "A Debate Over Crucifixes Provokes Larger Questions at Georgetown University." Georgetown officials indicated that the university was studying the matter while Cardinal James Hickey, head of the Archdiocese of Washington, D.C., admonished Georgetown to resolve the issue quickly "in favor of the university's professed Catholic identity." In the spring of 1998, Georgetown announced that it would place crucifixes in all but one of the classroom buildings. This type of controversy and the concerns of many faculty members in Catholic colleges and universities over Pope John Paul II's document, *Ex Corde Ecclesiae*, tends to further polarize the two sides in an ongoing dialogue about what it means to be a Catholic university. Although the purpose of *Ex Corde Ecclesiae* is to provide guidance for the preservation and development of the Catholic mission of colleges and universities, it is creating concern within American Catholic higher education. (1)

For DePaul, this struggle over identity is even more complex, given its experience of tensions between a quest for academic quality and being Vincentian and urban. Today these issues are debated within the institution. Some question whether DePaul can have a Vincentian mission given its selective admission policy and its tuition rates. Others wonder whether it can have an urban mission while creating a system of suburban campuses which offer expensive, highly selective graduate programs in the professional areas, or whether its traditional mission can be met while recruiting students nationally and internationally and seeking a Phi Beta Kappa chapter. Still others argue that DePaul cannot be truly a university, if it continues to give primacy to teaching and emphasizes applied research and service to the larger community. Some within the university have suggested that if DePaul is to achieve the visibility and recognition it deserves, it should stop using the words *Catholic, Vincentian* and *urban*. They suggest that such words can be misunderstood by those outside the university. (2) The term *Catholic* can carry negative connotations, especially over the issues of academic freedom and intellectual pluralism. *Vincentian* means little to most members of the larger society, and *urban* tends to carry negative inferences, particularly outside of the city. Thus there is pressure from many quarters for DePaul to abandon or reinterpret its unique historical identity.

As I noted earlier, DePaul's struggle to become a modern university has been marked by tensions that arise between the quest for academic quality and its distinctive identity. For most of its history this struggle was not very evident but the tensions were real. In the 1960s Father John R. Cortelyou, as president, and Father John T. Richardson, as executive vice president, led DePaul through a period of significant change that made it similar in many respects to other universities. At that time, they were confident that the institution's Catholic, Vincentian and urban identity would not be affected by such changes. Within ten years some Vincentians and others within the university argued that those values had disappeared. The resulting dialogue led Patricia Ewers, then dean of faculties and vice president for academic affairs, to articulate these tensions in the 1987 Self-Study Report for the North Central Association. She listed five tensions. Four of these resulted from the tension between DePaul's mission and the academic qualities of prestigious American universities: teaching (mission) versus research (academic prestige); professional education versus liberal learning; student access versus student quality; Catholic identity versus academic freedom. Ewers argued that these tensions could be turned to a creative advantage for the university. DePaul, by successfully responding to these challenges, could become a respected institution with a distinctive mission. (3) The events since 1987 have confirmed her optimism. The university in the 1990s continues to enhance its academic quality and to strengthen its distinctive mission and character.

Catholic Higher Education in the Twentieth Century

Philip Gleason's definitive study, *Contending with Modernity: Catholic Higher Education in the Twentieth Century*, published in 1995, places the history of Catholic colleges and universities in the context of the changes affecting American society and the Catholic Church. Within the

The Rev. John Minogue, C.M., president 1993–present.

larger society, the expansion of public education resulted in the democratization of higher education. This in turn brought about the disintegration of the classical curriculum. The explosion of knowledge and the emergence of the United States as a world power gave rise to the research university. The Catholic Church went through similar trauma and change. Periodic outbursts of anti-Catholicism and the increasing growth of the Church due to waves of European immigrants provided a reason for and the resources to support an institutional separatism among Catholics. (4)

DePaul's founding in 1898 and its early years as St. Vincent's College were similar to the experiences of scores of other Catholic institutions of higher education. Almost all were founded by religious orders and usually connected with high schools. They served the sons or daughters of upwardly mobile Catholic families. In some cases, the colleges also prepared students for study for the priesthood. The enrollments were usually a few hundred. However, in the first twenty-five years of this century, Catholic higher education changed dramatically. During that time most institutions ignored the divisions within the Roman Catholic Church that ultimately resulted in the condemnation of modernism (described by some as Americanism in the United States) in *Pascendi Dominici Gregis* by Pope Pius X in 1907. They moved ahead with modernizing their organizational structures, while repudiating the ideas of modernism. Many colleges, according to Gleason, especially those located in large cities, joined the university movement. They added medicine, law, business, social work, journalism, music, education and engineering. Enrollments in these professional programs increased very quickly. (5)

What happened nationally was reflected locally in Chicago. In 1926 DePaul had fewer than 300 students enrolled in the College of Liberal Arts and Sciences with 2,800, primarily part-time, in the professional programs; Loyola had 305 arts and science students compared with 3,140 in the professional programs. The university movement also led institutions to establish lay advisory boards and to become coeducational, especially in their professional or graduate programs. Some Catholic universities, like DePaul, adopted the modified elective system. Others, led by the twenty-six Jesuit institutions, remained committed to their 19th century curriculum. (6)

Gleason describes the period between World War I and World War II as a renaissance for Catholic intellectuals and Catholic universities. The National Catholic Educational Association became much more active and gained the respect of other national associations. The American Catholic Philosophical Association, which was founded in 1926, was only one of many Catholic professional organizations established during this time. These organizations gave Catholic academics and intellectuals a sense of legitimacy. The revival of Thomistic philosophy in the form of Neoscholasticism gave rise to more than twenty scholarly journals and a structured curriculum in philosophy that was adopted by virtually every Catholic college and university. It is noteworthy that during these decades it was philosophy, not the study of religion, that was the unifying agent of the curriculum. Religion courses carried fewer credit hours because they were seen as a means to moral development, not as academic courses. It was not until the late thirties that theology was introduced as a legitimate discipline of study within a Catholic university. Neoscholasticism became the foundation of an American Catholic culture and supported the intellectual and social action revival of these years. (7)

Catholic social teachings, supported by Pope Pius XI's *Quadragesimo Anno* in 1931, fostered the Catholic Action Movement. In Chicago the Interstudent Catholic Action organization, which was established in 1927, was active through the thirties at Loyola and DePaul. On Catholic college campuses student organizations supported an array of Catholic action movements, including pro-labor organizations, the Catholic Worker Movement, interracial programs and an interest in liturgy, as well the Legion of Decency and the censoring of films and publications. Catholic institutions were seen as providing much more than just education in Catholic religion. As Myles Connolly wrote, *"Catholic colleges are not only citadels of the Faith; they are centers of Catholic culture and tradition."* (8)

DePaul's history during this period was similar to what occurred nationally. Father Corcoran, who became president in 1930, led a Catholic Renaissance at DePaul. As Lester Goodchild has noted, DePaul became a center for scholarship on Catholic religious education. DePaul students were involved in local Catholic Action projects. As John Rury demonstrates in his discussion of student life at DePaul, they were involved in many related activities as well. But there was little question of DePaul's Catholic identity at this point in its history.

The consensus about Catholic culture in the universities peaked and then began to break apart during the years after World War II. Increasing opportunities for Catholic graduates to complete Ph.D.s—and then to return to teach in the rapidly expanding Catholic colleges and universities—began to make these institutions more like their secular counterparts. Priest and historian John Tracy Ellis also attacked the failure of American Catholics to produce significant intellectual leaders in his famous 1955 essay, "American Catholics and the Intellectual Life." This occurred at the time when some American liberals were attacking the Catholic Church as being tied too closely to McCarthyism and responsible for the attacks on the film industry and on freedom of speech. (9)

The questions did not abate in the years that followed. Movie censorship, the silencing of John Courtney Murray, S.J., the banning of speakers at Catholic University in 1963, and the firing of 31 faculty members at St. John's University in 1965 called into question whether a university could be Catholic and maintain academic freedom and intellectual integrity. Many saw the Church as an hierarchical, authoritarian institution more interested in moral supervision than in fostering academic excellence. Some Catholic intellectuals thought that perhaps Robert Hutchins of the University of Chicago was right in 1937 when he attacked Catholic universities for their athleticism, collegiatism, vocationalism, and anti-intellectualism. Many Catholic intellectuals during these years moved from being political and economic liberals to being theological liberals. This led to the increasing fragmentation of the Catholic community. (10)

By the 1960s Catholic universities were in disarray. Neoscholasticism was in decline. In the aftermath of Vatican II both the reality and the perception of a monolithic church disappeared. Over 5,000 religious left their orders between 1966 and 1975; the number of Jesuits declined 38 percent. At the same time, Catholic universities found themselves caught between two worlds. Most responded by endorsing the 1967 Land O'Lakes Statement that declared the need of autonomy to ensure academic freedom. At the same time many institutions also transferred control of the university to lay boards of trustees. The reasons for the laicization of the boards, according to Gleason, were the spirit of Vatican II, which encouraged the participation of the laity in the Church, and the need of new board leadership and new sources of funds. (11) As Anna Waring notes in chapter 3, there was also fear of the loss of federal aid. In the 1966 *Horace Mann* decision, the federal courts put Catholic institutions on notice that their religious affiliation might preclude support by the government. Although the *Tilton v. Richardson* decision in 1971 reduced this threat, the movement to institute greater lay control continued.

Similarities, Differences and the Distinctiveness of DePaul

Philip Gleason concludes his book on a pessimistic note, decrying the loss of consensus about what it means to be a Catholic university. As Charles Strain points out in his chapter, David J. O'Brien, a historian at Holy Cross College, and others take issue with Gleason's argument that Americanization resulted in the secularization of Catholic higher education. O'Brien sees that period of Catholic revival between the wars as one of abnormal consensus that is unlikely to be repeated. According to him, we are entering a new phase, a pluralistic world, and Catholic institutions have much to contribute through academic excellence and their commitment to peace and justice. Lester Goodchild, yet another historian of Catholic higher education, examined the strategic policy decisions that allowed Notre Dame, Loyola and DePaul to evolve from 19th century Catholic religious colleges to modern American Catholic universities (early 20th century into the 1960s), and then to very distinctive models of Catholic institutions. According to Goodchild, following Vatican II and, in particular,

Elie Wiesel, noted author and Nobel Peace Prize Laureate delivers commencement address, June 1997.

the establishment of lay boards of trustees, Catholic universities in the midwest followed distinctive paths of development. (12)

Gleason, O'Brien and Goodchild all agree that Catholic colleges and universities were more similar than different up to the 1950s. And this was true for DePaul. As a Catholic institution, DePaul was influenced by the changes within the larger Catholic community and the institutional church. Being Vincentian also influenced DePaul's values and culture, for example, in the emphasis given to the dignity of the individual person, concern for the poor, and the commitment to providing educational opportunities to those who might not otherwise have them. Serving an urban constituency made DePaul more entrepreneurial, more pragmatic, and more tolerant than many of its peer institutions. These three characteristics, Catholic, Vincentian and urban, were and still are inseparable. The nuances of each affect the others and each builds on the others.

The factors that influenced DePaul's early history later give rise to DePaul's distinctiveness, especially evident since the 1960s, a period of radical change in Catholic higher education. An example of its early distinctiveness is the university's 1907 charter, which did not include the word Catholic and which explicitly prohibited the applying of any religious test for admission or for employment. This undoubtedly made DePaul more open and tolerant, even through the Catholic revival years. And this legacy influenced the drafting of the 1967 mission statement, discussed in Anna Waring's chapter. The mission statement also did not identify DePaul as Catholic; rather it emphasized the university's Judaic-Christian tradition and its Vincentian character. The 1907 charter and the 1967 statement reflect DePaul's openness, and as a result the percentage of Catholic students, faculty, and religious have been lower than at most other Catholic institutions.

DePaul's distinctiveness is also reflected in its willingness to provide programs needed by the local community. This is most evident in its professional and graduate programs. Despite abortive early attempts, DePaul did not establish a medical, dental or an engineering school; such professional programs were expensive to initiate and sustain and they would, if established, serve a limited number of students. DePaul's professional programs in law, business and computer science, although having developed reputations for quality, are among the largest in the United States. As John Rury notes in his chapter on students, these programs have traditionally attracted a religiously diverse groups of students. DePaul's programs were more open to accepting Jewish and African American students and women. DePaul was also much slower to strengthen its College of Liberal Arts and Sciences and to develop doctoral programs. More recently, DePaul's emphasis on the fine and performing arts, through the School of Music and the Theater School, and the studio art and creative writing programs in the College of Liberal Arts and Sciences, give it curricular distinctiveness, and also require significant support from the external community.

One way DePaul sought to manifest its Vincentian character was through its commitment to provide access to higher education to an urban population. Father Comerford O'Malley, the university's seventh president, emphasized DePaul's determination to be the provider of low-cost degree programs to a large number of students. Partially as a result of this commitment, DePaul had, prior to the 1960s, less than adequate facilities, no residential campus to support a college of liberal arts and sciences, a small endowment, and the dependence on large enrollments in its professional programs. The results of this legacy are evident today. Unlike most large contemporary universities, DePaul's student body is almost evenly divided between full-time and part-time students. Of the latter, the vast majority are over twenty-four and enrolled in terminal master's programs. This reflects the university's continuing responsiveness to society's demand for professional programs.

DePaul has experienced phenomenal growth over the past twelve years; it has moved from being the fifth to the second largest Catholic university in the United States. DePaul's traditional strength in professional programs, especially at the master's level is one reason for this growth. The second reason is the development of the Lincoln Park campus. Both the university's undergraduate and graduate enrollments have increased by 45 percent between 1984 and 1997, while other large Catholic universities in total have experienced a 9 percent decline in undergraduate enrollment and only an increase of 20 percent in graduate enrollment. (13) DePaul's historical commitment to being responsive to the demand for professional education, along with considerable investment in facilities and programs on the Lincoln Park campus, have contributed to DePaul's reputation for academic excellence. And this excellence continues to enhance the university's enrollment growth.

As Thomas Croak indicates in his chapter, research is also a necessary and vital component of the modern university. Between 1985 and 1997 the university significantly increased its support for research. At the same time, faculty members were quite successful in obtaining federal funds to support their research. A group of about a dozen faculty members received over $5 million in competitive grants to support their research. These included well established scholars who taught in the Ph.D. program in psychology, and younger scholars in mathematics and the sciences. Their efforts have advanced DePaul's academic reputation.

However, external funding also has supported other programs, many of which are directly linked to the university's distinctive Catholic, Vincentian and urban mission. The university, for instance, received through a competitive process nearly $2.5 million from the Department of Education in Title III and Title IV funds to improve the academic services needed to support student success, especially students at risk. National Science Foundation and NASA funds were received to advance science education and to increase the numbers of minority students in the sciences. A $2.5 million matching grant from the National Endowment for the Humanities provided funds to support the construction of a new library and to endow collections. Other grants included $2 million to support the outreach efforts of the library, $2.5

million from the Department of Housing and Urban Development to the Egan Center to provide training for mid-level HUD administrators and to establish the West Humboldt Park/DePaul Community Alliance, $4.8 million from the Department of Agriculture for the McGowan Biological and Environmental Sciences facility and $350,000 for an urban forestry program, and over $1 million in United States Information Agency funds for the training programs offered by the International Human Rights Law Institute. (14)

As noted in the previous chapters, a critical element of DePaul's distinctiveness is its Vincentian heritage. This legacy continues to flourish. The Vincentian presence on the faculty has increased in recent years from one to seven, with Vincentians serving on the faculties of three schools. As a part of the capital campaign, the Midwest Province gave over $900,000 to endow a Vincentian Fund. Each year more than $50,000 is distributed to support programs that foster the university's Catholic and Vincentian mission. DePaul also became the home of the Vincentian Studies Institute and the library received over 100,000 volumes from the collections of closed Vincentian seminaries in Denver and Perryville.

But it is the urban programs that manifest most visibly the Catholic and Vincentian character and DePaul's distinctive mission. In 1996–1997, the university invested over $2 million and generated more than $14 million in grants and contracts to support 21 centers, institutes, and programs that reached out in partnership with or provided service to the larger community. In 1998, eleven programs are fully or primarily funded by university funds. Four of these, the Legal Clinic, the Reading Clinic, the Mental Health Center, and the Theater School's Playworks, provide service through the clinical or performance requirements of their degree programs; they are also the oldest of the university's outreach efforts, and involve both students and faculty. The oldest outreach program, driven by the Vincentian mission, is STEP (Students, Teachers, Educators, and Parents). This program, founded in 1982 by Rafaela Weffer, a faculty member in the School of Education, with a grant from the Joyce Foundation, provides course work on Saturday mornings to more than 200 high school students. Since the late eighties almost all the funding for this program came from the university. The other six programs—the Center for African American Research (now the Center for Culture and History of Black Diaspora), the Center for Latino Research, the Health Law Institute, the Institute for Business and Professional Ethics, the Small Business Institute, and the Driehaus Center for International Business—provide services that indirectly support academic programs and involve students and faculty. Although some outreach occurs, external funding is nominal. (15)

Six programs, most of which had been established between 1986 and 1996, received approximately $600,000 in institutional funds in 1996–1997 to support their administrative infrastructure. These generated approximately $3.5 million in grants and contracts to deliver programs to external constituencies. They are the Msgr. John Egan Urban Center, the Center for Urban Education, the Center for Church/State Studies, the International Human Rights Law Institute, the Chaddick Center for Metropolitan Development and the Kellstadt Market-

DePaul's Naperville campus opened in 1997.

ing Center. The largest and oldest of these is the Center for Urban Education, which was founded by Barbara Radner, a faculty member in the School of Education. (16)

Another four programs are fully funded through grants and contracts. These programs received $6 million in grants and contracts in 1996–1997 to deliver educationally related programs and generated about $400,000 to support the indirect costs associated with having these programs as a part of the university. The most traditional of these is the School of Music's Community Music Program, which was established in 1988. The Student Achievement Structure Program, founded by the dean of the School of Education, Barbara Sizemore, received nearly $3 million through contracts with almost thirty Chicago schools to assist the teachers, students and parents in raising the test scores of underachieving students. The McPrep Program, begun in 1993, with a $900,000, three-year grant from the Ronald McDonald's Children's Fund, provides junior high students with a Saturday and Summer program. The Office of Applied Innovations, joining DePaul in 1995, provides workforce education programs, especially for welfare-to-work participants. In 1997–1998, it received more than $4 million in contracts. (17)

These many and diverse programs extend and broaden DePaul's educational mission. The university nurtures and supports them because of its Vincentian mission and the underlying Catholic values and traditions. For DePaul University to continue to thrive well into the 21st century, it must be successful as a university and as one that is Catholic, Vincentian and urban. The major challenge in DePaul's hundredth year is whether the university can deliver high quality, innovative, educationally related programs that serve the larger society, whether these programs can provide learning and professional opportunities for students and faculty, and whether they can be sustained through external support.

DePaul as the New American Catholic University

In this last decade of the 20th century, higher education in the United States is recognized as the best in the world. From the vantage point of the larger global society, the United States is the model for how education must serve society. Hundreds of thousands of international students come to our universities to study. Many American faculty and administrators spend time abroad sharing their best practices. Yet higher education, especially public higher education, is facing increasing criticism from the American public, legislators, and business leaders. Some believe that higher education, especially in the public sector, is no longer "a public good" but a "private benefit." It is ironic that private religious colleges and universities are seen as having a much stronger commitment to becoming partners with institutions, communities and individuals in order to meet the challenges facing society. This was evident at the session, "The University in Engagement with Society," of the 1998 annual meeting of the Association of American Colleges and Universities. At one point, in response to a request that those in the audience share examples of their institutions engagement with society, the first six speakers came from Catholic or sectarian colleges or universities. Most Americans believe that such civic engagement is at the core of what it means to be an educated person and is a prerequisite for a democratic society.

Despite the efforts of many in public higher education to develop programs that serve the larger society, there is increasing concern as to the extent of the commitment of higher education in general to meet the needs of society. As seen in the earlier chapters by Meister and Strain, in response to this concern, the late Ernest L. Boyer called on higher education to create the New American College. Such a college would emphasize teaching, define scholarship broadly, and create a synergy with the larger society. (18) What Boyer called for partially describes what DePaul has represented in its recent history. More importantly, it provides the framework for DePaul's vision for the future.

Although Catholic institutions, including DePaul, offer a range of programs that respond to the needs of society, many question whether Catholic higher education is viable or sustainable over the long term. As we have seen throughout this volume DePaul University has and is, through its distinctive values, demonstrating ways in which a value-driven mission can be sustained. Can DePaul continue to shape and nurture its Catholic character in the future? First as a professor and dean and now as DePaul's chief academic officer, I struggle with the question: what does it mean for DePaul to be a Catholic university? On some days I succumb to the pessimism expressed in an essay by Marvin R. O'Connell, an historian at Notre Dame, who concludes that "little can be done to reverse what has happened. Now . . . we have in the name of pluralism become like everybody else." (19) However, most of the time, I am hopeful that an institution that recognizes and is serious about its religious character can define anew what that means. It can recover the unity that links John Henry Newman's "religion and secular knowledge."

The William G. McGowan Biological and Environmental Sciences Center under construction. This highly modern science facility will open in September 1998.

If we focus on trying to enforce a common faith and belief on those in the university community, we will fail. We know that no litmus test can be applied. Each of us have experienced how our own or our colleagues' religious perspectives have changed. Faith and belief are not absolute. Catholic higher education can only survive by recognizing that its value system and its traditions are responsible for this engagement with the larger society. It is our strength. At the same time this engagement with the larger society can only continue if the DePaul community nurtures and respects its Catholic and Vincentian values and traditions. Being Catholic, Vincentian and urban cannot be separated into three missions. The three words represent one mission. DePaul's programs that manifest its engagement with society are only the most visible manifestation of its Catholic and Vincentian values and traditions.

George M. Marsden, a Notre Dame scholar of a Reformed theological heritage, traces American higher education from its Protestant establishment to its present established nonbelief, and offers a ray of hope for Catholic universities. He does not call for a return to the past, but rather he argues that we must understand the forces that have shaped American education. The authors of this book trust that we have contributed to this understanding. (20)

Epilogue Notes

1. Theodore M. Hesburgh, ed., *The Challenge and Promise of a Catholic University* (Notre Dame, Indiana, 1994); *The Chronicle of Higher Education*, 28 November 1997, A43, A45.

2. Institutional Advancement Task Force, "Recommendations," in "Strategic Planning: Report of the Task Forces," (DePaul University: January 1994), 1–7.

3. Self-Study Report for the North Central Association (DePaul University, December 1996), I, 11–13.

4. Philip Gleason, *Contending with Modernity: Catholic Higher Education in the Twentieth Century* (New York, 1995).

5. Ibid., 95–102.

6. Ibid., 84–85.

7. Ibid., 105–169.

8. Ibid., 145–152, quoted p. 145.

9. Ibid., 261–304.

10. Ibid., 247, 305–322.

11. Ibid., 305–322.

12. Lester Goodchild, "The Mission of the Catholic University in the Midwest, 1842–1980: A Comparative Study of Strategic Planning at Notre Dame, Loyola University of Chicago and DePaul" (Ph.D. dissertation, University of Chicago, 1986), 816, see also 792–878; David J. O'Brien, *From the Heart of the American Church: Catholic Higher Education and American Culture* (Maryknoll, New York, 1994).

13. Office of Enrollment Management, DePaul University, Comparative Study the Twelve Largest Catholic Universities in the United States, 1997.

14. Office of Academic Affairs, DePaul University, Report on Programs, Centers and Institutes, Office of Academic Affairs, 1997. Located in the Office of Academic Affairs.

15. Ibid.

16. Ibid.

17. Ibid.

18. Ernest L. Boyer, "Creating the New American College," *The Chronicle of Higher Education*, 4 March 1994, A48.

19. Marvin R. O'Connell, "A Catholic University, Whatever That May Mean," in *The Challenge and Promise of a Catholic University*, edited by Theodore M. Hesburgh (Notre Dame, Indiana, 1994), 241.

20. George M. Marsden, *The Soul of the American University: From Protestant Establishment to Established Non-belief* (New York, 1994) *passim*.

CONTRIBUTORS

Thomas Croak, C.M. is associate vice president for donor relations and associate professor of history at DePaul. From 1992 to 1997 he served as chair of the history department. He holds a Doctor of Arts from Carnegie-Mellon University and a Juris Doctoris from DePaul's law school. He has been a Vincentian priest since 1965.

Albert Erlebacher received his Ph.D. in history from the University of Wisconsin. After teaching high school and at the University of Wisconsin—Oshkosh, he came to DePaul in 1965 as a member of the history department. Besides holding a variety of administrative appointments, he also represented DePaul on the Advisory Committee to the Illinois Board of Higher Education between the mid-1970s and the 1990s.

Dennis P. McCann is professor of religious studies at DePaul, and executive director of the Society of Christian Ethics. He received an STL from the Gregorian University in Rome in 1971, and a Ph.D. in theology from the University of Chicago Divinity School in 1976. During his sixteen years at DePaul, he has taught in the fields of Roman Catholic studies, religious social ethics, and business ethics.

Richard J. Meister is professor of history and executive vice president for academic affairs at DePaul. After receiving his Ph.D. in American history from Notre Dame, he taught at Xavier University and the University of Michigan—Flint before joining DePaul in 1981 as dean of the College of Liberal Arts and Sciences. His publications include *Cities in Transition* (1979) and two edited works, *The Black Ghetto* (1972) and *Race and Ethnicity in America* (1974).

John L. Rury is professor of education at DePaul, where he also was a faculty member in the School for New Learning for ten years. He holds a Ph.D. in educational policy studies and history from the University of Wisconsin. He has served as president of the History of Education Society (USA) and vice president, Division F (History and Historiography) of the American Educational Research Association.

Charles S. Suchar is a 1967 graduate of DePaul. He received his Ph.D. in sociology from Northwestern University, and has been a faculty member at DePaul since 1971. He is currently professor of sociology and associate dean for undergraduate studies in the College of Liberal Arts and Sciences. His interests range from the study of deviant behavior to visual sociology, documentary photography, and the study of changing urban communities.

Charles R. Strain is professor of religious studies at DePaul, where he has taught since 1976. He is the coauthor, with Dennis McCann, of *Polity and Praxis: A Program for an Ameri-*

can Practical Theology (1985) and the editor of *Technological Change and the Transformation of America* (1987) and *Prophetic Visions and Economic Realities* (1989). He has worked extensively in the area of curricular change at DePaul, beginning in 1980.

Anna L. Waring is assistant professor in the Public Services Graduate Program at DePaul. She received her Ph.D. from Stanford University. She teaches courses in nonprofit management, leadership, and policy analysis. Her research interests include leadership and management in colleges and universities and other nonprofit organizations.

ACKNOWLEDGMENTS

The editors would like to express their thanks to a number of people who made this study possible. Like many other academic enterprises, this project quickly became rather large and complicated, and many people contributed to its development. Although it is not possible to identify everyone who participated, we would like to acknowledge those who made important contributions to the success of the DePaul history project.

The idea for a centennial history of the university started with a series of conversations in the early 1990s. Father Paul Golden, C.M., vice president for university mission and secretary of the board of trustees at the time, provided support and encouragement from the beginning. Father Golden helped to secure funding for the study and oversaw the early stages of its development. Father John Richardson, C.M., who was president of the university, was also instrumental in identifying sources of support for the project, particularly at the point of its inception. These two men, important leaders of the university, shared a vision of the contribution a book such as this may make to the future of the institution and to the study of Catholic and urban higher education. We hope that this volume in some respects fulfills that expectation.

Following Father Golden's departure to assume the presidency of Niagara University, the task of fiscal oversight for the project fell to Tom Fuechtmann, who had recently been appointed director of the university's centennial celebration. Since that time Tom has been a constant source of encouragement and advice, prodding all of the authors to observe deadlines and to make use of funding to pursue their research. Tom also participated in discussions of key findings and ideas in the book, and played an important role in assisting the editors' work of preparing the manuscript for publication. His many contributions have been indispensable to the success of the study. Elaine Watson, the university's vice president for administration, oversaw key budgetary questions, and played an important role in negotiations with the publisher. Together, Tom and Elaine were integral to the evolution of this project.

No historical research project of this magnitude is possible, of course, without the support and assistance of librarians and archivists. Kathryn DeGraff, director of special collections and university archives at the John T. Richardson Library, was unstinting in her support for this study. Kathryn and her extremely capable staff assisted each of the authors in researching different facets of the university's history. They were adroit in finding relevant materials, and even in suggesting additional sources. They cheerfully photocopied items and stored research materials from one day's work to another. Kathryn and her staff members Elisa Addlesperger and Joan Mitchanis, along with student assistant Adrienne Godfrey, also proved indispensable to the task of identifying and reproducing photographs for the book. They located hundreds of images for the editors to select from, and participated in discussions about which ones were most appropriate. Altogether, Kathryn DeGraff and her colleagues in the library played a vital role in the development of the book.

There were yet other people who helped with the book as a whole, in addition to individuals who assisted with research or performed other tasks in connection with particular chapters. Jean Gottlieb and Dan LeBrun provided helpful editorial suggestions on the manuscript as a whole. John Burton, director of academic support in the university's office of academic affairs and himself a historian of higher education, provided advice for the editors and feedback on particular chapters in the book. Philip Gleason, professor of history at Notre Dame and noted authority on Catholic higher education, met with the project authors and answered questions about themes in the history of other institutions. Les Goodchild, yet another noted historian of higher education and author of an important study of DePaul, also was a source of advice for the editors. David Sims of DePaul's publication services helped with the design of the front and back covers of the book and provided advice on particular visual images. Kris Gallagher of the university's public relations office helped locate photographs of DePaul's contemporary buildings and places. Philip Puckorius, Vito DePinto and Dan LeBrun provided critical advice and support during the production process. Each of these individuals contributed to the quality of this volume; problems which remain, of course, are the responsibility of the editors and the authors.

Additionally, the editors would like to express their gratitude to the other authors of chapters in the book. Although we occasionally grumbled about missed deadlines and the need for yet another revision, all of the chapter authors proved up to the challenge of producing a well documented history of DePaul's experience in time for the university's centennial celebration. Looking back at this, we would like to acknowledge the fact that it was no small accomplishment. Without the hard work, thoughtfulness and creativity of each of our chapter authors, this book would not have been possible.

Finally, a word of thanks is due to the scores of DePaul students, faculty members and administrators—past and present—who contributed in one way or another to research for this study. Many of them were the subjects of interviews. Other offered insights, or sent us documents or photos. All shared a keen interest in preserving the past, and passing it on to others. This book is in large part their history, and it represents the story of their institution. We would like to dedicate it to each of them, to their peers in the past and present, and to the future generations of DePaulians who will use it to comprehend their unique heritage.

John L. Rury
Charles S. Suchar

INDEX